Teaching Religion and Healing

AMERICAN ACADEMY OF RELIGION

TEACHING RELIGIOUS STUDIES SERIES

SERIES EDITOR
SUSAN HENKING, HOBART AND WILLIAM SMITH COLLEGES

A PUBLICATION SERIES OF
THE AMERICAN ACADEMY OF RELIGION
AND
OXFORD UNIVERSITY PRESS

TEACHING LEVI-STRAUSS
EDITED BY HANS H. PENNER

TEACHING ISLAM
EDITED BY BRANNON M. WHEELER

TEACHING FREUD
EDITED BY DIANE JONTE-PACE

TEACHING DURKHEIM
EDITED BY TERRY F. GODLOVE, JR.

TEACHING AFRICAN AMERICAN RELIGIONS
EDITED BY CAROLYN M. JONES AND THEODORE LOUIS TROST

TEACHING RELIGION AND HEALING
EDITED BY LINDA L. BARNES AND INÉS TALAMANTEZ

AMERICAN ACADEMY OF RELIGION

Teaching Religion and Healing

Edited by
LINDA L. BARNES
INÉS TALAMANTEZ

UNIVERSITY PRESS
2006

OXFORD

UNIVERSITY PRESS

Oxford University Press, Inc., publishes works that further
Oxford University's objective of excellence
in research, scholarship, and education.

Oxford   New York
Auckland   Cape Town   Dar es Salaam   Hong Kong   Karachi
Kuala Lumpur   Madrid   Melbourne   Mexico City   Nairobi
New Delhi   Shanghai   Taipei   Toronto

With offices in
Argentina   Austria   Brazil   Chile   Czech Republic   France   Greece
Guatemala   Hungary   Italy   Japan   Poland   Portugal   Singapore
South Korea   Switzerland   Thailand   Turkey   Ukraine   Vietnam

Copyright © 2006 by The American Academy of Religion

Published by Oxford University Press, Inc.
198 Madison Avenue, New York, New York 10016

www.oup.com

Oxford is a registered trademark of Oxford University Press

Library of Congress Cataloging-in-Publication Data
Teaching religion and healing/Linda L. Barnes and Inés Talamantez, editors.
p. cm.—(AAR teaching religious studies series)
Includes bibliographical references and index.
ISBN-13 978-0-19-517643-8; 978-0-19-517644-5 (pbk.)
ISBN 0-19-517643-X; 0-19-517644-8 (pbk.)
1. Religion—Study and teaching.   2. Medicine—Religious aspects—Study and teaching.
3. Spiritual healing—Study and teaching.   I. Barnes, Linda L.   II. Talamantez, Inés.
III. AAR teaching religious studies.
BL41.T43 2006
203'.1'071—dc22   2005020916

1 3 5 7 9 8 6 4 2

Printed in the United States of America
on acid-free paper

To beloved friend and colleague Kimberley C. Patton,
a luminous teacher in her own right, and a brilliant
scholar in the comparative study of religion.
—Linda Barnes

To honor the memory of Meredith Begay,
NADEKLESHEN, beloved sponsor and teacher
1937–2006.
—Inés Talamantez

Acknowledgments

Many people played a part in bringing this book to completion. In particular, we thank our contributors for their commitment to teaching as an inherent aspect of their scholarship, and to their explorations into the study of religion and healing. This volume has grown out of the years of scholarly engagement by many of them in the Religions, Medicines, and Healing Consultation of the American Academy of Religion. In some cases, we found our contributors through a conference called "Religion and Healing in America" held in 2001 at the Center for the Study of World Religions and the Boston Medical Center that was organized by Linda Barnes and Susan Sered—a project that resulted in an edited volume by the same name. We have valued coming to know these scholars as teachers.

On all our behalves, we express our gratitude to our anonymous reviewers for helping us to deepen and sharpen the content and writing of this collection. We also thank Susan Henking, Cynthia Read, and Theo Calderara for their support throughout the process of publishing this volume.

Barnes is grateful to John B. Carmen for his ongoing support over the years of her work in the study of religion and healing, and to Arthur Kleinman and Tom Csordas for introducing her to the cross-cultural study of healing. She owes a great debt to Raymond Williams and Barbara DeConcini for involving her as the consultant and ethnographer for the teaching workshops offered through the American Academy of Religion and the Wabash Center for Teaching and Learning—forums within which she met and learned from religion faculty from around the United States for over nine years. She is grateful, as well, to Susan Sered, a steadfast colleague in the field of religion and healing.

Talamantez is grateful for the students in the religion and healing courses that she has taught, for their challenging contributions to the traditions of Native American healing. To Vernon Kjonegaard for introducing her to Sarita Macias, who convinced her that in order to understand the process of transformation in this tradition, she should go through the initiation, and who assisted with proofreading this manuscript; to Pilulaw Khus for her generous conversations on Chumash healing systems; to Benneta Jules Rosett, expert scholar on Pentecostals in Africa; and to Diane Bell, Karen McCarthy Brown, Christine Thomas, and Ann Braude for their work on women, culture, and healing and their generous intellectual exchange.

We thank our ancestors—intellectual, familial, and communal—for the roots they have given us, out of which our work and our ceremonies have grown.

Finally, we extend our deepest hearts' thanks to Devon Thibeault and Vernon Kjonegaard for their love, companionship, and engagement in our lives.

Contents

Contributors

PAULA K. R. ARAI (Religion Department, Carleton College) teaches about the religions of East Asia. Her special interests include Japanese Buddhist rituals and practices, women's experiences and contributions, and healing. She is the author of *Women Living Zen: Japanese Soto Buddhist Nuns* (1999) and several book chapters and journal articles, and is now working on a manuscript entitled *Polishing the Heart: Japanese Buddhist Women's Rituals of Healing and Transformation*.

LINDA L. BARNES (Departments of Family Medicine and Pediatrics, Boston University School of Medicine) directs the Boston Healing Landscape Project, an institute for the study of religions, medicines, and healing at Boston University School of Medicine. She founded and co-chairs the Religions, Medicines, and Healing Group in the American Academy of Religion (AAR). Her books include *Variations on a Teaching/Learning Workshop: Pedagogy and Faculty Development in Religious Studies* (1999), *Religion and Healing in America* (co-edited with Susan S. Sered, 2005), and *Needles, Herbs, Gods, and Ghosts: China, Healing, and the West to 1848* (2005).

CHRISTOPHER CARR (School of Human Evolution and Social Change, Arizona State University) has primary research and teaching experience in anthropological archaeology, the archaeology of sociopolitical organization and belief systems, the analysis of style in material culture, mortuary practices, quantitative methods, material technological analyses, and Eastern U. S. prehistory. His publications include *For Concordance in Archaeological Analysis* (1985), *Style, Society, and Person* (with J. Neitzel, 1995), and *Identify-*

ing the Mineralogy of Rock Temper in Ceramics Using X-Radiography (with J.C. Komorowski, 1995).

SUZANNE J. CRAWFORD (Religion Department, Pacific Lutheran University) teaches courses that explore Native American religious traditions and the interrelation and interaction of religion and culture in a variety of world religious traditions. She co-chairs the Religions, Medicines, and Healing Group in the AAR. Her books include *American Indian Religious Traditions: An Encyclopedia* (co-edited with Dennis F. Kelley, 2005) and *Native American Religions: Traditional Religions of the World* (co-edited with Richard Hecht, forthcoming).

KAJA FINKLER (Department of Anthropology, University of North Carolina, Chapel Hill) teaches courses on medical anthropology, gender and health, economic anthropology, political economy, globalization, Mexico, and Latin America. Her publications include *Women in Pain* (1994), *Spiritualist Healing in Mexico: Successes and Failures of Alternative Therapeutics* (1994), and *Experiencing the New Genetics: Family and Kinship on the Medical Frontier* (2000).

FRED GLENNON (Department of Religious Studies, Le Moyne College) teaches and researches in the fields of religion, social ethics, and society, particularly their interrelationship with public policies on welfare, poverty, and labor markets. He serves on AAR's Steering Committee for the Academic Teaching and Study of Religion Section, and chairs the Academic Relations Task Force (2005–2007). His publications include "Experiential Learning and Social Justice Action: An Experiment in the Scholarship of Teaching and Learning," in *Teaching Theology and Religion* (2004), and *Introduction to the Study of Religion*, with Nancy Ring, Kathleen Nash, Mary MacDonald, and Jennifer Glancy (1998).

INÉS HERNÁNDEZ-ÁVILA (Native American Studies, University of California, Davis) is an accomplished poet, whose research, writing, and teaching interests include Native American women's literature; Native American religious traditions; and Native American and indigenous/Chicana feminisms, womanisms, and spiritualities. She served as a consultant for the Smithsonian Institution to help envision and elaborate the inaugural exhibits for the opening of the new National Museum of the American Indian in Washington, D.C. Her edited books include *Reading Native Women: Critical/Creative Representations* (2004), *and Entre Guadalupe y Malinche: Tejanas in Literature and Art* (co-edited with Norma E. Cantú, forthcoming).

CLAUDE JACOBS (Anthropology Department, University of Michigan-Dearborn) directs the Center for the Study of Religion and Society, University of Michigan-Dearborn and serves as an affiliate of Harvard's Pluralism Project, which maps the religious landscape of Detroit. His publications include "Folk for whom?: tourist guidebooks, local color, and the spiritual churches of New

Orleans," in *Journal of American Folk-lore* (2001); "Healing and prophecy in the black spiritual churches: a need for re-examination," in *Medical Anthropology* (1990); and *The Spiritual Churches of New Orleans: Origins, Beliefs, and Rituals of an African American Religion* (with Andrew Kaslow, 1991).

PAMELA E. KLASSEN (Department and Centre for the Study of Religion, University of Toronto) researches and teaches about Christianity in North America (nineteenth and twentieth centuries), gender, health and healing, anthropology of religion, and ritual. Her recent publications include *Blessed Events: Religion and Home Birth in America* (2001), "The Scandal of Pain in Childbirth" (2002), "The Robes of Womanhood: Dress and Authenticity among African American Methodist Women in the Nineteenth Century" (2004), and "Agency, Embodiment, and Scrupulous Women" (2004).

LARA MEDINA (Department of Chicano and Chicana Studies, California State University, Northridge) researches the spiritualities and theologies of U. S. Latinas. She is particularly interested in explorations of faith or belief systems through traditional or official as well as nontraditional or unofficial practices, and explorations through rituals, stories, art, and other means. An Associate Editor of *Chicana/Latina Studies: The Journal of Mujeres Activas en Letras y Cambio Social*, she is also the author of *Las Hermanas: Chicana/Latina Religious-Political Activism in the U. S. Catholic Church* (2004).

STEPHANIE Y. MITCHEM (Department of Religious Studies, University of South Carolina) has a commitment to liberatory educational practice. She teaches contemporary theology and women's studies, emphasizing the experiences and perspectives of black women. Mitchem is Contributing Editor of *Crosscurrents* and Co-Editor of the *Journal of Feminist Studies in Religion*. She is author of *African American Women Tapping Power and Spiritual Wellness* (2004), *Introducing Womanist Theology* (2002), and numerous essays.

LUCINDA A. MOSHER (Adjunct Faculty at Fordham University, General Seminary, the University of Michigan-Dearborn, and St. Francis College) is a Christian ethicist, who focuses on interreligious concerns. Mosher chairs the Episcopal-Muslim Relations Committee for the Episcopal Diocese of New York Ecumenical Commission, and serves as a Staff Assistant for the Network of Inter Faith Concerns of the Anglican Communion. Her publications include *Living Stones: A Jerusalem Seminar Journal and Reflections on the Israeli-Palestinian Peace Process* (1994), and *Belonging (Faith in the Neighborhood)* (2005).

RONALD Y. NAKASONE (Center for Arts, Religion and Education, Graduate Theological Union), a Buddhist cleric, academic, ethicist, and *sho* (calligraphy) artist, teaches Buddhist thought and aesthetics. Rev. Nakasone studied with Morita Shiryu (1912–1999), a leading avant-garde *sho*-master, for seven years in Kyoto, Japan. In addition to exhibiting his works in Japan, China, and the

U. S., Rev. Nakasone is associated with the Stanford Geriatric Education Center and Ryukoku University's Center for Humanities, Science, and Religion in Kyoto, Japan. He has addressed his Buddhist reflections on aging, cloning, organ transplants, and other dilemmas in contributions to the *Encyclopedia of Ethical, Legal, and Policy Issues in Biotechnology* (2000).

VASUDHA NARAYANAN (Religion Department, University of Florida) researches the Sri Vaishnava tradition; Hindu traditions in India, Cambodia, America; Hinduism and the environment; and gender issues. She has served as the President of the Society for Hindu-Christian Studies from 1996–1998, and of the American Academy of Religion, from 2001–2002. She is the author and editor of five books, including *The Hindu Traditions in the United States: Temple Space, Domestic Space, and Cyberspace* (2004), and more than eighty articles, chapters, and encyclopedia entries. She is currently working on Hindu temples and Vaishnava traditions in Cambodia.

ARVILLA PAYNE-JACKSON (Department of Sociology and Anthropology, Howard University) has taught at Howard University for twenty-eight years. Her primary areas of interest are in the fields of medical anthropology, sociolinguistics, and ethnographic evaluation. She has conducted fieldwork in the United States, the Caribbean, Latin America, and Africa. She is the Executive Producer of the first comprehensive documentary on African American folk medicine ("African Roots to American Roots: A Story of Folk Medicine in America"). Her books include *Folk Wisdom and Mother Wit: John Lee—An African American Herbal Healer* (1993) and *Jamaican Folk Medicine: A Source of Healing* (with Mervyn C. Alleyne, 2004).

AMANDA PORTERFIELD (Department of Religion, Florida State University) is a historian of American religion interested in the interplay between religion and culture. She served as President of the American Society of Church History in 2001. Porterfield has written books on the New England Puritans, Protestant women missionaries in the nineteenth century, and the transformation of American religion after 1960. She also has wider interests in the history of Christianity and in the comparative study of world religions. Her most recent book is *Healing in the History of Christianity* (2005).

KWOK PUI-LAN is William F. Cole Professor of Christian Theology and Spirituality at Episcopal Divinity School in Cambridge, Mass., where she teaches and researches Christian theology, world Christianity, spirituality, religion and culture, Asian religions, women's studies, and postcolonial criticism. Her books include *Postcolonial Imagination and Feminist Theology* (2005), *Introducing Asian Feminist Theology* (2000), *Discovering the Bible in the Non-Biblical World* (1995), and *Chinese Women and Christianity* (1992). She coedited *Postcolonialism, Feminism, and Religious Discourse* (2002), and *Beyond Colonial Anglicanism: The Anglican Communion in the Twenty-First Century* (2001).

INÉS M. TALAMANTEZ (Department of Religion, University of California Santa Barbara), who comes from an Apache background, is a leading expert on Native American philosophy and religion, with expertise also in women in religion, religion and ecology, and healing and religion. Her publications include "In the Space Between the Earth and the Sky" in *Native Religions and Cultures of North America: Anthropology of the Sacred* (2000), "Vine Deloria Jr., Critic and Coyote: Transforming Universal Conceptions," a Festschrift for Vine Deloria Jr. (forthcoming), and "The Presence of Isanaklesh. The Apache Female Deity and the Path of Pollen," in *Unspoken Worlds: Women's Religious Lives* (2000).

EDITH TURNER (Department of Anthropology, University of Virginia) teaches courses on ritual and symbol, anthropology of performance, comparative healing, ritual and arctic survival, life story, shamanism, healing, experiential anthropology, the anthropology of consciousness, the anthropology of religion, and fieldwork and ethnography. She has researched the field of symbol and ritual for fifty-eight years, formerly in collaboration with Victor Turner. Her most recent books include *Heart of Lightness: The Life of an Anthropologist, Autobiography* (forthcoming), and *Among the Healers: Stories of Spiritual and Ritual Healing around the World* (2006).

IVETTE VARGAS-O'BRYAN (Department of Religious Studies, Austin College) researches South Asian and Tibetan Buddhist Studies, with a subfield in Hinduism. Her particular interests are in the interaction of doctrine and ritual practice, the rhetoric of illness in Asian literature, and the study of religion and science in Indian and Tibetan medicine. She is also exploring the role of women in Tibetan medical history and the use of the rhetoric of violence in Asian religious traditions. She teaches courses on scientific and cultural perspectives of infectious disease, and illness and medicine in Asian religions.

MICHAEL WINKELMAN (Department of Anthropology, Arizona State University) has longstanding interests in shamanism, medical anthropology, psychological anthropology, and intercultural relations and communication. His applied work focuses on interethnic relations in the U. S., particularly in medical, legal, and educational settings. He is the director of the Summer Ethnographic Field School held in Ensenada, Baja California, Mexico. His publications include *Shamanism: The Neural Ecology of Consciousness and Healing* (2000), and a guest edited issue of *Cultural Survival Quarterly* on "Shamanisms and Survival."

Teaching Religion and Healing

Introduction

Linda L. Barnes

The study of healing traditions is well developed in the discipline of anthropology. Much as religion scholars have uncoupled the term "religion" from an unexamined association with any one tradition, so have medical anthropologists—who engage in the cross-cultural study of medicine and healing traditions—challenged the popular assumption that "medicine" is synonymous with "biomedicine," the dominant, biologically based system of practice. They have argued, instead, that biomedicine is only one of many rich and diverse healing systems developed by human societies, and that biomedical illness categories, therapeutic responses, and meanings of efficacy are not universal. Some of these scholars, however, have been less successful in avoiding the reduction of religious systems to economic, political, psychological, or sociological substrata, with corresponding implications for studying the diversity of religious healing. Nevertheless, at the national meetings of the American Anthropology Association, sessions dedicated to the cross-cultural study of medicine and healing traditions—many of them grounded in religious traditions, worldviews, and practices—occupy approximately one fifth of the program each year.

Religious studies scholars, in turn, have often been unaware of the enormous body of scholarship in medical anthropology. Like many in the broader culture, they frequently equate "medicine" with "biomedicine," and assume that discussions of religion and medicine are therefore necessarily about faith healing in relation to biomedicine and/or about bioethics. (Both assumptions have been routinely represented in the American Academy of Religion program book for years.) Many scholars have also assumed that religious healing refers to the practices of only a few groups like Christian

Scientists or Pentecostals. Yet most religion scholars, when actually reflecting on the traditions about which they teach, quickly recognize the pervasive presence of healing matters. A small but growing number are beginning to focus their scholarship on such issues. Some have developed related courses.

Within the last several years, a number of American medical schools have offered elective courses on "medicine and spirituality." A significant part of this work has been funded by the Templeton Foundation, which has also offered faculty grants to medical schools to develop courses in "medicine and spirituality." In general, however, such courses focus on the health-outcomes literature and treat "spirituality" as a generic term—again, much as occurs in popular culture. Such courses do not usually address issues of race or class, and culture is often relegated to a single session, presented together with religious pluralism.

Twenty-One Questions

This book brings together a collection of different ways of conceptualizing and teaching about religion and healing, based on courses designed and taught by faculty in the humanities and the social sciences. It also proposes examples of alternative ways of teaching such issues to health care providers and other caregivers. Many of the authors are the very scholars whose scholarship has served as key touch points for other researchers. They also share a passion for teaching. Others are writing from earlier in their careers, with healing as a core issue in their larger intellectual projects. The synergy generated by bringing together the scholarship of these authors, as expressed through their teaching, illustrates different curricular approaches to broadening and redefining the concept of religious healing.

For this collection, each author was asked to address a set of questions in relation to his or her course. The questions grew out of issues raised in the series of yearlong workshops, initiated by Raymond Williams of Wabash College and supported by the American Academy of Religion in the early 1990s, which focused on mentoring faculty in relation to their teaching (see Barnes 1999). The function of these questions was to provide thematic continuities throughout the book. Should one choose to focus on any of these issues, one could thereby draw on these cross-cutting discussions and ideas:

1. Conceptualize the chapter as a concise manual designed to mentor someone else in how to teach this course.
2. Define the way(s) in which you are using the term "healing"
3. In what kind of setting have you taught the course, and how has that setting influenced the course design?
4. Who have your students for this course been, and how has who *they* are informed the course's design and implementation?
5. What theoretical issues inform the course design?
6. What pedagogy or pedagogies inform the design?

7. What are the learning goals of the course, and how is the course designed to accomplish them?
8. How do you address the cosmologies and epistemologies of the traditions about which you teach?
9. Discuss the *process* of teaching the course: What has been most successful and why? What didn't work and why not? What did you do about the less successful aspects?
10. How have you incorporated nontextual resources?
11. How is gender addressed?
12. How does the course address issues of pluralism (within a tradition, between traditions, and involving different cultural, racial/ethnic, and socioeconomic groups)?
13. Does the course address issues of structural violence (e.g., racism, classism, sexism, homophobia, colonialism, imperialism)? If so, in what ways?
14. Does your course address issues arising from the interaction between the tradition(s) represented and biomedicine as another medicine culture? If so, in what ways?
15. Do you use any web-based resources? If you do, what are they, how do you use them, and how have they worked?
16. Does the course draw on any regional resources? If so, how have you done this, and what has made doing so work well? Does the region where you teach have any other impact on how you present the course?
17. Are there any features of the course that you think are unusual/distinctive that could in some way be adapted to other contexts?
18. What have you found to be (uniquely?) problematic about teaching this course, and that other faculty would do well to keep in mind?
19. Given how you have approached the teaching of religion and healing, how do you think that our (and students') understanding of religion changes when we focus the topic of religion and healing?
20. Correspondingly, how does our understanding of healing change when we focus on healing within the framework of various religious traditions?
21. Do you have suggestions for readings for each class session that would serve someone else in preparing lectures, etc.?

Each author addresses these questions differently. Together, their responses flesh out our understanding of religion and healing, yielding important and transferable guides to designing and teaching courses of many different kinds.

On a basic level, this book is a manual on how to teach different kinds of courses on religion and healing. Some authors focus primarily on this dimension. On another level, the book raises some of the recurring issues involved in conceptualizing—as well as teaching—religion and healing. The authors themselves represent a culturally pluralistic group who bring diverse approaches to bear, including historical, ethnographic, sociological, and experiential methodologies, as well as diverse pedagogies. Some employ methods focused on race, gender, and class as primary tools of analysis. Those who write as feminist, womanist, *mujerista*, and Native American women scholars help us to arrive at a fuller understanding of women's interpretations of the traditions the book addresses. Finally, where possible, different approaches to teaching similar topics have been included, in order to illustrate what we know in practice—namely, that there are many ways to present the same kinds of material.

Definitional Challenges—"Religion" and "Healing"

For many of the authors, healing serves as a fruitful entrée to the study of religion, because it is integral to many if not most religious traditions. "Therefore," notes Paula Arai, "there is often no clear boundary between the therapeutic and the religious." If, she adds, "the study of religion is a cornerstone of the study of healing . . . one could argue, the reverse holds true as well." Fred Glennon adds:

> The focus on religion and healing has had a significant impact on our understanding of religion. We often conceptualize religion narrowly as a set of orthodox beliefs and practices that require participants to believe and act in certain ways. By looking at religion's role in healing, restoring balance and finding meaning even in face of the threats to oneself or community that illness brings, we begin to see the powerful way in which religious belief and practice—especially ritual practice—bring together the spiritual, ethical, and behavioral dimensions of human experience.

Yet, just as religion scholars face the difficulty of defining "religion," a corresponding challenge arises when one attempts to define the overarching topic "healing." Part of that challenge derives from the plethora of contexts in which it is used. One confronts the need to avoid a definition so broad as to be useless or so particular as to exclude critical dimensions of other traditions. One could, however, suggest that healing refers to theories of transformation or change seen as addressing or resolving some form of affliction or suffering. Yet even then, *what* kinds of change are considered significant depends on the tradition, as well on as the group or individual within that tradition, in a given time and place.

A second, and related, challenge entails students' frequent assumption that they already know what "religion" is (their own tradition), and what medicine is (biomedicine). If they have, in one way or another, turned away from both, they may refer, instead to "spirituality" and "healing"—frequently taken to mean something universal and a-historical. How one chooses to relativize these assumptions—including what Kaja Finkler refers to as "demystifying" biomedicine—can govern much of one's course organization. Suzanne Crawford, for example, begins by eliciting student definitions of religion to illustrate the range of meanings they themselves assign the term. Finkler compares and contrasts *emic* (insider) and *etic* (outsider) perspectives. Vasudha Narayanan, in her course in Hinduism and healing, leaves Āyurvedic medicine until late in the course, knowing that students generally expect it to function as the focus. Healing, she suggests, involves much more. The ordering of her topics—deities, ritual, journey, relationships to time and space, bodily disciplines, textual traditions and traditional medicine systems, women's traditions, health tourism, and the arts—indicates a rich conceptualizing of a broader theme. Lucinda Mosher and Claude Jacobs introduce the notion of religion as a *worldview*, of which healing is a part, whose intricacies "are informed by *conviction*."

Addressing Pluralisms

The very act of decentering student assumptions about religion and medicine leads directly to the need to address issues of plural systems, or pluralism. This encounter presents a very real challenge for some of our students on religious grounds, as Finkler and Arvilla Payne-Jackson both note, that challenge reflecting postures taken by sectors of the larger population. In a story on religious bias at the United States Air Force Academy, National Public Radio reporter Jeff Brady interviewed the academy's former Lutheran chaplain, who said that a cohort of senior officers publicly and routinely equated character formation with the virtues of evangelical Christianity and targeted religious pluralism as an enemy. This is a far cry from Diana Eck's (2001) definition of pluralism as an encounter between commitments. Our book's premise is that religious pluralism is not only a reality but a good, and that engagement with pluralism presses us not only to understand others, but also ourselves, in deeper ways that serve us all.

Some of this book's authors organize their courses around pluralism *within* traditions. As Mosher and Jacobs remind us, "No religion is a monolith." For that reason, they make the strategic decision to organize site visits to branches of a given tradition with which their students are less likely to be familiar. In this way, they observe the dictum to make the strange familiar, and the familiar strange. Other authors discuss the coexistence and interplay *between* traditions in a given cultural world. Ronald Nakasone, for example, characterizes Japanese American traditions as "porously laminated," with new layers entering an already layered framework. He uses the story of a one-eyed pheasant to illustrate how different Japanese religious groups interpret issues related to a shared commitment to filiality, even as they grapple with other differences that are not always so easy to resolve.

Some authors have chosen to teach about multiple traditions of healing originating from different regions of the world. Ivette Vargas-O'Bryan, for example, teaches about Indian, Tibetan, and Chinese systems, grouped under the rubric of "Asian religious traditions." Others choose different numbers, for different reasons. Mosher and Jacobs make the point, in their weeklong intensive course, by opening with a discussion of optical illusions to show how the same object can—when viewed from different angles—look like different things, and of a series of maps, to illustrate how cartographers inform how we visualize our world. Their point is to introduce perspectival issues early on.

Behind all discussion of religion and healing looms the influence of the culturally dominant system, biomedicine. Yet, just as religious systems are pluralistic, so is biomedicine, not only in its many subdisciplines—each with its own characteristics—but also in its relation to other alternative and complementary therapies, some of which define themselves as spiritual in orientation. As Marie Griffith notes, even when not construed as overtly religious, some American healing practices have "dense and unavoidable religious convergences" (Griffith 2003:16). Biomedicine itself, while resolutely denying any connection with religion, could be said to have its own religious overtones (McGill 1980). Moreover, as the cultural and religious pluralism of the country intensifies, biomedical caregivers—whether the physician assistants who take Glennon's course, or the doctors who take the courses taught by Nakasone, Mosher and Jacobs, or Barnes—find themselves confronted by the need to understand how religious systems of healing interface with biomedicine in clinical contexts. Hence the burgeoning field of "cultural competence" discussed by Glennon and Barnes. Similarly, as Kwok Pui-lan's course illustrates, chaplains working in biomedical settings, along with priests and ministers committed to introducing approaches to healing into their congregations, are drawn to understand how these issues configure in multiple traditions.

Pluralism also appears in the hybrid outcomes of the interactions among different systems of healing. Nakasone quotes Edward Said, who wrote: "All cultures are involved with each other. None is single and pure. All are hybrid, heterogeneous, extraordinarily differentiated, and unmonolithic" (1994:xxv). Nakasone himself illustrates the point by describing the introduction of sermons into Buddhist mortuary and memorial observations in San Francisco—a custom transposed from Christian practice. Narayanan elevates the word "custom," using it to discuss how Hindus *customize* their own configurations of practices from within a tradition, but in response to influences in the surrounding culture, whether in India or the United States.

Comparative Challenges

Pluralism almost invariably raises the impulse to compare, leading one into the thorny thicket of debates over comparative religion, and the efforts by some religion scholars to debunk and dismantle the enterprise. Yet here I am inclined to agree with Wendy Doniger, who wrote, "I am unwilling to close the comparativist shop just because it is being picketed by people whose views I happen, by and large, to share" (Doniger 2000:66). I suggest, therefore, that it is more useful to draw on scholarship in religious studies and medical anthropology, which views the undertaking as a necessary, albeit difficult one.

Nor, as the collection edited by John Carman and Steven Hopkins (1991) makes clear, is the issue new to faculty in religious studies.

Religion scholar Kimberley Patton describes the experience, some years ago, of presenting her plans for a course in comparative religious studies to a group of religion faculty. One of them spluttered, "But that's like my taking sixteen different birds and hacking out their livers and laying them out in a row! All you end up with is sixteen dead birds!" Her colleague Lawrence Sullivan, when he heard the story, riposted, "How did he know that all the organs were livers?" (Patton 2000:160). Or, for that matter, that all the creatures were birds?

Critiques of comparison focus on the perils of flawed abstractions and superficial similarities. The history of comparative study, with its roots in colonialism and imperialism, has generated arguments that the undertaking is irreparably tainted. Further complicating the issue are constructs of "religion" frequently grounded in Protestant Christian paradigms. (Doniger dryly quotes Mr. Thwackum in Henry Fielding's *Tom Jones*: "When I mention religion, I mean the Christian religion; and not only the Christian religion, but the Protestant religion; and not only the Protestant religion, but the Church of England" [Doniger 2000:64]). Dependence on such definitions yields an emphasis on selected aspects of religious life and practice that often do not represent other religious traditions or forms of religiosity. The result can be the hierarchical arrangement of traditions, or other alignments according to criteria that do not correspond to the internal order and pluralism of particular traditions. A related problem involves comparative courses, which rarely satisfy either designers or their critics. Framed as introductory courses, they make it difficult to avoid superficiality, or what Patton has been known to call "drive-by religion."

And yet, as scholars from many subdisciplines within religious studies have argued, the comparative project is intrinsic to human physiology and intelligence, making it "an inextricable component of our scholarly method" (Holdredge 2000:77). Even were the comparative impulse not physiologically and neurologically inborn (Sullivan 2000), our circumstances would inspire, and even impel us to it. As Diana Eck (2000) has observed, we find ourselves in increasingly complex religious settings in which native-born, immigrants, and refugees live together, their traditions encountering, influencing, resisting, and reconfiguring each other. This reality also calls us to attend to traditions as *processes* and to how we conceptualize change (see Trimble 2003; Berry 2003) as groups assimilate, accommodate, acculturate, and/or resist in response to their encounters with those different from themselves.

Taxonomies and Comparisons

How to compare? Any academic field functions through classificatory schema and taxonomies, requiring characterization and differentiation. William Paden suggests, "Wherever there is a theory, wherever there is a concept, there is a comparative program" (2000:182). The operative question is whether the categorization illuminates the phenomena so differentiated. The risk, as Barbara Holdredge notes, is when "certain paradigms of religious tradition are accorded a privileged status as the dominant discourse over against which specific religious traditions are to be judged and hierarchized," resulting in what Michael Polanyi characterized as "the tyranny of taxonomies" (Holdredge 2000:84).

Before his untimely death, religion scholar Kendall Folkert argued that the field of religious studies often relies on "implicit" and unexamined taxonomies in its analysis, and he challenged its scholars to engage in a more conscious and intentional formulation of thematic categories. Among those he targeted as problematic was "healing," writing, "The subject of healing seems to me to be an example of the worst sort of approach: whatever turns you on and is momentarily relevant, with insufficient effort to *reduce* the subject (in the best sense) to essentially comparative/comparable themes" (1991:24).

Although I cannot be sure, I suspect that Folkert assumed a popularized notion of healing, perhaps colored by New Age influences. Still, the comment illustrates the frequent and persisting lack of familiarity among religion scholars with the extensive taxonomic work that has been conducted in the field of anthropology and by medical anthropologists in particular. Prompted by questions of what different cultures mean by healing, these researchers realized decades ago that illness and disease categories that made sense in one cultural setting did not necessarily mean the same thing in another culture—if they existed at all. Cross-cultural psychiatry, for example, delved into whether depression existed across cultures and, if it did, how it manifested. What categories of experience corresponded to, exceeded, and undercut this biomedicalized category? The sophistication with which this other field has mined comparative taxonomies illustrates, of course, that no single list of categories or themes proves to be comprehensively cross-cultural or interreligious. At the same time, if one works toward clearly articulated thematic clusters, one can analyze each complex, dynamic system in its own right, and then look at how its parts are both similar to, and distinct from, analogous parts in another system.

For the most part, scholars in religious studies have not formulated taxonomies related to healing. Of course, given that religious studies is itself an interdisciplinary field that draws on methods formulated within many other disciplines, it begins to be a circular question of chickens and eggs. This is particularly so insofar as some of the major theoretical frameworks employed in religious studies derive from anthropology—just not yet from medical anthropology. I should add that, with the exception of Tom Csordas and Edith Turner, relatively few medical anthropologists are particularly interested in the phenomenology of religiosity or religious experience per se. But within the broader field of the anthropology of religion, the taxonomic and theoretical work of medical anthropologists like Arthur Kleinman, Byron Good, Kaja Finkler, Susan Sered, and many others contributes to a nuanced analysis and understanding of what, in human cultures, can be conceptualized as religious, *through* the complex phenomena of illness and healing.

Comparison operates on at least two levels in the study of religion and healing. As noted earlier, there is the level of the pluralism operative *within* a given tradition; there is also the level of differences and similarities *among* traditions (for which it becomes even more important to understand the pluralism characterizing each tradition in its own right). One must therefore be clear about the kinds of comparison in which one is engaging. One must know not only how to recognize and analyze the different parts and wholes, but also how to understand the internal connections and dissonances between them, and to scrutinize them for "their own further differentiation, subtypologization, and problematization through historical analysis" (Paden 2000:186). Moreover, the analysis of cultural shifts, reflected in different taxonomies over time, is in itself a useful comparative project.

Critics of comparative studies have challenged the focus on similarities—a view with which I have frequently found myself in sympathy, especially when the similarities insist on otherwise unconnected realities and try to argue for equivalence of meaning. Indeed, this focus on similarities can function in particularly pernicious ways when it supports the unauthorized appropriation of one group's traditions by another, based on ostensible similarity. This sort of impulse frequently appears, for example, in the assumption that, at the level of "mysticism," all religions are fundamentally the same, bypassing the underlying premises of each tradition and their crucial differences and discontinuities. Rather, as Doniger observes, "Similarity and difference are not equal, not comparable; they have different uses. We look for similarity for stability, to build political bridges, to anchor our own society, while we spin narratives to deal with our uneasiness at the threat of difference" (Doniger 2000:65). At the same time, it is worth noting that popular religiosity for many folks from various traditions involves the perception of similarities, the assumption of identity, and the merging of the multiple phenomena under broader symbolic rubrics. This process must be part of the comparative inquiry.

Comparative Frameworks

[*This section draws on previously published material* (Barnes, 2006).] Given such realities, what do we do with the very notion of taxonomies, without lapsing into utter nihilism? Or how do we balance the question, "How did he know that all the organs were livers?" with the effects of interchange between groups for whom "liver" may mean many different things, not least of them, being clustered with other organs in ways that "liver" is no longer the most operative term? All attempts at an answer can be, at best, provisional—contingent, again, on the specifics of the particular comparison. The endeavor calls us to hold in creative tension the classifying of things with the characterizing of change—something along the lines of talking concurrently about matter and energy, particles and waves. Indeed, insofar as categories tend not to name *processes*, I suggest that our notion of classification must include representations of change.

Finkler regularly reminds her students not to lose sight of the forest, because of too intent a focus on the trees. "Forest" and "trees" become an important metaphor, pointing to the need to analyze the connections between parts, as a critical part of the comparative undertaking (Finkler). Winkelman and Carr characterize their pedagogy as "cross-cultural and comparative" as well as "biopsychosocial"—a term developed by physician George Engel (1977) to promote attention to such factors in relation to bodily processes. Mosher and Jacobs use Alan Race's (1983) and Lochhead's (1988) theories regarding groups' attitudes and dispositions toward other groups.

Drawing on Csordas's work, Crawford develops a comparative framework focused on different constructs of embodiment. Kwok, in contrast, hopes to challenge theologies of the body influenced by Gnosticism and its descendents by positing "the body as a locus of spiritual wisdom." By body, she means that part of us "that actually eats or breathes." Mosher and Jacobs introduce discussion of customs related to health, healing, and death—as does Payne-Jackson—focusing on "the way each religion constructs the body in terms of its corporeal and incorporeal dimensions and the relationship between the two, especially in healing and death."

In my own teaching, I have found it useful to employ a comparative framework that draws on the work of medical anthropologists like my own mentors Arthur Kleinman and Tom Csordas (see, for example, Kleinman 1981 and Csordas and Lewton 1998). From them, I derive an approach to a taxonomic subdivision within the broader category of "healing." I find the following seven categories helpful, reminding readers that, in practice, each of these categories entails further complex subdivision and fine-tuning.

Paradigms of Healing: Ultimate Human Possibility

Paradigms of Healing—with a capital "H"—refer to understandings of ultimate human possibility. Healing here represents a tradition's deepest hopes and promises. It may be a way of talking about a person's relation to a highest reality, whether known as God, Yahweh, Allah, Atman, Nirvana, Obatalá, kamis, Tian, or other names. It may take the form of salvation, a place in heaven, life in a world to come, Paradise, Nirvana, freedom from cycles of rebirth, immortality, sagehood, revered ancestral status, eternal life through human memory, or something else not related to any particular tradition.

Healing thus conceptualized relativizes everything else about human life. It provides a frame of reference within which someone may interpret all other experiences, including the meaning of health in this lifetime. The influence of such visions of ultimate possibility are often read back into how people conduct their lives, leading them to try to live in ways that will bring about this kind of Healing.

Many traditions and related systems of healing represent some aspects of Healing as occurring after death. Death, therefore, becomes a transition, marking a change of state. Conversely, biomedicine is a tradition with no way of talking about what follows death, since the demise of the body represents the end of biomedical intervention. As a result, death can only represent failure, and is often experienced as such by biomedical clinicians.

Paradigms of Suffering and Affliction

Arthur Kleinman and Donald Seeman note, "the problem of suffering is everywhere, in one way or another, at the heart of religious experience" (1998:244). "Suffering" writ large may be assigned multiple explanations, not only between traditions, but also within a single tradition. Specific experiences then become embodied expressions of these often more cosmic explanations. Just as Healing is directly related to Suffering—Healing overcomes Suffering—so healing, in its different forms, addresses the particularities of individual episodes of suffering. Religions, Geertz argues, make suffering "sufferable" (1973:104). Their various approaches to ritual healing posit that the specific episode of suffering is relative and finite, as is the individual act of healing, where Healing, understood as ultimate, is not. This relativity is part of what renders suffering sufferable. Meanings of efficacy are formulated in relation to these understandings of Healing and healing.

Paradigms of Suffering and Affliction represent explanations for why suffering and affliction happen. Many traditions, for example, explain Suffering as the fruits of earlier actions, whether as a sign of judgment, punishment, and/or testing. The explanation may reiterate core narratives of a tradition: Some early individuals behaved in a forbidden way, as a result of which all subsequent humans suffer. Within the trajectories of Buddhism, the very nature of reality is characterized as impermanent. The human desire to hold on to things is routinely frustrated, causing suffering. Consequently, Suffering constitutes a fundamental human experience, until one learns how to disengage from its causes. Generally, paradigms of Suffering and Affliction are offset by paradigms of Healing. The former attempt to explain why we suffer; the latter offer possible responses and ultimate alternatives.

Such paradigms may frame how each party interprets specific experiences. "Am I being punished? Am I being tested?" "Am I to learn something from this?" In such instances, Suffering may function as the impetus for seeking transformation. On the other hand, actual experience may lead individuals to reject a paradigm as inadequate to account for a particular reality and to struggle to find some other reason for the reality that is happening. In such cases, the person is still searching for a paradigm adequate to the experience. Some of these paradigms may be experienced as punitive. If a family is told, for example, that God doesn't give them more to bear than they can handle, it is hard not to think, "If we were weaker, would our beloved family member not be living with this condition? Would he still be alive?" The sacred may be represented as indifferent or punishing. Yet the paradox of many traditions is that the sacred is represented as both merciful and loving, and as a force of judgment that is sometimes terrifying. The challenge may involve navigation through such paradoxes.

The Parts of Personhood

Virtually no tradition defines a person only in relation to bodily dimensions. Even biomedicine includes "mind," although often in relation to neurological structures. American popular culture, through the influence of New Age thought, has oriented many people to conceptualize "the whole person" as a combination of "body, mind, and spirit." Because these categories have taken such deep root in the culture, they can seem self-evident. But not every culture or tradition understands "body, mind, and spirit" to be the only parts or aspects constituting a person. Thus, one must address the question of a tradition's anthropology (or anthropologies). What is it to be human? What are the meanings of the Self, if indeed there is such a notion?

In some traditions, the key element may be a vital force. In Chinese systems, for example, *qi* (pronounced "ch'ee") is a subtle force that has both energetic and material dimensions, and of which all reality consists. Rocks are *qi*, winds and clouds are *qi*, blood is *qi*, and so is everything else about the body and all its subtle aspects. Chinese systems often emphasize patterns of process, change, and transformation. A clear division between "body" and "mind," therefore, does not pertain. Even though there are words for both things, their meanings are not the same.

For that matter, some traditions include one or more souls (which may be differentiated from the spirit). Here, the religious tradition involved makes a difference. "Soul" in the Christian tradition is not the same thing as "soul" in the Confucian tradition. If the culture or tradition views reincarnation as a process intrinsic to human life, then a person is conceptualized not only in terms of this life, but also of previous lives that may underlie who he or she is. In some West African traditions, when elders die, they reincarnate back into the family line. Grandchildren may then be recognized not only as themselves, but also as a returned grandparent.

One particularly powerful and normative model of personhood in many Western cultures privileges the stand-alone individual. Yet this is *not* an ideal in all cultures, some of which value the capacity to sustain interconnectedness. For systems that view family, clan, tribe, or analogous networks as the ground from which, and within which, a person emerges and finds meaning, the relational and communal is yet another intrinsic part of personhood. Gender provides another key variable in thinking about meanings of self and person, and may often highlight ways in which the self is understood in relational terms, as opposed to a cultural ideal promoting the autonomous individuated person. Authors like Talamantez and Glennon who foreground cooperative learning styles are presenting such an anthropology through their pedagogy.

Illness and Disease

Why does it matter to know how the parts of personhood are conceptualized? Because if we do not know the parts of a person, we do not know all the ways a person can get sick or be afflicted. Generally, each aspect of a person is conceptualized as susceptible to particular kinds of illness or affliction. Etiologies and causal factors point, on the one hand, to broader paradigms of suffering. As has been elaborated by medical anthropologists like Kleinman and others, there are also key differences between "illness"—the term used to refer to the lived experience—and "disease," the classification of that experience according to a medical system (Kleinman 1988). Each reflects different illness models, related to different forms of narrative about the etiology—the cause or causes understood to have generated the problem. As Finkler notes, "beliefs in the causality of sickness can elucidate broader social processes."

Things get complicated when the parties involved conceive of the person in different and even conflicting terms. A now classic example is Ann Fadiman's narrative about the Hmong child, Lia Lee, in *A Spirit Catches You and You Fall Down*. From infancy, Lia suffered from epilepsy. According to her pediatricians, for whom her physiology and neurology were the key aspects involved, the initial problem arose in these domains, and needed to be addressed in these domains. For Lia's parents, however, a radically different key aspect involved Lia's souls, which could be stolen or lost. Similarly, in traditional Chinese thought, each person had multiple souls, all of them various forms of qi. After death, certain souls entered the ground with the corpse. If not properly tended, they could become hungry ghosts and afflict the neglectful descendant.

Healers

People identify different kinds of healers as best qualified to address different kinds of problems. Frequently, they will resort to more than one—sometimes sequentially, sometimes concurrently. The very term "complementary and alternative medicine" reflects this reality in the United States. Questions about healers involve asking who are the healers, how do they acquire their healing power and authority, and by what processes is it recognized—as well as by whom? In what domains does their expertise function, and how? For example, healers arrive at their identity sometimes through culturally and religiously recognized forms of calling, or by taking steps recognized as conferring a professional identity often modeled after the process of becoming a physician. Healers may not only be individuals, but also communities and groups, as Nakasone's chapter illustrates.

In many cases, the divine or the sacred bestow healing *via* a human agent, sometimes living and sometimes dead. The role of the dead, in particular, is important because, as Lara Medina, Payne-Jackson, and Nakasone point out, they represent the living's connection with the past. If neglected or angered, they can make one sick, while in some traditions, they become the healers—as with Arai's discussion of the deceased, who are now Buddhas.

Related Interventions

Just as people classify health conditions in different ways, so they identify specific interventions as appropriate and/or necessary for each one. The identification of necessary or desirable interventions is culturally shaped. As Martin Rein and Donald Schön (1994) have suggested, *how* a problem is framed is also directly related to what people think can and should be done for it. What should be done for it is, in turn, related to each of the aspects discussed so far. Each therapy touches on these multiple levels, with different layers of hope, expectation, and things at stake. The hopes and expectations are tied in with normative ideas of personhood. This aspect becomes particularly clear when one looks at cases involving persons with disabilities and with how the disability is construed (Barnes and Coulter 2006). At the same time, it is important to make clear to students that financial and political realities also intervene, influencing the kinds of care to which a person or family has access (see Garro 1998).

Meanings of Efficacy

It is a common question to ask whether a therapeutic intervention has "worked." However, this apparently simple question can hold many meanings. For example, which aspect of personhood was suffering, and to what was the suffering attributed? What intervention or interventions were deemed necessary, and what was expected of each one? If the larger framework of Healing is factored into the picture, then the most meaningful kinds of change—of "working"—may be understood to happen after the person's death. The expectation of some life after death modifies the time frame of healing. Other frameworks of hope operate similarly.

Efficacy is another way of talking about the form of change that is recognized and valued. It may be assessed as the process engaged in by the healer; it is also related to whatever is meant by an outcome. To grasp the different meanings of efficacy involved in a situation, we must know how both Healing and Suffering are understood. We must understand the concept of the person at work, along with *which* aspect of the person is viewed as having been affected. We must grasp the nature of the afflicting force, whether a germ, another individual, an oppressive social dynamic, a deity, or something else. And we must know how the person and his or her family and social network envision all the necessary healers and interventions, in order for both healing and Healing to happen (see Barnes 2005b). As Vargas suggests, we must take into account the levels of experience in question, whether they be personal balance, social order, or cosmological liberation. And Talamantez points out the importance of land and biosphere in the particular equations of balance.

Teaching Experience

As many religious studies faculty quickly discover, students are often drawn to religion courses not only out of an academic interest in the course content, but also because they hope that the course will provide a forum in which to pursue their own personal search. If, as Crawford suggests, healing is a matter of self-making, it is not surprising that the same happens with courses on religion and healing. Different faculty acknowledge this reality differently. Some view such pursuits as falling outside the purview of an academic course. They teach the application of conceptual material—or, as Crawford puts it, how to apply abstract ideas to real-life scenarios. Yet they may be less likely to promote participation or practice. Others make room for it in discussions outside the classroom. Still others build it into the design of the course itself—but even there, in different ways.

The underlying issue is the role and understanding of experience as part of one's pedagogy. As Glennon observes, educator John Dewey emphasized the primacy of experience in relation to learning. In general, the anthropological method of participation and observation through fieldwork has become the sine qua non in the discipline. It is assumed that the experience of immersion in another cultural setting is the primary way to learn about that culture's traditions. Turner and her husband, the late Victor Turner, built on Dewey's discussions of experience in their theory and practice of anthropology (see, for example, Turner and Turner 1985; Turner and Bruner 1986). The Turners—and Edith in particular—privileged the religious experience that the researcher might undergo while engaging in anthropological fieldwork. This orientation is quite different from, say, that of history or literature, in which texts constitute the foundation of one's inquiry. Religious studies, as a discipline, falls across the spectrum insofar as it encompasses both historians and anthropologists. Also not surprisingly, therefore, faculty in religious studies hold wide-ranging opinions about the meanings and functions of experience in their pedagogies.

These opinions cannot be separated from the type of learning a given teacher hopes to engender. Arai and Barnes (in her medical school course) engage students in reflection related to their own cultural formation and self-awareness to prepare them to enter more consciously into interactions with others. For Mosher and Jacobs, the experience deriving from site visits aims to equip students to engage in what they call "intelligent interreligious dialogue." For Turner, healing is central to human consciousness. Her goal is "to awaken a sleeping faculty," the "faculty for religion." Kwok argues that engagement with the body is intrinsic to her objective of nurturing and sustaining "students' interest in the spirituality of healing and to integrate classroom learning with their daily lives."

Some teachers also incorporate theories of learning and of different types of intelligence into their course design and their approach to experience. Crawford, for example, draws on Benjamin Bloom's taxonomy of cognitive thinking and questioning—a transition from the acquisition of knowledge to comprehension, application, and analysis (Bloom 1956). Her goal is to foster active participation and engagement with increasingly complex levels of questioning and thinking. Glennon applies active-learning pedagogy, particularly its emphasis on learners' formulating their own learning goals and contracting their goals with the instructor. This approach, he argues, "culminate in cognitive, affective, and behavioral learning goals that address the content and the skills needs of the students." Arai uses Howard Gardner's discussion of three types of intelligence—linguistic, interpersonal, and intrapersonal (Gardner 1991). Kwok, in addition to using approaches to embodiment, also turns to the theories of Parker Palmer and Jane Tompkins, the latter emphasizing the importance of experiential learning in relation to the inner life of students (Tompkins 1996). Miriam Greenspan's work on healing through the "dark emotions" (Greenspan 2003) further informs Kwok's pedagogy.

Narayanan focuses on lived religion as course content. Unlike other courses on Hinduism that may begin with a discussion of classical Sanskrit texts, Narayanan helps her students to understand the ways in which textual content enters people's daily lives on a daily, experiential basis. Concomitantly, she avoids focusing on narrow understandings of illness by raising the more important existential issue of "being in the world"—which can include not being well.

In an attempt to approximate experience, many of the authors bring in speakers and show videos. Yet, as Mosher and Jacobs note, even films can be experience-far rather than experience-near. They therefore try to select films "informed by a phenomenological rather than a history-of-religions methodology." Some instructors draw on their own fieldwork experience, thereby becoming something of a living text themselves. Nakasone and Barnes turn to community advocates and residents as community faculty. Turner has healers come to her class to show students how to practice a particular form of healing.

Having students visit religious sites and attend healing rituals functions along an experiential spectrum for various instructors. Payne-Jackson has her students attend a ritual unfamiliar to them, after first clearing it with her, in order to expand their understanding and appreciation of ritual as a religious phenomenon. Glennon, too, includes attendance at a healing practice or ritual with roots in a spiritual or religious tradition. For Mosher and Jacobs, these group visits are grounded in an experiential, phenomenological, interactive methodology "by which we encourage seminar participants to become 'empathic visitors' who stand 'imaginatively within' the various worldviews we explore." Kwok, in contrast, includes the creation of ritual in class, recognizing that her students are also practitioners of liturgies, and will be responsible for generating rituals in their professional lives. Winkelman and Carr mix didactic presentations with experiential activities. In particular, the latter are "designed to produce personal experiences of the shamanic world view routinely produced in the context of shamanic practices."

Teaching Shamanism

In Western cross-cultural literature on traditional healing, the shaman has often stood as the paradigmatic healer. Several of our authors organize course units—and, in some cases, entire courses—around the phenomenon and experience of shamans, illustrating how a topic can provide multiple interpretive frames. Porterfield, for example, defines the term "shaman" broadly, noting that it first appeared in English late in the seventeenth century in reference to "priest-doctors" among Asian tribes. Later, in the eighteenth and nineteenth centuries, usage extended to include Native American "medicine men." More recently, the term has come to figure as a more generic term for "healers, prophets, and mediums who diagnosed ills and prescribed remedies by embodying and interacting with spirits." Winkelman and Carr join Mircea Eliade's work on shamans with Michael Harner's concept of "core shamanism," defining the term as involving altered states of consciousness, and interaction with a spirit world to divine and heal.

Porterfield finds that shamanism provides a useful model with which to think about the phenomenon of religious healing and to compare different kinds of religious healing. From there, she moves to a focus on healing in the history of Christianity. Finkler discusses shamanism in relation to the Kalahari iKung, Mexican spiritualists, and Hmong healers. She uses these discussions to illustrate the differences between emic and etic perspectives. Winkelman and Carr are interested in exploring tensions between what they characterize as universal variables, rendered active in specific contexts. They view shamanic experience as rooted in human physiology and, therefore, "a part of the human heritage." They remind their readers that Europe had its own shamanic traditions, and they argue that no single tradition group can claim exclusive rights to shamanism. This argument comes in response to Native Americans who have challenged non-Indians teaching about shamanism—a position responding, in turn, to cultural appropriation by some European Americans engaged in "playing Indian" (Deloria 1998). Winkelman and Carr reply that, instead, their interest lies in "core shamanism," a substrate to all particular versions.

Both they and Turner address the aspect of shamanism that involves interacting with spirits, but do so in quite different ways. Winkelman characterizes them as cognitive and emotional projections onto the unknown. Like Jungian psychologist James Hillman, he views spirits as extensions of the human unconscious "that represent important information for psychological integration and healing," and he explicitly avoids other kinds of ontological speculation.

Turner, in contrast, insists on the ontological reality of the spirit forces described by anthropological subjects. More pointedly, in her writing and teaching she describes her own experiences of the same, arguing that this is not uncommon among other anthropologists who, anticipating ridicule from their colleagues, omit such narratives from their ethnographies (see Turner 2005). In line with her goal of awakening the "religious faculty" in her students, she encourages them to attend to dreams, memories, spirits, angels, and other forms of consciousness. She challenges the distinction between the subjective and the objective, arguing that "a participant in religion may be overcome with the magnificent sense that the religion is objectively true. The spirit is 'out there,' real, and not a subjective construction of the mind."

Religious studies, still a relatively young discipline, has felt the need to differentiate itself from theology, and to assert itself as an interdisciplinary field spanning the humanities and social sciences. Its scholars, therefore, have studiously avoided such ontological discussions, opting instead for a phenomenological stance that begs the question. One studies, instead, what people say, think, feel, and do, striving to become the empathic visitor who, while speaking from an etic perspective, learns to approximate an emic one. Ontological statements of any kind generally elicit ferocious, often furious critique. And yet, as Patton asks—and Turner would surely agree—"If we maintain a relentlessly closed mind toward the claims of religious traditions to describe what is real or true, how on earth can our descriptions of how they work, however 'thick,' be authentic?" (Patton 2000:166).

By encouraging students to participate in ritual activities designed to engage such forces—whether understood as projections or as aspects of the real, Winkelman, Carr, and Turner deploy a pedagogical strategy that has not gone uncontested, as Winkelman and Carr themselves acknowledge. Critics raise the question of authorization—who, that is, has authorized them to transmit such teachings? Turner points to cases of anthropologists who learn from within a particular tradition and then are bidden to go and heal others. Do they then honor the bounds of secrecy inherent in that tradition, circumscribing their teaching accordingly? Winkelman and Carr flag challenges to the prospect of students' having powerful experiences which, for a less than stable individual, may prove damaging. Readers may differ in their assessment of the authors' response to the question. Is it different for Hernández-Ávila to invite her students to a sweat lodge? Does it make a difference that she does so as an insider?

The Embodiment of Structural Forces

Anthropologist-physician Paul Farmer (1997) signals the importance of analyzing the varieties of "structural violence"—what Kwok defines as "the larger social and political issues that make people and the society sick, such as racism, poverty, pollution, homophobia, and patriarchy." The impact of these pervasive forms of violence translates into institutional and interpersonal expressions and acts. It also, Farmer adds, plays out in individual bodies, registering as health disparities. Unless students are taught to recognize and analyze these structural dimensions, it becomes all too easy to reduce these issues to individual failings. Crawford, accordingly, attends to political and economic contexts, as well as to the cosmological dimensions of the traditions about which she teaches.

Kwok points to the imperative to show the relationship between individual and systemic dimensions of healing. "As students begin to see that healing has personal, interpersonal, cultural, institutional, and spiritual dimensions," she writes, "they are more open to discussing the difficult issues of racism, homophobia, and gender discrimination in society." This imperative governs Barnes's team-taught first-year medical school course as well, with the goal of helping students come to an awareness of their own biases which, if unattended, may contribute to perpetuating health disparities. Both Kwok and the members of Barnes's team teach that all racial/ethnic/cultural groups have a stake in this inquiry, building on the notion that oppressive practice harms all parties in different ways.

The project of situating oneself, therefore, becomes more than an intellectual conceit. Rather, it functions as part of a process of reclaiming those parts of self truncated by perpetuating, or being the target of, the different forms of structural violence. Our authors who do so view it as part of their own praxis, invested in challenging such forces as misogyny and colonization, as described by Talamantez, Hernández-Ávila, and Medina. Mosher and Jacobs introduce their students to progressive voices speaking from within different traditions, to illustrate ways in which traditions themselves are addressing these forces. Others highlight women's participation in healing traditions, the effects of illness on women, and the loci of power through healing. For some, this involves a larger project of reclaiming one's gendered identity. Religious traditions are analyzed both as having inflicted injury and having provided tools for healing.

Payne-Jackson requires her students to engage in service learning within disenfranchised communities, to understand experientially that healing is a communitywide concern. Nakasone's course involves community advocates, pointing to the ways in which advocacy itself can also be an act of healing. Other reclamation projects involve what Hernández-Ávila calls "reindianization"—the challenge to the stripping away of identity perpetrated through colonialism. She, like Talamantez, emphasizes the imperative for non-Indian scholars to learn Native American languages in order to study Native practices. She also emphasizes the reclamation of language for Native Americans themselves as a core part of reconnecting with the multiple dimensions of their traditions in a crucial act of recovering identity. Here, healing is defined as both individual and communal. Similarly, Kwok cites Greenspan (2003) to argue that personal healing and global healing are integral to each other.

Narratives and Arts

Illness and healing are often expressed through stories, or what Arthur Kleinman calls "illness narratives" (1988). These narratives speak to the particularities of a person's suffering, and to the meanings and effects of sickness on all the lives involved. When a biomedical clinician takes that narrative and translates it into a "case," Kleinman argues, the existential dimensions are stripped away, leaving only the physiological underpinnings. Many of our authors recognize the centrality of story to the enterprise of understanding how illness experience is configured. Arai, for example, has her students work with a "collaborator" to elicit such stories. Both telling and hearing such stories have therapeutic meaning. Turner bases her entire course on stories of healers at work. Talamantez points to the ways in which individual experiences of suffering are relocated within mythic frameworks, which serve to remind the afflicted individual of her place in a larger balance, helping her to recover her awareness of that location.

Glennon observes that students are rarely encouraged to develop their creative abilities through artwork, journaling, and similar activities. A number of our authors incorporate such activities into their course design. Narayanan shows how the theological and the mythological take embodied form in sculpture, architecture, painting, and dance. Medina, herself an artist, has her students create an *ofrenda*—an altar for a deceased person, in the Mexican tradition of the *Días de los Muertos*, or Days of the Dead. Kwok invites students to create a "centerpiece" for each class, finding that it evokes "a rich visual memory." In each case, the arts become an important vehicle for learning.

Like Medina, Hernández-Ávila, as a poet and dancer, emphasizes core Nahuatl concepts related to artistry and creativity as critical components of religious engagement. She writes, "I wanted students to encounter and discover the humanistic and liberating aspects of the Nahuatl cultural, spiritual traditions which foreground the autonomy of the creative self, and possible wholeness in the intimate relationship of that creative self to the Giver/Creator of Life." Both she and Medina lift up the role of the *tlamatinime*—in Nahuatl tradition, the wise teacher whose purpose is to encourage the awakening of consciousness (the *conscientización*) of the learner. From this perspective, teaching itself promotes creative processes as a part of restoration and healing (see Barnes 1991).

Conclusion

Clearly, some vital cultures and traditions are not represented in this collection. For example, despite extensive networking and searches, drawing on the resources of the AAR, other professional organizations, colleagues, and the wonders of Google, no courses related to Judaism, Islam, or African traditions surfaced. Some of these matters are addressed in units in some of the courses discussed in this volume. To encourage faculty to develop courses related to healing, resource bibliographies have been both included and placed on the AAR syllabus Web site, representing Jewish, Christian, American Mind Cure and New Thought, and other African and African Diaspora systems of healing. Useful anthologies and journals have been included as well, as a way of getting a head start on theoretical and methodological issues.

If this collection is any evidence, there is enormous promise for an emerging field in the study of religion and healing. I invite our colleagues across their respective disciplines to mine the literature within their own areas of scholarship in order to develop courses, and I predict that they will be surprised at how much they find. It is to be hoped that embarking on course development in this rich area may inspire others to turn their scholarly eye toward including related issues in their own research. In all of these endeavors, I wish our readers the same fulfillment that the authors of this collection have found through our own engagement of the topic.

BIBLIOGRAPHY

Abu-Lughod, Janet. 1991. Going Beyond the Global Babble. In *Culture, Globalization and the World-System: Contemporary Conditions for the Representations of Identity*, ed. Anthony D. King. Binghamton: State University of New York at Binghamton.

Barnes, Linda 1991 "Healing" as a Theme in Teaching the Study of Religion in a Liberal Arts Setting. In *Tracing Common Themes: Comparative Courses in the Study of Religion*, ed. John B. Carman and Steven P. Hopkins, pp. 81–99. Atlanta: Scholars Press.

————. 1999. *Variations on a Teaching/Learning Workshop: Pedagogy and Faculty Development in Religious Studies*. Atlanta: Scholars Press.

————. 2005a. Multiple meanings of Chinese healing in the United States. In *Religion and Healing in America*, ed. Linda L. Barnes and Susan S. Sered, pp. 307–331. New York: Oxford University Press.

————. 2005b. American Acupuncture and Efficacy: Meanings and Their Points of Insertion. *Medical Anthropology Quarterly* 19(3): 239–266.

———— and David Coulter. 2006. Concepts of holistic care. In *Development and Disabilities: Delivery of Medical Care for Children and Adults*, 2nd ed. I. Leslie Rubin and Allen C. Crocker. Baltimore: Paul H. Brookes Publishing Co., Inc.

Berry, John W. 2003. Conceptual Approaches to Acculturation. In *Acculturation: Advances in Theory, Measurement, and Applied Research*, ed. Kevin M. Chun, Pamela Balls Organista, and Gerardo Marín, pp. 17–37. Washington, DC: American Psychological Association.

Bloom, Benjamin. 1956. *Taxonomy of Educational Objectives: The Classification of Educational Goals*. New York: Longman and Green.

Bowker, Geoffrey C., and Susan Leigh Star. 2002. *Sorting Things Out: Classification and Its Consequences*. Cambridge, MA: MIT Press.

Brady, Jeff. 2005. Non-Christians Claim Bias at Air Force Academy. On *Day to Day* National Public Radio (May 4).

Carman, John B., and Steven P. Hopkins. 1991. Thematic Comparison in Teaching the History of Religion. In *Tracing Common Themes: Comparative Courses in the Study of Religion*, ed. John B. Carman and Steven P. Hopkins, pp. 1–18. Atlanta: Scholars Press.

————, ed. 1991. *Tracing Common Themes: Comparative Courses in the Study of Religion*. Atlanta: Scholars Press.

Connor, Linda L. 2001. Healing Powers in Contemporary Asia. In *Healing Powers and Modernity: Traditional Medicine, Shamanism, and Science in Asian Societies*, ed. Linda H. Connor and Geoffrey Samuel, pp. 3–21. Westport, CT: Bergin & Garvey.

Csordas, Thomas J., and Elizabeth Lewton. 1998. Practice, Performance, and Experience in Ritual Healing. *Transcultural Psychiatry* 35(4): 435–512.

Deloria, Phillip J. 1998. *Playing Indian*. New Haven, CT: Yale University Press.

Dirlik, Arif. 2000. Reversals, Ironies, Hegemonies: Notes on the Contemporary Historiography of Modern China. In *History after the Three Worlds: Post-Eurocentric Historiographies*, ed. Arif Dirlik, Vinay Bahl, and Peter Gran, pp. 125–156. New York: Rowman & Littlefield.

Doniger, Wendy. 2000. Post-Modern and -Colonial -Structural Comparisons. In *A Magic Still Dwells: Comparative Religion in the Postmodern Age,* ed. Kimberley C. Patton and Benjamin Ray, pp. 63–74. Berkeley: University of California Press.

Eck, Diana L. 2000. Dialogue and Method: Reconstructing the Study of Religion. In *A Magic Still Dwells: Comparative Religion in the Postmodern Age,* ed. Kimberley C. Patton and Benjamin Ray, pp. 131–149. Berkeley: University of California Press.

———. 2001. *A New Religious America: How a "Christian Country" Has Now Become the World's Most Religiously Diverse Nation.* San Francisco: HarperSanFrancisco.

Eckel, Malcolm David. 2000. Contested Identities: The Study of Buddhism in the Postmodern World. In *A Magic Still Dwells: Comparative Religion in the Postmodern Age,* ed. Kimberley C. Patton and Benjamin Ray, pp. 55–62. Berkeley: University of California Press.

Engel, George. 1977. The Need for a New Medical Model: A Challenge for Biomedicine. *Science* 196: 129–136.

Farmer, Paul. 1997. On Suffering and Structural Violence: A View from Below. In *Social Suffering,* ed. Arthur Kleinman, Veena Das, and Margaret Lock, pp. 261–283. Berkeley: University of California Press.

Featherstone, Mike. 1995. *Undoing Culture: Globalization, Postmodern and Identity.* London: Sage.

Folkert, Kendall W., edited by John E. Cort. 1991. A Thematic Course in the Study of Religion. In *Tracing Common Themes: Comparative Courses in the Study of Religion,* ed. John B. Carman and Steven P. Hopkins, pp. 19–36. Atlanta: Scholars Press.

Gardner, Howard. 1991. Cognition: A Western Perspective. In *MindScience: an East-West Dialogue,* ed. Daniel Goleman and Robert A.F. Thurman, pp. 82–84. Boston: Wisdom.

Garro, Linda C. 1998. On the Rationality of Decision-Making Studies. Part 1—Decision Models of Treatment Choice. *Medical Anthropology Quarterly* 12(3): 319–340; Part 2—Divergent Rationalities, 12(3):341–355.

Geertz, Clifford. 1973. *The Interpretation of Cultures.* New York: Basic Books.

Greenspan, Miriam. 2003. *Healing through the Dark Emotions: The Wisdom of Grief, Fear, and Despair.* Boston: Shambhala.

Griffith, R. Marie. 2003. Born Again Bodies: New Thought, Evangelicalism, and American Body Regimens. Oral presentation, Society for the Anthropology of Religion, Providence, RI, April 25.

Gupta, Akhil, and James Ferguson. 1997. Culture, Power, Place: Ethnography at the End of an Era. In *Culture, Power, Place: Explorations in Critical Anthropology.* Durham, NC: Duke University Press.

Holdredge, Barbara A. 2000. What's Beyond the Post? Comparative Analysis as Critical Method. In *A Magic Still Dwells: Comparative Religion in the Postmodern Age,* ed. Kimberley C. Patton and Benjamin Ray, pp. 77–91. Berkeley: University of California Press.

Hungerford, Harold. 1987. *Sheep, Goats, and Chinese Encyclopedias.* Chicago: Chicago Literary Club.

Juergensmeyer, Mark, ed. 1991. *Teaching the Introductory Course in Religious Studies: A Sourcebook.* Atlanta: Scholars Press.

Kleinman, Arthur. 1981. The meaning context of illness and care: reflections on a central theme in the anthropology of medicine. In *Science and Cultures: Anthropological and Historical Studies in the Sciences.* Everett Mendelsohn and Yehuda Elkana, ed., pp. 161–176. Dordrecht, the Netherlands: D. Reidel.

————. 1988. *The Illness Narratives: Suffering, Healing, and the Human Condition*. New York: Basic Books.

Kleinman, Arthur, and Don Seeman. 1998. The Politics of Moral Practice in Psychotherapy and Religious Healing. *Contributions to Indian Sociology* (n.s.) 32(2): 237–252.

Kroes, Rob. 2000. Advertising: The Commodification of American Icons of Freedom. In *"Here, There and Everywhere": The Foreign Politics of American Popular Culture*, ed. Reinhold Wagnleitner and Elaine Tyler May, pp. 273–287. Hanover, NH: University Press of New England.

Langridge, D. W. 1992. *Classification: Its Kinds, Systems, Elements, and Applications*. London: Bowker-Saur.

Lochhead, David. 1988. *The Dialogical Imperative: A Christian Reflection on Interfaith Encounter*. Maryknoll, NY: Orbis

McGill, Arthur C. 1980. The Religious Aspects of Medicine. In *Medicine and Religion*, ed. Donald W. Shriver, pp. 77–93. Pittsburgh: University of Pittsburgh.

Paden, William E. 2000. Elements of a New Comparativism. In *A Magic Still Dwells: Comparative Religion in the Postmodern Age*, ed. Kimberley C. Patton and Benjamin Ray, pp. 182–192. Berkeley: University of California Press.

Patton, Kimberley C. 2000. Juggling Torches: Why We Still Need Comparative Religion. In *A Magic Still Dwells: Comparative Religion in the Postmodern Age*, ed. Kimberley C. Patton and Benjamin Ray, pp. 153–171. Berkeley: University of California Press.

Race, Alan. 1983. *Christians and Religious Pluralism: Patterns in the Christian Theology of Religions*. London: SCM.

Robertson, Roland. 1995. Glocalization: Time-Space and Homogeneity-Heterogeneity. In *Global Modernities*, ed. Mike Featherstone, Scott Lash, and Roland Robertson, pp. 25–44. London: Sage.

Said, Edward W. 1994. *Culture and Imperialism*. New York: Random House.

Saks, Mike. 1999. Beyond the Frontiers of Science? Religious Aspects of Alternative Medicine. In *Religion, Health, and Suffering*, ed. John R. Hinnells and Roy Porter, pp. 381–398. London: Kegan Paul.

Schön Donald, and Martin Rein. 1994. *Frame Reflection: Toward the Resolution of Intractable Policy Controversies*. New York: Harper Collins.

Starr, Paul 1982. *The Social Transformation of American Medicine*. New York: Basic Books.

Sullivan, Lawrence. 2000. The Net of Indra: Comparison and the Contribution of Perception. In *A Magic Still Dwells: Comparative Religion in the Postmodern Age*, ed. Kimberley C. Patton and Benjamin Ray, pp. 206–234. Berkeley: University of California Press.

Sullivan, Winnifred Fallers. 2000. American Religion is Naturally Comparative. In *A Magic Still Dwells: Comparative Religion in the Postmodern Age*, ed. Kimberley C. Patton and Benjamin Ray, pp. 117–130. Berkeley: University of California Press.

Tompkins, Jane. 1996. *A Life in School: What the Teacher Learned*. Reading, MA: Addison-Wesley.

Trimble, Joseph E. 2003. Introduction: Social Change and Acculturation. In *Acculturation: Advances in Theory, Measurement, and Applied Research*, ed. Kevin M. Chun, Pamela Balls Organista, and Gerardo Marín, pp. 3–13. Washington, DC: American Psychological Association.

Turner, Edith. 2005. *Among the Healers: Stories of Spiritual and Ritual Healing around the World*. Westport, CT: Praeger.

Turner, Victor W., and Edith L. B. Turner, eds. 1985. *On the Edge of the Bush: Anthropology as Experience*. Tucson: University of Arizona Press.

Turner, Victor, and Edward M. Bruner, ed. 1986. *The Anthropology of Experience* Urbana: University of Illinois Press.

Tweed, Thomas A. 1999. Night-Stand Buddhists and Other Creatures: Sympathizers, Adherents, and the Study of Religion. In *American Buddhism: Methods and Findings in Recent Scholarship*, ed. Duncan Ryūken Williams and Christopher S. Queen, pp. 71–90. Surrey: Curzon.

Welsch, Wolfgang. 1999 Transculturality: The Puzzling Form of Cultures Today. In *Spaces of Culture: City, Nation, World*, ed. Mike Featherstone and Scott Lash, pp. 194–213. London: Sage.

PART I

Theoretical Frames

I

Religion, Healing, and the Body

Suzanne J. Crawford

> Put your feet down with pollen.
> Put your hands down with pollen.
> Put your head down with pollen.
> Then your feet are pollen;
> Your hands are pollen;
> Your body is pollen;
> Your mind is pollen;
> Your voice is pollen;
> The trail is beautiful.
> Be still.
> —Washington Matthews, 1897

At the center of my scholarship are questions about embodiment: how bodies in movement, in society, in symbol, and in expression, create and are created by religious experience. At the heart of religiosity is a move toward wellness—physical, spiritual, intellectual, social, ecological. Spiritual lives are dominated, overwhelmed at times, by a need for healing. Through enacting ritual, religious practitioners and adherents re-create the world, re-create the self, re-create the body. I would argue that, at the heart of every religious tradition, are practices of healing. Healing and medical traditions within every culture are intensely concentrated arenas in which foundational notions of the sacred and the ultimate (whether explicit or implicit) come into play within lived daily life. In this chapter I reflect upon my course *Religion, Healing and the Body*, a topics course taught under the wider rubric of Religion and Culture. "Religion and Culture" could encompass virtually any mode of human experience so, one might ask, why *religion and healing* in particular? It is a fundamental argument throughout all my courses that questions of ultimate meaning and ultimate concern can be expressed and accessed within virtually any cultural arena, not simply within churches or synagogues. And, as this class goes on to argue, one of the most powerful spaces for accessing and negotiating the sacred can be found in approaches to healing. I also chose religion and healing as a focus because a course such as this is uniquely situated to meet what I see as the fundamental educational goals of the liberal arts curriculum and the goals of religious studies as a discipline more specifically: to disrupt students' preconceived worldviews, present them with multiple alternative perspectives, and to challenge them to critically evaluate these perspectives within the context of the political inequalities and conflicts that emerge when multiple perspective collide (or coexist).

This course has been taught as a general education requirement in the humanities at both a large state university (University of California, Santa Barbara), and at a small private religiously affiliated liberal arts university (Pacific Lutheran University in Tacoma, Washington). Despite these schools' obvious differences of class size and religious affiliation, the goals of the course remained essentially the same: to enable students to reflect upon their own philosophical assumptions about the body, medical care, healing, and spirituality with a new critical distance, seeing these assumptions as a product of our own historical and cultural context; to appreciate and critically empathize with alternative perspectives on the body and healing; and to analyze the power relations that emerge when different perspectives (often linked to class, gender, and ethnicity) come into contact with one another.

The structure of the course is designed to facilitate two major pedagogical goals: active participation in and engagement with increasingly complex levels of questioning and thinking. Active participation is essential for every aspect of this course. I want to convey information to them, but I also want them to develop analytical skills that enable them to make connections among traditions, apply theoretical ideas across cultures, and question established ways of thinking. This requires their consistent active engagement with the material, and with each other. A single class session will commonly involve a reflection question (which students are asked to write on for five minutes, and then discuss), a brief lecture, guided dialogue about assigned reading, and active interpretation of some kind of visual representation, such as slides or video. Reflection questions in particular allow students to integrate these ideas on a personal level and engage in what Ninian Smart referred to as *critical empathy*—the ability to empathize with ideas and experiences outside of one's culture while simultaneously viewing them through a scholarly lens.

In order to promote increasingly sophisticated modes of thinking and questioning, course assignments throughout the semester are designed to follow Benjamin Bloom's taxonomy of cognitive thinking and questioning. Bloom's now-classic work argues for a progression from knowledge (observation and recall of information); comprehension (understanding meaning, translating into new contexts); application (using information in new situations); analysis (seeing patterns, recognizing hidden meanings); synthesis (using old ideas to formulate new ones); and evaluation (comparing and discriminating between ideas). The course as a whole and assignments in particular move through this taxonomy as it transitions from unit to unit, demanding of students an increasingly sophisticated level of thinking (Bloom 1956).

The course is divided into seven units, each of which builds upon the previous in terms of knowledge base, theoretical analysis, and scholarly questioning. The units, oriented around particular views of the embodied subject, are Biomedical Bodies; Complementary Bodies; Porous Bodies; Active Bodies; Sacred Bodies; Gendered Bodies; and Political Bodies. The first three units are guided by theories from medical anthropology on the cultural specificity of healing traditions (Arthur Kleinman, Robert Hahn); units four and five emphasize questions of the phenomenology of embodiment (Thomas Csordas); and units six and seven are guided by theories of the body and power (Michel Foucault, Denise Riley, Susan Bordo). Each unit works to guide students to a place in which they can critically and knowledgably reflect upon approaches to health and wellness, perceiving their underlying spiritual, philosophical, and political implications, and negotiate ways in which cultural differences can be creatively navigated.

Unit One

Why Biomedical Bodies?

The first unit, Biomedical Bodies, is devoted to disrupting established categories of thought, introducing key theoretical principles, and enabling students to reflect critically upon their own biomedical tradition as a product of culture and historical location. The first goal of this unit is to give students the tools with which they can begin to see even Western biomedicine as an inherently *religious*, ritual-bound phenomenon, one that emerges from a particular culture-bound worldview. The second goal is to give students theoretical tools and terminologies to begin discussing multiple healing systems. In particular, this unit focuses on the distinction between *illness* and *disease*, and definitions of *healing*. And finally, this unit seeks to provide students with an opportunity to critically reflect upon their own medical experiences, considering the symbols, rituals, and messages that have been conveyed within them.

Challenges

One immediate challenge that must be addressed involves justifying why a course in Religion and Culture should take as its focus religion and healing. Unit one presents a rationale for this decision through its definition of "religion," "illness," and "healing." Students are first challenged to rethink their definitions of religion, expanding their understanding to include as "religious" those elements of cultural experience that may at first glance appear purely secular. A variety of scholarly definitions of religion are discussed at length, such as those of Emile Durkheim, Robert Bellah, Clifford Geertz, Paul Tillich, and D. T. Suzuki. Consideration of these definitions is intended to open possibilities in which seemingly mundane spheres of existence might in fact be spaces of religiosity, where the sacred might be experienced and expressed in surprising ways—and within healing systems in particular. It is at this point that I also encourage students to begin rethinking fundamental understandings of healing and illness. Having read selections from Arthur Kleinman's *The Illness Narratives*, and Robert Hahn's *Illness and Healing*, students are guided through a discussion of how we define "healing," "illness," and "disease." I return to these definitions throughout the course, emphasizing the important distinction between "disease" (the material and physiological ailment as diagnosed by a practitioner), and "illness" (how individuals and their social networks perceive, live with, and give meaning to the symptoms, disability, and treatment that accompany the disease) (Kleinman 1988: 13). As Hahn further argues, illness can be seen as "an unwanted condition in one's person or self," as an inability to be one's self, an inability to fully engage with one's appropriate identity (Hahn 1996: 5).

This unit also sets up the rationale and theoretical positioning for studying other cultural traditions and perspectives. As Hahn and Kleinman suggest, in order to make sense of cross-cultural notions of healing, one must first begin with an understanding of culturally distinct notions of *self*, because such notions lead to culturally distinct approaches to healing. As Hahn notes, "For example, whereas disturbances in the capacity for independence may be regarded as pathological in the West, disturbances in the capacity for interdependence may be regarded as pathological elsewhere" (Hahn 1996: 5). And, in addressing the whole self, the illness and not the disease, healing incorporates physical, psychological, and spiritual approaches to wellness. What those approaches will be, how they will take shape, and what ultimate goals will shape them, are determined by cultural, political, and social locations. As Kleinman further argues, "Illness takes on meaning as suffering because of the way this relationship between body and self is mediated by cultural symbols of a religious, moral, or spiritual kind"(1988: 13, 27). Hahn concludes, "The soul of sickness is closer to the self than the cell" (1996: 5). This broader picture of illness conveys a sense of *healing* as a religious activity, one that is fundamentally about self-making, about restoring a sense of one's self, through ritual, symbol, and storytelling. Having disrupted common assumptions about where issues of ultimate concern and meaning can be experienced, where ritual, ethics, and meaning can be constructed, and how we might distinguish between disease and illness, the students have tools with which to reconsider assumptions about their own sacred healing system—Western biomedicine. Class texts present a compelling argument that Western biomedicine can itself be viewed as a religion, insofar as it is constructed around ritual practices, ethics, faith, symbol systems, and a sacred hierarchy of authority from patients, to nursing staff, to physicians. Getting students to see biomedicine as a religious system and a product of culture, based upon certain philosophical, spiritual, and cultural assumptions, is not an easy task. Students tend to continually return to a sense of biomedicine as "real" medicine, and other traditions as superstitious, inferior, or less evolved. To facilitate this necessary critical distance and reflection upon their own culture, students read "Body Ritual of the Nacirema," a traditional anthropological analysis of the strange and mystical world of the primitive *Nacirema* (American), their body rituals, and the obsessive faith with which they endow their *latipsoh* (hospital). The piece introduces students to the notion that our own culture is as bound by ritual, ceremonially structured, and faith-driven as any "exotic" culture we might discuss in class. Another valuable text in getting across the notion of biomedicine-as-religion is Robbie Davis-Floyd's *Birth as an American Rite of Passage*. Davis-Floyd's critique of biomedical birthing traditions crafts a compelling depiction of biomedicine as ruled by ritual, faith, and cultural hierarchies of patriarchy and technocracy.

If the goal of this unit is to disrupt students' fundamental assumptions about religion and healing, this notion is put into practice in their own illness narratives. In this assignment they begin this process of critical reflection upon their own standpoint by writing about an experience they have had with illness and how it affected the way they viewed their body, their faith, or medicine in general. In particular, students are asked to apply Kleinman and Hahn's notions of illness and disease, and to reflect upon the rituals, symbols, and meaning conveyed within their medical care.

Unit Two

Why Complementary Bodies?

Having established these notions of illness, disease, and selfhood, and having disrupted the a priori certitude of biomedicine, this unit provides students with an alternative perspective, traditional Chinese medicine, in which the fundamental philosophical assumptions of biomedicine are virtually inverted. Here students begin the process of critical empathy, understanding the rationale and reasoning behind other worldviews and traditions: seeing through someone else's eyes. Without necessarily adopting that position, students come to a place where they understand the system and the worldview upon which it is predicated. The first goal is simply knowledge of another tradition, that students will be able to identify and recall the physiologies, etiologies, and modes of cure that are here involved. The second goal is for students to demonstrate their comprehension of Kleinman and Hahn's theoretical precepts by applying them to the Chinese model.

Challenges

The theoretical orientation of this unit is to introduce students to the notion that there are multiple ways of perceiving the body, causes of disease, illness, and approaches to healing, and that these differences are primarily based on culturally distinct notions of the self. Before students can make knowledgeable comparisons between traditions they need a firm grounding in the logic and rationale of each. This requires presenting students with a clear understanding of the underlying worldviews, interpretations of illness, and approaches to healing found within each system. This can be a difficult undertaking, because for many students this is their first introduction to a different approach to the body and the embodied subject. In contrast to the mechanistic body found in biomedicine, traditional Chinese medicine approaches a body that is perceived as "an open system linking social relations to the self, a vital balance between interrelated elements in a holistic cosmos," where the self is "an organic part of a sacred, sociocentric world, a communication system involving exchanges with others (including the divine)" (Kleinman 1988: 11–12). The emphasis in this unit is upon notions of *complementarity and correspondence*, of bodies existing in interrelationship to the natural world, mirroring the landscape, and ordered by laws of elemental balance and harmony of opposites. Students are easily overwhelmed when confronted with an entirely new way of seeing the body and illness. One of the best ways to ensure their comprehension is through application of this knowledge. In this instance, students are presented with a chart of the five phases, a fundamental ordering structure of the Chinese cosmos. Each phase corresponds to seasons, sensations, foods, organ systems, and so on. Following a lecture on the ideas of complementarity and correspondence and the importance of maintaining balance among the five phases, students are given a variety of patient biographies. They are asked to "diagnose" the patient's imbalance and recommend lifestyle adjustments. Although I have emphasized that this is a simplified and inaccurate mode of diagnosis, not what they would receive from a professional practitioner, students have experienced a genuine sense of accomplishment (a true "aha!" moment) when they were able to diagnose "actual patients." A woman visiting her doctor in late fall, for example, who lived in a particularly damp climate, worried incessantly about her financial instability, and was suffering from muscle aches and stomach cramps was suffering from "blocked spleen chi," they decided, and they recommended that she move to a warm, dry climate and eat spicy foods.

Unit Three

Why Porous Bodies?

The goal of this unit is to continue the application of Hahn's and Kleinman's theories of the culturally specific notions of illness and the embodied self, by exploring two additional traditions: Tibetan Buddhist medicine and Diné ceremonials, or chantways.[1] Each of these traditions has a particularly complex view of the embodied self, and its relationship to the surrounding cosmos. As the title of the unit suggests, these are *porous* bodies—bodies and selves that are essentially interdependent and interconnected with the human, spiritual, and ecological communities. This view of the embodied self directly instructs the healing traditions within both these cultures. The goal of this unit, then, is to make further explicit how the cultural understanding of the embodied self is reflected in disease etiologies, healing techniques, and ultimate concern of the healing process.

Challenges

Tibetan Buddhism's notion of an interdependent, impermanent self directly constructs the method and outcome of Tibetan medicine. The ultimate concern here is the realization of one's true nature: a self that is a constellation of experiences, a constant process of becoming, rather than something finite and unchanging. For Tibetan Buddhists, ignorance of this notion of an interconnected self is the ultimate cause of illness. Healing is thus a spiritual endeavor; through somatic medicine, tantra, and dharma, the individual moves closer to enlightenment and genuine wellness.[2] This unit is also concerned with Diné conceptions of the embodied subject, a body and self that are intricately bound to the sacred landscape of the Diné people, a tie that is maintained through complex ceremonial chantways and storytelling. The sacred geography of the Diné, bounded by the four directions, each with its sacred mountain, holy people, associated plants, animals, colors, minerals, stories, and familial clans, is represented within Diné sandpaintings. The human self, physiologically, energetically, and spiritually is intertwined with this landscape and the human community of the Diné people. Healing thus becomes a ceremonial process of restoring the individual to balanced and harmonious relationships with the spiritual, ecological, and ancestral forces in the Diné landscape.

    Diné and Tibetan Buddhist healing systems both incorporate sandpainting mandalas into their meditative and spiritual practice, images that are used as a means of expressing this sense of interconnection with a sacred cosmos. Understanding a sense of self that is fundamentally intertwined with one's landscape can be a very alien concept to students, many of whom may never have considered the importance of place within personal identity. To bridge this gap, students are asked to create a mandala of their own. Using whatever visual media they prefer (from crayons to Photoshop to knitting), students have crafted fantastically creative sacred geographies representing landscapes that give them a sense of identity, location, and meaning.

Unit Four

Why Active Bodies?

Having introduced students to a variety of healing traditions outside of Western biomedicine and established the multiplicity of views of the embodied self, the purpose of this unit is to provide a space for comparison between traditions. Drawing from phenomenological studies of embodiment that emphasize the view from within, the experiential reality of being *in* a body, this unit focuses on the importance of movement and performativity in these healing traditions, and the transformative power of such movement. Once students have demonstrated their knowledge of a variety of traditions, this unit provides them with the opportunity to find points of connection between them, specifically, through the notion of *subtle physiologies.*

Challenges

Most centrally, this unit reinforces the notion of subtle physiologies: bodily systems existing between pure matter and pure spirit which appear to be present in nearly every healing tradition outside of Western biomedicine. The unit compares four bodily practices and their concurrent subtle physiologies. In each, a subtle physiology exists whereby energy is generated, preserved, and moved throughout the body upon established pathways or meridians through visualization, ritual, breathing, and dance. These traditions include: Diné chantways as a means of coordinating holy winds; the role of *taiqi* (a Chinese martial art) as a means of cultivating *qi* (pronounced "ch'ee"—vital force) within Taoist traditions; yoga, breathing, and meditation within Tibetan tantric healing traditions; and finally, healing dance (or *num chai)* among the Kalahari iKung. All of these traditions involve physical practices. Such practices occur within a ritualized context, and are always accompanied by meditation and breathing techniques designed to effect changes within subtle physiologies which, in turn, affect the material and spiritual selves. However, difficulties arise as students grapple with these comparisons. Nearly all of these traditions are new to them, and attempts at comparisons can quickly lead to confusion. I find that visual representations of these physiologies are vital for student comprehension. I present the students with hand-drawn diagrams of each of these systems' subtle physiologies, demonstrating the remarkable parallels existing within and among them. The visual images do the trick: students are always profoundly stuck by the similarities. The second challenge that must immediately follow is to recontextualize each tradition, emphasizing the distinctiveness of worldview, and the particularity of selfhood as it is approached and experienced in each cultural tradition.

Unit Five

Why: Sacred Bodies?

One primary goal of this course is for students to begin a process of critical reflection upon the nature of healing and what it means to achieve wellness. Having disrupted established biomedical assumptions about health and wellness, and having been presented with a variety of traditions with markedly different views, students can begin to formulate their own definitions of healing. This unit continues a phenomenological look at healing, here emphasizing the role of healing traditions in formulating a sense of self, of personal identity. The purpose of the unit is both to find points of connections with healing traditions in the West and to continue this process of critical reflection upon the meaning of healing.

Challenges

This unit focuses on healing as self-making within Rarámuri, Christian, and Jewish healing traditions, all of which emphasize healing as the realization of a working identity. This unit draws its theoretical approach from Thomas Csordas's *The Sacred Self*. Csordas argues that charismatic healing in Catholic congregations centers on a re-creation of a sacred self, the self that one was created to be. Healing of physical, emotional, and spiritual wounds all work toward this larger goal of realizing the self, becoming a "sacred self" united with Christ. This unit illustrates this point through texts and films that highlight Christian faith healing, Jewish Orthodox ritual and ceremony, as well as the re-creation of the self within recovery from drug and alcohol addiction. We conclude the section with a viewing of the film *Jesus' Son*. This film provides a stirring depiction of a young man's addiction to and recovery from narcotics. Not overtly "religious," the film is a stirring illustration of Christian themes of redemption and the remaking of self. Throughout, these narratives of Christian faith emphasize healing as a process of remaking the self, of locating and embodying a new identity.

Healing as self-making is a difficult concept for many students to grasp. To facilitate this, students are asked to apply the concept to a "real life" individual. Working in groups, students create a patient biography (based on an actual or fictitious patient), and research biomedical and alternative treatment options. As they reflect upon their research and compose treatment recommendations for the patient, they are asked to consider the role of self-making in their patient's healing process. What is the self this person is meant to embody? What stands in the way? How can these obstacles to wellness be overcome? Collaborative group work such as this is always fraught with pedagogical dangers. Often, for instance, one student ends up carrying the weight of less motivated students in the group. I have sought to remedy such potential pitfalls by making each person of the group responsible for particular aspects of the research, and grading them based both on their individual contributions and their ability to work together as a whole. I have also incorporated into the semester collaborative group workdays, as students often find it difficult to coordinate their schedules outside of class, and required periodic progress reports. As a whole, such projects help students to apply abstract ideas to real-life scenarios, thus expanding their understanding of course material.

Unit Six

Why Gendered Bodies?

Having looked at healing traditions in their idealized form, this unit seeks to locate these traditions within the real world of political and social inequalities. Who has access to care and to roles as healers? What kinds of power relations exist between doctors and patients? Who gets to make decisions about care? How do structural violence and social inequalities affect the way in which illness and healing are perceived or accessed? Social hierarchies of gender, ethnicity, and class may determine one's access to care, power of choice, and ability to control the way in which care is given, practiced, or integrated into society. This unit concentrates on gender and the way it affects one's bodily experience and approach to wellness.

Challenges

This unit primarily emphasizes women's participation in healing traditions within patriarchal structures such as Saudi Arabian Islam and Orthodox Judaism. The challenge here is to bring students to recognize the covert ways in which women maintain power and control over their wellness and spirituality even within settings in which they are seemingly disempowered. Additionally, students may find it difficult to make connections between their own position as women and men in twenty-first-century America and what might seem to them to be alien notions of gender. It thus becomes important to note the ways in which biomedicine too alienates women from positions of authority and decision making, and to return to Robbie Davis-Floyd's feminist critique of biomedicine, finding places of connection with the essays in this unit. It is also deeply important to raise issues of masculinity and the effects that a society's construction of the masculine has on male well-being. As a way of making this connection, students read a deeply moving piece by Howard Harrod, "Essay on Desire," in which he reflects upon the impact that his battle with cancer has had on his sexuality and sense of self. Throughout, this unit highlights the necessary negotiations of power relations and gendered hierarchies that both women and men must navigate in seeking healing, and the ways in which gender complicates and transforms this process.

Unit Seven

Why Political Bodies?

As with the previous section, the goal here is to complicate students' notions of healing traditions by pointing out the way in which they must seek to operate within what are often highly charged spaces of political, cultural, or ethnic conflict. Healing systems pulled out of context and looked at under the glass present a partial and distorted view of such traditions. If healing is truly about self-making, then the lived reality of that self must be considered. What does it mean for an individual to create a working identity, if that identity is compromised by poverty, despair, cultural alienation, or the historical legacy of colonialism? The goal of this unit is thus to take students from simple comprehension of the variety of healing traditions to a sense of the deeply complex political climate within which healing must take place and to which healing must respond.

Challenges

The final unit concentrates on a careful reading of Anne Fadiman's *The Spirit Catches You and You Fall Down*. This book narrates the story of Lia Lee, a Hmong child with epilepsy, and the cultural conflicts between her biomedical doctors in Merced, California, and her traditional Hmong parents. The book vividly concludes the class, illustrating virtually all the key thematic and theoretical issues raised throughout the semester. It demonstrates how understandings of the self, the body, illness, and healing are culturally distinct; it presents Hmong approaches to healing, disease etiology, and the philosophical assumptions upon which these rest. Without demonizing biomedicine, the book illustrates how, for all its incredible knowledge, biomedicine can itself be a form of religious ethnomedicine, working from culturally determined assumptions about the self, the body, and curing that can complicate and disrupt effective patient care—especially when working across cultures. The book illustrates healing as self-making, as part of a larger process of negotiating the unequal power relations and cultural stresses of a newly immigrated Hmong family. It highlights inequalities of gender, class, and ethnicity as the family engages in power struggles with Lia's doctors and Child Protective Services. And finally, as they read and interpret the book, students are able to distinguish between curing a disease (isolated, specific, body-bound) and healing an illness (the human experience of the ailment and its treatment).

A significant challenge here is for students to truly engage with the dilemmas at hand. A 1998 National Public Radio archive, "Faith Healing," which describes conflicts between state authorities and parents who withhold medical care for children on religious grounds, can inspire students literally to enact these power inequalities in the classroom. I assign students to role-play, taking on the positions of Child Protective Services, Lia Lee's parents, and Christian Science practitioners who insist that parents, not the state, should determine children's health care. By debating the positions, students gain a better sense of the complex issues involved in such cultural negotiations.

Conclusion

At the conclusion of this class, it is hoped that students no longer see religion as an activity that merely takes place within a church or synagogue, but one that is found within virtually every arena of culture in which one seeks to respond to, comprehend, and engage with an ultimate concern and in which one finds faith, ritual, symbol. Further, healing has become an entirely different animal. As defined and discussed throughout the class, healing is about self-making, it is about navigating and coping with illness, that broadly defined experience of material disease as well as its effects on and meaning within every aspect of one's experience. Healing involves ritual, ceremony, storytelling, community, and a sense of one's location in the cosmos. And it may be seen to take place within subtle physiologies, not merely biochemical systems. The final essay for the course helps students express these concepts. By synthesizing their understanding of the broad array of traditions we have studied, students evaluate claims made in a 2000 *Los Angeles Times* article that religion and health care should remain separate. To answer the question, students draw from a new sense of "religion" and "healing." They demonstrate an ability to reflect critically upon their own cultural background and biomedical tradition, display knowledge of other approaches to health and wellness, evaluate points of connection and dissonance between them, and suggest ways in which multiple perspectives on wellness might be brought together, both within their own lives and within contemporary culture as a whole. Thus, as I suggested at the outset, a course such as this uniquely meets the demands and pedagogical goals of religious studies as a discipline: it encourages students to reflect thoughtfully upon their own preconceived assumptions, it provides them with multiple alternative perspectives, and it gives them the tools with which to meaningfully evaluate those assumptions and perspectives.

Syllabus: Religion and Culture: Religion, Healing, and the Body

Course Objectives

- To challenge one's definitions of "religion," "illness," and "healing."
- To consider healing as a fundamentally spiritual and religious activity.
- To critically reflect upon one's own worldview and biomedical system.
- To gain an understanding of a variety of religious healing traditions, and their philosophical foundations.
- To synthesize, evaluate, and apply knowledge gained in this class to a case study and to one's own life and approach to wellness.

Required Texts

Course Reader (all readings other than Fadiman and Davis-Floyd are in the Course Reader)
Anne Fadiman, *The Spirit Catches You and You Fall Down*
Robbie Davis-Floyd, *Birth as an American Rite of Passage*

Grading and Assignments

- 15% Class participation
- 10% Reading journal
- 25% Written assignments
- 5% Illness narrative: Narrative of a personal experience you have had which has affected the way you feel about health, healing, spirituality, and your body. This may be an illness or trauma that you or someone close to you experienced.

- 5% Sacred geography narrative: Describe your sacred geography, identifying key locations and the stories, memories, and associations that enable those locations to make you who you are. This piece should be accompanied by an illustration of your "mandala."
- 15% Patient case study: History and Physical. Research write-ups of biomedical and alternative treatments. Critique, evaluation, and treatment recommendations.
- 25% Midterm exam: The exam will take place in class.
- 25% Final exam: A take-home final essay exam will be distributed two weeks before the end of the quarter.

Course Timeline

WEEK 1

Wednesday: Introduction to the Course
Unit 1. Biomedical Bodies: Understanding Healing and Illness

Friday: Defining Sickness, Illness, and Embodiment
Reading: Kleinman, "The Meaning of Symptoms and Disorders," in *The Illness Narratives*, pp. 3–30

WEEK 2

Monday: Western Biomedicine: Ritual and Practice
Reading: Miner, *Body Ritual of the Nacirema*, pp. 37–41

Wednesday
Reading: Davis-Floyd, *Birth as an American Rite of Passage*, pp. 1–43

Friday
Reading: Davis-Floyd, *Birth as an American Rite of Passage*, pp. 73–153, 252–291

WEEK 3

Monday: Group Workday
Unit 2: Complementary Bodies: Traditional Chinese Medicine

Wednesday: Introduction to Philosophy of Traditional Chinese Medicine

Friday: Complementarity and Correspondence: Body and Landscape
Readings: Kaptchuk, "Medicine East and West: Two Ways of Seeing, Two Ways of Thinking," in *The Web That Has No Weaver*, pp. 1–40; and "Meridians: The Warp and Woof," in *The Web That Has No Weaver*, pp. 105–142

WEEK 4

Monday: Guest Speaker
Illness Narrative Due
Unit 3: Porous Bodies: Self, Community, and Ecology

Wednesday: Philosophy of Tibetan Buddhist Medicine

Friday: Porous Bodies: Tibetan Subtle Physiologies
Reading: Donden, "The Body" in *Health through Balance*, pp. 29–51, 55–70

WEEK 5

Monday: Buddhist Healing: Somatic Medicine, Tantra, Dharma
Reading: Clifford, "Tantric Medicine," in *Tibetan Buddhist Medicine and Psychiatry*, pp. 64–88

Wednesday: Mandalas and Healing: Locating the Self

Friday: Diné Physiology and Nilch'i
Reading: Schwarz, "The Cultural Construction of the Nihookáá Dinéé," in *Molded in the Image of Changing Woman*, pp. 61–112

WEEK 6

Monday: The Role of Sacred Geography in Diné Healing: Sandpaintings
Video: *Sandpainting: A Navajo Tradition*
Unit 4: Active Bodies: Movement, Healing, and Performativity

Wednesday: Diné Ceremonialism: The Coyote Chantway
Readings: Luckert, selected prayers from *Coyoteway*; and Wheelwright, "The Myth of the Coyote Chant," pp. 97–107

Friday: Diné Healing and Community
Reading: Lewton and Bydone, "Identity and Healing in Three Navajo Religious Traditions: Sa'ah Naagháí Bik'eh Hózhǫ́," pp. 476–498
Sacred Geography Due

WEEK 7

Monday: Ritual, Dance, and Healing: Kalahari iKung
Reading: Katz, "The iKung Approach to Healing," and "Wa Na, 'A Healer among Healers' " in *Boiling Energy*, pp. 33–57, 222–228

Wednesday: Subtle Physiologies: Taiqi and Yoga
Midterm Review

Friday: Midterm Exam
Healing and Self-Making: Finding a Working Identity

WEEK 8

Unit 5: Healing and Self-Making: Finding a Working Identity
Monday: Introduction and Review

Wednesday: Recovering Community: Revisioning Healing
Reading: Levi, "The Embodiment of a Working Identity," pp. 13–47

Friday: Healing in Christianity: Nineteenth-century Protestantism and Catholicism: Remaking the Self

WEEK 9

Monday: Film: *Jesus' Son*
Wednesday: Discussion of *Jesus' Son*
Friday: Holiday—No Class

WEEK 10

Monday: Christian Faith Healing and Remaking the Self
Reading: Wacker, "The Pentecostal Tradition," in *Caring and Curing*, pp. 513–548

Unit 6: Gendered Bodies: Faith, Childbirth, and Sexuality in Islamic and Jewish Communities
Wednesday: Healing and Identity in Orthodox Judaism
Video: *In Her Own Time*

Friday: Discussion of *In Her Own Time*

WEEK 11

Monday: Infertility and Ultraorthodoxy
Reading: Kahn, "Rabbis and Reproduction," in *Infertility Around the Globe*, pp. 283–297

Wednesday: Women Healers in Islam
Readings: Doumato, "The Healing Power of Words," pp. 130–146; and "Engaging Spirits," in *Getting God's Ear*, pp. 130–146, 147–150

Friday: Multicultural Perspectives on Childbirth, Infertility, and Sexuality
Readings: Harrod, "An Essay on Desire"; and Abu-Lughod, "A Tale of Two Pregnancies" in *Women Writing Culture*, pp. 339–349

WEEK 12

Unit 7: Political Bodies: Conflict, Resistance, Adaptation
Monday
Reading: Fadiman, *The Spirit Catches You and You Fall Down*, pp. 1–77

Wednesday: Healing as Political Resistance
Friday: Group Workday

WEEK 13

Monday
Reading: Fadiman, *The Spirit Catches You and You Fall Down*, pp. 78–153

Wednesday: Faith Healing and Legal Issues: "Faith Healing," NPR, Nov. 25, 1998, Student Debate

Friday
Reading: Fadiman, *The Spirit Catches You and You Fall Down*, pp. 154–224

WEEK 14

Monday
Reading: Fadiman, *The Spirit Catches You and You Fall Down*, pp. 224–end

Wednesday: Final Comments

NOTES

1. The Diné are more commonly known as Navajo. I prefer to use the term Diné, as that is the name the people themselves use.

2. For a detailed description of Tibetan medicine, see Yeshi Donden, *Health through Balance*. In contrast to somatic medicine, which addresses the physical body, "tantra" within this tripartite system of medicine refers to those healing practices that address the subtle body such as yoga, meditation, the construction of mandalas, and the reciting of mantras. "Dharma" refers to spiritual practice that addresses the karma-body, seeking to improve one's karma or to restore good relationships with ancestral spirits or other supernatural beings.

SOURCES AND RESOURCES

Books and Articles

Abu-Lughod, Lila. 1996. A Tale of Two Pregnancies. In *Women Writing Culture*, ed. Ruth Behar and Deborah Gordon, 339–349. Berkeley: University of California Press.

Associated Press. 2000. "Mixing Health Care, Faith Criticized," *Los Angeles Times*, June 24,B2.

Bloom, Benjamin. 1956. *Taxonomy of Educational Objectives: The Classification of Educational Goals*. New York: Longmans, Green.

Clifford, Terry. 1984. *Tibetan Buddhist Medicine and Psychiatry: The Diamond Healing*. New York Beach, ME: Samuel Weiser.

Csordas, Thomas. 1994. *The Sacred Self: A Cultural Phenomenology of Charismatic Healing*. Berkeley: University of California Press.

Davis-Floyd, Robbie. 1992. *Birth as an American Rite of Passage*. Berkeley: University of California Press.

Donden, Yeshi. 1986. *Health through Balance: An Introduction to Tibetan Medicine*. Ithica, NY: Snow Lion Press.

Doumato, Eleanor Abdella. 2000a. The Healing Power of Words. In *Getting God's Ear: Women, Islam, and Healing in Saudi Arabia and the Gulf*, 130–146. New York: Columbia University Press.

———. 2000b Engaging Spirits: Prophylaxis, Witchcraft, Exorcisms, Trial by Ordeal, and Zar. In *Getting God's Ear: Women, Islam, and Healing in Saudi Arabia and the Gulf*, 147–184. New York: Columbia University Press.

Fadiman, Anne. 1997. *The Spirit Catches You and You Fall Down: A Hmong Child, Her American Doctors, and the Collision of Two Cultures*. New York: Farrar, Straus, and Giroux.

Farella, John R. 1984. *The Main Stalk: A Synthesis of Navajo Philosophy*. Tucson: University of Arizona Press.

Hahn, Robert A. 1996. *Sickness and Healing: An Anthropological Perspective*. New Haven, CT: Yale University Press.

Harrod, Howard. 2003. Essay on Desire. *Journal of the American Medical Association* 289: 813–814.

Kahn, Susan Martha. 2002. Rabbis and Reproduction: The Uses of New Reproductive Technologies among Ultraorthodox Jews in Israel. In *Infertility around the Globe: New Thinking on Childlessness, Gender, and Reproductive Technologies*, ed. Marcia Inhorn, 283–297. Berkeley: University of California Press.

Kaptchuk, Ted. J. 2000. *The Web That Has No Weaver: Understanding Chinese Medicine*. Chicago: Contemporary.

Katz, Richard. 1982. *Boiling Energy: Community Healing among the Kalahari iKung*. Cambridge, MA: Harvard University Press.

Kleinman, Arthur. 1988. *The Illness Narratives: Suffering, Healing, and the Human Condition*. New York: Basic Books.

Levi, Jerome M. 1999. The Embodiment of a Working Identity: Power and Process in Rarámuri Ritual Healing. *American Indian Culture and Research Journal* 23, no.3: 13–47.

Lewton, Elizabeth, and Victoria Bydone. 2000. Identity and Healing in Three Navajo Religious Traditions: Sa'ah Naagháí Bik'eh Hózhǫ. In *Ritual Healing in Navajo Society, Medical Anthropology Quarterly* 14, no. 4: 476–498.

Luckert, Karl W. 1979. *Coyoteway: A Navajo Holyway Healing Ceremonial*. Tucson: University of Arizona Press.

Matthews, Washington. 1897. *Navajo Legends*. Boston: Houghton Mifflin.

McNeley, James K. 1981. *Holy Wind in Navajo Philosophy*. Tucson: University of Arizona Press.

Miner, Horace. 1956. Body Ritual of the Nacirema. *American Anthropologist* 58: 3 (June): 37–41.

Schwarz, Maureen Trudelle. 1997. *Molded in the Image of Changing Woman: Navajo Views on the Human Body and Personhood*. Tucson: University of Arizona Press.

Wacker, Grant. 1986. The Pentecostal Tradition. In *Caring and Curing: Health and Medicine in the Western Religious Traditions*, ed. Ronald Numbers and Darrel Amundsen, 514–538. New York: Macmillan.

Wheelwright, Mary. 1988. The Myth of the Coyote Chant. In *The Myth and Prayers of the Great Star Chant and the Myth of the Coyote Chant*, 97–107. Tsaile, AZ: Navajo Community College Press.

Films and Audiotapes

"Faith Healing," audio archives, National Public Radio, November 25, 1998.

Hinn, Benny. 2003. *"This Is Your Day."* Trinity Broadcasting Network.

Littman, Lynne, director. 1985. *In Her Own Time: The Final Fieldwork of Barbara Myerhoff*. Direct Cinema.

Maclean, Alison, director. 1999. *Jesus' Son*. Lion's Gate Films. *In Search Of History: Lourdes: Shrine of Miracles*. History Channel.

Marshall, John. 1966. *Num Chai: The Ceremonial Dance of the iKung Bushmen*. Documentary Educational Resources.

Winkler, Merrie. 1990. *Sandpainting: A Navajo Tradition*. INTERpark.

2

Teaching Religion and Healing at a Southern University

Kaja Finkler

An Overview

Because religion is an emotionally charged subject, teaching about it and about healing traditions in entry-level college courses requires different approaches than do topics that do not always touch on a student's personal feelings. Consideration must therefore be given to the specific backgrounds of the students, particularly if many come out of traditions characterized by fundamentalist Christian beliefs, as is the case at the southern university where I teach. Inasmuch as students with strong fundamentalist backgrounds may be sensitive to evaluations of religious beliefs and practices from an analytic rather than theological perspective, dealing with these topics requires a corresponding sensitivity from the instructor. At the same time, other students—many of whom are biology and science majors bound for medical school—are influenced by a powerful strain of discourse based on science and scientific rationality. Teaching about the mystical aspects of religious healing, including the use of altered states of consciousness, calls for equally subtle forms of navigation through these different currents in American society.

Insofar as both streams of influences shape students in different ways, the topic becomes even more complicated. Various students may also have had exposure to complementary medicine, although not necessarily of a religious nature. Their parents may be physicians, chiropractors, or massage therapists, some of them interested in New Age medicine. Most of the students know little about anthropology, but some have heard of or been exposed to New Age thinking. For this reason, I inform them that the class does not deal with New Age medicine but with the nature of traditional healing systems, most of which are embedded in a religious ideology and practices.

I have taught two courses dealing with religious healing. Both have similar content, but different settings and designs. The first, "Comparative Healing Systems," is an entry-level course in medical anthropology, usually with 130 students. It consists of minimal lectures and a great deal of discussion. The second, "The Art of Healing and the Science of Curing," is a freshman seminar consisting of twenty students, and it is based entirely on discussion. The latter allows me to develop ideas about healing and curing that can be addressed only on the surface in the larger class.

Pedagogically, no matter what size the class, I use the Socratic method. In fact, the most successful feature of the course has been the emphasis on class discussion that engages the students in debates. The least successful has been when I attempt to lecture. I am always surprised by how well the students retain the materials discussed in class and how much less they garner from the readings if these are not discussed. In both classes I ask students to present a summary of the reading for the day, what they found most interesting about a particular reading, and the questions it has raised for them. These summaries and questions serve as a kickoff for other topics that we explore, which may not be covered by a given reading. The class, however, consists always of a dialogue among the students, the reading materials, and me. Therefore it is not rigidly structured, since one cannot anticipate all the points the students will raise during a given period.

Because students are asked to think critically about all the readings and topics brought up in class, I indicate on the syllabus that the first and foremost requirement is for each of them to "shake up his or her head." Specifically, this means that the student is asked to rethink his or her basic assumptions about healing systems in general and about those we study in particular. Students may come in with stereotypical views about the nature of religious healing—either rejecting it as quackery or idealizing it along the lines of the "noble savage." My aim is to disabuse them of either view. It becomes necessary for them to evaluate the materials and recognize the multidimensional nature of all healing practices, including biomedicine, and to understand that all healing systems may be effective in some cases and ineffective in others.

I stress that when studying healing systems, they must distinguish "the forest from trees," a metaphor they seem to remember years later better than any specific point discussed in class. By this I mean that while we focus on specific healing systems—the trees—each one opens a window onto the broader society of which it is part, the forest. Since I have done extensive fieldwork in Mexico (see Finkler 2001), where I studied biomedical practices and spiritualist healing along with the efficacy of the healers' ministrations, and where I was trained to become a healer, I refer to examples from my fieldwork. Drawing on these materials, students learn how beliefs in the causality of sickness can elucidate broader social processes. For example, in Mexico a major cause of sickness is thought to be anger. It is widely believed that if a person gets angry he or she may fall ill. While attributing sickness to anger is, in and of itself, significant, we also discuss how anger represents moral statements in response to injustice or improper actions by others, reflecting the society's values about justice and social expectations. Etiological beliefs related to anger may also suggest a form of social control. That is, if one does not control one's anger, one may fall ill—suggesting, in this context, how medical beliefs have wider societal consequences. In short, one goal of the classes is not only for students to be exposed to different kinds of healing systems but also to understand them in the broader social and cultural contexts. I wish them to recognize how any healing system, whether religious or secular, is embedded in a society, and reflects major themes of that society. Much as Western technological medicine mirrors the technological society in which we live, just as the iKung healing system of the Kalahari Desert in Africa—particularly as expressed in dances—reflects that society's egalitarian nature, its lack of technology, its aesthetics, and its emphasis on community.

I have found that the comparative method in anthropology is an especially useful approach to take to the teaching of religion and healing. My focus has been on comparing biomedical beliefs and practices with religious healing in selected societies to demonstrate the symbiotic relationship between the two approaches to healing. I discuss both in their social and cultural contexts and, in the case of biomedicine, I address the historical forces that contributed to its divergence from religion. I emphasize the ways in which religious healing addresses etiological and profound phenomenological questions—such as "Why me?"—and provides meanings to sickness that biomedicine does not and cannot address, given its epistemology and history. I include a discussion of medical pluralism and its practical consequences, such as the clashes that may arise between biomedicine and religious healing when symbiotic relationships between alternative healing systems—especially religious healing—are ignored or devalued. Such clashes also lead to ethical dilemmas that I address.

I formulate one of the major aims of both courses through the following question: Given the burst of interest in alternative healing in the United States, with more and more people seeking alternative healers, why do twenty-first-century Americans resort to alternative healers in light of the great advances made by contemporary Western medicine? I indicate that to answer this question is to explore the nature of several healing systems cross-culturally, including biomedicine.

The Sequence of the Course

Inasmuch as both courses are designed as entry level, and most beginning students are not familiar with anthropology, I begin the class with a brief overview of the richness of the field. I focus on the notion of culture as a central unifying theme in the cross-cultural study of human beliefs and practices, and its role in human life. I underscore the symbolic nature of culture, which is most revealed in religious and healing practices. Inasmuch as it is common in Western society to regard symbols as lacking a "true" reality, as being things that exist only in one's head, I impress upon the students that symbols are as real as any material substance or physical act.

Following an overview of anthropology and discussion of the meaning of culture and symbols I introduce the notions of *emic*[1] and *etic*,[2] which are extremely useful both for pedagogical and analytical reasons. Pedagogically, whether students have a fundamentalist orientation or a science background, they readily accept that one must understand any society and culture from an emic perspective, even though it may clash with their own comprehensions. This approach opens to them the possibility of understanding their own religious practices, as well as the Other's, without necessarily threatening their personal beliefs. I stress however that the etic perspective is actually our Western (emic) approach, rooted in the scientific revolution and its emphasis on rationality, objectivity, and empiricism. I discuss the scientific revolution and the Enlightenment to make the point that, arguably, these intellectual movements forged a separation in Western history between sacred and secular beliefs that has informed how we think about healing.

The introduction of the concepts of emic and etic leads to a discussion of the differences between relativism and universalism. I emphasize that we must always understand religious healing from an emic view within its cultural context in ways that lead to a relativistic stance. Yet I also note the fascinating phenomenon that many religious healing beliefs and practices are shared by peoples from disparate parts of the world as, for example, in the practice of altered states of consciousness, or beliefs in witchcraft as the source of sickness. Thus in approaching the different ethnographic descriptions of religious healing systems, students are asked to find similarities and differences between sacred and secular healing form; how, that is, they differ and how they are the same. We examine the role of symbols in human life, including those used in both sacred and secular therapeutics, and we analyze the healing process, the difference between healing and curing, and how to assess the efficacy of any healing system. We also address the ethical consequences resulting from the difference between emic and etic approaches as, for example, when biomedicine attempts to impose its curing practices on practitioners of Christian Science, who may refuse biomedical treatment, or on Jehovah's Witnesses, who refuse blood transfusions.[3] Does the larger society have a right to do so? Moreover, the book *The Spirit Catches You and You Fall Down* raises many of these ethical and practical questions as well.

I hasten to add in the theoretical discussion of relativism and universalism that although we need a relativistic approach to understand our subject, relativism has its limits. The problem lies in defining these limits. Whereas we cannot relativize Nazi medical practices,[4] we might, one could argue, examine the practice of female circumcision from a relativistic perspective.

An understanding of emic and etic, relativism and universalism, affords students theoretical constructs with which to approach and wrestle with the course materials. The first of these involves the multiple definitions of the word "healing." Generally speaking, the word "healing" stands in opposition to the word "curing." Whereas healing addresses the treatment of the whole person, including existential states of *dis-ease,* and *dis-order,* curing refers to the alleviation of physical symptoms. I give an example from my own work on the efficacy of spiritualist healing in Mexico. When patients initially arrived at the temple, they were feeling sick. After having received treatments and participated in temple rituals, they reported that they had completely recovered and felt well, even though they continued to experience the same symptoms for which they had sought treatment. In short, they had been healed by temple rituals and ministrations, but they may not have been cured.

With these understandings, we begin with the medical system with which the students are most familiar, biomedicine, and its notions of the body, health, and disease. There is an extensive literature on the nature of biomedicine, including the book *From Doctor to Healer* by Robbie Davis-Floyd and Gloria St. John. I discuss the nature of biomedicine, using examples from an updated version of *Birth in Four Cultures* by Brigitte Jordan and Robbie Davis-Floyd. The latter is an excellent introduction to biomedical practices. It also deals with a topic that engages all of the female students, while many of the male students find it compelling, especially the freshman, who may know little about the birthing process. The book also leads to a discussion of the definition of "sickness," which in Western society includes birthing, unlike most other societies where it is a natural event in human life. This leads the student to realize the cultural nature of the meanings of sickness. Although this book tends to idealize traditional birthing methods and tends to be overcritical of biomedicine, it generates an enormous amount of debate. For most students, reading this book marks the first time they confront and question their idealizations of their own medical system. By demystifying biomedicine, religious healing systems become more approachable and less "weird."

To introduce religious healing, I explore with them the nature of religion in general and religious experience. We seek to identify the major characteristics of most religious systems, including attempts to explain how the universe works; how the world was created; how humans came to be on this earth; and how and why adversity happens, with sickness and suffering being central concerns. All religious systems promote ways of knowing and being in the world. Since I dwell on spiritualist healing, I discuss how one of the major ways that spiritualist healers know the world is through spirit possession.

We then move to different systems of religious healing. We use Richard Katz's *Boiling Energy,* which describes in great and excellent detail the iKung of the Kalahari Desert, their culture, religion, and healing;[5] my own book *Spiritualist Healers in Mexico* and the efficacy of those healers from both the emic and etic perspectives; and Anne Fadiman's *The Spirit Catches You and You Fall Down,* which brings us back to Western medicine and also gives us a fine view of the Hmong's traditional healing beliefs and practices. This last book is exceptionally appropriate for this class, because it brings into bold relief the clash between American and Hmong cultural beliefs about sickness and Hmong shamanistic practices, while also raising numerous ethical issues.

Since so many religious healing systems—including the iKung, the spiritualists, and the Hmong—resort to altered states of consciousness, I spend considerable time discussing this phenomenon from cultural and experiential perspectives. We explore the reasons for the desire to know reality through an altered state (the emic view), and the scientific or etic analysis of what happens to human consciousness when people are in a trance or become possessed by spirits, at which time their brain waves deviate from the usual patterns. Since many cultures resort to altered states of consciousness in their religious and healing rituals, I ask why human beings desire to seek transcendence through altered states.

This section on altered states of consciousness is both near and far for students. It is far when we speak about altered states of consciousness as forms of apotheosis and transcendence in which a person confronts the "true reality," as the iKung say. In such instances, the students recognize that they live in a society dominated by skepticism and disenchantment, which makes it difficult for them to comprehend such mystical ideas. It is near when the discussion turns to forms of altered states achieved by using drugs, including marijuana and LSD. Occasionally students may note having entered an exalted state when attending a sport event that is similarly a communal event, but in such instances they also quickly recognize that such a state lacks the sacred context to give it deeper significance. Indeed, even though students may understand altered states better when they are discussed in the context of drug use or sports (including running), I usually underscore that when such states are reached in the context of a religious ritual or healing—as is the case among the iKung and the spiritualists—they are achieved under extremely controlled and usually communal conditions. Students come to recognize that such states have meaning within the religious context, whereas in many Western contexts altered states are sought for recreational purposes and are devoid of meaning. In the final analysis, however, it is difficult to teach issues associated with sacred healing that border on the mystical and the enchanted, simply because the students themselves seem to acknowledge that it is alien to them. They lack a genuine point of reference; one exception is the occasional student who comes out of a charismatic religious tradition.

Although I do not foreground this course with issues relating to gender, I do have opportunities to focus on gender from several perspectives. For example, in our discussion of iKung healing dances it is quite evident that these dances depend on the complementarity of gender roles. The dances can be performed only if the women clap and provide the rhythmic stimulation for the men to *do* the dance and enter into trance. I call attention to how, in a traditional iKung society, there exists interdependence between men and women, and gender relations are cemented by this interdependence, unlike in contemporary Western society where the emphasis is usually on the individualism of each member of the pair. Significant discussions ensue regarding the possible consequences of these differences in gender relations.

The subject of gender also arises in the discussion of spiritualist healers, who are primarily women. We discuss dissident religious movements, such as Mexican spiritualism, in which spiritualist healing systems are embedded. Such movements attract women for various reasons, one of which is access to positions of leadership. Generally speaking, the dominant religions, such as Catholicism, may block avenues to power for women. I also discuss gender in the context of religiously oriented altered states of consciousness. I use I. M. Lewis's discussion, *Ecstatic Religion,* which discusses religions of the powerless. Inasmuch there is no greater power than control of the spirit world, women may be attracted to movements that promote altered states of consciousness because these change ordinary powerless people into repositories of power. Spiritualist healers serve as a good example of this phenomenon.[6]

We discuss the concept of medical pluralism, particularly under conditions of globalization. Biomedicine has penetrated most of the world and has usually been at the vanguard of the colonial enterprise. One can expect to find medical pluralism, including both biomedicine and native healing traditions, almost anywhere. In this context, we return to comparisons between traditional modes of healing and biomedicine, and how people usually turn first to biomedicine when they have access to it and, when it fails, then go to their own traditional healers. Here it is important to distinguish between emic notions about grave and non-grave illnesses. Generally speaking, people will seek treatment from biomedical practitioners for grave sickness and infectious diseases and for disorders caused by accidents, because biomedicine has been most successful in treating effectively infectious and contagious disease, excepting AIDS and emergency medicine. Sacred healing is often sought when biomedicine fails and usually this applies to chronic illnesses, conditions assessed as non-grave, or typical illnesses, as, for example, *susto* in Mexico.[7] There are, of course, many other reasons for seeking sacred healing, as students learn from my article comparing biomedicine and sacred healing (see Finkler 1994a).

We revisit the initial question posed in the syllabus that relates to medical pluralism in America. As in most societies, people in the United States tend to resort to alternative healing systems when they have unsuccessfully been treated by physicians, and when biomedicine has failed them. We also explore the meaning of efficacy of any healing system, including biomedicine. As I point out, and as is discussed in *Spiritualist Healers in Mexico,* biomedical standards view efficacy of any healing system in relation to eliminating the cause of a particular disease. Biomedicine has been successful in eliminating the causes of infectious diseases with antibiotics, and arguably with surgery or transplants. In the majority of disorders, however, biomedicine treats the symptoms, and its ministrations are primarily palliative. Similarly, in sacred healing, using the spiritualists as an example, most treatments do not eliminate the causes of the disorder. Rather they address symptoms that may be associated with traditional etiological understandings, including witchcraft, evil, and suffering.

My interest is to engage the students in ideas. I therefore concentrate class time on discussion and I use visual materials only to complement the readings—to give students visual representations of what they read. I supplement the reading of the Kalahari iKung with the film *N/untchai: Ceremonial Dance of the iKung Bushman.* It depicts their all-night healing dances and parallels closely the book's description of these activities, giving students visual conceptualizations of what they had read. Similarly, I use slides from my own collection to show the spiritualist healers in trance and their healing techniques.

I do not use Web-based resources. I encourage students to use them only to gather factual materials, and I caution them that surfing the Web does not lead to knowledge. In the freshman seminar, each student is required to write a paper based on fieldwork of an alternative healing system. Some of these are associated with religious traditions as, for example, in charismatic churches. Others may explore nonreligious alternative healing practices, including chiropractic or homeopathy.

Though we do not draw on any one regional source in the course itself, students are encouraged to do so for their field research project, given that many originate from small towns in the South, with traditions of Native American sacred healing, herbalism, and Christian charismatic healers. A special feature of the course is to invite advanced undergraduates, or recent graduates who have taken these classes, to give presentations that serve as role models for the younger students. For example, one student who is now in her third year of medical school had written an award-winning honors thesis on Australian aboriginal healing and health, based on her own fieldwork. Another of my students had written an award-winning honors thesis on Mongolian shamanism, based on fieldwork in Mongolia. Whenever available, using senior undergraduates who have done fieldwork in the areas of traditional healing or biomedicine, rather than professional speakers, serves the students well.

These entry-level courses have led many students to major in anthropology. So some students find the study of sacred healing to be a sufficiently compelling reason to change their majors.

Though I have not encountered anything especially problematic when teaching these classes, one must be aware that students in the twenty-first century tend to be skeptics. They may have difficulty understanding mystical practices, which seem strange to many. In all likelihood, more than one course is required for them to appreciate the richness of other traditions. Most important, I indicate to the students at the beginning of the class that I wish them to savor ideas and especially questions, which I find always more interesting than answers. I suggest that thinking anthropologically is good, which essentially means thinking comparatively—contextualizing situations and placing themselves in the shoes of those often conceptualized as Other. Teaching about religious healing allows them to begin learning about the Other and, for this reason, I regard this enterprise as a moral endeavor. As the philosopher Levinas suggests, empathy may be the core of much of human morality.

Syllabus

Aim of the Course

There has been a burst of interest in alternative healing in the United States, with more and more people in the United States seeking alternative healers. In this seminar we will pose the question "Why do twenty-first-century Americans seek alternative healers in light of the great advances made by contemporary Western medicine?"

To answer this question, we will learn about different kinds of healing beliefs and practices in the United States and in other cultures, as well as about social, economic, political, and ethical aspects of our lives that relate to health and healing. We will explore how the various healing systems we will be studying are the same and different from Western medical practices and what they tell us about ourselves and about different cultures. We will therefore focus on curing in Western medicine and healing in sacred healing systems. We will begin the course by exploring the relationship between health, ecology, and culture.

Readings

Strathern and Stewart, *Curing and Healing*
Jordan and Davis-Floyd, *Birth in Four Cultures*
Katz, *Boiling Energy*
Finkler, *Spiritualist Healing in Mexico*
Finkler, "Sacred and Biomedical Healing Compared"
Fadiman, *The Spirit Catches You and You Fall Down*

Outline of the Course

I.   Introduction
     What is anthropology?
     What is medical anthropology?

II. Sickness, healing, and curing in a cultural context
     Reading: Strathern and Stewart, *Curing and Healing*

III. The art of curing: Birthing in Western and non-Western cultures
     Reading: Jordan, *Birth in Four Cultures*

IV. The art of healing
     a. Healing as a community practice
        Reading: Katz, *Boiling Energy*
     b. Healing and religion
        Reading: Finkler, *Spiritualist Healing*
     c. The role of altered states of consciousness in healing

V.   When healing systems collide: Sacred and secular healing compared
     Reading: Fadiman, *The Spirit Catches You and You Fall Down*
     Finkler, "Sacred and Biomedical Healing Compared"

The readings will be supplemented by one film and slides of spiritualist healers in Mexico. The film we will see is *N/untchai* (Curing among Bushman). If available, we will have one or two speakers to discuss their work on healing. Ideally, these will be advanced undergraduates who have taken these classes and have written either an honor's thesis or a longer paper on issues raised in the course. We will also have two or more outside speakers who will discuss their work on healing.

NOTES

1. In its simplest form, *emic* refers to folk, or cultural, comprehensions of a particular belief or practice.

2. *Etic* relates to the scientific explanation of the same phenomenon. For example, in Mexico the emic, or widespread cultural understanding is that diabetes (usually adult onset diabetes or Type II) is caused by an unexpected fright, or *susto,* whereas the etic, or biomedical, explanation is that diabetes mellitus (Type II) results when the body fails to produce sufficient insulin to sustain normal blood sugar levels.

3. The conflict occurs mainly in cases involving children. Pediatricians have a legal obligation to serve as advocates for minors' health, and the question is whether a child can give informed consent to refuse a given intervention. Children are assumed to be incapable of understanding fully the consequences of these refusals, and therefore incapable of being fully informed.

4. For an excellent description of Nazi medical practices see *Deadly Medicine: Creating the Master Race,* published by the United States Holocaust Memorial Museum 2004.

5. When discussing this book, I impress on the students that owing to changing political and economic processes the practices described in the book may no longer exist in the twenty-first century. In fact, the book calls attention to the gradual changes in the healing practices, a topic that often leads to a discussion of the role of economic and political changes influencing healing traditions.

6. For an in-depth discussion of this phenomenon, see Finkler, "Dissident Religious Movement in the Service of Women's Power."

7. For a discussion of these types of sicknesses and patterns of resort to treatment in Mexico, see Finkler *Physicians at Work, Patients in Pain* and *Spiritualist Healers in Mexico.*

REFERENCES

Davis-Floyd, Robbie, and Gloria St. John. 1998. *From Doctor to Healer.* Piscataway NJ: Rutgers University Press.

Fadiman, Anne. 1997. *The Spirit Catches You and You Fall Down.* New York: Noon Day.

Finkler, Kaja. 1981. Dissident religious movement in the service of women's power. *Journal of Sex Roles* 7:481–495

———. 1994a. Sacred and biomedical healing compared. *Medical Anthropology Quarterly* 8(2):179–198.

———. 1994b. *Spiritualist Healers in Mexico.* 2nd ed. Salem, WI: Sheffield.

———. 2001. *Physicians at Work, Patients in Pain.* 2nd ed. Durham, NC: Carolina Academic.

Holocaust Memorial Museum. 2004. *Deadly Medicine: Creating the Master Race.* Washington, DC.

Jordan, Brigitte and Robbie Davis-Floyd. 1998. *Birth in Four Cultures: A Cross-cultural Investigation of Childbirth in Yucatan, Holland, Sweden, and the United States,* 4th ed. Prospect Heights, IL: Waveland Press.

Marshall, John, narrator and photographer. *N/untchai: Ceremonial Dance of the iKung Bushman,* ed. Frank Galvin. Distributed by Documentary Education Resources: Watertown, MA, 1966.

Lewis, I. M. 1971. *Ecstatic Religion.* Middlesex: Penguin.

Katz, Richard. 1982. *Boiling Energy.* Cambridge, MA: Harvard University Press.

Strathern, Andrew, and Pamela Stewart. 1999. *Curing and Healing.* Durham, NC: Carolina Academic.

PART II

Hindu, Tibetan, and Chinese Traditions

3

Shanti: Peace for the Mind, Body, and Soul

Vasudha Narayanan

To study health and healing in the Hindu traditions is to learn about the larger concepts of well-being and happiness in human life. "Well-being" (*su asti* or *svasti*, from which the word *svastika* is derived) is dependent on a harmonious relationship with the earth, the planets, and the stars; appropriate balances between the various elements within the body, family, and society; and a good relationship with the natural world, ancestors, and deities. Imbalances and disharmony are, alas, a part of life—one's astrological chart may be flawed, one catches viruses, one's children may not do what one desires. All of these cause a lack of well being—particularly the virus—and the many Hindu traditions have thousands of ways to remedy the situations.

To study heath and healing in the Hindu traditions is to study notions of medicine; gender, caste, and class; diet; karma; a human being's perceived connections with the stars and planets; issues of the mind-body-soul relationships; conceptions of reality; boundaries between religious traditions; postcolonial revival of traditional systems of knowledge; turf wars on intellectual property; and issues of theory and method in the study of religion. To study health and healing in the Hindu traditions is to have a clear trajectory to the many moving centers of local communities, castes, language groups, generations, narratives, and activities that collectively and cumulatively form the dominant religious culture of India. In other words, it serves as a good introduction both to one particular religion and to the study of religion.

Although Hindus all over the world participate in and are, in fact, at the cutting edge of health care processes, their traditional notions of well-being, disease, and health are frequently seen in a religious context. The many rituals to maintain well-being and health and systems of medicine that Hindus press into practice are all understood in a religious framework. Thus, the post-Enlightenment divisions between religion and the sciences seen in the West are found only in some contexts in India. The framing of medicine in a religious context is done in several ways in Hinduism. At least three of these ways are particularly significant. The first is to consider Āyurveda ("the knowledge of a [long] life"), a complete, complex, and sophisticated system of medicine, as an ancillary, or branch, of the Vedas. This secures its connection with the sacred texts. The second is by presenting the knowledge, in the customary format, as having some kind of divine origin. Thus, an entire treatise on astrology or medicine may be presented as a conversation between deities and/or holy people. For instance, a certain god may ask a goddess for information on how one maintains a state of well-being, and the goddess may explain the techniques. The following passage from the first chapter of Charaka's (ca. third century BCE) *Compendium* is a typical example:

> Desirous of long life, Bharadvaja of austere penances repaired to the supreme deity Indra, regarding him worthy of court. Since the Science of Life, as declared by Brahman was received by Prajapati [a deity] in its entirety, the Asvins [divine physicians in Hindu narratives] then from him, from the Asvins the illustrious Sakra [i.e., Indra, the god of the celestial beings] alone had received (it), therefore, requested by the *Rsis*, Bharadvaja repaired to Sakra. (Chandra Kaviratna and Sharma: 2–3)

In this text, a holy man is requested by sages (the *rishis*) to go to the various gods who have themselves received the teaching from the supreme being itself. A third way is to understand specific deities as presiding over particular functions in medicine or one's destiny. This may take several forms and include several categories of gods and goddesses. The deities who are imputed with curative powers range from Vishnu, Shiva, or Shakti, that is, the well-known, pan-Indian deities to the personifications of various planets and stars, as well as lesser known local deities. Some diseases are also seen to be a result of the wrath of the deity; a concept that is present in many other world religions.

Custom Narrative and Practice

Perhaps the first thing that is to be emphasized in a course like this is that the materials on which we focus, like the Hindu traditions themselves, are *not* just based on the written Hindu texts. While arguably there are many deeply moving and philosophically sophisticated texts in the Hindu tradition, the enduring experiences that most Hindus have of their traditions come through what one may call *custom narrative and practices* that are deeply connected with their embodied cosmologies. The term "custom" is used primarily as an adjective but also as a noun; it refers to received narratives and practices that are all *customary*, that is, part of tradition, and *customized*; Hindus of every stripe are actively engaged in choosing and adapting stories and practices, customizing them, making them relevant. Hindus encounter and embody these narratives and practices through their relationships, both synchronic and diachronic, with families, communities, nature, and deities. Thus, although there may be many texts of Āyurvedic healing, most Hindus who know them would have learned of them through a grandmother, a neighbor, or a friend. Many South Indians would tell you that there are particular times, each day of the week, called *Rahu kalam* ("the time of the planet Rahu") that are inauspicious; these are times when one does not embark on new or important ventures. They may even be able tell when these times occur on every day of the week, but would be hard-pressed to say if it is in a text, and if so, which one. But it is important enough that South Indian Hindus in Chennai, Mumbai, or New York would avoid those times to start on a new project. And it is important enough that, based on the general principles of *Rahu kalam*, the latitude and longitude of New York, and the times when the sun rises and sets in New York, a new set of Rahu Kalam timings that are relevant for this city has been calculated and disseminated through local calendars from the Flushing temple in Queens. Similarly, most people will tell you that turmeric and neem have antiseptic properties and are powerful healing medicines; but today, some people may opt to buy them in ointment form in local pharmacies. The *customary* knowledge in both cases has been *customized* to fit dwellers in America (using New York City as the norm) or urban dwellers who prefer to get their traditional medicine in a local drugstore. And the list of such old remedies in new bottles—shampoos, body washes, and so on—being packaged, marketed, and sold is very long.

Thus the many rituals, practices, and narratives pressed into use for well-being and healing may have some origin in texts, but these original texts may not be the ways that Hindus get to know about the remedy. Rather, in the case of a specific remedy or ritual, we can say that one hears about it, remembers it was done by one's family, and then continues a family tradition. One may acknowledge it is in the text or that a holy person authorized it, but the details of such authority are frequently vague. Custom narrative and practice is both textual and oral; I emphasize here not the body of knowledge itself but the individual who (or family unit which) exercises agency in picking and choosing and practicing a custom. In recent years such customized traditions have been rendered into text format (as in the New York calendar) and into hypertexts/ Web pages thereby becoming sources for the diaspora Hindu. Much of the reading for this course is from Web pages, which as constantly modified sources, resemble glorified oral traditions. These Web pages, of course, have to be used with abundant caution.

The course is divided into (1) an introductory week, (2) a section on deities and votive rituals, (3) practices for general maintenance of well-being and good health which can be connected with or accelerated to (4) remedial and therapeutic measures. Thus forms of Āyurveda and Siddha medicine, which are best known in the Western world are dealt with in the course but only in the larger context of well-being and health.

Many of the early segments are framed with the power of narratives. There are thousands of stories in India and many variations to each story. Some details change by region and over time; some parts remain constant. New stories, cast with old molds, come into being. Some of them accompany rituals, others glorify a holy person, deity, or sacred place through whom or where a cure takes place. The present illness, the present cure, becomes part of the narrative, part of the lore, instilling faith and hope in those who wish to hear, those who wish to belong to the paradigm.

Various complicated rules of ritual purity and pollution, together with dietary rules are seen in the many Hindu communities. Though many Hindus eat meat (except beef), others may eschew it completely. Some communities may even avoid some spices and vegetables such as garlic and onions. These rules are followed as long as one wants to maintain good health, or is in normal circumstances—however, if one is ill, these rules are overruled in the preparation of certain medicines. Hindus have been careful about religious regulations but are very practical people as well.

In the course of preparing this syllabus, several interesting phenomena have been regretfully left out because of time constraints. I mention these here because others may find it possible to weave them in by cutting short another segment or by adding them to graduate readings. Segments that can be added to the syllabus are: the roles and status of physicians in traditional Hindu societies in precolonial India; snakebites; intellectual property rights; and special cures. Though I deal briefly with new reproductive technologies, others may want to spend more time on this unit. This course is designed for upper level undergraduates, but the readings can be adjusted for a graduate audience by making the extra readings mandatory.

Much of the ethnographic information in some sections of the course comes from the state of Tamilnadu in South India where I have done a lot of my research. The readings, however, are more general and are geographically more diverse.

Charaka (c. third century CE), who wrote one of the earliest and most powerful texts on healing, puts good health and general well-being in the broadest possible context. He says that a human being should, above all, have the will to live. Next, the person should have a desire for prosperity; and finally, for liberation from the cycle of life and death. It is in this context that we can understand the systems of health.

Week 1: Diversity, Commonalities in Hinduism

The plan during the first week of classes involves rehearsing some of the historical context for the study of the Hindu traditions and redirecting the students to think of methods and paradigms other than texts in the study of the Hindu traditions. During this week, we specifically highlight (a) the diversity of Hindu traditions; (b) the common elements in the worldviews—particularly the plurality of authority chains and leadership, and the emphasis on "this worldly" happiness; and (c) notions of auspiciousness/ inauspiciousness, and purity and pollution.

Week 2: Gods and Goddesses of Healing

In week 2, we do an overview of the pluralistic theism of the Hindus, getting to know deities who actively intervene in human affairs and help a human being stay healthy. There is an initial discussion on pan-Hindu gods: Vishnu, Shiva, the goddesses, Ganesha, and others, followed by a focus on local deities. Many local goddesses in South India, especially, are strongly connected with healing. I do not start the course with the Vedas—especially the Atharva Veda, which does, in fact, have large sections on healing. If one starts with the Vedas, the students are left with the impression that these are the most important texts in healing that Hindus refer to regularly, and that knowledge is written. By starting the course with the deities, we properly signal to the students that the Hindus in daily life are not, in fact, obsessed with the Vedas or notions of karma, liberation or *moksha*, or the three ways to liberation, topics that are dealt with at length in the easily available textbooks. If Hindus think of karma at all, it is only insofar as it affects issues such as chronic disease, and then only so they can "fix" it with rituals recommended to them by family, friends, or a family priest.

The mental blocks that come in this week are connected with local deities. It is not just difficult for the students to think of the supreme being or infinity in the plural, but to think of them as having local manifestations with colorful personalities. The range, therefore, is broad: from classical Hindu deities to local deities, we look at their healing power and the human being's agency in healing.

There are many deities of healing and medicine within the Hindu traditions. On a pan-Hindu level, Shiva and Vishnu have special manifestations in local temples in which they are known as divine physicians, and we look at traditional mantras and prayers addressed to them in their healing roles. Dhanvantari, a minor incarnation of Vishnu, is considered to be the paradigmatic physician. In a powerful narrative known as the "churning of the ocean of milk," he appears from the ocean holding a jar which contains the nectar of immortality. Goddesses in various forms and with various names have special functions—protecting the womb and fetuses, as well as expressing ambivalent relationships with specific diseases such as measles and chicken pox. And then there are the lesser known "divine twin physicians"—the Ashvin/s—in Sanskrit narratives, who are invoked ritually in some prayers but who are not the object of direct devotion.

The regional manifestations of Shiva and Vishnu command the devotion of those who need cures. Shiva is known as Vaidyanatha—lord of healing or lord of the physicians in Vaideeswaran Koil, Tamilnadu, a temple town with a flourishing mail-order devotee list. We also look at some Sanskrit prayers for Shiva and compare them with the songs and prayers addressed to goddesses.

Vishnu is known as Vira Raghavan in the little town of Tiruvallur (near the city of Chennai) and as Guruvayur Appan in the state of Kerala; in these, and other manifestations, Vishnu is considered to be a divine physician. A small pond of water near the Tiruvallur temple is said to have special properties. In the course of votive/simulative rituals (referred to in earlier anthropological literature as imitative or homeopathic magic), pilgrims frequently dissolve little clumps of jaggery (a natural sweetener made from concentrated sugarcane juice) in the water and believe that through divine grace, cysts and tumors will dissolve in the body.

The students focus on four goddesses plus a "goddess construct," and then move on to the issues of possession. These four goddesses are regionally known: Garbha Rakshambika ("The mother who protects the womb"), Adi Para Shakti, and Mariamman are known in Tamilnadu, and Sitala Devi is worshiped in Bengal. Worship for the first goddess is Sanskritic and brahmanical in texture; the prayers to her are in Sanskrit. Mariamman is also worshiped in the same neck of the woods, and manifestations of this local goddess are found in many parts of South India. She is a goddess who is said to intrinsically carry the "heat" of the universe in her body, and devotees carry jars of water or milk to bathe and "cool" her—and thus "cool" the heat of disease that lurks in people's bodies. Many of her manifestations or siblings have local names and local shrines; in recent years, large temples have been built for her in Tamilnadu. Although worshiped as both inflector and healer of smallpox in earlier days, she is propitiated extensively for various diseases. Most of her devotees are Tamil speakers; crowds line up to worship her in local temples.

Sitala Devi ("the cool goddess") is also a goddess of smallpox, chicken pox and other infectious diseases. She is worshiped predominantly in Bengal but is also popular in many other places; many see her as a North Indian counterpart to Mariamman. Complex reciprocal relationships between the devotees and the deity have to be nuanced with considerable sensitivity; she is seen as the cause and the cure of the disease. A selection of websites as well as Ed Dimock's classic article on this theme are part of the required reading.

The fourth goddess has a pan-Indian name, "Adi Para-Shakti" ("the Primordial Supreme Power"), but is a local, new goddess in Melmaruvatur, near Chennai. Ritual impurity connected with menstruation is not observed in her worship—men and women rotate on and off in groups, conducting the prayers. Men and women who worship her wear red clothing, for this goddess is supposed to have said that she does not discriminate between people of various castes, classes, gender, and races. She is supposed to have spoken through a devotee and said that though the outer packaging of skin color is different, the color of blood that flows under the skin is red for all human beings—and thus equality of all is an important feature for the thousands of devotees who flock to her for the well-being of self and good health for the family.

A new goddess who was "constructed" by a local science teacher is called Aids-Amma. Modeled after Mariamman and Sitala Devi, Aids Amma is taking a life of her own. A science teacher, noticing how many of the votive rituals to Mariamman promoted hygiene and healing, decided to actually create a new goddess and introduce devotional songs that encourage prevention of the disease in various ways.

There is not much written material on Garbha Rakshambika, the goddess who protects the womb, on Adi Para Shakti, or on Aids Amma. The reading in the syllabus are two short documents—a kind of "white paper"—I wrote after visiting their shrines in 1998 and 1999 and a small section on Aids Amma in one of my papers (Narayanan 2001). For Adi Parashakti of Mel Maruvatur, I use slides taken during a short ethnographic study I did, along with a booklet written by a devotee. (These will be posted on the Web and available to all teachers.)

After dealing with deities, we focus on the issue of "possession." There are several kinds of possession, but we begin with a simple binary model— the good kind, in which one may be possessed by the local goddess, and the bad kind, which involves being possessed by evil spirits, resulting in illness of various kinds. Goddesses frequently possess human beings—often, but not exclusively, a female—and while using a human frame indulge in various activities, including that of curing. When a woman's body is occupied by a goddess, her eyes may seem glazed and she may dance with vigor and rhythm. Devotees understand the goddess to be temporarily possessing a human body to make herself manifest in this world—she is said to speak through the human body she has occupied to give instructions on how problems can be resolved. The mental, physical, family, and professional problems are all considered to be interconnected. The goddess, speaking through the human being, may give directives on pilgrimages, home remedies, fasting schedules, and votive rituals.

A second kind of possession is one in which an evil spirit is perceived to have occupied a vulnerable body, resulting in physical and mental illness. Evil spirits include, but are not limited to, some ghosts; besides the occasional ghost, there are several categories of spirits who lurk near the earth. These beings—among them *brahma rakshasas* and *yakshis*—have no direct counterparts in the Western world. This kind of possession is said to occur in any number of ways—through physical or moral impurity or even a simple act such as walking near a graveyard. Instances of these kinds of possession are described in both Sanskrit and vernacular texts; there are brief references from Tamil texts from the third and fourth centuries and interesting ones from biographical literature in the thirteenth century. Saints are described as curing many of these cases with sacred symbols of the deities. With the cure, the person who was afflicted (and sometimes the family members as well) begin to worship this new deity through whose grace the cure was effected.

An optional film that can be seen at this point or which the students can see on their own time involves possession, dance, and Hinduism in the diaspora. The film, *Divine Madness: Trance, Dance, and Healing in Guyana*, by Philip Singer (1978), is about an hour long.

Week 3: Votive Rituals

The study of deities moves into a discussion of votive rituals in Hinduism. This segment examines ritual pacts between devotees and deities; issues of gender; miracles; and the porous boundaries among religious traditions (Hinduism, Islam, and Christianity) in connection with effecting cures through the grace of holy men and women.

Most Hindus pray explicitly for the fulfillment of specific wishes and make various pacts with the deities. If the wish is fulfilled—or in order for it to be fulfilled—they may go on a pilgrimage, shave their heads, have dietary regulations (various kinds of fasting), or perform an assortment of rituals at home. Some of these acts are gendered; women do specific kinds of fasting for the well-being of the families good health, a long life for their husbands, or other such purposes. The works of Tracy Pintchman, Mary McGee, and Anne Pearson introduce the student to domestic votive rituals within the Hindu world and how women, particularly, practice them. The periodic fasting and feasting by women, is accompanied by the retelling of narratives and performance of rituals.

The second segment in votive rituals focuses on pilgrimages taken for good health and for curative purposes. Visiting specific temples where the deity is said to be known as a healer, bathing in sacred waters, and other rituals are introduced here.

The last part of this section deals with the porous boundaries between many religious traditions in India. There are, of course, strong boundaries within religions and between them, especially in connection with marriage. But when Hindu devotees want specific wishes fulfilled—cures effected—they move seamlessly among religious groups and practices, petitioning Catholic saints, the Virgin Mary, and Muslim holy men and women. Historically, Hindu kings and patrons donated land and monies to these religious personnel when they were cured of a disease or obtained progeny. These votive rituals still take place and frequently involve pilgrimages. In some holy places, vendors sell silver models of various body parts. If one wants a cure for stomach ailments, a pilgrim may buy a silver facsimile of a person's torso and drop it into the donation box.

Thus, Hindu devotees flock to the temples for Hindu deities in Nagapattinam and then may go to Nagore, about ten kilometers away, to venerate the sixteenth-century Muslim saint, Shahul Hamid. From here, they may go on to Velankanni to worship Arogya Mata ("the Mother [goddess] of Good Health), the local name by which the Virgin Mary in known in this town. Both Shahul Hamid and Arogya Mata in Velankanni are known for effecting miraculous cures and people of all faiths flock to these shrines. The discussions can explore the juxtaposition of miracles cures, holy men and women, and religious boundaries.

Week 4: General Well-Being and Remedies to Problems—Part 1

Many Hindus believe that planets and stars, the magnetic energies of the earth, gems, among other forces, affect human beings. Astrologers, experts in gems, scholars in positioning of homes, and ritual specialists propitiating the planets all hold court in India. All these forces can create good health and harmony; imbalances can cause major problems. Hindus, therefore, may adopt practices involving some of these forces either to maintain a sense of well-being or as a remedy to specific problems.

The second part of this section looks at other better known ways by which one maintains good health are adopted for relief from stress or specific ailments like hypertension. These stress reduction techniques include yoga and meditation. An important part of the course will be to have two visiting speakers—one who practices yoga as part of a spiritual regime and another who teaches yoga in the local YMCA or health club. One can do the same on the issue of meditation. Two questions frame this discussion: Is yoga part of a religious structure, or can it be pried away and used as a physical excercise? If it is done as a physical exercise, does it still give rise to spiritual experiences?

In addition to the regular reading, students can also read articles from Web sites on Transcendental Meditation, its promoters' studies on reduction of stress, the claims of Isha Yoga, and so on.

VASTU

While the concept of *vastu* is not as famous as feng shui, it is slowly becoming popular both in India and the Western world. *Vastu* literally means "dwelling," or "plot of land." Though Hindus in India and Southeast Asia followed several rules—generally passed on through oral tradition and apprenticeship of traditional architects—in the building of temples, people were ordinarily more flexible in the building of homes. In the late twentieth century, there has been a revival in the traditional knowledge system known as *vastu*—a system that governs the positioning of houses, offices, places of study and work.

The correct positioning—which is incumbent on several factors—is generally connected with the eight cardinal directions, measurements, spaces, and so on, but in recent years it has been associated with colors and interior decoration as well. All these are closely linked to one's mental and physical well being. A plot shaped in an inauspicious way, jutting in the wrong directions, positioning the house in a manner that is not harmonious with the earth, or having clutter in the wrong direction may result in ill health, and/or mental and physical stress. Although *vastu* is poised to take off in pop culture in the United States with several popular books, many of the rules have been passed on through oral traditions in several Hindu communities

Vastu is said to work on several principles: the building must be "dweller friendly" and be convenient for the purpose for which it was built. It should be aesthetically pleasing—thus the ratio of measurements, materials used for construction, and so on should be appealing to the senses. Finally, the building should make the person who dwells in it feel good. Aligning rooms to cardinal directions, such as placing the kitchen in the southeast, which is ruled by the fire god Agni, is an important feature of *vastu* design.

While *vastu* principles have been generally followed in the building and design of dwellings in India, in recent years there have been different opinions about its practice and applications. An orthodox view is that these principles should be followed from the very beginning in the design and building of the house; others are more flexible and practical, holding that one may take remedial action on existing structures with interior decoration, such as positioning little water fountains or candles in appropriate places. The mental and physical calm that comes through living in these structures that are at peace with the magnetic forces of the earth are said to bring about harmony and a sense of well-being in one's life.

This segment has scope for interesting discussions on comparative issues. Feng Shui comes up as an immediate point of comparison. However, in China, feng shui positioning is related to configurations of *qi*. Early on it had to do with the positioning of graves to ensure that the dead would not be uncomfortable and return as angry ghosts to afflict the living. Although *vastu* is not based on the positioning of graves, some directions and positions are associated more with death than others.

It is also interesting to ask students to think comparatively with notions of the sacrality of the earth in some indigenous religions. In the context of *vastu*, the sacrality of the earth is not the central issue—it is an acknowledgment of the natural forces of the earth, a recognition of minor but powerful deities who preside over the various directions and harness these powers for the well-being of human beings.

The requirement for this section is for students to design a house, apartment, or business offices keeping some *vastu* principles in mind and explaining them. They should also give copies of the Web sites or relevant pages from the books they used for citations to make the checking easier.

Week 5: General Well-Being—Part 2

ASTROLOGY, HEALING POWER OF GEMS, MEDICINAL ASTROLOGY,
PRAYERS TO THE NINE PLANETS

In ancient India, Jyotisha or the study of lights, referred to the study of astrology, astronomy, and the mathematics that made this study possible. This, of course, is similar to the Western world, where astronomy and astrology were closely connected until the seventeenth century. Indeed, in the first few centuries before and after the common era, there was considerable give-and-take and mutual influencing between Greek and Indian astrology. Astrology was also considered to be one of the ancillaries to the Vedas. Between the middle to the end of the first millennium CE, nine "planets" with presiding deities came to be recognized in India and in the larger Hindu world that was then seen in Cambodia, Thailand, and Indonesia. Panels with sculptures of these deities are seen all over South and Southeast Asia. Seven of these "planets" are known to us—the Sun, Moon, Mercury, Venus, Mars, Jupiter, and Saturn. Two celestial bodies called Rahu and Ketu, described as the ascending and descending nodes of the moon, are added to this list. These are the places where the apparent path of Sun and Moon intersect—the points where eclipses can occur—and not really planets. Nevertheless, they are said to have a strong effect on the health of a human being.

Natal astrology, the horoscope of an individual based on his or her birth, is extremely important and may have come, as the Indians themselves acknowledged in their texts, from the Greeks. The texts were cast in a religious framework with the instruction coming from various Hindu gods. Despite this, Hindu/Indian astrology is largely nonsectarian; Buddhists and Jains, Vaishnavas, and Shaivas all had ownership of this "science." Astrology, in earlier days, was divided into several branches—the art of choosing the right moment for activities, marriage compatibility, horary astrology (the time when a question is asked is as important as the question itself), omens and interpretation of dreams, and military astrology. In the twentieth century, however, Hindus focus on marriages, careers, and medicinal astrology.

The last area focuses on how one may maintain good health and effect cures by attending to planets that are in unfavorable houses. The readings include a brief history of Indian astrology, which includes the correlation of the nine planets venerated in India and various parts of the human body and health, and the propitiation of these planets to get through the bad periods. Modern astrologers in India have co-opted scientific technology and have powerful computers charting horoscopes and predictions, but ultimately rely on instinct and human variables to assess the prospects of a client.

Astrology is tied in with the votive exercises we studied earlier and the study of gems. Gems are supposed to balance malefic planetary influences, but wearing the wrong gems could result in negative energies being mobilized in one's life. Internet sites are useful as introductions; these tend to advertise themselves with statements that "planetary gemology is an ancient healing and protective art that can be used to one's advantage with the help of a Vedic astrologer."

Vastu, food, astrology, and gems are all connected for Hindus. Nine kinds of gems (*nava ratna*) and nine kinds of grains (*nava dhanya*) are said to correlate to the nine planets. According to some interpreters, the nine gems are supposed to correspond to nine substances in one's body. While building houses, these nine gems and nine kinds of grains are buried in relevant directions in the plot to enhance the state of well-being for the inhabitants.

Some kinds of astrology and palmistry, known as *naadi josyam*, involves the retrieval, reading, and interpretation of palm leaf manuscripts held in some temples in South India. These are divided into various sections and address issues of serious illness for an individual. *Naadi josyam* is one of the few places where the karma of past lives is actively discussed, and the afflicted individual is told why precisely he or she is suffering now. Few resources are available in this area other than the recent doctoral dissertation of Martin Gantsen of Sweden.

Week 6: Yoga and Meditation

This section moves from "maintenance" to therapeutic issues. Though all the topics discussed so far have both maintenance and remedial aspects, meditation has specifically been touted for both purposes. It also helps that yoga, as it is claimed in reviews, is "as mainstream as Madonna." A new frame that we add here for discussion is that of appropriation, particularly appropriation without context. There is, of course, a plethora of reading materials on these subjects—literally thousands of books, articles, and Web materials—and a few dozen experts in every town. Amazon.com alone brings up more than fourteen thousand references to yoga.

An important question we discuss in this section is the "religious" dimension of yoga and meditation. Some proponents of these practices think they are spiritual disciplines; others think of them as stress-reduction physical and mental exercises. There is no agreement if these practices automatically, and without intent, lead to spiritual experiences.

An interesting dimension can be added if you get two or three practitioners of meditation or yoga to talk to students. It is particularly useful if you get two people with different viewpoints—say, a yoga teacher from the local health and fitness center and someone who practices yoga as part of his or her spiritual discipline. The two viewpoints on meditation or yoga—as a "natural" stress reducer or as a spiritual discipline that also results in relaxation and other secondary health benefits—frequently end up with discussions on the constructions of religion and culture.

There are many studies on meditation, but perhaps the most well-documented body of literature on stress reduction effects is found in the Transcendental Meditation movement. These studies and Web sites devoted to Transcendental Meditation are useful resources.

One strategy is to make the students hunt out articles and books on their own and present their findings in class. The instructor can then tabulate them on the board under various categories (*hatha*, *raja*, the kinds of yoga found in the Bhagavad Gita). To maximize the benefits, it is helpful to make a list of analytical questions or possible points for discussion and ask the students to think about them. For those who are nervous about this approach, any book by B.K.S. Iyengar (*Yoga: The Path to Holistic Health*, for instance) can give an "insider's" body-mind-soul perspective. Books by Feurstein or Desikachar are also useful to start discussion. Popular books like *A Morning Cup of Yoga: One Simple, Balanced Routine for a Lifetime of Health and Wellness,* by Jane Goad Trechsel and Rodney Yee, are fun to discuss. Linking health with yoga and meditation draws far less student skepticism than does linking it with *vastu,* astrology, and gems.

Weeks 7–9: Systems of Medicine: Āyurveda *and* Siddha

The last major section focuses on topics that the students have been anticipating since the first week and that some of them may have thought would be
the only focus of the course: Āyurveda and Siddha. These forms of medicine
are traditional health care systems of India and, at least in the case of Āyurveda,
do indeed date back more than three thousand years. Āyurveda is like a "para"-
veda and is ordinarily translated as the "knowledge of a [long and healthy] life."
A history of Āyurveda would entail a history of medicine in India and usually
invokes a sense of admiration for the advances made so early in this field. The
works of Caraka and Susruta, both of whom lived in the first few centuries of
the common era, are usually seen as foundational.

As with *vastu* and yoga, there are several hundreds of Web pages on Āyurveda. The works of Dominik Wujastyk are considered to be standard scholarly
resources, and the writings of Prakash Desai and Robert Svoboda are interesting focal points for discussion. The introductory chapters of Vasant Lad's book
combined with some Web pages usually also give a good introduction. Lad's
approach is just one of many, but it is as good as any to get into the field. His
Text Book of Āyurveda gives the philosophical underpinnings of some Hindu
systems and a very detailed look at the major principles that govern Āyurveda.
Basic to its understanding is a trifold division—the three *doshas* that underlie
many medical problems. Although *dosha* is frequently translated as "mistake"
or fault, it is used in the sense of organizing principles. The Sanskrit words
for these three principles are *vata, pitta,* and *kapha,* frequently translated as
"wind," "bile," and "phlegm." Since these are very approximate and in some
ways misleading translations, most writers explain them in detail and then use
the original words.

Popular approaches range from treating Āyurveda as a completely independent medical system and body of knowledge to integrating it with astrology,
yoga, and other healing disciplines. Thus Lad's Web pages describes one of his
program's goals as an "integration of Āyurveda with modern medicine, yoga,
Jyotish (Vedic astrology), other healing disciplines, and the individual Self to
bring about total health, awareness, and harmony" (The Āyurvedic Institute;
http://ayurveda.com/about). Āyurvedic principles and practices are said to
bring peace and balance to the body, mind, and soul.

There are far fewer materials on Siddha medicine, a predominantly South
Indian system, than on Āyurveda. In Siddha medicine, the physician bases the
diagnosis on pulse readings taken from different parts of the body at different
times. Val Daniel's article is a good introduction to this system.

Vastu, Āyurveda, Siddha, and other systems thrived in local communities
and as family practices in the nineteenth and twentieth centuries. It is in the
last quarter of the twentieth century that they have become more widely popular in India. One may seek the reasons for the retrieval and recognition of
these customs and practices. Possible answers lie in the assertion of indigenous and traditional systems of knowledge and wisdom in the postcolonial era.
There is a strong perception that these systems were devalued by Europeans

and Indians during the colonial era and that they were bulldozed by the "scientific" paradigms of education and practice. Another possible reason may be the "pizza" effect—it is said that Italians did not think of pizza as an exciting dish until the Americans showed interest in it. The spotlight on traditional systems of wisdom as well as on New Age religions certainly could have fueled interest in Āyurveda; the revival of *vastu*, however, is a local phenomenon which is only now going transnational.

Those interested in the history of medicine in India can choose to focus one or two lectures on the advances made by Charaka and Susruta in medicine and surgery.

Week 10: A Woman's Body: Menstruation, Childbirth, and Religion

In Hindu traditions—as in other religions—the woman's body is celebrated in some rituals and subjected to patriarchal aggression in others. Although there is considerable focus on women's traditions in this course, this week's discussions focus directly on women's knowledge, women's bodies. Much of this knowledge is local. In theorizing about this, women writing on women's health urge us to look at sources that are not Sanskrit and brahmanical, which are frequently androcentric. Instead, they urge us to focus on local traditions. One such example is recent anthropological work focusing on the work of midwives, their knowledge of pressure points, and the theology of birth.

"Upper" caste Hindus think of menstruation, childbirth, and death as ritually polluting. The axis of purity and pollution is distinct from, though there is occasional overlap with, the poles of auspiciousness and inauspiciousness.

Week 11 (First Class): Health Tourism: Visiting India for Massages, Oil Therapies, Puttur Bone Setting, and More

There is just one class in which we can explore the exploding "health tourism" business in South India—health spas with special oil massages from Kerala, *pancha karma* remedies from Āyurveda, and the esoteric paste used for the unique "bone setters," the folks who cure complex fractures by using a special herbal paste and rudimentary splints. This form of tourism can be seen again as a commodification of traditional knowledge systems. But the class is also introduced to some traditional forms of oil massages that are part of daily living in India. Massages are seen as therapeutic and invigorating, not as a luxury or sign of decadence, as they are often thought of in the West. Oil massages are included in religious frames; women, for instance, traditionally had oil massages on Tuesdays and Fridays because those days were sacred to the goddesses. On auspicious events such as their wedding day, women have "oil baths," in which their bodies and heads are massaged with fragrant oil and then washed off with herbal powders including turmeric. Turmeric is a symbol of well-being and "auspiciousness"—in South India, a symbol of a married woman whose husband is alive. It also has antiseptic properties. In the postcolonial revival of these customs, there has been a perception that many of the traditional practices did have medical benefits. All this has led to an increased pride in the religious, cultural, and medical heritages of India.

Week 11: (Second Class and Part of Week 12) Focus on Food

Student projects identify specific properties in foods according to various systems of thought and healing with which they become familiar through the Materia Medica, books on Āyurveda and Siddha systems, Web resources, and so on. Many of these sources give both general and specific information. They may ask one, for instance, to avoid caffeinated foods and drinks in general and also give very precise directions on how to make healthy drinks.

There are, of course, several ways of classifying foods. The trifold Āyurvedic system with its divisions of *kapha*, *pitta*, and *vata* is one system. There are also categories of "auspicious" and "inauspicious" foods. Some of these classifications are regionally known or specific to communities; others followed categories better known through an Āyurvedic framework. In some regional classifications, foods may be thought of as "heating" or "cooling." Others divide up food into what is loosely and misleadingly translated into English as "raw" and "cooked." These translations are misleading because they do not refer to "cooking" in the ordinary sense of the word but rather refer to a range of specific treatments to which the food is subjected. In some North Indian communities, food cooked in water is sometimes considered to be "raw" (kaccha), and food cooked in clarified butter or oil is "fine" and "cooked" (pakka). While some of these regulations are lost in the process of modernization, practicality, convenience, and migrations, a number of them linger on and are specially pressed into use on ritual occasions or when one is suffering from ill health.

Another system is to classify foods according to the traditional Hindu philosophical system of *sattva* (purity), *rajas* (movement/energy/passion), and *tamas* (darkness, sloth, stupor).

Students can either work individually or in groups to classify foods, suggest modifications to everyday food intake in the United States, identify possible foods that would help common ailments like digestive disorders or colds, or just theorize about the categories.

Week 12 (cont.): The Healing Power of Dance and Music

A special feature of Indian musical system is the belief that some *ragas* (literally, a scale of notes or series of motifs) not only create special effects but also reduce stress and induce cures. The literature on this is rather general, but there is enough for discussion in one class. Dances are also considered to be therapeutic—professional dancers sometimes speak of dance sessions as helping a whole range of mental and physical problems, from grief to migraines.

Above all, many dancers speak of dance as a kind of yoga—they see it as an activity that seeks well-being for the body, mind, and soul and that can bring about mental and physical health. But what is interesting according to some theories of Indian aesthetics is that dance lifts into higher levels of consciousness not just the dancer but also the audience.

Week 13: Wrapping Up

The final week of class discussions before the actual student presentations is devoted to putting all these healing systems in perspective and comparing them with other systems of healing.

Weeks 14–15: Student Projects

How Hindus understand well-being and how their practices reinforce these beliefs, therefore, is based on their worldviews and their understanding of human beings and their place in the universe. The laws that govern the physical body are frequently seen to be contiguous with or homologous to other natural laws. As in every other matter, there is great diversity; and for every rule there may be someone who practices the exception or who may be ignorant of it. Nevertheless, over centuries, certain concepts regarding deities, votive rituals, positioning of houses, constituents of the body, nature of bodily processes, medical treatments, and food have endured in some ways and drastically altered in other ways. For most Hindus, traditional worldviews regarding well-being and health do not form an alternative model to a worldview infused with modernity but are complementary to it. Thus, most of them would tend to put an "and" as a conjunction between the so-called scientific worldview and the traditional ones instead of seeing them as an "either/or" dichotomy. Perhaps it is in this process that we can see the lingering power of the Hindu religious and cultural tradition—as coloring and being an integral and important part of one's life.

Syllabus: Well-Being, Health, and Healing in the Hindu Traditions

- Reading List

Selected visual resources will be available on my home page at http://www .clas.ufl.edu/users/vasu.

GENERAL WORKS AND INTRODUCTIONS

- Short chapters and articles

David Knipe. "Hinduism and the Tradition of Āyurveda." In *Healing and Restoring*, ed. Lawrence Sullivan. New York: Macmillan, 1989.
Dominik Wujastyk. "The Science of Medicine." In *The Blackwell Com-*

panion to Hinduism, ed. Gavin Flood, pp. 393–409. Oxford: Blackwell, 2003.

- Books

Prakash N. Desai. *Health and Medicine in the Hindu Tradition: Continuity and Cohesion*. New York: Crossroads, 1989.
Jean Filliozat, ed. *The Classical Doctrine of Indian Medicine*. Delhi: Munshiram Manoharlal, 1964.
R. C. Majumdar. "Medicine." In *A Concise History of Science in India*, eds. D. M. Bose, S. N. Sen, and B. V. Subbarayappa, pp. 213–273. New Delhi: Indian National Science Academy, 1971.
G. Jan Meulenbeld and Dominik Wujastyk, eds. *Studies on Indian Medical History*. Dehli: Motilal Banarsidass, 2001.
P. V. Sharma. *History of Medicine in India*. Delhi: Indian National Science Academy, 1992.
Dominik Wujastyk. *The Roots of Āyurveda*. New York: Penguin Books, 1998.
Kenneth Zysk. *Religious Medicine: The History and Evolution of Indian Medicine*. New Brunswick, N.J.: Transaction Books, 1985.

WEEK 1: DIVERSITY, COMMONALITIES IN HINDUISM
Readings

Vasudha Narayanan, *Hinduism: Origins, Beliefs, Practices, Holy Texts, Sacred Places*, chaps. 1 and 2. New York: Oxford University Press, 2004.
E. Valentine Daniel. Introduction to *South Asian Systems of Healing*, eds. E. Valentine Daniel and Judy F. Pugh. Vol. 18 of *Contributions to Asian Studies*, pp. ix–xii. Leiden: Brill, 1984.

WEEK 2: GODS AND GODDESSES OF HEALING
Readings

- Mariamman

Margaraet Trawick Egnor. "The Changed Mother, or What the Smallpox Goddess Did When There Was No More Smallpox." In *South Asian Systems of Healing*, eds. E. Valentine Daniel and Judy F. Pugh. Vol. 18 of *Contributions to Asian Studies*, pp. 24–45. Leiden: Brill, 1984.

- Sitala

Edward Dimock. "The Myth of the Goddess Sitala." In *The Divine Consort: Radha and the Goddesses of India*, eds. J. S. Hawley and D. M. Wulff, pp. 184–203. Boston: Beacon, 1986.

- Aids Amma

See relevant section of Vasudha Narayanan, "Diglossic Hinduism: Lentils and Liberation." *Journal of the American Academy of Religion* 68, no. 4: 761–779.

- Possession

B. S. Bharathi. "Spirit Possession and Healing Practices in a South Indian Fishing Community." *Man in India* 73, no. 4: 343–352.

Peter J. Claus. "Medical Anthropology and the Ethnography of Spirit Possession." In *South Asian Systems of Healing*, eds. E. Valentine Daniel and Judy F. Pugh, pp. 60–72. Vol. 18 of *Contributions to Asian Studies*. Leiden, Brill: 1984.

Philip Singer. *Divine Madness: Trance, Dance, and Healing in Guyana* (film). Southfield, MI: Traditional Healing Productions, 1978.

Kathleen M. Erndl. "The Mother Who Possesses." In *Devi, Goddesses of India*, eds. John Stratton and Donna Marie Wulff, pp. 173–194. Berkeley: University of California Press, 1996.

Kalpana Ram. "The Female Body of Possession: A Feminist Perspective on Rural Tamil Women's Experiences. In *Mental Health from a Gender Perspective*, eds. Bhargavi V. Davar, pp. 181–216. New Delhi: Sage.

WEEK 3: VOTIVE RITUALS: WOMEN'S RITUALS FOR THE WELL-BEING OF THE FAMILY

Readings

- Choose from

Mary McGee. "Desired Fruits: Motive and Intention in the Votive Rites of Hindu Women." In *Roles and Rituals for Hindu Women*, ed. Julia Leslie, pp. 71–88. Rutherford, NJ: Farleigh Dickinson University Press, 1991.

Anne Mackenzie Pearson. *Because It Gives Me Peace of Mind: Ritual Fasts in the Religious Lives of Hindu Women*. Albany: SUNY Press, 1996.

- Porous Boundaries in Pilgrimage Traditions

Vasudha Narayanan. "Religious Vows at the Shrine of Shahul Hamid." In *Dealing with Deities: The Ritual Vow in South Asia*, eds. Selva J. Raj and William P. Harman. Albany: SUNY Press, 2006.

Vasudha Narayanan. "Shared Ritual Spaces." *Religious Studies News*, February 1998, pp. 15, 30, 41.

Paul Younger. "Velankanni Calling Hindu Patterns of Pilgrimage at a Christian Shrine." In *Sacred Journeys*, ed. Alan Morinis, pp. 89–100. Westport, CT: Greenwood.

WEEK 4: GENERAL WELL-BEING AND REMEDIES TO PROBLEMS—PART I:
FOCUS ON *VASTU*

Readings

> Kathleen Cox. *The Power of Vastu Living.* New York City: Fireside, 2002.
> http://www.experiencefestival.com/index.php/topic/vastu
> http://www.experiencefestival.com/index.php/topic/ef-teachers/teacher/
> 758 (This Web site provides a number of useful links.)

WEEK 5: GENERAL WELL-BEING—PART 2: FOCUS ON ASTROLOGY, HEALING
POWER OF GEMS, MEDICINAL ASTROLOGY, PRAYERS TO THE NINE PLANETS

Readings

> Hart DeFouw and Robert Svoboda. *Light on Life.* Twin Lakes, WI: Lotus,
> 2003.
> Judy F. Pugh. "Astrology and Fate: The Hindu and Muslim Experi-
> ences." In *Karma: An Anthropological Inquiry*, eds. Charles F. Keyes
> and E. V. Daniel, pp. 131–146. Berkeley: University of California Press,
> 1983.
> Judy F. Pugh. "Concepts of Person and Situation in North Indian Coun-
> seling: The Case of Astrology." In *South Asian Systems of Healing*, eds.
> E. Valentine Daniel and Judy F. Pugh, pp. 85–105. Vol. 18 of *Contribu-
> tions to Asian Studies.* Leiden: Brill, 1984.
> Valerie Roebuck. Introduction to *The Circle of Stars: An Introduction to
> Indian Astrology.* London: Vega, 2002. (This is an interesting discus-
> sion on the history of astrology in India.)
> Komilla Sutton. *Indian Astrology.* New York: Viking Studio, 2000. (Lovely
> picture book but nonacademic, tending toward New Age religion.)
> Michio Yano. "Calendar, Astrology, and Astronomy." In *The Blackwell
> Companion to Hinduism*, eds. Gavin Flood, pp. 376–392. Oxford:
> Blackwell, 2003.

> • Gems

> http://www.astrologer-drsudhirshah.com/gemsastrology.html

WEEK 6: YOGA AND MEDITATION

Readings

> T.K.V. Desikachar, with R. H. Cravens. *Health, Healing, and Beyond: Yoga
> and the Living Tradition of Krishnamacharya.* New York: Aperture,
> 1988.
> Georg Feuerstein. *The Yoga Tradition: Its History, Literature, Philosophy,
> and Practice.* Prescott, AZ: Hohm Press, 1998.
> Georg Feuerstein, trans. and ed. *Teachings of Yoga*: Boston: Shambhala,
> 1997.

Georg Feuerstein and Jeanine Miller. *The Essence of Yoga: Essays on the Development of Yogic Philosophy from the Vedas to Modern Times.* Rochester, VT: Inner Traditions, 1998.

WEEKS 7–9: *ĀYURVEDA* AND *SIDDHA*

Readings

- Āyurveda

David Knipe. "Hinduism and the Tradition of Āyurveda." In *Healing and Restoring*, ed. Lawrence Sullivan, pp. 89–109. New York: Macmillan, 1989.
Lad Vasant. *The Complete Book of Āyurvedic Home Remedies.* New York: Harmony Books, 1998.
_____. *Textbook of Āyurveda: Fundamental Principles.* Alberquerque, NM: Āyurvedic Press, 2002.
Dominik Wujastyk. *The Roots of Āyurveda.* New York: Penguin Classics, 2001.

- Web sites on Āyurveda.

Āyurveda http://www.webindia.com/india/Āyurveda.htm
http://www.ayur.com/about.html

- Siddha Medicine

Daniel E. Valentine. "The Pulse as an Icon in Siddha Medicine." In *South Asian Systems of Healing*, eds. E. Valentine Daniel and Judy F. Pugh, pp. 115–126. Vol. 18 of *Contributions to Asian Studies*. Leiden: Brill, 1984.
http://www.healthmantra.com/siddha/siddha.htm
http://www.healthmantra.com/siddha/siddha2.htm
http://www.webhealthcentre.com/altmed/siddha/index.asp

- For those who would like to spend a class on surgery:

Guido Majno. *The Healing Hand: Man and Wound in the Ancient World.* Cambridge, MA: Harvard University Press, 1975.
Girindranath Mukhopadhyaya. *Surgical Instruments of the Hindus.* Dehli: New Bharatiya Book Corp., 2000

- Extra Reading

Larson, Gerald. "Āyurveda and the Hindu Philosophical Systems." *Philosophy East and West* 37, no. 3 (July 1997): 245–259.

- For those who want to do some really intense reading:

Daniel Cohen. "Murugan. A God of Healing Poisons: The Physics of Worship in a South Indian Center for Pilgrimage." Ph.D. dissertation, Department of Anthropology, University of Chicago, 1984. X, 264 l.BL9999.M79, University of Chicago Library.

WEEK 10: A WOMAN'S BODY: MENSTRUATION, CHILDBIRTH, AND RELIGION

Readings

Janet Chawla. *Child-bearing and Culture: Women-Centered Revisioning of the Traditional Midwife: The Dai as a Ritual Practitioner.* New Delhi: Indian Social Institute, 1994.

Anu Gupta, Bharati Roy Choudhury, Indira Balachandran et al. *Touch Me, Touch-Me-Not: Women, Plants and Healing: Women's Beliefs about Disease and Health.* New Delhi: Kali for Women, 1997.

I. J. Leslie. "Some Traditional Indian Views on Menstruation and Female Sexuality." In *Sexual Knowledge, Sexual Science*, eds. R. Porter and M. Teich, pp. 63–81. Cambridge: Cambridge University Press, 1995.

- Āyurvedic explanations for failed births and miscarriages:

Dominik Wujastyk. "Miscarriages of Justice: Demonic Vengeance in Classical Indian Medicine." In *Religion, Health, and Suffering*, eds. John Hinnells and Roy Porter, pp. 256–275. London: Kegan Paul, 1999.

- Advanced Reading

Main texts of Āyurveda on conception, embryology, and birth:

Selected chapters TBA:

S. Suresh Babu. *Astanga Samgraha.* Delhi: Chaukhamba Orientalia, 1st ed., 2004.

Caraka. *Caraka samhitā*, 2nd ed. Trans. A. Chandra Kaviratna and P. Sharma. Delhi: Sri Satguru Publications, 1996.

G. D. Singhal and T.J.S. Patterson. *Synopsis of Ayurveda: Based on a Translation of the Suśruta Samhitā (The Treatise of Suśruta).* Delhi; New York: Oxford University Press, 1993.

Vagbhata. *Astanga Hridaya of Vagbhata: The Book of Eight Branches of Ayurveda.* Trans. Board of Scholars. Delhi: Sri Satguru Publications, 1999.

WEEK 11 (FIRST CLASS): HEALTH TOURISM: VISITING INDIA FOR MASSAGES, OIL THERAPIES, PUTTUR BONE SETTING, AND MORE

- Web sites
- Short newspaper articles and Web sites promoting health tourism— the commodification of health

http://123world.com/india/health/
http://www.expresstravelandtourism.com/200309/lookin01.shtml

http://www1.timesofindia.indiatimes.com/cms.dll/articleshow?msid=
50409
http://rajasthan.eindiatourism.com/nature/rajasthan-swasthya-yog
-parishad.html

Web searches will bring up the latest Internet sites.

Puttur Bone Setting
http://www.hinduonnet.com/folio/fo0010/00100420.htm
http://www.hindu.com/thehindu/mp/2002/11/13/stories/
2002111300420100.htm

WEEK II: (SECOND CLASS AND PART OF WEEK I2): FOCUS ON FOOD

WEEK I2: THE HEALING POWER OF DANCE AND MUSIC

Readings

Guy Beck. *Sonic Theology: Hinduism and Sacred Sound.* Columbia: University of South Carolina Press, 1993.
http://www.aquarius-atlanta.com/september/dance1.shtml (New Age Web page)

WEEK I3: INTEGRATIVE DISCUSSION

Readings

Lawrence Sullivan, ed. *Healing and Restoring.* New York: Macmillan, 1989.

WEEKS I4–I5: STUDENT PROJECTS

4

Keeping It All in Balance: Teaching Asian Religions through Illness and Healing

Ivette Vargas-O'Bryan

The Search

Initially, my fascination with teaching a course on illness and healing in Asian religions grew out of my experience of working with undergraduate students in religious studies and the sciences at Harvard University who wanted to learn about the cultural beliefs and customs of Asia in unconventional ways, crossing disciplinary boundaries and creating a net of interconnections between various fields like religious studies, medicine, anthropology, and sociology. Intersecting with my own doctoral work at the time on illness and renunciation in Tibetan Buddhist biographies, I was thrown into a search for what I saw as an exciting field of inquiry—illness, healing, and religion. I found that these themes appear throughout a number of traditions within Asia, have an overarching human element that crosses cultural boundaries, and have historical and current-day prominence. Thereafter, teaching several courses on the topic as junior tutorials at the same university and as undergraduate courses at two liberal arts colleges helped me consider large pedagogical questions: How do I teach an engaging yet informative introductory course on Asian religions year after year? How do the lenses of illness and healing help students understand Asian religious traditions? How do I engage responsibly in comparative and interdisciplinary studies? This essay discusses how the journey of teaching a course on illness and healing in selected religious traditions of India, Tibet, and China from a large urban setting to smaller isolated liberal arts colleges led to several revelations. The most crucial of these is that it is important to set broad course goals that utilize the lenses of illness and healing; to tailor courses to the specific teaching setting, taking into consideration the student population, local area, school programs and resources; and to use interdisciplinary materials. Because of their diverse interpretations and viable applications, the themes of illness and healing provide unique ways to engage with religious traditions cross-culturally and create intersections across disciplines.

Course Goals and the Thematic Approach

Setting broad learning goals helps ensure that students develop a basic foundation and critical thinking skills within the study of religion and Asian traditions in particular. This course, on one level, is an introduction to the study of religion and to the religious traditions of India, Tibet, and China. Therefore, as many central ideas within the field of religion are introduced, assumptions of what constitutes an academic study of religion (as opposed to other ways of approaching religion) are addressed. Currently teaching in a liberal arts college in the Bible Belt, this consideration is taken very seriously. Having the students think through their expectations and assumptions about religion and Asia the first day of class is a useful exercise to weed out or at least give voice to biases and misinterpretations.

On another level, through the lenses of illness and healing students are exposed to the values within these traditions and their interactions with Western biomedical traditions in historical and current-day circumstances. Through thematic and case study approaches, students gain knowledge about how particular traditions and values are played out within these themes. Since illness and healing are often integral parts of a religious tradition, this course explores ways in which people attempt to find meaning in their lives through these themes such as understanding the sacred, life, pain, suffering, death, human and divine agency, the role of the individual and community, the authority of healers, and how tradition and modernity affect these views.

Students also tackle different ways traditions define illness and health through the study of "institutional" medical traditions and other healing traditions (which may or may not involve an apprenticeship and/or an institution). Not only does the course cover the complex medical theories and applications of Āyurvedic medicine, Indian Buddhist medicine, Tibetan medicine, Chinese medicine, and Western medicine within Asia, which have distinctive and well-developed medical curricula and pharmacological training, but also other ways in which healing is manifested in the rituals of mediums or shamans, monks and priests, ordinary people in homes and villages, and even political leaders. In terms of India, Tibet, and China, health is examined as maintaining the balance of humors and elements or maintaining order in the environment or society as a whole or achieving liberation. The causes of illness are analyzed in terms of the fruits of personal or collective action (karma), the forces of spirits or demons, the effect of jealousy or envy, the influence of the natural environment, and the effects of political or cultural upheavals or abuse. Studying illness and healing during China's Cultural Revolution, we get a view of the Confucian ethic of maintaining order in society and how this idea and others are redefined through Mao's fight against Confucian culture and schistosomiasis. Anthropological studies and debates on how the terms *illness, disease,* and *religion* are used, such as Robert A. Hahn's "Rethinking 'Illness' and 'Disease,'" provide theoretical background and assistance for comparative study. Each individual or group in a tradition plays a role in defining illness and healing within her own context; considered altogether, these divergent conceptions provide an array of options that may either complement or contradict one another.

Through discussion of illness and healing as themes, students are led to look at the appropriateness (and inappropriateness) of such categories in their own experiences, a process that leads to critical rethinking of categories like "religious" and "secular." Helaine Selin's work *Medicine across Cultures* provides helpful studies on the diverse ways of thinking about healing from a crosscultural perspective. Paul Tillich's monograph on health is useful for its discussion on the correlation of health with salvation. Donald Schriver's essay "Medicine and Religion" provides a theoretical account of the relation between medicine and religion. These studies show the metaphorical force of these terms and how they have been understood in relation to religious and political transformations in different countries.

Studying the effects of illness on the individual and society leads to discussions of stigma in terms of class distinctions, gender, sexual orientation, and racism in religious traditions. Understanding illness in a positive light also helps students view the diverse ways in which a tradition defines its categories. Studies of the smallpox and AIDS goddesses in India and the story of the contraction of leprosy by a Kashmiri Buddhist nun in Tibetan texts help students understand illness as a mark of being a chosen devotee (and therefore a sign of honor), as a way of helping women achieve higher social status, as a means of achieving liberation (the notion of *via dolorosa*), and as an educational tool for prevention. Overall, illness functions as a means for achieving health on multiple levels.

The course goals are therefore accomplished in three ways: (1) reading primary and secondary source materials concerning illness, healing practices, and medical traditions in Asia, and reading theoretical studies by Asian and Western scholars; (2) viewing and discussing films; and (3) engaging in panel discussions and debates. The course carefully considers the teaching setting, since that setting dictates available resources and course content.

Teaching Setting

How do I design a course on religion, on Asia, and on illness and healing that is enticing, informative, and a great learning experience for students within a liberal arts context? These are goals that every teacher has in mind, but in a small, isolated, religiously affiliated liberal arts college, the challenges are even greater because the course is competing with courses that may be considered more practical in terms of career development and less threatening in terms of challenging local religious values. Students may assume at the outset that these traditions are "superstitions," and they may have unexamined postcolonial views about the Other; thus a teacher will need to draw attention to the ways that ideas in the traditions are just as "scientific" and viable as those within our own society. Drawing from the traditions and strengths of the college or university and local setting in the design of one's course attracts the attention of the student body, the college community, and the larger community. For example, five factors were at play when I designed a course on illness and healing in Asian religions for my current college: (1) the religious affiliation of the school, student body, and people in the region; (2) students' exposure to Asia; (3) the academic programs to which students are most attracted; (4) special programs at the school; and (5) the resources at the school and in the community.

The first factor, the religious affiliation of the student body and the population around the school, affects how the students react to the material. In the Bible Belt, some students have set ideas about what constitutes religious values and therefore have either a strong aversion to the traditions they encounter or a real curiosity about something different. Their decision to take the course shows that, despite their personal convictions, they have a genuine curiosity to learn. The second factor can be of special importance in a school such as mine: many of these students have never been exposed to these traditions and, further, know little about different parts of Asia. This is a great opportunity to break down their biases and build new knowledge by introducing these traditions through themes that the students can relate to, namely illness and healing. During some points in their lives, students are exposed to such experiences. Their challenge is to learn that these traditions are just as concerned with the meaning and quality of life as the Jewish and Christian traditions with which the students were brought up, deriving knowledge and theories from different conceptions about existence, the body, and the divine.

The third factor involves considering the academic programs at the particular school and how they inevitably influence course offerings. For example, a strong pre-med program certainly can shape some of the course content. In the present course, I define healing broadly, to encompass different healing modalities, like medicine in an allopathic setting, medicine in diverse Asian medical non-allopathic settings, and traditional healing using herbs, spells, mantras, and mediums. Readings address (1) modern Western allopathic physicians trained in alternative, complementary, and integrative medicine, who incorporate Asian religious-medical traditions into modern Western medical practices, and (2) current research on Asian medicine by the Office of International Health (NCCAM/NIH-CAM). The Samueli Institute, the World Health Organization, and the Osher Institute at Harvard Medical School draw students' attention to the applicability of the material to their current career interests. In addition, I work with scholars from the sciences and social sciences, and with the pre-med advisors, whose collaboration on panel discussions and through lectures helps students understand the diversity of illness and healing theories and practices cross-culturally.

Special programs at the school also contribute to the design of the course. Lilly Grants for the Theological Exploration of Vocation, January terms, and study abroad programs greatly enhanced my course. For example, the current course is funded under a Lilly grant allowing a faculty member to discuss the themes of a course in light of vocation, broadly defined. Not only are students made aware of medicine cross-culturally as a vocation, which greatly strengthens their background in the sciences; they also explore how vocation can be perceived in much larger, philosophical terms, such as dealing with one's goals in life. How does thinking about illness and healing help us understand our lives better? How do these traditions help us grasp large ontological categories such as death, karma, and rebirth? January terms and study abroad programs bring students' knowledge to the experiential level—they can visit hospitals, view rituals firsthand, and talk with religious practitioners.

Finally, tapping into the resources at my school and in the community has created mutual awareness on the part of students and the community at large. Inviting local acupuncturists, traditional Chinese and Tibetan doctors, *taiqi* and *qigong* masters, Buddhist monks, yoga instructors, chaplains, and physicians who practice integrative medicine to class to give a lecture or conduct a panel discussion gives students firsthand encounters with various practices, engagement in fruitful discussions, and possible future internships. In addition, audiovisual materials through Powerpoint presentations, slides, and films provide a visual learning experience for students who have never experienced Asian cultures and their healing practices. Films presented in class include "The Annual Visit of the God Vishnumurti," which provides a powerful presentation of a traditional healer-medium in an Indian village. "The Medium is the Masseuse" displays the healing practices of a female medium in a Hindu Balinese context. The "Knowledge of Healing" exposes students to the Tibetan healing traditions, and Dr. Herbert Benson's video on *tummo* research in the Himalayas provides students a view of the interaction of Tibetan and Western medical theories and practices. Bill Moyers's "Healing and the Mind: The Mystery of Chi" provides an on-the-ground account of Chinese medicine "To Taste a Hundred Herbs: Gods, Ancestors, and Medicine in a Chinese Village" discusses a variety of Chinese indigenous healing practices. Finally, "Good Medicine: How to Turn Pain into Compassion with Tonglen Meditation" focuses on the role of meditation in healing among Tibetan Buddhists. These materials also engage students' visual learning styles.

Methodological, Theoretical Issues, and Pedagogy

A course on theories of illness and healing practices in Asian religious traditions requires attention to methodological and theoretical issues and provides great opportunities for comparative study. The course includes materials that (1) provide foundational theoretical background within the study of religion and other disciplines such as anthropology, ethnography, medicine, and sociology; and 2) provide case studies of illness and healing theories within Asian and Western contexts.

The works of Clifford Geertz, Emile Durkheim, Paul Tillich, and Andrew Weil enable students to reflect on how the themes related to healing work with religion as part of a cultural system, as a function of society, or as the salvific or liberative function. Case studies of Asian cultural and medical frameworks, in interaction and collaboration with Western biomedical ideas, provide material for comparative analyses. Issues of pluralism and interaction between medical traditions are briefly considered through analyses of case studies of Āyurvedic, Tibetan, and Chinese medical traditions, and other healing practices. For example, one case focuses on an Indian patient who consults multiple healers such as Indian mediums, Āyurvedic doctors, and Western-trained biomedical practitioners in order to find an explanation for his ailment. Another involves Tibetan patients in Lhasa who have access to Tibetan medical physicians and traditional healers, Chinese medical practitioners, healers who integrate Tibetan and Western medical ideas, and Tibetan monks performing healing rituals. Arthur Kleinman's *Patients and Healers in the Context of Culture* provides examples of case studies from Chinese society of folk systems, traditional Chinese medicine (TCM), and Western encounters. Other comparative case studies address Western appropriation of Asian religious healing concepts and techniques into a Western context, as in Herbert Benson's study of Tibetan *tummo* meditation, Mark Epstein's psychoanalytic study of Buddhist ideas, and a cancer research study utilizing Tibetan yoga in one Texas hospital. The debate between doctors Arnold Relman and Andrew Weil about integrative medicine provides a useful context through which to structure students' own debates about the materials, and current uses of Asian healing practices in comparison with Western techniques. Ming Ho Tak's historical study of Chinese medicine and its encounter with the West provides informative background on this subject.

Course Structure

The structure of a course like this can vary, depending on the level of the group, and can address different learning styles (visual, reading, and auditory) through lectures, small class, and blackboard discussions, viewing and discussion of audiovisual materials, and panel discussions and debates. Assignments and tests include brief writing assignments, quizzes, longer papers, and a group project. In the past, the course required at least five 1–2 page reflection papers, three or four quizzes on each of the three traditions, one group project, and a 12–15 page final paper.

For the most part, I deliver six to eight introductory lectures, which include a discussion of the goals of the course and basic concepts in the study of religion and history of the Asian traditions. The next five to seven classes cover the three major Asian religious traditions' theories of illness and healing practices. Two classes address issues of pluralism and interactions between Asian traditions and biomedicine through case studies, and two other classes focus on Asian healing practices in the West. A concluding lecture reiterates the main goals of the course and the lessons learned.

Written and discussion exercises are an integral part of the course. The short response papers help in reflecting upon these theoretical frameworks and how they can be applied to various Asian contexts. Discussion groups provide in-depth explorations of the theories of illness and healing practices in the Asian religions. Role-play debates help students reflect on a personal level some of the positions taken by key thinkers in the course, and allow them to integrate the material, exercise their creativity, and experience the views of others. The debate may focus on a set of central questions, such as how they would deal with the presence of an infectious disease from a religious perspective, or how they would choose between Asian and Western remedies. A discussion of the AIDS epidemic in Thailand and of how Thai monasteries act as hospices for people dying with the disease, provides a perfect scenario for this discussion. Finally, panel discussions by Asian and Western medical practitioners who integrate Asian religious and/or medical systems in the West can both include and promote debate.

Challenges and Benefits

I have encountered a number of challenges when teaching this course. One involves determining how many Asian religious traditions to cover in this course, given the setting and the nature of my students. Limiting the course to two or three traditions may allow students to arrive at a better understanding of unfamiliar traditions and related theories of illness and healing. I have found, in contrast, that when teaching the course in a school environment that is more pluralistic and diverse, studying three or more Asian religious traditions works well, so long as readings are not too long (less than 100 pages a week), and can be comprehended by college-age students with some assistance from the instructor. Teaching about traditions that have some historical connections among them can also help students see both continuities and disjunctions in their theories and practices.

Another challenge can arise in relation to resources for student research papers. Requiring a research paper is not realistic, for example, in a small liberal arts college that does not have sufficient resources to support it—for example, one in which interlibrary loan policies are limited. I find it more useful to assign short twelve- to fifteen-page papers and brief essays in which students are expected to utilize some of the class and/or supplemental reading; to direct students to Web-based resources (e.g., the Chinese medicine Web page www.albion.edu/history/Chimed/, which includes a bibliography of works on Chinese medicine, links to Web pages, and current events); and to have students conduct ethnographic studies on Asian healing practices in the local region.

Another challenge is student participation. Small group discussions every week and group projects help address problem issues with the readings, breaking down difficult concepts to digestible levels and reinforcing a sense of independence and creativity. Projects devised and presented to the class by students at Grinnell College, for example, included researching acupuncture through websites; discussing Buddhist concepts of healing through modern action films; and studying yoga in Asian and Western settings, which included a film clip and class exercise of yoga.

Syllabus

Religious Studies 295–03: Illness and Healing in Asian Religious Traditions

> The first priority in Tibetan medicine is to restore harmony to each person in the context of his or her life experiences
> —Helaine Selin, *Medicine across Cultures*, p. 95

Course Description

We may often ask: Why do we suffer? Why are we ill? How do we heal? In addressing these themes, Asian cultures often uniquely break down barriers between the secular and sacred in an effort to locate meaning and effect physical and spiritual transformation within larger soteriological frameworks. This introductory interdisciplinary course explores the different ways Hindu, Buddhist, Chinese, and Asian folk traditions understand illness and healing. Emphasis is placed on pain and suffering; illness and stigma; agency and karma; the body; ritual; gender; and the role of healers and "shamans," demons, gods and goddesses, monks, and gurus. The course culminates in a study of the conflict and coexistence of modern Asian and Western religious and medical systems. We explore the role of the individual in society, the significance of community, the ethical questions that bridge religion and medicine, tradition and modernity, and the balance that must be achieved with the outside environment. This course is meant to challenge, intrigue, and reorient us into new ways of thinking about ourselves and our relationship with the universe.

CLASS I: INTRODUCTION: RELIGION, CATEGORIES, AND THEORETICAL FOUNDATIONS

Clifford Geertz, "Religion as a Cultural System"
Paul Tillich, *The Meaning of Health*

CLASS 2: INDIAN RELIGIONS: ILLNESS AND HEALING CATEGORIES

Hahn, Robert A., "Rethinking 'Illness' and 'Disease,' " pp. 1–23

CLASS 3: INDIAN RELIGIONS, ĀYURVEDA AND THE BODY

Gregory Fields, *Religious Therapeutics: Body and Health in Yoga, Āyurveda, and Tantra*, pp. 1–31
David Snipe, "Hinduism and the Tradition of Āyurveda," pp. 89–110

CLASS 4: ĀYURVEDA

CLASS 5: KARMA AND STIGMA: THE CASE OF LEPROSY

Julia Leslie: "The Implications of the Physical Body," in *Religion, Health and Suffering*, pp. 23–45
Hanne de Bruine, *Leprosy in South India*, pp. 33–51

CLASS 6: DISEASE GODDESSES AND LOCAL HEALERS

David Kinsley, *Hindu Goddesses*, pp. 151–160, 197–211
Tony Stewart, "Encountering the Smallpox Goddess," in *Religions of India*, pp. 389–397
Films on local healers: *The Annual Visit of the God Vishnumurti* and *The Medium Is the Masseuse*

CLASS 7: IN-CLASS ESSAY QUIZ; INDIAN BUDDHISM: SHAKYAMUNI AND CONCEPTS OF HEALING

Donald Lopez, ed., *Asian Religions in Practice*, pp. 56–87 [Indian Buddhism]
Skorupski, "Health and Suffering in Buddhism," in *Religion, Health and Suffering*, pp. 139–165
Frank Reynolds, "Cosmology and Healing," in *The Life of Buddhism*, pp. 161–176

CLASS 8: INDIAN BUDDHIST MEDICAL HISTORY

Joseph Mitsuo Kitagawa, "Buddhist Medical History," in *Healing and Restoring*, pp. 9–32

CLASS 9: TIBETAN RELIGIONS: BUDDHA'S HEALING

Donald Lopez, ed., *Asian Religions in Practice* [Tibetan Religions]
John Avedon, *The Buddha's Art of Healing*, pp. 21–41

CLASS 10: FILM ON TIBET: *THE KNOWLEDGE OF HEALING*

CLASS 11: TIBETAN MEDICINE AND MEDITATION OF MEDICINE BUDDHA

Film: *Good Medicine* (on Tonglen meditation)

CLASS 12: IN-CLASS ESSAY QUIZ ON TIBETAN RELIGIONS; CHINESE
RELIGIONS: CONFUCIANISM AND SYSTEMATIC CORRESPONDENCES

Paul U. Unschuld, "Unification of the Empire, Confucianism, and the
Medicine of Systematic Correspondences." In *Medicine in China*
Background Reading: Ted J. Kaptchuk, *The Web That Has No Weaver:
Understanding Chinese Medicine*, pp. 51–100

CLASS 13: CHINESE RELGIONS: THE BASICS OF TAOISM

Donald Lopez, ed., *Asian Religions in Practice*, pp. 88–122 [Chinese Relig-
ions]
Francesca Bray, "Chinese Health Beliefs," pp. 187–211

CLASS 14: TAOISM AND THE BODY

Livia Kohn, *Taoist Meditation and Longevity Techniques*, chaps 2 and 8

CLASS 15: TAOISM HEALTH AND DRUGS THERAPY

Paul U. Unschuld, "Taoism and Pragmatic Drug Therapy." In *Medicine
in China*, pp. 101–116.
Kohn, *Taoist Meditation*, chap 3
Film: *To Taste a Hundred Herbs*

CLASS 16: CHINESE BUDDHISM AND BODHISATTVAS

Raoul Birnbaum, *The Healing Buddha*, pp. 3–26, 115–124; and "Chinese
Buddhist Traditions of Healing and the Life Cycle." In *Healing and Restoring*, pp. 33–58.

CLASS 17: THE PLAGUE GOD ONG IA KONG

Katherine Gould-Martin, "Ong ia kong: The Plague God as Modern Physician" In *Culture and Healing in Asian Societies*, pp. 41–67.

CLASS 18: RELIGION AND POLITICAL IDEOLOGY

Judith Farquhar, "Re-writing Traditional Medicine in Post-Maoist China."
In *Knowledge and the Scholarly Medical Traditions*, pp. 251–257.

CLASS 19: CLASS PROJECT AND EVENING PANEL DISCUSSION

CLASS 20: IN-CLASS ESSAY QUIZ, CHINESE RELIGIONS AND MEDICINE

Arthur Kleinman and J. Gale, *Patients and Healers in the Context of Culture*
Linda L. Barnes, "The Psychologizing of Chinese Healing Practices in
the United States"

CLASS 21: EAST MEETS WEST: HO TAK MING, *DOCTORS IN THE EAST: WHERE EAST MEETS WEST* DISCUSSION—HISTORICAL STUDY OF CHINESE MEDICINE AND THE WEST

CLASS 22: CLASS PROJECT DAY

CLASS 23: MARK EPSTEIN, *GOING TO PIECES WITHOUT FALLING APART* DISCUSSION

CLASS 24: FILM: *HERBERT BENSON AND TUMMO MEDITATION*

Nov. 29: Debate

Arnold Relman and Andrew Weil, "Is Integrative Medicine the Medicine of the Future? A Debate between Arnold S. Relman, MD, and Andrew Weil, MD," pp. 2122–2126

CLASS 25: CONCLUSION: DEBATE AND CONCLUDING REMARKS

CLASS 26: REVIEW DAY

Dec. 7: Final Exam

(I thank Sarah McKinley, Linda Barnes, Vincanne Adamas, TJ Hinrichs, Eric Jacobson, and Arthur Kleinman for their inspiration and valuable ideas about sources and materials for my courses.)

BIBLIOGRAPHY

Books and Articles

Avedon, John, et al. 1998. *The Buddha's Art of Healing: Tibetan Paintings Rediscovered.* New York: Rizzoli.

Barnes, Linda L. 1998. The Psychologizing of Chinese Healing Practices in the United States. *Culture, Medicine and Psychiatry* 22: 413–443.

Bates, Don, ed. 1995. *Knowledge and the Scholarly Medical Traditions.* Cambridge: Cambridge University Press.

Birnbaum, Raoul. 1979. *The Healing Buddha.* Boulder, CO: Shambhala.

Clark, Barry. 1995. *The Quintessence Tantras of Tibetan Medicine.* Ithaca, NY: Snow Lion.

de Bruin, Hanne M. 1996. *Leprosy in South India: Stigma and Strategies of Coping.* Vol. 22. Pondicherry: Institut Français de Pondichery.

Donden, Yeshe. 1999. *Healing from the Source.* Ithaca, NY: Snow Lion.

Epstein, Mark. 1999. *Going to Pieces without Falling Apart: A Buddhist Perspective on Wholeness.* New York: Broadway.

Fields, Gregory. 2001. *Religious Therapeutics: Body and Health in Yoga, Ayurveda, and Tantra.* Albany: State University of New York Press.

Geertz, Clifford. 1977. *The Interpretation of Cultures.* Boston: Basic Books.

Hahn, Robert A. 1984. Rethinking "Illness" and "Disease." *Contributions to Asian Studies* 18: 1–23.

Hinnells, John, ed. 1999. *Religion, Health, and Suffering*. London: Kegan Paul.

Kaptchuk, Ted J. 2000. *The Web That Has No Weaver: Understanding Chinese Medicine*. Chicago: Contemporary.

Kinsley, David. 1997. *Hindu Goddesses: Visions of the Divine Feminine in the Hindu Religious Tradition*. Berkeley: University of California Press.

Kleinman, Arthur, ed. 1978. *Culture and Healing in Asian Societies: Anthropological, Psychiatric, and Public Health Studies*. Cambridge: G. K. Hall.

Kleinman, Arthur, and J. Gale. 1980. *Patients and Healers in the Context of Culture*. Berkeley: University of California Press.

Kohn, Livia. 1989. *Taoist Meditation and Longevity Techniques*. Ann Arbor: University of Michigan Press.

Lopez, Donald, ed. 1999. *Asian Religions in Practice: An Introduction*. Princeton, NJ: Princeton University Press.

————. 1995. *Religions of India*. Princeton, NJ: Princeton University Press.

Ming, Ho Tak. 2001. *Doctors in the East: Where East Meets West*. Selangor Darul Esang: Pelanduk

Reynolds, Frank, ed. 2000. *The Life of Buddhism*. Berkeley: University of California Press.

Scheid, Volker. 2002. *Chinese Medicine in Contemporary China*. Durham, NC: Duke University Press.

Schriver, Donald. 1980. *Medicine and Religion: Strategies of Care*. Pittsburgh, PA: University of Pittsburgh Press.

Selin, Helaine, ed. 2003. *Medicine across Cultures: History and Practice of Medicine in Non-Western Cultures*. London: Kluwer.

Sullivan, Lawrence, ed. 1989. *Healing and Restoring: Health and Medicine in the World's Religious Traditions*. New York: Macmillan.

Tillich, Paul. 1961. *The Meaning of Health*. Chicago: University of Chicago Press.

Unschuld, Paul U. 1985. *Medicine in China: A History of Ideas*. Berkeley: University of California Press.

Zysk, Kenneth G. 1991. *Asceticism and Healing in Ancient India: Medicine in the Buddhist Monastery*. Oxford: Oxford University Press.

Films

Good Medicine: How to Turn Pain into Compassion with Tonglen Meditation (www.shambhalamountain.org/giftstore/product_info.php?c)

Healing and the Mind: The Mystery of Chi (www.documentary-video.com/displayitem.cfm?vid)

Teyyam: The Annual Visit of the God Vishnumurti (www.der.org/films/)

To Taste a Hundred Herbs (www.tsquare.tv/longbow/ttahh.html)

The Knowledge of Healing (www.tcfilm.ch/heilen_txt_e.htm)

The Medium is the Masseuse: A Balinese Massage (www.der.org/films/)

Tummo Meditation and Dr. Herbert Benson at the Mind-Body Medical Institute (Mind-Body Institute, Boston)

5

Teaching the History of Chinese Healing Traditions

Linda L. Barnes

Setting the Stage

Nothing in my formal training prepared me to teach about the history of Chinese healing traditions. As a religion scholar I had, to be sure, studied the history of Chinese religions and, as an anthropologist, had explored the entry of Chinese healing practices into the United States, particularly in Boston, but it was not the same thing. Still, I had friends and colleagues who were historians of Chinese medicine. When offered the chance to design a course of my choice for my spring semester as visiting faculty in the Religion Department at Brown University in 1999, it seemed like a good time to fill in this rather substantial hole in my own background.

As many of us have done, I turned to these friends and colleagues, picking their brains and borrowing their syllabi to pull together both the resources with which to write a syllabus and the backup sources with which to learn enough to keep a few steps ahead of my students. Much of the semester saw me scrambling to get through the required readings myself—many of them new to me—and to pull together lectures, sometimes based mostly on a few articles the students had not read. It was, to say the least, an adventure in just-in-time teaching. All by way of saying that designing a course on a subject to which one is relatively new is a viable venture, and one that many faculty regularly face.

Challenging Matters

From teaching other courses in religion and healing, I anticipated that students would come with three erroneous but related expectations: first, that the course would involve my bringing in Chinese medicine practitioners to give treatments; second, that they themselves would be learning Chinese healing practices; and third, that because they had already encountered something called "traditional Chinese medicine" in the United States, they had a good handle on the topic to begin with.

By putting the word "history" in the course title, I hoped to disabuse students of the first two expectations. That I was not altogether successful became evident when one student, after the first three weeks of the course, came to me with visible resentment to tell me she was dropping it because of all the things it was not. The third expectation was one I knew would take the course as a whole to address. In part, it reflected the influence of New Age approaches to healing, which tend to Orientalize and essentialize Asian and South Asian practices, viewing them in highly ahistorical terms. (The same type of thing happens with "Tibetan medicine" and with Āyurveda.) American practitioners of acupuncture in particular often refer to their practice as "traditional Chinese medicine." The term (frequently shortened to the acronym TCM) refers to the version of Chinese medicine systematized by the government of the People's Republic of China since the 1950s as a national medicine of the Marxist state. To create this system, the PRC government stripped older texts of terms and practices seen as "superstitious" (often a way of talking about religious dimensions).

The sharpest critics of the results point out that never, in its documented history, has Chinese medicine been fully dominated by a single school of thought. Rather, interacting theories and approaches to practice have always coexisted, with little overall synthesis. The government's need to present an ostensibly coherent system came in response to biomedical logic, which often calls for one or the other of two conflicting statements to be authoritative (Unschuld 1987, 1992). Even so, the results in China have not been unified (Scheid, 2002). In some cases, it took the full semester for students to understand the difference between what they have encountered as "Chinese medicine" in the United States—which they largely took to be acupuncture and maybe herbs—and the larger world of Chinese approaches to healing.

Likewise, American students familiar with racialized notions of "Asian" or "Chinese" rarely think of China as multiple and multicultural. They tend to know little about Chinese religious pluralism other than to associate Confucianism with patriarchy and foot binding and to idealize Daoism as a form of mysticism (making it, in their minds, universal). Feng shui, although a term they had perhaps heard, referred to interior decorating or perhaps to maximizing one's luck through adjustments to one's environments; it held no associations with the positioning of graves or with precautions against angering the dead and causing related affliction. I knew that the course would have to tackle all these dispositions to stereotype.

A different kind of challenge proved to be logistical. The preregistration numbers were pushing 45 when I approached the chair of the department to ask for teaching assistance if I were to allow that many students or more to take the course. After receiving assurance that such assistance would be forthcoming, I decided not to cap the enrollment. Soon, more than 85 students had signed up. However, a decision from higher up that "it was not a good idea to provide teaching fellows for a part-time visiting faculty" (I was, the memo said, free to cut back the enrollment if I chose) led the department to reverse its decision. The course that I had envisioned as one lecture a week and one discussion session had just become a twice-a-week lecture course. Despite not having assistance, I decided not to turn students away, but to try to adapt to these new circumstances—a large lecture hall, students ranging from freshmen to seniors and, for the most part, with no background in Chinese religious history or in the history of medicine of any kind. It was a largely novice audience, which was probably just fine, given that I was a novice to much of the content of the course.

To promote discussion, I drew a large seating chart of the lecture hall and asked students to sit in the same seats each time. I then provided a Polaroid camera in the religious studies office for students to take pictures of themselves. I cut out the heads and stuck them on the chart, which enabled me to learn people's names and call on students by name. To my surprise, many of them promptly assumed I knew who they were, leading them earnestly to inform me when they were going to have to miss a lecture.

In fact I implemented the course's attendance and participation requirements by having students turn in a signed comment and/or question at the end of each class session. I borrowed a method from a colleague of asking what point(s) remained "muddy." Collecting these questions allowed me to record attendance and to get an idea of how the students were interacting with the material. I used the questions turned in after the first class session in a given week to structure the beginning of the following lecture and, when possible, to refer to individuals as the authors of particular questions. Gradually, students began to raise questions in class. The major difficulty became one of turning around the muddy-points discussion relatively briefly so as not to compromise the balance of my lecture. Still, I tended to feel that the importance of student engagement outweighed getting through a lecture.

As a final challenge, it did not help that I had been diagnosed with breast cancer at the turn of the year. I booked my chemotherapy sessions for Fridays, so that by my Monday lectures I was ready to perform. I use the word "perform" deliberately. For me, teaching is, among many things, a performance art. My lecture notes function as my script. I rehearse them accordingly, to maximize my ability to use them minimally, and to improvise as needed. Early on in my teaching, I witnessed the difference between students' responses to exclusively oral presentations—the standard lecture—and to sessions thick with images, music, and in some cases, tastes and smells. It is, perhaps, a truism to say that there are different styles of learning—visual, auditory, olfactory, gustatory, and kinesthetic—but I have become convinced that teaching involving multiple styles goes deeper, because the content is transmitted on multiple levels. Nor do I think that this multisensory approach dilutes academic and intellectual content or rigor.

Contrasts in Change

In general, I intentionally avoid the term "medicine" and use "healing" instead, because the former sometimes intersects so uneasily with "religion," and because it tends to prompt associations and/or comparisons with biomedicine. Healing, on the other hand, allows for everything from the more erudite elite practices to talismans nailed to the door. It can include gods, goddesses, demons, and ghosts, as well as teleological and soteriological kinds of questions. One way to get at pertinent intersections and overlaps is to introduce conceptual paradigms that have emerged over the course of Chinese history. In particular, I have in mind a persisting interest in understanding the nature of change, given that healing involves the pursuit of particular forms of change

I introduced the issue of change in two key ways. First, and most obvious, the course was historically oriented. As a scholar cross-trained in history and anthropology, I have developed a quasi-allergic reaction to histories of particular phenomena isolated from discussions of broader social and cultural processes. This disposition revealed itself in the design of courses like this one. Operating on the assumption that most of the students had never studied Chinese history, I had them read Charles O. Hucker's *China's Imperial Past*. I could just as easily have used Patricia Ebrey's *Cambridge Illustrated History of China*, which has the advantage of wonderful illustrations. (Since I needed to rely on Ebrey at that point for some of my lecture material, I opted to have the students read Hucker.) I also assigned Daniel Overmyer's *Religions of China* to provide a more focused overview of Chinese religious history.

I cannot say that all my students appreciated these sections of their required reading. One person complained that he "hadn't realized that the course was going to have so much history," course title not withstanding. Still, these sources provided frames of reference and at least introduced students to the broad periods of Chinese history, to the roles of different religious traditions in historical context, and to the coexistence and interchange between traditions in particular periods. Had I been teaching the course in the Boston area, I would have taken students on local field trips, both to the China exhibits in the Museum of Fine Arts and to Chinatown. Providence, however, had neither, making such forays difficult.

Scholars in the history of Chinese medicine generally concur that although there are many outstanding works on specific periods and on particular issues, virtually no single source provides an overarching history. One of the few available is Paul Unschuld's *Medicine in China: A History of Ideas*. The book presents several difficulties as a source for an undergraduate course. It is, in some sections, fairly technical and difficult for students to understand. Although largely divided into dynastic periods, it is interrupted in the middle by two long chapters—one on Buddhist approaches to healing, the other on Daoist versions. Although roughly historical in their internal organization, neither one is integrated into the rest of the book's historical sequence. Finally, perhaps under the influence of Michel Foucault, Unschuld attempted to relate social structures and medical metaphors in ways that are sometimes, at best, heavy-handed. Still, the work provided something of an overview and had the virtue of containing translations of original texts.

Second, I used the underlying theme of change to illustrate how the different religious traditions in China have configured their understandings of change on the one hand, and of continuity and connection on the other. This approach took students beyond thinking just about acupuncture and herbs by relocating both within larger dynamic cosmic frameworks. Conceptually, the work of François Jullien proved useful in this connection. The Chinese word *shi*, Jullien writes, refers to a "configuration or disposition of things operating through opposition and correlation, and which constitutes a working system" (1995:17). It is central to many Chinese religious and medical systems, according to which reality is a dynamic process, articulated through terms like *yin* and *yang*. Though many American students have encountered these two words and their related images in popular culture, rarely do they really know what they mean. Students tend, rather vaguely, to talk about the unity of opposites, the light and dark of things, but with echoes of Manichean dualism. They do not know that, within all *yin*, *yang* is constantly emerging, and vice versa, or that both are expressions of a larger process known as the *Dao*.

Shi, Jullien adds, also refers to Chinese understandings of the *propensity* of things to change in patterned ways. "At the most embryonic stage," he notes, "the tendency toward the fullness of actualization is already latent. It is this tendency that one must examine attentively from the very beginning, from the first hint of its existence, for it gives us certain information regarding the evolution of things and provides us with a dependable basis for success" (223). He contrasts *shi* with Aristotelian concerns for primary causes and principles. The formula *rerum cognoscere causas* (to know the causes of things) has so guided pursuits of knowledge in the West as to seem self-evident.

Kant, Jullien reminds us, "tells us that causality is a general law of understanding that must be established a priori" (220). Chinese thought has instead often focused less on sequences of causes and effects and more on the configuration of forces at a given moment as typifying change of particular sorts. Divination diagrams, like those in the *Yijing* (the Classic of Change)—much like pulse readings—function as windows onto change in the midst of its making, and guide one in transforming one's fate. Such convergences illustrate the problems inherent in relying on taxonomies of "religion" and "medicine." The pursuit of change in response to affliction is sometimes a more complicated affair.

The course design was predicated on pluralism, not only within traditions, but also between them. It involved a geographic region in which a particular country—China—experienced centuries of reconfigured borders and related interactions with multiple cultural groups. This reality required inclusion of practices employed by different ethnic groups, at least as illustration of the cultural pluralism within China. In each unit, I selected additional readings to illustrate approaches to healing developed by different social constituencies not only within Confucian, Daoist, and Buddhist contexts, but also in more popular and minority forms. I attempted to show which groups, traditions, or practices were relatively more marginal at particular times (as in the more rampant homophobia of the Ming) and to point to some of the influences of Western forces, particularly in nineteenth and twentieth centuries. I also tried, in as many sections as I could locate materials, to address women's traditions.

As I now do with all my lecture courses, I illustrated each lecture liberally with slides and video clips. Some of the slides came from the Image Bank collection housed at Harvard University's Center for the Study of World Religions. Others I had made from books on China, Chinese medicine, Chinese art, and any other source that provided images useful to conveying what I was trying to communicate. I have, over time, built up a collection of videos as well, some of which contain only snippets that pertain to the specific content of a lecture, but that still help it come alive. To organize lectures this way requires additional advance planning and coordination with a school's media services. It also means being prepared to ad-lib when technology fails. Nevertheless, student feedback consistently pointed to the value of a multimedia approach. At the time, I had not developed a trove of Web-based resources. Were I to teach the course again, I would enhance its resources accordingly.

Conclusions

The course worked. I think that the students came to see the many ways that healing was barely below the surface of many religious phenomena in China, once one began to look for it. During the next to last session, on the persistence of older traditions, I used excerpts from popular movies from Hong Kong, showing the continuing appearance of longevity practices, herbal elixirs, karmic healing, gods, and street practitioners. In the final class, I showed segments of Bill Moyer's television special in which Harvard Medical School professor David Eisenberg showed examples of practices related to qi, or vital force, as used in the PRC (the documentary was made in the early 1990s). By that time, students were able to differentiate and discuss how the content of both sessions illustrated continuities and disjunctures with earlier periods. Yet for all of that, I would have to conclude that it was I who emerged the real learner.

The History of Chinese Healing Traditions

(Instructor's Version with Supplemental Readings can be found on the AAR Syllabus Project Web site at http://www.aarweb.org/syllabus/default.asp.)

Class Hours: Tuesdays, Thursdays 10:30–12

This course explores the history of intersections between the religious and the medical through the study of healing traditions in China. We will examine the role of shamans and the persistence of traditions involving gods, ghosts, and ancestors; the emergence of classical medicine and canonical texts, together with the role played by Scholar-Physicians; the influences of Daoist approaches to healing, longevity, and alchemy; the introduction of Buddhist and Indian healing practices; the effects of an emerging biomedical practice brought in from the West; and the meanings of the revival of traditional Chinese medicine in the People's Republic of China. We will also examine different understandings of the body, of diagnosis, of categories of disease and affliction, and of healing, with attention to related gender differences. Course readings include primary texts in translation as well as secondary materials. No prerequisites.

Required Readings

Books are indicated by *; all other materials are in the Course Reader.

* Charles O. Hucker, *China's Imperial Past*. Palo Alto, CA: Stanford University Press, 1975.
* Daniel L. Overmyer, *Religions of China*. New York: Harper and Row, 1986.
* Paul U. Unschuld, *Medicine in China: A History of Ideas*. Berkeley: University of California Press, 1985.
CR: RS88 Course Reader

Schedule and Reading Assignments

WEEK 1: INTRODUCTION TO THE COURSE: BASIC CONCEPTS AND PROBLEMS IN THE STUDY OF CHINESE HEALING TRADITIONS

WEEK 2: ILLNESS AND HEALING IN SHANG CULTURE (EIGHTEENTH–TWELFTH CENTURIES BCE)

Required Readings

* Hucker, pp. 21–30
* Overmyer, pp. 11–25
* Unschuld, pp. 17–28
Chang, K. C. 1983. Shamanism and Politics. In *Art, Myth, and Ritual: The Path to Political Authority in Ancient China*, pp. 44–55. Cambridge, MA: Harvard University Press.
Keightley, David N. 1984. Late Shang Divination: The Magico-Religious Legacy. *Journal of the American Academy of Religion Thematic Studies* 50(2):11–34.
Kuriyama, Shigehisa, 1994. The Imagination of Winds and the Develop-

ment of the Chinese Conception of the Body. In *Body, Subject & Power in China*, eds. Angela Zito and Tani E. Barlow, pp. 23–41. Chicago: University of Chicago Press

WEEK 3: THE ZHOU PERIOD AND DEMONIC MEDICINE (12TH CENTURY BCE–404 BCE)

Required Readings

* Hucker, pp. 30–38, 48–68, 96–117
* Overmyer, pp. 26–27
* Unschuld, pp. 29–50
Schwartz, Benjamin I. 1985. Early Chou Thought: Continuity and Breakthrough. In *The World of Thought in Ancient China*, pp. 40–55. Cambridge, MA: Harvard University Press.
Chan, Wing-Tsit 1963. The Growth of Humanism. In *A Source Book in Chinese Philosophy*, pp. 3–13. Princeton, NJ: Princeton University Press.
Watson, Burton. 1962. *Early Chinese Literature*, pp. 40–43, 64–65. New York: Columbia University Press.

WEEK 4: UNIFICATION OF THE EMPIRE AND THE INFLUENCE OF CONFUCIUS (WARRING STATES: 403–221 BCE/QIN: 221–207 BCE)

Required Readings

* Hucker, pp. 69–95
* Overmyer, pp. 27–33
* Unschuld, pp. 51–66
Mencius. 1970. *Mencius*, trans. D.C. Lau. Book II, Part A, nos. 2, 6, Book IV, Part A, nos. 9–12, 15, Book VI, Part A, nos. 6, 8, Book VII, Part A, nos. 1–4, pp. 76–80, 82–83, 121–124, 162–165, 182. New York: Penguin Books.
Tu Wei-ming. 1984. Pain and Suffering in Confucian Self-Cultivation. In *Philosophy East and West* 34(4):379–387.
Raphals, Lisa Ann. 1998. The Textual Matrix of the *Lienü Zhuan*. In *Sharing the Light: Representations of Women and Virtue in Early China*, pp. 87–105. Albany: SUNY Press.
Harper, Donald. 1996. Spellbinding. In *Religions of China in Practice*, ed. Donald S. Lopez, pp. 241–250. Princeton, NJ: Princeton University Press.

WEEK 5: FUNDAMENTAL PRINCIPLES OF THE MEDICINE OF SYSTEMATIC CORRESPONDENCES

Required Readings

* Hucker, pp. 121–128, 149–159, 170–172, 176–177, 180–183, 187–189, 193–198, 221–227

* Unschuld, pp. 67–100, and Appendix, sections 1.1, 1.3, 1.4, 1.6, 1.9, 2.2, 2.4, 2.5, 2.7, 2.8

Sivin, Nathan. 1995. Text and Experience in Classical Chinese Medicine. In *Knowledge and the Scholarly Medical Traditions,* ed. Don Bates, pp. 177–204. Cambridge: Cambridge University Press.

Raphals, Lisa. 1998. The Treatment of Women in a Second-Century Medical Casebook. *Chinese Science* 15:7–28.

Cohen, Alvin P. 1979. Avenging Ghosts and Moral Judgement in Ancient Chinese Historiography: Three Examples from *Shih-chi.* In *Legend, Lore, and Religion in China,* pp. 97–108. San Francisco: Chinese Materials Center.

WEEK 6: RELIGIOUS HEALING: THE FOUNDATION OF THEOCRATIC RULE

Required Readings

* Hucker, pp. 128–133, 159, 161–167, 183, 190, 199–200.
* Overmyer, pp. 33–9.
* Unschuld, pp. 117–131.

Epler, D. C. 1988. The Concept of Disease in an Ancient Chinese Medical Text: The Discourse on Cold-Damage Disorders (Shang-han Lun). *Journal of the History of Medicine and Allied Sciences* 43(2):8–35.

DeWoskin, Kenneth J., trans. 1983. *Doctors, Diviners, and Magicians of Ancient China: Biographies of Fang-shih.* Fan Yeh's Introduction, pp. 43–49; #5, pp. 52–53; #10, pp. 60–61; Postscript to Part 1, pp. 66–67; #21–#26, pp. 74–81. New York: Columbia University.

WEEK 7: TAOISM AND PRAGMATIC DRUG THERAPY (PART 1) (LATTER HAN, THREE KINGDOMS, JIN, SIX DYNASTIES, SUI, TANG, FIVE DYNASTIES)

Required Readings

* Hucker, pp. 201–206.
* Unschuld, pp. 101–116, Appendix, Section 2.1, pp 277–280.

Bauer, Wolfgang. 1976. Freedom and Anarchy. In *China and the Search for Happiness: Recurring Themes in Four Thousand Years of Chinese Cultural History,* trans. Michael Shaw, pp. 131–152. New York: Seabury.

Stein, Rudolph. 1979. Religious Taoism and Popular Religion from the Second to the Seventh Centuries. In *Facets of Taoism,* ed. Holmes Welch and Anna Seidel, pp. 53–81. New Haven, CT: Yale University Press.

Roth, Harold D. 1996. The Inner Cultivation Tradition of Early Daoism. In *Religions of China in Practice,* ed. Donald S. Lopez, pp. 123–148. Princeton, NJ: Princeton University Press.

WEEK 8: TAOISM AND PRAGMATIC DRUG THERAPY (PART II)

Required Readings

Nickerson, Peter. 1994. Shamans, Demons, Diviners and Taoists: Conflict and Assimilation in Medieval Chinese Ritual Practice (c AD 100–1000). *Taoist Resources* 5(1):41–66.

Cahill, Suzanne. 1986. Performers and Female Taoist Adepts: Hsi Wang Mu as the Patron Deity of Women in Medieval China. *Journal of the American Oriental Society* 106(1):155–167.

Akahori, Akira. 1989. Drug Taking and Immortality. In *Taoist Meditation and Longevity Techniques*, ed. Livia Kohn, pp. 73–98. Ann Arbor: Center for Chinese Studies, University of Michigan.

Engelhardt, Ute. 1989. *Qi* for Life: Longevity in the Tang. In *Taoist Meditation and Longevity Techniques*, ed. Livia Kohn, pp. 263–296. Ann Arbor: Center for Chinese Studies, University of Michigan.

Ho Peng-Yoke. 1985. Chinese Alchemy. In *Li, Qi and Shu: An Introduction to Science and Civilization in China*, pp. 180–194. Hong Kong: Hong Kong University Press.

WEEK 9: BUDDHISM AND INDIAN MEDICINE (LATER HAN, THREE KINGDOMS, JIN, SIX DYNASTIES, SUI, TANG, FIVE DYNASTIES)

Required Readings

* Hucker, pp. 139–148, 153–155, 160–163, 167–169, 173–176, 178–180, 184–186, 191–192, 207–220

* Overmyer, pp. 39–48

* Unschuld, pp. 132–153

Lee, Lily Xiao Hong. 1994. The Emergence of Buddhist Nuns in China and Its Social Ramifications. In *The Virtue of Yin: Studies on Chinese Women*, pp. 47–64. Broadway, New South Wales, Australia: Wild Peony.

Birnbaum, Raoul. 1989. Chinese Buddhist traditions of Healing and the Life Cycle. In *Healing and Restoring*, ed. Lawrence Sullivan, pp. 33–57. New York: Macmillan.

Yü, Chün-fang. 1996. A Sutra Promoting the White-Robed Guanyin as Giver of Sons. In *Religions of China in Practice*, ed. Donald S. Lopez, pp. 97–105. Princeton, NJ: Princeton University Press.

Cohen, Alvin P. 1982. *Tales of Vengeful Souls: A Sixth Century Collection of Chinese Avenging Ghost Stories*, pp. v–xix, 33, 35–36, 45–47, 50. Paris: Ricci Institute.

SPRING RECESS (NO CLASS)

WEEK 10: SUNG NEO-CONFUCIANISM AND MEDICAL THOUGHT (960–1279 CE)

Required Readings (Plan carefully, and use the spring break)

* Hucker, pp. 267–287, 303–307, 315–316, 323–326, 329–334, 336–337, 342–346, 348–356, 358–373
* Overmyer, pp. 48–54
* Unschuld, pp. 154–188 and 321–324

Hymes, Robert. 1987. Not Quite Gentlemen: Doctors in Sung and Yuan *Chinese Science* 8:9–76.

WEEK 11: MEDICAL THOUGHT DURING THE MING DYNASTY (1368–1644 CE)

Required Readings

* Hucker, pp. 287–294, 317–323, 326–327, 334–335, 337–338, 346–347, 351–352, 373–376
* Unschuld, pp. 189–228

Leung, Angela Ki Che. 1987. Organized Medicine in Ming-Qing China: State and Private Medical Institutions in the Lower Yangzi Region. *Late Imperial China* 8(1):134–167.

Cass, Victoria B. 1986. Female Healers in the Ming and the Lodge of Ritual and Ceremony. *Journal of the American Oriental Society* 106(1): 233–240.

WEEK 12: MEDICAL THOUGHT DURING THE QING DYNASTY (1644–1911 CE)

Required Readings

* Hucker, pp, 294–302, 318, 327–328, 338–342, 376–384
* Overmyer, pp. 55–56
* Unschuld, pp. 324–340

Benedict, Carol. 1996. Nineteenth-Century Chinese Medical, Religious, and Administrative Responses to Plague. In *Bubonic Plague in Nineteenth-Century China*, pp. 100–130. Palo Alto, CA: Stanford University Press.

Bray, Francesca. 1995. A Deathly Disorder: Understanding Women's Health in Late Imperial China. In *Knowledge and the Scholarly Medical Traditions*, ed. Don Bates, pp. 235–250. Cambridge: Cambridge University Press.

Ng, Vivien. 1990. Madness in Chinese Culture. In *Madness in Late Imperial China: From Illness to Deviance*, pp. 25–62. Norman: University of Oklahoma Press.

WEEK 13: THE "MODERNIZING" OF HEALING IN CHINA

Required Readings

* Hucker, pp. 427–431
* Unschuld, pp. 229–251

Croizier, Ralph. 1968. Introduction and Growth of Modern Medicine in China, 1800–1949. In *Traditional Medicine in Modern China: Science, Nationalism, and the Tensions of Cultural Change*, pp. 36–56. Cambridge, MA: Harvard University Press.

Buck, Peter. 1980. Social Diseases and Contagious Disorders: Missionary Science and Medical Missionaries. In *American Science and Modern China, 1876–1936*, pp. 8–45. Cambridge: Cambridge University Press.

Andrews, Bridie J. 1997. Tuberculosis and the Assimilation of Germ Theory in China, 1895–1937. *Journal of the History of Medicine* 52(January):114–157.

WEEK 14: THE PERSISTENCE OF POPULAR TRADITIONS

Required Readings

Ahern, Emily. 1975a. The Power and Pollution of Chinese Women. In *Women in Chinese Society*, ed. Marjory Wolf and Roxane Witke, pp. 269–290. Palo Alto, CA: Stanford University Press.

————. 1975b. Sacred and Secular Medicine in a Taiwan Village: A Study in Cosmological Disorders. In *Medicine in Chinese Cultures*, ed. Arthur Kleinman et al, pp. 91–113. Washington, DC: U.S. Government Printing Office.

Anderson, E.N., and Marja L. Anderson. 1978. Folk Dietetics in Two Chinese Communities, and Implications for the Study of Chinese Medicine. In *Culture and Healing in Asian Societies: Anthropological, Psychiatric and Public Health Studies*, ed. Arthur Kleinman et. al., pp. 69–100. Cambridge: Schenkman.

Frick, Johann. 1951. How Blood Is Used in Magic and Medicine in Ch'inghai Province. *Anthropos* 46:964–979.

Gould-Martin, Katherine. 1978. Ong-ia-kong: The Plague God as Modern Physician. In *Culture and Healing in Asian Societies*, ed. Arthur Kleinman et al, pp. 41–67. Cambridge: Schenkman.

Harrell, C. Stevan. 1974. When a Ghost Becomes a God. In *Religion and Ritual in Chinese Society*, ed. Arthur P. Wolf, pp. 193–206. Palo Alto, CA: Stanford University Press.

Lu Xun. 1981. Medicine. In *The Complete Stories of Lu Xun*, trans. Yang Xianyi and Gladys Yang, pp. 19–29. Bloomington: Indiana University Press.

Wolf, Margery. 1990. The Woman Who Didn't Become a Shaman [Taiwanese village evaluates a resident's erratic behavior]. *American Ethnologist* 17:419–430.

TRADITIONAL MEDICINE (TAIWAN/HONG KONG)

Readings

Gale, James L. 1978. Patient and Practitioner Attitudes toward Traditional and Western Medicine in a Contemporary Chinese Setting. In
*Culture and Healing in Asian Societies: Anthropological, Psychiatric, and
Public Health Studies*, ed. Arthur Kleinman et. al., pp. 275–288. Cambridge: Schenkman.

Harrell, C. Stevan. 1991. Pluralism, Performance and Meaning in Taiwa-
nese Healing: A Case Study. *Culture, Medicine, and Psychiatry* 15(1):45–
68.

Kleinman, Arthur, and James L. Gale. 1982. Patients Treated by Physicians and Folk Healers: A Comparative Outcome Study in Taiwan.
Culture, Medicine, and Psychiatry 6(4):405–423.

Kleinman Arthur, and Lillian Sung. 1979. Why Do Indigenous Practitioners Successfully Heal? *Social Science & Medicine* 13B (1):7–26.

Lee, Rance P. L. 1980. Perceptions and Uses of Chinese Medicine
among the Chinese in Hong Kong. *Culture, Medicine, and Psychiatry* 4:
345–375.

Topley, Marjorie. 1970. Chinese Traditional Ideas and the Treatment of
Disease: Two Examples from Hong Kong. *Man* n.s. 5(3):421–437.

———. 1976. Chinese Traditional Etiology and Methods of Cure in
Hong Kong. In *Asian Medical Systems: A Comparative Study*, ed.
Charles Leslie, pp. 241–265. Berkeley: University of California Press.

Unschuld, Paul U. 1976. The Social Organization and Ecology of Medical Practice in Taiwan. In *Asian Medical Systems: A Comparative Study*,
ed. Charles Leslie, pp. 300–316. Berkeley: University of California
Press.

WEEK 15: MEDICINE IN THE PEOPLE'S REPUBLIC: THE EMERGENCE OF TCM

Required Readings

* Overmyer, pp. 103–117

* Unschuld, pp. 252–262 and 340–366

Xu Liangying and Fan Dainian. 1982. *Science and Socialist Construction
in China*, ed. Pierre M. Perrolle. pp. 55–71, 131–139. New York: M. E.
Sharpe.

Feuchtwang, Stephan. 1989. The Problem of "Superstition" in the People's Republic of China. In *Religion and Political Power*, pp. 43–68. Albany: SUNY Press.

Wu Naitao. 1994. China Offers Health Care Itinerary. *Beijing Review*
(Sept. 19–25):31–32.

Farquhar, Judith. 1995. Re-writing Traditional Medicine in Post-Mao
China. In *Knowledge and the Scholarly Medical Traditions*, ed. Don
Bates, pp. 251–276. Cambridge: Cambridge University Press.

Farquhar, Judith. 1996. Market Magic: Getting Rich and Getting Personal in Medicine after Mao. *American Ethnologist* 23(2):239–257.

Course Requirements

1. Attendance—25 grade points
2. Participation—35 grade points—The class will be conducted in a lecture and discussion format. Your engagement in both the lectures and discussions is extremely important to your own learning and to that of the group as a whole. Therefore, you will be expected to turn in a question or comment at the end of each class session, reflecting your thoughts on the material for that day. You are responsible for securing from your classmates any information missed in the form of in-class announcements, handouts, notes, and so on.
3. Take-Home Final Exam—40 grade points—The essay questions for the final exam, which will be open-book, will be handed out in class with instructions. There will be three sets of essays; you will answer one question from each set, and each essay will be worth up to 10 points. All sources used are to be documented (with related endnotes at the end of the exam). Each answer is to be *no longer* than three pages, not including endnotes. (Note: the endnotes are not intended to represent additional discussion of the question, but are merely to cite your sources.)

   Exams are to be typed, double-spaced, with 1-inch margins, and font size set at New York 10, Palatino 12, or roughly the equivalent. Completed exams will be due *no later than 5:00 on Friday, May 21*, and must be turned in at the Department of Religious Studies office.

A Professor's Goals

A profound person teaches in five ways. The first is by a transforming influence like that of timely rain. The second is by helping students to realize their virtue to the full. The third is by helping them to develop their talent. The fourth is by answering their questions. And the fifth is by setting an example others not in contact with one can emulate. These are the ways in which a profound person teaches.

—Mencius, Book VII, Part A, no. 40
(trans. D. C. Lau, modified by L. Barnes)

Acknowledgments

This syllabus presented in this chapter owes much to the good counsel of TJ Hinrichs and Bridie Andrews, and to examples provided by Paul Howard, Michel Strickman, and Nathan Sivin. All of them have taught their own versions of courses on Chinese healing traditions, and I have benefited greatly from their resources, insights, and experience.

REFERENCES

Barnes, Linda L. 2005. *Needles, Herbs, Gods, and Ghosts: China, Healing, and the West to 1848*. Cambridge, MA: Harvard University Press.

Jullien, François. 1995. *The Propensity of Things: Toward a History of Efficacy in China*. New York: Zone.

Scheid, Volker. 2002. *Chinese Medicine in Contemporary China: Plurality and Synthesis*. Durham, NC: Duke University Press.

Unschuld, Paul. 1987. Traditional Chinese Medicine: Some Historical and Epistemological Reflections. *Social Science and Medicine* 24:1023–1029.

———. 1992. Epistemological Issues and Changing Legitimation: Traditional Chinese Medicine in the Twentieth Century. In *Paths to Asian Medical Knowledge*, ed. Charles Leslie and Allan Young, pp. 44–61. Berkeley: University of California Press.

PART III

Native and Chicano/a American Traditions

6

Teaching Native American Religious Traditions and Healing

Inés M. Talamantez

Living in balance and harmony within one's Native culture is said to be at the heart of indigenous peoples' concerns for healing the community, the land, and the natural world. This chapter will discuss an interdisciplinary and comparative course about representative Native cultures of the American Southwest, and their different religiomedical systems. The course introduces students to these cultures' different understandings of experimentation, the long-term observation of nature, the historical evaluation of changes over time and place, and the sacralization of the biosphere in order to meet human physical and spiritual needs. Through this course, I attempt to guide students toward an understanding of diverse perspectives on the relationship between humans, the numinous, the biosphere and the multiple layers of meaning and experience in which healing is practiced and understood. We also examine the significant role of language in wellbeing, particularly through reestablishing the interconnectedness between oral traditions and the importance of taking responsibility for our actions. One of my larger objectives is to provide paradigms for decolonizing the minds of native and non-Native students, by deconstructing colonization, missionization and assimilation. In the process, I hope to offer contemporary possibilities for theories of resistance, wellbeing and survival in a multi-ethnic society.

The history of the American Southwest Indian cultures and peoples can be found throughout the states of New Mexico, Arizona, parts of Nevada, Utah, and Southern California. Native people there have survived by living close to the land and the natural world. They learned, through long-term observation, to consider, honor, and cultivate all of the living entities in their ecosystems—rocks, minerals, bodies of water, people, insects, animals and the plant world, as well as the unseen realms, including the air. Yet the peoples of these cultures also experienced recurring terror in their own lands, beginning with their first encounters with European groups. Since then, Indians have been intimidated by the American government, as well as by proselytizing missionaries attempting to force conversion to Christianity. Inconsistent policies on the part of the government have converged with missionizing over time to exercise unjustly severe and oppressive power, and these have regularly functioned to usurp Native sovereignty.

In spite of problems facing indigenous peoples, and the many arguments that such problems do not represent significant issues for the larger American society, this course affirms the continuing important role of healing in Native contexts for the present and future, as a social concern for all Americans and their families. To address these complex social and religious issues requires pulling together various aspects of American majority culture, Native American cultures, civil society, government agencies, education, and community life. The course posits that in our highly technological society, the well being of our families is crucial for the development of children and adults, as well as for the quality of life for America's diverse communities—many of which have survived for more than five hundred years—and for the preservation of the common good of the nation and democracy.

This orientation evokes important cultural questions that are especially relevant to traditional approaches to healing, within religious contexts that have been forced to respond to many historical changes, including displacement and relocation to new land bases. Despite the pervasive power of these forces of change, Native people have continued to cherish what has often been ignored by the surrounding culture—what can be called indigenous spirituality, and the rich complex of customs, ideas, and commitments that have kept this spirituality alive in urban areas as well as on reservations. In this connection, the course draws on two pedagogical models. The first involves an integrated approach to learning; the second, team teaching in small groups. In these groups, students critique each other's work and consult with members of the local Indian community.

Looking for Common Ground

At the heart of the courses I have taught on Native American traditions of religion and healing is my own commitment to correcting misinformation about indigenous peoples. As one way of doing this, I have focused on the nature of these religions' functions in Native American cultures of the Southwest, and on their healing systems regarding disease, change, and issues of decolonization. Bringing new light to old and deeply divisive debates about indigenous healing has been a challenge. There have been, and still are, many strong ideologies and cultural differences that have kept us from finding common ground regarding health issues. I continue to hold that what is needed is more dialogue, the kind that leads to compassion followed by action.

The course proposes that if we are all to be healthy we need a new sche-mata, one that frees us from the constraints of a Western patriarchal paradigm of control on the one hand, and that takes us beyond victim status and para-digms of blame on the other. We need a framework that enables us to under-stand our own cultures while allowing us to teach others about them without supporting or condoning appropriation. Through shared reflection on, and scrutiny of, the power of church and state, Native and non-Native men and women can share knowledge in a meaningful way. Nor can we forget that the dissemination of knowledge about Native cultures faces institutional barriers. The world of academia continues to exert control over the very substance of Native American research and the publication of our work, given its power to determine what counts as scholarship. Indeed, the deeper issue involves the control over what counts as knowledge—a critical question when exploring Native American epistemologies.

In the Light of Gender

Women are at a historical juncture where, as workers, mothers, scholars, heal-ers, and poets, we have the necessary tools to move forward. Our fight for religious freedom is a fight for life and for land. To fight for social justice is to fight for freedom. To raise children is to fight for freedom. To write as a woman is to fight for freedom. As a Native American woman, I choose to make gender one of the course's analytical frameworks. I speak to students about, and from, my own formation in Native American traditions. My female kin guided me along a path of even deeper reflection on the issues we discuss conceptually in class, teaching me about the diverse roles of women healers. By drawing on the tradition of the Sun Clan at the Mescalero Apache Reservation in New Mexico, I bring to my classes linkages between myself, my research, and my political activism as a woman.

In practice today, the lives of Native American women are shaped by the complex intertwining of several controlling regimes that discriminate against them in a variety of ways. Native women living on reservations are subject to the will of tribal governments, which are often under the control of the Bureau of Indian Affairs, an arm of the Department of the Interior. The concerns of women are often not a priority for the bureaucrats or elected officials, any more than they are in the dominant society. Urban Indian women who are not reg-istered in federal government records—that is, who have no number indicating that they are enrolled in a tribe, making them "legitimate Indians" according to the government—find social services and benefits difficult if not impossible to obtain. Those who make it through the school system and who plan to attend a junior college or university are denied access to scholarships unless they can prove that they are Indian. No one else in this country has to prove her eth-nicity. Why, then, do Native Americans?

Health care issues are also affected by such factors. Indeed, the discussion of religion and healing in Native American contexts is not complete without addressing them. For example, if a woman is enrolled in the federal records, she qualifies for federal Indian Health programs; if she is not enrolled, she is just another minority woman seeking health care. In reforming the health care system, the particular needs of those who are women and Native need to be addressed. We are, after all, not only American women; we are also indigenous women. We share many of the health concerns of other American women, but we have also been disproportionately exposed to additional health risks.

Many Christian churches, especially in areas largely populated by Indians, still require their parishioners to give up participating in their own religious traditions if they wish to be Christians. This discrimination has been met in a variety of ways. Some Native women continue to resist all forms of Christianity, practicing their own Native ways instead, beautifully blending culture, health, and spirituality in one complete worldview. Other women continue to follow their cultural ways but have worked out their own ways to be both Indians from a specific culture, as well as persons who also accept and embrace Christian dogma. And, of course, some Indian women have accepted Christianity completely and have opted for assimilation into the dominant American culture.

Church and state have combined in powerful ways to divide and conquer the Native women of the American Southwest. Yet the religious and medical practices of these women today demonstrate a rich, complex blend of ideas, commitments, and identities. Coatlicue (an Aztec female deity), Guadalupe (a melding of an Aztec deity and sixteenth-century Spanish Catholicism), *curanderas* (Mexican folk healers), *parteras* (midwives), and, more recently, Mexican and Chicana *espiritualistas* stand as a testament to the strength and creativeness of women of the borderlands who are in contact with the Native women of this area. Today, Chicana and indigenous women, in dialogue with women elders, are finding a place for themselves as they redefine the history of our religious and healing experience. Rigoberta Menchú, a Quiche woman of Guatemala, has brilliantly named our struggle the spirituality of the Western hemisphere.

It is important to acknowledge that Native women have had many roles as ceremonialists and healers and that they have played political and social roles in different times and in different indigenous cultures. Yet when we research American historical and ethnographic accounts, women are often invisible. Still, their influence pervades Native religious life. For example, speaking from my own background, ceremonies in which women are involved have evolved for every phase of Apache life from birth through adolescence, adulthood, old age, and death. These traditions are expressed in chants, sayings, songs—both social and sacred—and in ceremonial dances and other styles of performance. The ceremonies are the artistic expression of social interaction and explain Apache religious belief and culture. Through ceremony, the Apache keep in touch with the world of their ancestors. The resulting sense of communication with events of the past assures them that they have a path to follow throughout life.

Many Diné (Navajo) women today deal with these issues as part of an ongoing struggle for religious freedoms and social justice. To be a Diné woman requires living in, and practicing, the Diné way of life. The power manifested by Changing Woman—a female deity in the myth of the Blessingway ceremonial complex—is a power that Diné women call upon in their struggles today. This is especially so in their struggle for a land base, as they continue to be forced to relocate from what they consider to be their spiritual homeland. The ideas set forth in the concepts of Blessingway provide the sanctions for Diné peoples' roles in human life. Participation in ceremonial life in a specific land base is required in order to be healthy in body, mind, and spirit. According to a Diné woman traditionalist and friend involved in this political and religious struggle, to be moved away from her place means to be living an unhealthy life, out of balance and harmony.

The indigenous framework within which many of us work is grounded in the systems of relatedness, obligation, and respect that govern the lives of many Native women. There is a driving purpose behind our work; we know what we are expected to do. There are political commitments to social justice, concerns for what constitutes activism in our present day, and complex issues of health identity and naming ourselves. The political survival issues of the day—land claims, freedom of religion, environmental racism, and the lack of appropriate health care, education, and employment, for example—engage us as persons who labor under the twin oppressions of being women and Native. A narrative of inquiry into the meanings of these things in our own lives requires deep reflection. It is an exploration in both humility and authority. Insight is gained through analysis, interpretation, and a critique of colonialism.

To create a healthy environment, these women have resisted relocation by the federal government. In the face of danger, they have continued to care for essential plant medicines needed for healing ceremonies and to collect them from the land. These women often lead the fight against fast food, disposable diapers, the commodified and violent culture presented on television, and the use of excessive Western medicine. Even so, it will be a long time before Native American women can be equal partners in dialogue. The course makes a place for some of their voices not as a separate topic, but as threads woven throughout the whole—just as women's voices and lives occur within the traditions themselves.

Transforming Conceptions about Power and Authority

The tensions between the spiritual forces at work in Native America, the pressures of forced religious conversion, and the influence of newly introduced technologies have had a tremendous impact on the lives of the peoples of these cultures. One of the greatest tensions has involved the imposition of different constructs of authentic knowledge through alien forms and understandings of power. In many Native American traditions, power cannot be understood apart from sacred realities, or from specific notions of balance.

In the Apache context, for example, proper behavior within a religious and cultural context is expected of a person, in order to live a life in balance with one's environment as well as with the spirit world, and to assure the possibility of acquiring sacred powers—what Apache call *diyii*—and strength, *nhldzil*. These belief systems continue to reflect the spiritual and aesthetic dimensions predicated on the interconnectedness of the religious, social, cultural, healing and mythological categories of these societies. The biggest obstacles to the survival of these healing traditions continue to be Christian missionary efforts at religious conversion, and government policies that deny religious freedom and social justice for Native Americans.

In Mescalero life, the healer exerts a powerful presence. Her primary characteristic is her concept of herself as having power deriving from natural sources in the environment. She is continually searching for clues emanating from these and other sources—the stars, clouds, lighting, bears, snakes, coyotes, and owls. Once she has acquired one or more of these powers personally, she is always aware of her relationship to it. She learns to understand the symbolic value of her power, developing a ritual symbolism by which she becomes the intermediary between that supernatural power source and society. She sees things and interprets them to the people. Her knowledge allows her to interpret the signs through which the powers speak and to take the necessary steps demanded by the spirit message. This alternative understanding of experience and authority is an important alternative for students to learn, as is its relationship with a larger vision of the social and sacred world.

Landscape, Language, and Healing

Settlers who came later to this land felt the need to exploit it even further for natural resources, such as gold, in the name of what they believed to be civilization. Their attitudes differed from those of the diverse tribal societies they encountered. Sharp contrasts in ideals and values affected how the newcomers viewed the religious practices of these societies, in ways that are still felt today. The settlers often feared nature and wilderness, for example. They were, after all, from another land and ecosystem. Perhaps they were haunted by memories of former times and by fears that—if they were not successful in mastering this new, strange land and its peoples—they themselves might revert to earlier "uncivilized" states that had existed in Europe.

The colonists' actions toward the land had less to do with the natural world than with their own ideals of individualism and manifest destiny and their desperate need for a new beginning in a new world. In shaping their adjustment to this new environment, they inherited much from the Native American societies they encountered. They were, however, frequently more concerned with conquering than with understanding, and they used Native knowledge to that end—thereby distorting it, by dislocating it from the sacred contexts in which it had emerged. The settlers' belief that God had given them this natural world to exploit allowed them to rationalize their behaviors in the name of civilization and Christianity. Everywhere, in every direction, the consequence was the laying waste of souls and natural resources.

In contrast, knowledge of a sustainable environment is revealed in the language in which many of the Native American myths are told. Acknowledging the interconnectedness of all living entities is central to what it means to be indigenous to a place and to be of good health. The Sun Clan creation myth, when told in Apache, for example, relates in elaborate detail that, from the very beginning of time, the earth existed and was in a process of continuous change, which was seen and is seen as the manifestation of the cyclical powers of nature. An Apache knows, when she is ill, that it is because she is out of harmony with the universe. She knows that if a ceremony has effected a cure for someone else, it can also cure her. The performance reassures her that something can be done to reestablish a proper balance between her and the spiritual and physical environment. She is instructed, as well as informed, by the medicine man or medicine woman, that the cure will be achieved if the "patient" will behave in the prescribed way—the way the supernaturals behaved in the beginning of time.

In Apache culture, when young girls are initiated into the role of woman, they are taught about the sense of smell, taste, touch, sight, *and* about their responsibility for being healthy. They are taught the importance of studying the natural features of the earth's surface, land forms, and substrate, as well as the earth's responses to climate change and the biologically relevant characteristics of the soil. Such knowledge prepares them to understand how to live on the land in a good way. The ceremony itself is a portrayal of Apache reality, as it is still celebrated today.

This orientation to the land grounds the conceptual material I try to convey through the course. A land-based pedagogy involves helping students to understand the connections between Native American epistemologies and the different ways in which the traditions grow out of relationships with the land. This pedagogy helps them to situate the struggle for religious freedom and to reconfigure the roles of Native women and their distinctive contributions. We are looking at tangled historical processes and systems that continue to integrate cultural, political, and ecological dimensions.

Indians Schools and Native American Ways of Learning

Among the components of colonization that the course deconstructs are the Indian schools, as vehicles through which outside constructs of knowledge and authority have been imposed on Native American children. The history of these schools—their removal of children from the reservations, their suppression of Native languages, their efforts to disconnect children from their peoples and their heritage—represents one of the more pernicious dimensions of dispossession. The schools serve as a counterpoint to the ways in which learning is defined and communicated in Native contexts.

In class, we focus on Apache mythology and its corresponding code of ethics and ideology, both of which are used over and over again to reinforce who Apaches are as a people. The myths reaffirm that visions are worth pursuing and that this elaborate cultural history teaches morals, health, and appropriate behavior. The telling of myths, or sacred narratives, to children at a young age, and then repeating them again and again throughout the life cycle, maintains the teachings of these stories in people's minds and spirits until they reach a wise old age. Observing the corresponding ceremonies that mark different points along the life cycle makes it possible to live a good, healthy life. The ceremonies consist of useful teachings for the present and the future, especially for how to deal with disease, uncertainty, and unforeseen events.

To illustrate: in the *Kináálda*, or girls' initiation ceremony, Diné girls are instructed to live their lives modeled after Changing Woman. Women's beliefs about Changing Woman's attributes, and about the nature of her interconnectedness with all living entities, are profoundly significant. The ceremony clarifies for the initiates what their roles and responsibilities will be as Diné women. Female sponsors for the initiates derive their power from a codified body of ceremonial knowledge and personal experience. The ceremony itself requires the sponsors to be responsible for ritually guiding the initiates from childhood, through the doors of adolescence, into womanhood. This is a tremendous task that requires rigorous, dedicated religious commitment if the ceremony is to be effective. Initiated women will sometimes gain prestige in the community by learning from their own sponsors how to carry on the *Kináálda* ceremony. This, of course, takes years of apprenticeship, if it is to be done correctly. The important point is that initiated women often become the carriers of the Diné female tradition. Diné women are also known to perform the ceremonial roles of Hand Tremblers—diagnosticians who pray over a patient's body with trembling hands, as they discern answers, locate the source of an illness, and then refer the patient to the appropriate ceremonies. Women are usually not free to pursue these demanding roles until after menopause. In such ways, Native American traditions—with their foundation in the oral traditions of the past—serve to carry the people into the future.

Native American Healing Arts

The Southern Athapaskans arrived in the area from the north, probably in the 1400s. These Apache and Diné people gathered foods, hunted, and later participated in agriculture and trading for survival, exchanging whatever they could with other peoples. The religious beliefs of these groups were rooted in knowledge acquired from the land and the environment, with a belief that health and healing required knowing how to live in balance and harmony with all living entities. Today these religious and cultural customs are still passed from generation to generation by way of oral traditions. Chants, songs, and sacred narratives remain the most significant ways of accessing the divine powers for healing, harmony, and spiritual teachings. Elaborate ceremonies are still held, led by religious specialists with access to spiritual knowledge. Such knowledge is used for healing, based primarily on the use of power as an ethical precept that functions within a spiritual visionary domain, beyond the limits of ordinary experience. These specialists, who have access to super-natural power, function to maintain and promote health understood in com-prehensive ways that include long life, crops, rain, cultural unity, and survival.

In Mescalero culture, song is the verbal expression of successful formulas for maintaining a healthy, balanced world. The singers sing the song-prayers that were sung to them, as they know and remember them. Each singer has their own song(s) and will sing no others. Some variation and creativity is permitted, such that every performance also bears the singer's individual style and expression. Sometimes there are slight variations in their voices and in the texts themselves, yet they are all somehow singing together. Singers differ in their ability to evoke within their listeners an experience of the supernatural influences.

One of the important things that students learn is that although ceremo-nial structures do not change from generation to generation, the traditions themselves are dynamic. A corresponding fluidity within the context of cere-monies also exists, allowing for differences in healing techniques to emerge as required, for dealing with old and new ailments, cultural change and the ongoing struggle for sovereignty. Understanding this interplay of ongoing structures and fluid implementation helps overcome popular tendencies to reify and exoticize Native American religious traditions and, indeed, helps stu-dents to see how these arts embody the nature of traditions *as* living forms of continuity and change.

The Politics of Disease and Native American Responses

Widespread poverty resulting from colonization, dispossession, disenfran-chisement, and the usurping of Native authority has left a powerful impression on both the individual and on the collective body, particularly insofar as indi-vidual bodies embody the impact of poverty, and the collective reflects the resulting health disparities. In Native contexts, there is a corresponding des-perate need for health care improvement, especially in relation to diabetes. If suicide is the third leading cause of death for all people ten- to twenty-four years old in the United States, what does this mean for young Native Ameri-cans? Suicide for Native American youth is the second leading cause of death for those who are fifteen- to twenty-four years old.

In the course, we discuss not only such statistics, but also the impact of media in promoting unhealthy approaches to food and diet. Students reflect on ways in which media and community leaders should exercise their authority to challenge the kinds of food products fostered by television advertising, which contribute to the "sugar craze." This harmful influence is economically driven and devastating to American health as a whole and to Native health in particular because poor people tend to eat inexpensive starchy and sugary foods, contributing to obesity and its correlate, diabetes. Students also recognize that parents need to become more effective in monitoring their children's health and controlling the kinds of TV programs they are allowed to watch, especially young children who are vulnerable to violence and nutritional misinformation. We tie the discussion back into such media's effects on the health of young people in urban communities and on the reservation, and to the need for effective media to focus on healthy foods and healthy families.

Some students have felt that federal, state, and local governments should be required to do more to support initiatives to preserve and rehabilitate communities, especially with regard to poverty, drug policies, juvenile crime, foster care, teenage pregnancy, suicide, health problems such as diabetes and high blood pressure, and child mortality, all of which affect most segments of the American population directly or indirectly. In their research projects, some students opt to research comparisons between biomedicine and Native healing practices. A review of their research, carried out over the past two decades on many aspects of the cultures of the Southwest, shows that much of this research has addressed different aspects of healing. These students' findings demonstrate that a host of issues are interrelated, and have been extremely relevant for teaching these classes.

Conclusion

What have I learned from the way students have impacted my research and teaching? What do we gain by exploring this material together? Is it possible for us to step out of the worldview we have inherited, both to see our own strengths and weaknesses and to understand the beliefs of others? The course reaffirms my own conviction that, in seeking to heal our bodies, we look to religion, land, and medicine in ways that present-day health care systems often find difficult to accommodate. Yet, as Apache Medicine Woman Meredith Begay has taught me, medicine, health, and ceremony are all intertwined. Her work as a cross-cultural communicator and healer shows one path forward. The course is one of my own ways of communicating that these issues must be brought to the attention of the American public. It challenges romanticized notions of Native American religion and healing by positing, instead, that the fight for American Indian religious freedom is a human rights issue, as is the right to health care. The two are intimately related to the issue of survival, and to healing self, people, world, and biosphere.

Syllabus: Native American Religious Traditions and Healing

Course Readings

Basso, Keith H. 1996. *Wisdom Sits in Places: Landscape and Language among the Western Apache.* Albuquerque: University of New Mexico Press.

Grounds, Richard A., George E. Tinker, and David E. Wilkins, ed. 2003. *Native Voices: American Indian Identity and Resistance.* Lawrence: University Press of Kansas.

Nelson, Richard K. 1983. *Make Prayers to the Raven: A Koyukon View of the Northern Forest.* Chicago: University of Chicago Press.

Sullivan, Lawrence E. 2000. *Native Religions and Cultures of North America.* New York: Continuum.

Course Schedule

WEEK 1

Tuesday: Lecture: Living in Balance in a World Out of Balance: Healing the Community and the Land

- Readings

Harjo, *Native Voices,* pp. 3–4
Mohawk, *Native Voices,* pp. 20–34

Thursday: Lecture: Colonization and Resistance in the American Southwest: Decolonizing Methodologies—Old and Deeply Divisive Debates

- Reading

Smith, *Decolonizing Methodologies,* pp. 1–94

WEEK 2

Tuesday: Lecture: What Keeps Us from Finding Common Ground?

- Readings

Wilkins, *Native Voices,* pp. 81–96
Morris, *Native Voices,* pp. 97–154

Paper 1 due (3 pages)

Thursday: Lecture: The Process of Healing: Religious Studies and Native Studies

- Reading

Pesantubbee, *Native Voices,* pp. 209–222

WEEK 3

Tuesday: Lecture: Transforming American Conceptions about Power and Authority

- Readings

Talamantez, *Native Voices*, pp. 273–289
Grounds, *Native Voices*, pp. 290–317

WEEK 4

Tuesday: Guest Lecture: Jim Proctor—Religion and Science

- Reading

To be provided by lecturer

Thursday: Discussion of guest lecture

WEEK 5

Tuesday: Lecture: Images of Health and Illness: The Land Looks after Us

- Reading

Sullivan, *Native Religions and Cultures*, pp. 121–141

Thursday: Lecture: Is Science a God? Is Religion a Science?

- Reading

Sullivan, *Native Religions and Cultures*, pp. 142–159, pp. 208–237

WEEK 6

Tuesday: Lecture, Landscape, Language and Healing

- Reading

Basso, *Wisdom Sits in Places*, pp. xiii–70

Paper 2 due (3 pages)

Thursday: Lecture: Qualities of Mind, Smoothness of Mind

- Reading

Basso, *Wisdom Sits in Places*, pp. 71–152

WEEK 7

Tuesday: Lecture: The Watchful World

- Reading

Nelson, *Make Prayers to the Raven*, introduction and pp. 1–76

Thursday: Lecture: Principles of Koyukon World View, Healing, and Nature, and the Distant Time

- Reading

Nelson, *Make Prayers to the Raven*, pp. 225–237

WEEK 8

Tuesday: Lecture: Native American Experiences in Indian Schools

Readings

Nelson, *Make Prayers to the Raven*, pp. 238–260
Sullivan, *Native Religions and Cultures*, pp. 1–32

Thursday: Lecture, Passing on Traditional Knowledge

- Reading

Sullivan, *Native Religions and Cultures*, pp. 160–180

Paper 3 due (3 pages)

WEEK 9

Tuesday: Film and discussion.

Thursday: Guest Speaker, Julianne Cordero, Native American Healing Arts

- Reading

Cordero, "Reciprocal Terrain." Santa Barbara: University of California, Department of Religious Studies. Unpublished mss.

WEEK 10

Tuesday: Lecture: The Politics of Disease: Native American Responses

Thursday: Course Review
Turn in final paper and pick up take-home final exam.

REFERENCES

Grounds, Richard A. 2003. Yuchi travels: up and down the academic "road to disappearance." In *Native voices: American Indian identity and resistance,* ed. Richard A. Grounds, George E. Tinker, and David E. Wilkins, 290–317. Lawrence: University Press of Kansas.
Harjo, Joy. 2003. The psychology of Earth and sky. In *Native voices: American Indian identity and resistance,* eds. Richard A. Grounds, George E. Tinker, and David E. Wilkins. Lawrence: University Press of Kansas.
Mohawk, John. 2003. The power of Seneca women and the legacy of Handsome lake.

In *Native voices: American Indian identity and resistance,* eds. Richard A. Grounds, George E. Tinker, and David E. Wilkins, 20–34. Lawrence: University Press of Kansas.

Morris, Glenn T. Vine Deloria, Jr., and the development of a decolonizing critique of indigenous peoples and international relations. In *Native voices: American Indian identity and resistance,* eds. Richard A. Grounds, George E. Tinker, and David E. Wilkins, 97–154.Lawrence: University Press of Kansas.

Pesantubbee, Michelene E. 2003. Religious studies on the margins: decolonizing our minds. In *Native voices: American Indian identity and resistance,* eds. Richard A. Grounds, George E. Tinker, and David E. Wilkins, 209–222. Lawrence: University Press of Kansas.

Smith, Linda Tuhiwai. 1999. *Decolonizing methodologies: research and indigenous peoples.* New York: Zed Books, distributed by St Martin's Press.

Talamantez, Inés. 2003. Transforming American conceptions about Native America: Vine Deloria, Jr., critic and coyote. In *Native voices: American Indian identity and resistance,* eds. Richard A. Grounds, George E. Tinker, and David E. Wilkins, 273–289. Lawrence: University Press of Kansas.

Wilkins, David E. 2003. From time immemorial : the origin and import of the reserved rights doctrine. In *Native voices: American Indian identity and resistance,* ed. Richard A. Grounds, George E. Tinker, and David E. Wilkins, 81–96. Lawrence: University Press of Kansas.

7

Ometeotl Moyocoyatzin: Nahuatl Spiritual Foundations for Holistic Healing

Inés Hernández-Ávila

This essay is based on my initial experience teaching a course focused completely on the ancient and contemporary Nahuatl, or Aztec, tradition. I regularly offer NAS 157 Native American Religion and Philosophy (a core course for our Native American studies undergraduate majors and minors), with a focus on a grouping of traditions, one of which is usually the Nahuatl tradition. I have often wanted to create a course dedicated entirely to this tradition and its influence on contemporary Chicana/Chicano and Mexican spiritual expressions and understandings of healing, so this project provided me with the opportunity to use the space of NAS 157, in fall 2003, to design, teach, and reflect upon a new course proposal (NAS 159), which I have now drafted as a result of this experience.

As a core course for our program, NAS 157 enrolls students who have a cultural/historical basis for studying Native American religious traditions. At the same time, the course is listed as fulfilling our campus general education requirement, so I also tend to get some students who know little or nothing about anything Native American. My ideal goal is to encourage the NAS majors and minors to help me in the teaching of the material by raising the level of discussion conceptually and pedagogically. In this course I had a diversity of undergraduates (Euro-American, Chicanas/Chicanos, and Native American), several of them majors and minors. Our graduate program allows our graduate students to take some selected undergraduate upper-division courses, so this particular course often has some of our graduate students as well. In the fall of 2003, I had three graduate students in the class: Elisa Huerta from the University of California, Santa Cruz, and Ashley Hall and Jennie Luna from our own program. Hall and Luna signed up for independent study with me in order to be in the class, and all three are specifically committed to the teaching project because of their own research and teaching interests. These graduate students took leadership positions with the group work that was part of the course. My campus runs on a ten-week quarter schedule which, as those who teach along similar time frames know, goes by quite fast.

The main learning goals of the course were (1) to introduce students to some of the principle concepts emanating from the ancient Nahuatl philosophical and religious traditions; (2) to have students begin to understand the integrity, complexity, and beauty of these traditions *as* traditions of healing; (3) to have them consider the ways these teachings have been translated into contemporary settings, such as the ongoing reclamation by Chicanas/Chicanos of this particular indigenous heritage in their own lives and spiritual expressions; (4) to promote reflection upon how these teachings represent a recovery process, a healing process, which in certain ways can be used to address issues of identity, community, education, diversity, and difference in contemporary society. I kept my texts to a minimum because of the quarter system and because the main study that formed the basis of the course, Miguel León-Portilla's *Aztec Thought and Culture: A Study of the Ancient Nahuatl Mind* (one of the many works that have earned him the beloved title "Maestro"), is sometimes a challenge for students. My other texts were *In the Language of Kings: An Anthology of Mesoamerican Literature—Pre-Columbian to the Present*, edited by León-Portilla and by Earl Shorris, and a course reader designed to support the group work.

In the introduction to the course I emphasized the importance of understanding the historical processes of discovery, invasion, genocide, dispossession, ethnocide, and colonization. I asked students to consider the so-called Conquest as an ongoing tension between those who were subjugated and colonized (and thereby suffered systematic de-Indianization) and those who are still attempting to enforce assimilationist processes and policies among indigenous peoples. I introduced them to the work of Guillermo Bonfil Batalla, whose book *Mexico Profundo: Reclaiming a Civilization*, elaborates the intense social/political/cultural dynamic that still exists and reverberates between the imposed (Western) "imaginary Mexico," and the "profound Mexico" represented by Mesoamerican (and other) indigenous peoples as they undertake the processes of decolonization and re-Indianization. I also noted that the re-Indianization process is not essentialist but, on the contrary, is one that opens up the term "indigenous" to be both broadly contemporary and inclusive, yet rooted. I asked students to consider the different levels of healing that take place through the re-Indianization process happening today in indigenous communities, culturally, linguistically, academically, and otherwise, through the recovery and adaptation of ancient ways of naming, knowing, and being.

Since the late 1960s, the deep interest within the Chicana/Chicano community regarding the regaining of Aztec religious traditions has resulted in the creation of numerous Aztec dance groups and ceremonial circles throughout the United States. Chicana/Chicano artists, writers, and cultural workers have appropriated, employed, and reinterpreted many aspects and icons of the early Nahuatl cultural/spiritual traditions, such that there is a popular familiarity with terms such as Aztlan, the place of origin of the Mexica-Tenochca who migrated south to central Mexico to found Tenochtitlan; Tonatiuh, the name of *el Quinto Sol*, the Fifth Sun; *in tlilli in tlapalli*—the red and the black ink—the term for writing, as wisdom; the Toltecs, the supreme artists who anteceded the Mexica; and others who are discussed below. The names for the Supreme Being are many, designating the various aspects or manifestations of the Giver of Life: Ipalnemoani, the Giver of Life, the Mystery; in Tloque Nahuaque, Lord of the Close Vicinity; Yohualli Ehecatl, the One Who is Invisible and Intangible; Moyocoyani, the One Who Invents Himself/Herself; Ometeotl, the Duality of the Supreme Being, Female and Male; Quetzalcoatl, the Plumed Serpent, the Toltec god of wisdom known to all Nahuatl peoples (all of these concepts/terms are presented in *Aztec Thought and Culture*).

The course design reflected some of the ways that Nahuatl philosophical, religious concepts were embedded in the culture and belief system of peoples like the Mexica, the Texcocanos, the Tlaxcaltecas, and others.[1] The story of the creation of the Fifth Sun in Teotihuacan—beginning with the self-sacrifice of the humble Nanahuatzin in the sacred fire, the eventual self-sacrifice of the proud and egotistical Tecuciztecatl, concluding with the self-sacrifice of all the gods and goddesses, and even including the reluctant Xolotl (Quetzalcoatl's double)—provided one of the main foundations for the course. I asked the students to remember that, according to the Aztec calendar, the age in which we now live is called Nahui Ollin (Four Movement), and the Sun is known as Tonatiuh, the Fifth Sun of Movement. One of the main components of the course involved the existential ideal of encouraging students to "assume a face and a heart," which is tied both to the concept of autonomy (personal and collective), and to the centering and balancing of the individual with(in) society. I wanted to make sure that students had the time for contemplation and reflection on their own movement in relation to their own lives, and to this age. The Nahuatl word for heart, *yollotl*, has the same root as the word for movement, *ollin*. I underscored the potential healing journey that each student would take, inwardly and outwardly, for herself/himself, with me, and collectively with all of us in the class.

From the beginning, I made explicit my choice to focus on the tradition's humanistic teachings that foreground interrelationship—how a human being and a society come to healing, self-realization, and self-wisdom through contemplation, reflection, and sacred discourse with the self, with the earth, with the universe, and with the mystery who is the Giver of Life. I fully acknowledged the militaristic, imperialist, and hierarchical practices of Aztec society but addressed them as weaknesses of a culture that was otherwise noteworthy in its humanism. León-Portilla writes, "The popular and public cult of the gods as expressed in sacrifice and the mystical militaristic vision of the Aztecs was differentiated from the *tlamatinime's* [the wise teacher's] search for a new form of knowledge which might embody the truth."[2] I asked students to consider how, in our own society today, the United States is at war, and yet a strong

peace movement also manifests itself dramatically. In terms of the contemporary expression of neo-Aztec, or Mexica, religious traditions, I also asked
students to be cautious of settling for fundamentalist and rigid renditions of
the ancient belief system.

León-Portilla tells us that the Nahuatl poets questioned whether "anything
on earth [is] capable of satisfying the heart (the whole dynamic being)" of
humans "in a changing world."[3] The poets, and the *tlamatinime* (the wise teachers) also remind us that we come to suffer in this world. I asked the students
to keep in mind this idea of suffering throughout the course, especially as we
pursued the concept of *yoltéotl*, or speaking to the Supreme Being in ones'
heart. Suffering, in this tradition, has to do in part with the transitory nature
of life—the idea that life is relatively short, even for those who live long, and
especially for those who die unexpectedly at an early age, and the idea that
there is no guarantee about how long any of us will be here. Suffering also
involves the idea of the imperfection of humans and the often widespread
evidence of human ignorance. In this sense, suffering is not only material or
physical, but it has to do with *conciencia* (consciousness and conscience). I
asked the students to consider this as the root of the poets' search for truth in
this life on this earth. I even suggested that perhaps one of the implicit causes
for such deep yearning had its foundations in the questioning of the militaris-
tic/imperialistic aspects of Nahuatl society. This urge to know, to question, to
pursue, to unlayer, to dig, to always arrive more intimately at the truth(s) of
life is at the heart of the poet's work, the artist's work, the teacher's work, and
is the example they offer(ed) to humanity then and now.

These core issues informed the four dynamically interwoven concepts
guiding my explicit pedagogy throughout the course: (1) the concept of the
Supreme Being or Creator as Ometeotl Moyocoyatzin, the One Who Invents
Himself/Herself, and Who Manifests as a Female/Male Duality, and who
therefore manifests in everything else as a dual duality; (2) *in ixtli in yollotl*,
face and heart, the concept for education (good teaching and good learning) in
the ancient Nahuatl tradition; (3) *in xochitl in cuicatl*, flower and song, the
concept of poetry (and art or the creative act) as the path to truth; and (4) the
idea of *yoltéotl*, talking to the Supreme Being in the heart. When the individual
speaks truthfully to God in her or his heart, intuition is heightened and inspiration is possible, setting into motion the creative impulse. "God," when explored through the Nahuatl belief system, is revealed and named in many ways,
from the invisible and intangible to the concretely expressed and gendered
biodiversity of the earth. Through the subsequent artistic expression, the individual achieves *in xochitl in cuicatl*, thus bringing about a more defined *in
ixtli in yollotl* which, in turn, allows the individual to come closer, through his
or her own originality, to the Creative Spirit that is Ometeotl Moyocoyatzin.
The individual becomes *yoltéotl*, a deified heart. This ongoing process is the
path to truth, *conciencia*, intuition, self-discipline, ethics, and autonomy, and
the collective is better situated to achieve autonomy when the individuals have
achieved it for themselves.

León-Portilla explains how in the *calmecac*, or higher institutions of learning in early Nahuatl society, the *tlamatinime*, or wise teacher, had a central role in guiding the people through this process. A good *tlamatinime* shed light upon all that was possible, all that could be known on the path of the student. The *tlamatinime* did not hide points to benefit his or her interpretation, but rather shone a light even on areas that might complicate what he or she wanted to teach. Such a person is a mirror by which to contemplate the self in relation to the universe. Through prudence, care, and a rigorous discipline, the student is taught to strengthen his or her heart (with the heart as the center of the human), and to humanize his or her will. León-Portilla explains the word "*monotza*" which is translated as " 'he [she] calls to himself [herself],' 'he [she] enters within himself [herself],' 'he [she] disciplines himself [herself],' 'he [she] controls himself [herself].' "[4] Both the *tlamatinime* and the student seek the energy of Quetzalcoatl, as they resonate with the "yearning for a metaphysical investigation of truth."[5] In my course, the focus on Quetzalcoatl allowed the students to grapple with these ancient core teachings having to do with self-knowledge and the inherent relationship between creativity, originality, autonomy, and spirit. I was able to make a connection between what Nakota scholar Kathryn Shanley would call a thinking heart[6] and the Nahuatl concepts of being truthful with the self and being able to recognize truth, which requires sentience and compassion.[7]

The work of the *tlamatinime* was to "delve deeper into the meaning of [the] symbols"[8] contained in the myths. I had the students consider the connection between myths as oral tradition and as official stories, which each nation has (and which each religion has). These stories, the formal interpretations of ways of being and knowing, tend to be prescriptive as well as descriptive; in terms of religion, they become doctrine. But official stories have a way of blurring the idiosyncrasies of the individual stories (and ways of seeing) that constitute the larger picture. Because the *tlamatinime* is herself or himself a medium of contemplation who looks at things through the perforated mirror, this is a person who does "delve deeper," seeing a multiplicity of facets that deepen (and widen) her or his understandings of things. The *tlamatinime*, like the poets such as the famous Nezahualcoyotl (Fasting Coyote) from Texcoco, could not help but question, always seeking to go beyond. Even in the creation of the Fifth Sun, Quetzalcoatl's double, Xolotl, expresses fervently his resistance to self-sacrifice, although he does end up being thrown into the fire along with the others who offer themselves willingly. Xolotl's existence, however, affirms the value of the idea of doubt, doubt as friend, as ally, as teacher, because doubt can help a person remain open, rather than fixed. Doubt can be a door to the intuition and to the universe.

This doubt or ambivalence is present even in relation to the "mysterious dialectic process within the Divine concerning the creation of man," as León-Portilla notes, adding that "the internal struggle for and against the appearance of man takes place *within the supreme being*."[9] Mictlantecuhtli and Mictlancihuatl, as the sacred pair of the underworld, are manifestations of the Supreme Being who create the obstacles, or the tests, that Quetzalcoatl must overcome to retrieve the bones of humanity. Though Quetzalcoatl is the liberatory force (helped by Xolotl, by doubt) and is ultimately successful, and as such is related to Ometéotl as Giver of Life, it is important to remember that the struggle for Creation occurs within the Supreme Being himself or herself. This creative tension, this working through the blocks, has its correspondence in the creative processes of *yoltéotl, in xochitl in cuicatl*, and *in ixtli in yollotl*.

León-Portilla writes about the idea of people coming into the world "face-less," without an identity, with anonymity.[10] I reminded students how sometimes humans are taught or shown to discount others, especially those who are different in some way, perhaps according to class, race or ethnicity, disability, religion, age, language or accent, or sexuality. It would seem that, in the Aztec concept of education, once a person was aided in his or her pursuit of a face and a heart, then he or she would be able to recognize the face and heart of others. It is in the way we see others that they respond. I asked students to think about this in relation to their own life experiences, to think of the times they were made to feel invisible, or the times they felt acknowledged for who they really are. León-Portilla notes that the *tlamatinime* "approached the supreme social and personal ideals—the mainspring of Nahuatl thought and action—the divine spark in [the human's] heart which transforms him [her] into an artist, a poet, or a sage."[11] From anonymity to autonomy, from invisibility to presence, here is the visionary healing, rooted in originality, in difference. I asked the students to remember that we are all texts, noteworthy in our difference, and that the classroom itself was a text, all the subject of contemplation.

Regarding the assignments I required for the course, I had the students write one formal essay (as the midterm), for which I gave them a choice of multilayered questions to answer. This particular assignment proved the most difficult for them, particularly in relation to reflecting on the pursuit of a face and a heart in their own experience. Many reverted to their previous academic socialization as "analyzers," rather than draw on the understandings they were gaining through the more creative, intuitive aspects of the class. Such understanding is so rarely rewarded in the academic study of religion—or in the academy in general—that it was hard for students to trust either their own ability to engage in that way, or that their work would be accepted if they did. This is one of the challenges to the pedagogy I chose, in relation to the course content. The group work also turned out to be slightly uneven, with some group members more enthusiastically engaging in the collective effort, and those who had little background in Native American studies feeling (and sometimes being) more restricted in their ability to contribute. The groups had to present their findings through a class presentation in the final week of the quarter. The three graduate students each took charge of one of the following interrelated groups, each related to different dimensions of healing: song, dance, and ceremony; herbs and plants; and the ethics of the land.

Since I taught this course in the fall quarter, the group who worked on song, dance, and ceremony did a representation of an altar for *Día de los Muertos* (Day of the Dead), rooted in Aztec tradition. The altar was complete with the marking of the four directions, sacred images, family photos, and memorabilia, *copal* (incense), flowers, and offerings of food and drink. Some of the Chicana/Chicano students who are *danzantes* (traditional dancers) led the group in this work, complete with ceremonial songs from the contemporary Aztec dance tradition. This particular group affirmed the living spirits of the ancestors who continue to sustain the people, balancing the relationship between the living and the dead, even as they themselves are nourished by those who remember them. In the students' offerings of flower and song, they reminded the class of *in xochitl in cuicatl*.

The group who focused on herbs and plants examined them as natural medicines for the body, the spirit, the mind, and the heart. These medicines were seen as restoring balance to the individual and providing ways of purification, through indigenous forms of nutrition and wellness (prevention and treatment). Central to this group's work were the stories about how corn came to the people, and how certain plants, like the prickly pear cactus and the maguey, were and are precious for the many ways they serve human beings. The land-ethic group looked specifically at the sacred narrative of the migration from Aztlan as a framework for considering Aztec religion as sacred science and culture emerging from and informed by the land. They also considered the climate of the Valley of Mexico and the bases of environmental ethics and ecological knowledge in Aztec culture, most significantly the sacred pairing of Tlaloc/Chalchihuitlicue as manifestations of rain/earth/fertility and their correspondence to hydrologic cycles.

I was in charge of working with the group devoted to gender, specifically to notions of female power as it was expressed in ancient Nahuatl society, first through the representation of the Supreme Being as dual in Ometeotl, and then through the many distinct aspects of the female principle(s) of the universe. I called upon the work of both Mexican scholars such as Justino Fernandez's study of Coatlicue, and contemporary Chicana writers and artists who have been inspired by Coatlicue, the tremendous Mother Earth; Mayaguel, the lady of the Maguey; Coyolxauhqui, the moon; Tonantzin, otherwise known as the Virgin of Guadalupe; Tlazolteotl, the one who regulates the cycles of women and who hears the confessions of the people. We considered the various manifestations of these sacred beings, the interrelatedness of their stories, their connection to Ometéotl, and to the restorative healing of female identity.

I also offered the option (not a course requirement) to students to attend either a men's or women's sweat lodge ceremony, which united all of the four work groups, weaving together song and ceremony, herbs and plants, the earth, and women's power (the sweat lodge is seen as female in many indigenous traditions, including the Nahuatl, in which the sweat lodge is known as Temazcalteci, the grandmother sweat lodge), within a larger framework of healing. Again, the sweat lodge ceremony reinforced the idea of the inner journey that is, at the same time, one with the cosmos. While the altar for Day of the Dead could be adapted to another institution, the sweat lodge ceremony would probably be more difficult. The sweat lodge is the main regional resource I drew upon for the course. I also invited one of my colleagues, Martha Macri, to give a presentation on the Mexican codices, and I asked one of her graduate students, Michael Grofe, to talk about his work, through the codices, on cacao. The next time I teach the course, I will show many more digitalized color images from the codices and from the contemporary Conchero dance tradition.

Overall, perhaps the most successful aspects of the course were the creative projects, the journal entries, and the final reflections. The creative projects provided a way for students to connect with the creative process as a path to truth, broadening slightly the idea of *in xochitl in cuicatl, floricanto*, flower and song, which is the *difrasismo* (doubly stated expression) to designate poetry. Students were able to use whatever artistic medium they chose to express their face and heart, and their own holistic realization of the concepts we studied throughout the quarter. Several produced family codexes; one Mixtec young woman replicated her family's journey from Oaxaca to California, using the Mixtec codex as her model. One young woman did a tile self-portrait of her face and heart; another paired her own photography with major Nahuatl philosophical concepts. Another young woman turned in a collection of poems written in Nahuatl and translated into English (she had been studying Nahuatl through our program). Several students worked in acrylics, in pastels, in watercolor, in collage, from the abstract to the concrete. Others offered songs and instrumental music. One person did an enormous mobile representing the thirteen levels of heaven of the Nahuatl universe, using elements from nature to designate the different realms.

The journal entries provided a space for the reflection that was a major tenet of the course. With their consent, I began to post their contributions to the course website. As they read each other's impressions of the material and of the prompts I gave them, the students gained in confidence. I was elated to see how most students began to *read* each other. They literally created their own discourse on the materials and concepts. One student, Amber Hill, responding to another student's entry, wrote:

> The image this person has created of "our personalities and hearts like spiral galaxies with long reaching arms" is beautiful. This line and the line after it, "The more we are exposed to, the more matter we can pull to the core of our beings, becoming more solid and assured or autonomous." This relates to the Nahuatl concept of finding the face. Through interaction (Danza) with the world and other people, we can begin to find our own face[s].

Another student, Robert Farahmand, made an impressive connection between the deified heart and Nanahuatzin at the time of the creation of the Fifth Sun:

> When considering the event at Teotihuacán when the sun was created, a connection can be made with the right heart and the attainment of harmony. Tecuciztecatl was unable to create harmony among the elements because he would not sacrifice himself. This could be interpreted as a fault of his heart, which was not rooted firmly enough in God or the Gods to obey their command. Only after Nanahuatzin bravely displayed the nature of his true heart by

sacrificing himself, could the sun be made and set into motion. It could be said then that Nanahuatzin was *yoltéotl*, while Tecuciztecatl was not. The heart of the former was able to create (as the good artist does), while the latter even though he did eventually sacrifice himself, had not displayed a steadfast heart.

Student Jesús Sanchez wrote:

Moyocayani says I can create my world on my own terms. This class has been for many of us an eye opener. . . . We have become the subjects our own studies, learning from ourselves, and later relating this to the context provided by our short glances into Nahuatl philosophy. . . . We have benefited from a new form of learning, where education begins with the understanding of ourselves. Each student will walk away, I hope, with universal notion of how we can ordain the people we become, and how to treat ourselves at all levels of our health.

And student Jorge Gonzalez wrote:

As we move along the course I begin to see the effects of this healing process. As I walk into the class my spirit finally gets to rest and travel inside of me. It expands my imagination, opening my pores of inspiration, and then eventually sending me to my own place of Omeyocan, . . . to where it all began.

In the end, I believe that the focus I chose was unexpected and welcome for the majority of the students. I was clear that I was not trying to convert them to Aztec religion, and in fact, I spent only a portion of time in class discussing the sacred beings otherwise called gods and goddesses of the Nahuatl tradition (I would probably do more of this the next time I teach the course). Instead, I wanted students to encounter and discover the humanistic and liberating aspects of the Nahuatl cultural and spiritual traditions that foreground the autonomy of the creative self, and possible wholeness in the intimate relationship of that creative self to the Giver/Creator of Life. This point is important because it is an ancient reminder that what humans make of themselves and of this world, this life on earth—how they heal themselves—is up to them. The importance of being firmly rooted, even when it seems that nothing is stable or lasting, comes back to the individual who leaves "at least flowers, at least songs," that is, she or he leaves the creativity that has emerged from her or his internal dialogue (and search for the truth) with the Giver of Life.

Syllabus: NAS 157 Native American Religion and Philosophy

TR 2:10–4:00 PM
Instructor: Dr. Inés Hernández-Ávila
e-mail: *ighernandez@ucdavis.edu*

261 Olson
Office: 2415 Hart
Office Hours: T, 4:15–5:30 PM and
    by appointment

Phone: 752-4394; 752-3237 (NAS office)

Course Description

Religious and philosophical thinking of Native American people with emphasis
on North America

Course Goals

To introduce students to the emerging interdisciplinary area of Native American
ican religious studies, including the conceptualizations, methodologies, pedagogies, and ethical considerations inherent in the study and representation
of indigenous religious traditions from a Native American academic and
community-centered perspective. To read texts which introduce basic religious
and philosophical/cosmological perceptions from the early Nahuatl tradition
and to consider how this tradition has sustained itself in a contemporary setting
within the United States and Mexico. To provide a sense of the context in which
Nahuatl religious/spiritual/ceremonial traditions are expressed and negotiated
in contemporary society. To consider how the tradition known as Nahuatl,
Aztec, Mexica, in its various forms, including "Danza Conchera," represent a
tradition of religion and healing from past times to the present. As the occasion
permits, to meet and have conversation with recognized elders or representa-
tives of the Aztec or Nahuatl tradition, or with scholars working in the field of
Native American religious traditions. This course is a core course for the NAS
major, and as such, students will be presumed to have a sound background in
the multi/interdisciplinary area of Native American studies.

Required Texts

> Miguel León-Portilla, *Aztec Thought and Culture: A Study of the Ancient
>   Nahuatl Mind*, trans. Jack Emory Davis. Norman: University of
>   Oklahoma Press, 1990.
> Miguel León-Portilla and Earl Shorris, eds., *In the Language of Kings: An
>   Anthology of Mesoamerican Literature—Pre-Columbian to the Present*.
>   New York: Norton, 2001.
> *The Five Suns* (film)
> Personal video, *Danza Conchera*
> Course Reader

Recommended Readings

Gloria Anzaldúa, *Borderlands-La Frontera: The New Mestiza*, 2nd ed. San Francisco: Aunt Lute Books, 1999.

Guillermo Bonfil Batalla, *Mexico Profundo: Reclaiming a Civilization.* Trans. Philip A. Dennis. Austin: University of Texas Press, 1996.

Justino Fernandez, *Estética del arte Mexicano: Coatlicue,* 2nd ed. Mexico City: Universidad Nacional Autónoma de Mexico, 1990.

Elizabeth Hill Boone, *Stories in Red and Black: Pictorial Histories of the Aztecs and Mixtecs.* Austin: University of Texas Press, 2000.

Antonio Velasco Piña, *Tlacaelel: El Azteca entre los Aztecas.* Mexico City: Jus, 1979.

Grading and Course Requirements

Journal	20%
Mid-Term (take-home)/Essay	20%
Creative project/research project	20%
Group work/project	20%
Final Exam/reflection (essay)	10%
Class attendance and participation	10%

Topical Outlines (Partial List of General Themes Addressed in Class)

1. Definitions of the sacred, including the idea of religion/spirituality as a path to healing
2. Moyocoyani, Ometeotl Moyocoyatzin
3. The Aztec/Nahuatl tradition as a land-based geocentric sacred science
4. Cultural pedagogy; the development of a face and heart
5. Poetry as the path to truth
6. The role of song, dance, music, ceremony in healing
7. Women's power and men's power
8. Dreamers, healers, "medicine people"
9. The role of tricksters; humor and the outrageous
10. Nahuatl philosophy and creativity; the deified heart
11. Oral tradition and Nahuatl language preservation
12. The teaching of autonomy through Nahuatl religious/spiritual traditions
13. Contemporary religious/spiritual movements based on the early Nahuatl traditions

Format

The class structure is a circle, with students expected to give value to each other's comments as well as the professor's. Each class period will be a combination of lecture/commentary by the professor and discussion that is focused on themes generated from the readings. Reading assignments will be supplemented by guest speakers, films, exercises, and some (optional) field trips. Students will be evaluated on the quality of the assignments they turn in, but also in relation to the careful, thoughtful attention and articulation by which they contribute to the learning process in this class.

NOTES

1. The term "Nahuatl" allows for an acknowledgment of not only the Mexica, but of the other important Nahuatl-speaking peoples/cultures.

2. Miguel León-Portilla, *Aztec Thought and Culture*, p. 74.

3. Ibid., p. 5.

4. Ibid., p. 119.

5. Ibid., p. 31.

6. Kathryn Shanley develops the trope of the "thinking heart" in her essay "The Thinking Heart: American Indian Discourse and the Politics of Recognition," in *Race, Ethnicity, and Nationality in the United States: Toward the Twenty-first Century*, ed. Paul Wong, pp. 256–276 (Boulder: Westview, 1999). For a brief and corollary discussion of the idea of the center of thinking residing in the heart, see my essay "The Power of Native Language(s) and the Performance of Indigenous Autonomy: The Case of Mexico," in *Native Voices: American Indian Identity and Resistance*, eds. Richard Grounds, George Tinker, and David Wilkins, pp. 35–74 (Lawrence: University Press of Kansas, 2003).

7. I take the liberty of gendering the *tlamatinime*, so that he or she is represented as a wise male or female teacher.

8. León-Portilla, *Aztec Thought and Culture*, p. 25.

9. Ibid., pp. 109–110. Emphasis mine.

10. Ibid., p. 104.

11. Ibid., p. 105.

8

Chicanos/as, Religion, and Healing: Traditions and Transformations

Lara Medina

I have taught a course on Chicana and Chicano religiosity since 1992, first at the University of California, Los Angeles and now at California State University, Northridge. These are both large public universities in Southern California. The students in the course are primarily of Mexican ancestry although, as the demographics in Los Angeles change, more students with Central American heritage are now attending. The course counts toward general elective credit, which ensures an average of 40 students, a few coming from non-Latino ethnic groups who are preparing for a teaching profession in public elementary schools. I began teaching this class shortly after I completed a master's in theology. The pleasure I experienced in teaching in a secular university a course that I view both as *about* healing and as *promoting* healing persuaded me to pursue a doctorate in history and religious studies.

In part, the course draws on my own experience related to religion and healing. I am a third-generation Chicana raised in the San Francisco Bay area. I attended Catholic schools for 12 years. I am the product of a devout Catholic mother and a father who converted so that they could marry within the Catholic Church. By the time I had turned 17, I had left the church because of the weight of religion on my life. As a young woman, religion did not offer healing. Rather, it became something that I needed to heal from. It would take another decade before I could reconcile with the limitations that the church had placed on me and the faith that my parents still practiced. I share this biographical information in this essay on teaching about Chicanas/os, religion, and healing because my life experience gives me the advantage of understanding where the majority of my students are "coming from." Most have been raised Catholic but are on the margins of the church. Yet there are always a few who are very satisfied in the Catholic Church and may even participate as youth ministers. Some have turned to Evangelical and Pentecostal traditions for the answers to their questions of ultimate meaning. Others (re)turn to an Indigenous spirituality. The latter offers not only a spiritual tradition, but also (re)connects them to their own Indigenous ancestral roots, which offers healing from the wounds of spiritual colonization. Healing, in this sense, is related on many levels to the effects of historical process.

Many of my students are searching. They are searching for more knowledge about themselves and about how to understand the notion of God. They express great interest in knowing more about their Indigenous roots; knowledge that has been denied them in the Western educational system. Most have never studied religion as an academic enterprise. Many have not been allowed to question Christian doctrine. I offer them the opportunity to question religious "truths" constructed within historical and gendered contexts so they may think critically about their own traditions and their own cultures. I suggest that it is through the process of critical thinking about religion that healing can occur. My emphasis on Indigenous epistemology challenges the majority to confront their learned internalized biases against non-Christian and non-Western worldviews. For Chicanos/as and Latinos/as who are products of biological and cultural *mestizaje*—hybridity resulting from a historical violent encounter between cultures, reconciling the differences and discovering the similarities between Christian and Indigenous traditions offers healing. Healing, in this context, is about bringing forth self-knowledge and historical consciousness in order to claim religious agency—the ability to determine for oneself what is morally and ethically just, and what enables communication with spiritual sources. For the young women in the class, discussions about moral authority in relation to one's body constitute another central part of the healing process. The personal nature of the students' interest in religion definitely influences the course design, as I attempt to address their searching process while also providing a scholarly understanding of how religion shapes Chicano/a culture.

My learning objectives for the course are clearly stated in the syllabus. The first involves teaching about religious diversity within Chicano/Latino communities. Though the majority of these remain Catholic, I also address the historical presence of Chicanos and Latinos within mainline Protestant denominations (primarily Methodist), Evangelical and Pentecostal faith communities; the growing numbers in *indigenista* and Chicana spiritual feminist circles; and the participation in traditions such as Islam and Santería. Utilizing the more personal and reflective writings of Latinas/os within some of these spiritual paths helps to paint a broad picture of the "religious landscape" within our communities. This is also the starting point to insert gender within patriarchal religions, which quickly leads to discussions about transformations that Chicanas/Latinas are making in religious discourse and practices. The works of Gloria Anzaldúa, Yolanda Tarango, Jeanette Rodriguez, along with my own writing on Chicana/Latina spirituality, are useful here. Beginning the course around multiple religious identities, and including my own story, helps to create a space that encourages diversity, dialogue, critical thinking, and reflection.

The second objective is to provide a basic understanding of Mexican Indigenous epistemology, which provides a framework to understand contemporary Chicano/a religiosity. A central theoretical issue in the course is that *mestizaje* shapes the foundation of Mexican and Chicano religiosity. One cannot understand this *mestizaje* unless one begins with a basic understanding of Mesoamerican Indigenous epistemology and cosmology. I emphasize the concepts of duality, fluidity, balance, sacred nature, metaphorical language, corporeal/spiritual animistic sites, circular time, interdependency, reciprocity, sacrifice, *flor y canto* (flower and song), and *cara y corazón* (face and heart) to sketch the fundamentals of a Mesoamerican Indigenous worldview. When contrasted with a Western European worldview, the students are often better able to grasp these concepts. Sylvia Marcos's article "The Sacred Earth" in *Concilium* is extremely helpful here, as are many of the publications of Miguel León-Portilla and Davíd Carrasco. Grounding the course in these concepts is important because when we look at the merging of Indigenous and Spanish Catholicism, and later Chicano religiosity, we enter into what I call *Nepantla* spirituality. *Nepantla* is a Nahuatl term, meaning "in the middle." Through the lens of *Nepantla*, students can identify Indigenous concepts that continue to be active today. They can then recognize how Indigenous epistemology and practice exists in much of their familial religiosity, as in the construction of altars or domestic sacred centers, or the making of promises or *mandas* to divine beings in acts of reciprocity between humanity and divinity—a phenomenon that cuts across both the Indigenous and Christian roots. What might have seemed "superstitious or old-fashioned" can now be understood as reciprocal actions to maintain familial spiritual and cosmic balance.

Studying the origin mythologies of the Toltec and the Mexica helps to explain the cosmology of a sacred universe with distinct levels, and the role of divine sacrifice in the creation of the world. We consider how this cosmology was replicated on Mesoamerica's geographical landscape to create sacred space. Pyramids as sacred mountains created sacred centers and unified a community. The patriarchal "mystico-militaristic" theology of the Mexica or Aztecs is critiqued for the purpose of understanding the multifaceted role of human sacrifice. A warrior culture requiring sacrifice did ensure its domination over a broad territory; it also revealed Mexica animistic understandings of the body that perceived the heart as a vessel of efficacious sacred energy that had to be returned to the divine forces to ensure the continuation of life. Reciprocity between humanity and divinity was at the basis of human sacrifice.

We also examine the writings of the elite intellectuals and artists, the *tlamatinime*, within the Mexica domain, who protested human sacrifice and rejected the martial-mystical interpretation of the world. These Indigenous philosophers and theologians developed sophisticated doctrines concerning the divine and promoted alternative offerings in the form of poetic expression, or *flor y canto*. The extensive research of Mexican philosopher Miguel León-

Portilla permits the study of the rich theological heterogeneity in Mexica society "making it possible for one to hear, once more, the voice of an ancient, alternative form of wisdom" (León-Portilla 1992: 189)—recovering, for many students, what they had been taught to devalue.

Analyzing the Mexica mythology of the sun god, Huitzilopochtli, and his sister the moon goddess, Coyolxauhqui, reveals how mythology can easily be manipulated by subsequent generations to construct unequal gender relations and misogynist cultural practices. Although the original intent of the myth explained the duality of day and night, it has been used to justify the violent subordination of women. An analogy can be made between Coyolxauhqui and Eve in the Genesis mythology: both use their creative powers, yet are interpreted as evildoers. We explore how patriarchal societies interpret myths for male advantage. Cherríe Moraga's (1993) revisionist mythology of Coyolxauhqui, "En busca de la fuerza feminine," provides a feminist archetype for a Chicana/o spiritual heritage. Discussion about La Malinche, whose real name was Malintzín Tenepal, also enters here as another primary archetype of how women have been demonized in Mexicano/Chicano culture. The work of numerous Chicana writers on Malintzin offers a deconstruction of her history and a reconstruction of her identity as victim, survivor, translator, and the reclaimed Indigenous mother of all *mestizos*.

The experience of *mestizaje* and the discussion of how cultures and religions confronted, clashed, and ultimately adapted to one another throughout Latin America provides a theoretical framework for understanding the process of conquest, colonization, and adaptation that occurred in the religious history of Chicanos/as. Davíd Carrasco's article "Jaguar Christians in the Contact Zone" discusses shared symbol systems and *double entendres* to illuminate how Indigenous peoples reshaped Christian icons and rituals, adapting them to their own cosmological understandings. His example of the Christ figures sculpted primarily from cornstalks by Indigenous artisans represents the "ancient Indigenous pattern of refashioning plants to illustrate the powers of the sacred and its regeneration" (76). In these *cristos de caña*, Christ is merged with the "cosmo-magical powers" of the sacred corn. The icon becomes a symbol with shared meanings that are forced to enter a dialogue with one another. Yolanda Broyles-Gonzalez's "Indianizing Catholicism" also exemplifies how native peoples incorporated Christianity yet maintained an Indigenous sacred worldview and ritual practices. Broyles-Gonzalez's Yaqui Catholic grandmother felt closest to the divine while tending to her garden. "The powerfully healing *sábila* (aloe vera) plant is thought of as a substitute for Jesus, as the teacher of the 'Apóstoles' " (Broyles-Gonzalez 2002: 124).

At this point I introduce the concept of *Nepantla* spirituality—a spirituality at the biological and cultural crossroads, where diverse elements converge, at times in tension and at other times in cohesion. My use of *nepantla* differs somewhat from how Gloria Anzaldúa and others use the term to connote a psychic and physical state, limited by confusion and conflict because of contradictory cultural forces. I suggest that there are different aspects to *nepantla*, as a state of being born out of *mestizaje* or cultural and racial mixture. *Nepantla* spirituality is not a simple syncretic mixture of spiritual traditions, but is rather an example of transculturation, or a continuous encounter of two or more divergent worldviews. Rather then being limited by confusion or ambiguity, Chicanas/Latinas act as subjects or agents in deciding for themselves how diverse religious and cultural forces can or cannot work together. They creatively maneuver the fissures, boundaries, and borders and consciously make choices about what aspects of diverse worldviews nurture the complexity of their spiritual and biological *mestizaje*, and what for them enables communication with spiritual forces. Once the tensions of *nepantla* are understood and confronted, and the native Self is recovered and continuously healed, *nepantla* becomes a psychological, spiritual, and political space that Chicanas/os and Latinos/as transform as a place of meaning-making. I argue that much of Mexicano/Chicano religiosity reflects *Nepantla* spirituality, a creative mixture of symbols, rituals, and meanings that allow the Indigenous, European, African, and Asian to "have voice" and coexist. This explicit and dynamic coexisting is, by its very nature, about healing voices that have been silenced in multiple ways.

A section on Our Lady of Guadalupe follows as a fundamental expression of *Nepantla* spirituality, as her image embodies the coexistence of the Spanish Catholic and the Mesoamerican Indigeous symbol system. Louise Burkhart's "The Cult of the Virgin of Guadalupe in Mexico" (1993) offers a critical historical perspective of the Guadalupe mythology. My goal is to enhance the students' understanding of the social construction and evolution of this central mythology in Mexican identity. Stafford Poole (1995) and Jacques Lafaye (1976) are also useful sources. I balance a scholarly treatment of Guadalupe by emphasizing the significance of oral tradition and the element of mystery, in what Virgilio Elizondo calls "the Guadalupe event." Faith and the testimonies of Guadalupanas (devotees of Guadalupe) receive equal treatment with the lack of historical evidence for the apparition. I provide a timeline beginning in 1521 when the apparition is dated and ending in 2003 with the canonization of St. Juan Diego by the Roman Catholic Church to reinforce the power that this religious mythology has on a culture and a global church. I emphasize Guadalupe as a multivocal symbol whose identity is tied to the individual devotee's interpretation. She can be the mother of Jesus in Mexican colors; Tonanztin, the Nahuatl revered divine mother; or both. As journalist Ruben Martinez states in "God is Alive" in the *LA Weekly*, "She is both, the epicenter of the tremendous clash between Old and New Worlds, a blend of Nahuatl mythology and Christianity" (1992: 27). I require the students "to read her image" as a Nahuatl codice, one that speaks with metaphors through its colors and symbols. Elizondo's *Guadalupe Mother of the New Creation* (1997) is central here. Gender must also be addressed, as Guadalupe has historically been used as a symbol of liberation in revolutionary struggles, yet for Mexicanas and Chicanas she continues to be used as an archetype of the "good woman" who is an all-sacrificing mother who negates her sexuality. The visual art of Ester Hernandez, Yolanda Lopez, and Alma Lopez is extremely useful here to show the revisionist work being done on Guadalupe by Chicana feminists. Guadalupe indeed has multiple identities.

With so much focus on the Virgin, the next logical step is to deal with religion and sexuality. Karen Torjesen (1995) illuminates the religious process that demonized female sexuality, beginning with the writings of St. Augustine. Sylvia Marcos's article "Missionary Activity in Latin America" clearly shows how Augustine's teachings on sexuality were brought to the Americas and imposed on the sexual understandings of native peoples. A discussion of contemporary sexuality and spirituality develops, with a connection made between the high rate of Latina teenage pregnancy and the silencing of female sexuality in Latino cultures because of the influence of a patriarchal religious discourse that attempts to control women's bodies. I also discuss the denigration of homosexuality in traditional Chicano/Latino cultures and how the Christian Western paradigm supplanted native understandings of the fluid nature of sexuality. Paula Gunn Allen's *The Sacred Hoop* (1992) helps here as well as the anthology, *Que(e)rying Religion* edited by Gary David Comstock and Susan Henking (1997). My goal is to make sexual orientation and religion an even more significant part of the course, as Latino cultures continue to foster homophobia.

The course returns to the discussion of *Nepantla* spirituality in order to address Mexican/Chicano Catholic popular religiosity, or the faith and practices of the people. Orlando Espín's work helps to theorize popular religiosity, and Timothy Matovina's and Gary Riebe-Estrella's anthology *Horizons of the Sacred* (2002) provides three ethnographic studies on popular religiosity from contemporary Mexicano/Chicano Catholic communities. David Carrasco's concepts of "world making, world centering, and world renewal" discussed in *Religions of Mesoamerica*, explicate the significance of ritual action in popular religiosity. In contemporary rituals such as *Días de los Muertos* (Days of the Dead), *Via Cruces* (the Way of the Cross), or devotional processions to various saints and madonnas, the sacred universe is continually reconstructed, a community maintains its center, and life is renewed. Here, healing is discussed as a renewal—giving something form in a variety of ways.

A significant amount of time is spent on understanding the Mexican Indigenous/Chicano tradition of honoring and communing with the dead. Even though the tradition of *Días de los Muertos* is gaining popularity in mainstream culture, many Chicano/a students remain unaware of its richness. Assimilation forces within the Catholic Church and U.S. society compelled at least two generations of Chicanos to lose the tradition. As in many Indigenous cultures around the world (exceptions exist, of course), the dead or the ancestors play a key part in cultural continuity and communal healing. The ancestors guide the living and offer protection. Constructing sacred space in their honor, leaving them gifts of food and drink, spending time with their spirits, and sharing in oral tradition ensures family stability and, more important, reminds the living of their historical lineage.

For marginalized peoples in the United States, the simple act of remembering their family history holds spiritual and political significance, especially when history has been systematically rendered invisible and represented as inconsequential. Whether celebrating the dead takes place in public processions and gatherings in cultural centers or in the privacy of a family altar, the tradition rejects mainstream attempts to ignore the histories and traditions of nonwhite and mixed raced peoples. Through public processions and public altars honoring the dead, marginalized Others claim public space and reject any efforts to dismiss their presence in an increasingly segregated society. For Chicanos/as, Days of the Dead express a spirituality "forged in the struggle against domination." The tradition also challenges a society that privileges youth and fears aging and the dead. Western cultures enclose death in gated cemeteries devoid of color and merrymaking. The dead are silenced shortly after a funeral. In sharp contrast, Days of the Dead values ancestral wisdom and the interconnectedness of the living and the dead. Teaching about this tradition underscores the distinctiveness of non-Western epistemologies, and illustrates how healing transects boundaries of life and death.

The time spent on teaching the historical influences, both Indigenous and Christian, of Days of the Dead and how Chicano communities reinvent the tradition provides a foundation for a key assignment in the course. At the end of the semester, students are required to construct *ofrendas* (offerings) in honor of a deceased member of their family or community. The *ofrenda* can be designed in a crate or box that can be easily carried to class. They must decorate the container with symbols and photos that represent the life of the deceased. In their oral presentations, they must introduce the person to the class including a brief biographical sketch followed by an explanation of the symbols they chose to represent the deceased. For many of the students, building the *ofrenda*, explaining it to the class, and writing a two-page summary enables them to talk about a loved one and confront the pain of loss. Many students express how meaningful the assignment is not only for themselves but also for their families. Oftentimes they will have to ask a parent to tell them more about a deceased family member and the exchange brings about a sharing of family history previously untold. One student recently communicated that doing the assignment with her mother helped to relieve the nightmares her mother had experienced since the death of the grandmother. For some students, it is the first time that they speak publicly about the deceased, and the sharing promotes a process of healing memory. For students who have lost kin or friends through violence, the sharing can be particularly healing. Some students will choose to honor those who died in public catastrophes, such as the attack on the World Trade Center in 2001 or the student massacres at Tlatelolco in Mexico City in 1968. *Ofrendas* are excellent tools to teach family history as well as world history. I have also successfully used this assignment in a world religion class, and students from various ethnic groups benefited from talking about their dead. In Mexicano/Chicano culture, communing with the dead renews and heals the living.

Requiring the students to creatively construct an *ofrenda* brings to the surface another significant theoretical issue in the course: the role of the creative arts in expressing spiritual truths. Drawing from the Mesoamerican Indigenous tradition of *flor y canto* as the only true way to commune with the deities, I am able to illustrate how the artist continues to play this role in contemporary expressions of Chicano/a spirituality. Showing the work of Chicana artists such as Santa Barraza, Yreina Cervantez, and Amalia Mesa Baines or the performance art of Raquel Salinas and En Lak Ech exemplifies the changing consciousness of Chicana feminists toward religion. Contemporary Chicana/o art is a most effective tool to show how spirituality remains a central aspect of Chicano/a culture while undergoing essential revisions. The art reinforces what Chicanas/os are challenging and articulating. As Mesa Baines states, "Art is about healing" (Portillo and Muñoz 1988).

The section on Chicano Catholic Church history maps out the role of the church in the Southwest following the Treaty of Guadalupe Hidalgo in 1848 when one million Mexican Catholics found themselves under the authority of the U.S. Catholic Church. European-born clergy from France, Germany, Spain, and later Ireland ministered to these people, now Mexican Americans, and a legacy of discrimination ensued. The legacy is traced through subsequent historical periods up to the 1970s when Chicano Catholics, priests, sisters, and laity openly challenged the Church for its overtly racist actions. Jay Dolan's and Gilberto Hinojosa's *Mexican Americans and the Catholic Church, 1900–1965* (1994) is particularly useful here. My own work (2004) on *Las Hermanas*—a national organization of Latina Catholic feminists—brings to light the efforts of Chicanas and Latinas to challenge the patriarchy and Eurocentrism of the Church. The organization's efforts to create church beyond the boundaries of the institution provide a model of feminist strategies for transforming patriarchal religion and healing the wounds it has caused.

Liberation theology always receives attention as a catalyst for change in both Catholic and mainline Protestant denominations. A brief overview of the revolutionary struggles that ground the theology explains its extensive influence on the global church. Exposing the students to the writings of Gustavo Gutierrez, Leonardo Boff, and Juan Luis Segundo and others provides only a glimpse of a central part of Christian history. The film *Romero* helps the students to visualize and better understand the social context of liberation theology and its ongoing challenge to all people of faith.

In order to explore the role of Protestantism in Chicano history, I utilize the works of Daisy Machado, Paul Barton, and David Maldonado. Arlene Sanchez Walsh's *Latino Pentecostal Identity* (2003) is sure to strengthen and diversify this part of the course. A group like Victory Outreach has influenced Chicano communities significantly, and its success in improving the lives of ex-gang members and drug addicts cannot be ignored. Many of the students have family members or friends who have benefited from Victory Outreach. Gender again receives attention here when we consider the growth of Latino Pentecostal churches. Ana Adams's "Perception Matters: Pentecostal Latinas in Allentown, Pennsylvania" (2002) highlights the advantages and disadvantages for women in these tightly knit faith communities.

My third objective is to expose students to how women are transforming male-dominated aspects of Christianity. We explore Latina feminist theology, for example, through Protestant and Catholic Latina theologians, who are making significant contributions to rethinking Christianity from the perspective of racialized women. I find that starting with a basic discussion of "feminism" helps to address the resistance that many students have toward the term. After asking them to define the word, it is clear that many have internalized the negative connotations of feminism that the media have fostered. Ironically, as we get further into the discussion, it becomes clear that they support the praxis of equality and self-determination for women. Explaining my own identity as a feminist, and the indebtedness I owe to the feminist movement, frequently inspires them to rethink their assumptions about it, and it encourages a process of critical thinking. I highly recommend the first text on Latina theology by Latinas, Ada María Isasi-Díaz and Yolanda Tarango's 1988 book, *Hispanic Women: Prophetic Voice in the Church*, and a more recent anthology entitled *A Reader in Latina Feminist Theology*. For the sake of time, I focus on the articles in the latter text by Rodriguez, Guardiola-Sáenz, Machado, Lozano-Díaz, and Pineda-Madrid.

I also want students to understand how Chicanas are retrieving cultural archetypes for the empowerment of women and the reconstruction of culture. One of the primary archetypes in Chicano culture is the *curandera*, the wise healer, usually an elder, who knows the medicinal properties of plants, corporeal energy sites, and/or ways to mediate with the dead. *Curanderas* understand healing as a holistic process. Many of the students have internalized Western ignorance regarding *curanderismo* and have been socialized to think of *curanderismo* as witchcraft. Much of this misunderstanding also comes from their own families. In reality, however, *curanderismo* is a complex healing system utilizing natural medicines that has its own theoretical, diagnostic, and therapeutic aspects. *Curanderismo* addresses psychological, spiritual, and physical ailments as a unified whole, and it draws from Spanish, Indigenous, Arabic, and Greek healing methods and medicinal knowledge. *Curanderismo*, by Robert T. Trotter II and Juan Antonio Chavira (1997), offers an accessible analysis of the tradition in South Texas and can be adapted to *curanderismo* in an urban context. The authors describe the various types of healers or specialists and clarify the complexity of the numerous healing methods utilized. When possible, I invite a healer to speak to the class. The numerous *botánicas* in the Los Angeles area also make it possible to require students to visit selected sites in order to demystify the material culture used in ritual practices. The article by Luis León titled "Soy una Curandera y Soy una Católica" sheds light on the work of a *curandera* in East Los Angeles. Her profile can also be used to exemplify *Nepantla* spirituality.

Chicana/o writers frequently use the archetype of the *curandera* as a powerful symbol of healing, to underscore the value of Indigenous knowledge and the use of intuitive and cognitive skills, and to challenge gender norms. As Chicana literary theorist Tey Diana Rebolledo explains in *Infinite Divisions*, "Thus, like the Virgin, the *curandera* has the capacity for intervention between earth and spirit, but her world is a much more equal one, where accepting patriarchal rule is not the norm" (1993: 195). Assigning a novel that includes *curanderismo* can also offer a closer look into a tradition that remains shrouded in mystery for many students. The novels *Bless Me Ultima* by Rudolfo Anaya (1994) and *So Far From God* by Ana Castillo (1993) can be considered as classics in Chicana/o literature that revisit the role of the *curandera*. A sampling of other novels addressing the traditional and transformative nature of Chicano religiosity and spirituality include *La Maravilla* by Antonio Vea (1993), *Thirteen Senses* by Victor Villaseñor (2001), *The Flower in the Skull* by Kathleen Alcalá (1998), and *The Miraculous Day of Amalia Gómez* by John Rechy (1991). These are just a few examples of the numerous creative works by Chicano and Chicana writers who address religion and culture, and in which one can also find multiple elements that point to the different layers of healing discussed above.

This course evolves differently each semester, depending on the mix of students and the issues they identify as deserving more time and attention. Requiring students to maintain learning journals in response to questions and issues raised in class challenges them to engage more deeply with the material. It also encourages the quiet students to articulate their thoughts. Having the students present summaries of readings has not worked, as it discourages the others from reading the materials themselves. Small group discussions lasting 10 to 15 minutes on specific text-based questions, followed by a class discussion, seems to work the best. Some semesters I require a 10- to 12-page research paper on a specific topic of the student's choosing. They must also summarize their research for the entire class. I try to integrate small group discussion, lecture, and visual aids in each class session. A new website, www .Chicanoart.org, designed by art historian Sybil Venegas, looks very promising as an aid to teaching about Indigenous cosmology and *nepantla* spirituality in contemporary Chicano/a art.

At the end of the course, I ask the students to write a short essay on what, for them, was most beneficial to them in the course. Many students find empowering the concept of *nepantla* spirituality, as it validates their participation in both Indigenous and Christian traditions. In essence it validates their search for reconciliation between the oppressor and the oppressed, in which that process helps to heal the felt imbalances in their identity. As one student stated:

> I feel more at peace with myself now, there is nothing wrong with me trying to practice indigenismo. . . . I don't see myself as only Catholic. . . . I don't want to leave Catholicism but, I have always felt a strong connection to the earth, to herbs, and especially to the ocean, I now feel at peace being in the middle, being in *nepantla*.

Or as another student wrote:

> *Nepantla spirituality* is a useful concept because many people feel that the Catholicism alone will not satisfy their spiritual needs. *Nepantla* is the common ground, where both Indigenous and Christian religions can meet.

To be in *nepantla* is to exist on the border, on the boundaries of cultures and social structures, where life is in constant motion, in constant fluidity. To be in *nepantla* also means to be in the center of things, to exist in the middle places where all things come together. The center point is a point of balance, a point of equilibrium or, as discussed earlier, a place of chaos and confusion. Border people, *las mestizas y los mestizos*, constantly live in *nepantla*. We can never leave the middle space, as that is where we were created, in the meeting of cultures and religions. How we choose to occupy the middle space is crucial. *Nepantla* spirituality offers a choice. One can choose to exclude or to include, to remain fragmented or to heal. Overall, I try to have fun with the subject matter. Mexicano/Chicano religiosity is full of magic and mystery, and it is rich in material culture. Faith has sustained the majority of my student's families, but religion has been passed on without room for questioning. I emphasize that questioning one's beliefs leads to self-knowledge, and self-knowledge leads to healing.

Syllabus: CHS 350: Chicanas/os and Religion in Society: Traditions and Transformation

Dr. Lara Medina

Course Description

This course examines the role of religion in Chicana/o history and culture with an emphasis on Mesoamerican cosmology, Mexican Catholics and Protestants, liberation theology, *indigenismo* and Chicana feminist spirituality. Attention will be given to the diversity of Chicano/a religious identities; religion and social change; popular religiosity; and Chicana/o spiritualities and ritual.

Objectives

1. Students will obtain a broad understanding of the diversity of religious perspectives and experiences within Chicano/a communities.
2. Students will obtain a basic understanding of Mexican ondigenous spirituality that provides a framework for contemporary Chicano/a religiosity.
3. Students will be exposed to how Chicanas are challenging and transforming patriarchal or male-dominated religion within Chicano culture to empower themselves as women and to reconstruct Chicano mythology and culture.
4. Students will enhance their public speaking and oral presentation skills.
5. Students will develop further their research and writing skills.

Required Texts

> Timothy Matovina and Gary Riebe-Estrella, eds. 2002. *Horizons of the Sacred: Mexican Catholic Traditions in the U.S.* Ithaca, NY: Cornell University Press.
>
> Robert T. Trotter II and Juan Antonio Chavira. 1997. *Curanderismo* Athens: University of Georgia Press.
>
> Reader compiled by professor, or use Luis León. 2004. *La Llorona's Children: Religion, Life, and Death in the U.S.-Mexican Borderlands* Berkeley: University of California Press.

Requirements

Students are required to: (1) attend class sessions having completed reading assignments, (2) contribute to class discussions and small-group assignments, (3) present to the class one reading for analysis and discussion and submit a two-page summary of your presentation, (4) maintain a learning journal throughout the semester, (5) complete one midterm exam, (6) construct and present an *ofrenda*, (7) write a two-page summary of the *ofrenda*, (8) attend a Day of the Dead event and submit a two-page written summary, and (9) complete one final exam.

Grade Distribution

> Class Attendance: = 50 pts. (Each absence is minus 5 pts.)
> Participation: = 50 pts.
> Learning Journal = 50 pts.
> Midterm = 100 pts.
> Ofrenda and written summary = 50 pts. each = 100 pts.
> Attend a Day of the Dead event and written summary = 50 pts.
> Final exam = 100 pts.
> Total possible pts. = 500 pts.

Your final grade will be determined by the total number of points you accumulate in the course:

600-575=A	376-350=C
574-550=A−	399-375=C+
549-500=B+	349-325=C−
499-449=B	326-300=D+
448-400=B−	299-250=D
249-200=D−	199-below=F

Midterm and Final Exam: Exams will be two or three essay questions.

Learning Journal

You are required to keep a journal in a notebook separate from your class notes. These journals will consist of spontaneous, informal writings in response to questions or ideas raised in class. I will regularly ask you to write in your journals during class time, so bring your notebooks to class. Your journals will not be graded, but you will receive credit for turning them in. Incomplete journals will receive less than full credit.

Ofrenda Project

Construct and present to the class a symbolic offering in honor of *your life* according to the Mexicano/Chicano tradition of altar making. This will be explained further in class. You must also submit a two-page typed summary of your *ofrenda,* explaining why you chose the specific symbols. Or you may construct an *ofrenda* in honor of someone who has died. You may choose to honor a family member, friend, public figure, or event that caused the death of many people. You must also submit a two-page typed summary of your *ofrenda,* explaining why you chose the specific symbols. You will be assigned a presentation date during the last two weeks of class.

Class Schedule

This schedule is subject to change. Attendance is mandatory, so stay informed of possible changes.

WEEK 1: WHO ARE U.S. LATINOS/AS? TERMINOLOGY AND DEMOGRAPHICS

- Reading

  Miguel A. De La Torre and Edwin David Aponte, eds. 2001. U.S. Hispanics: Who are They? In *Introducting Latino/a Theologies.* Maryknoll, NY: Orbis.

WEEK 2: CHICANO/A RELIGIOUS EXPERIENCES AND IDENTITIES

- Reading

  Ruben Martinez. 1992. God Is Alive. *LA Weekly,* July 31–August 6: 14
  Vicki Larson. 1990. The Flight of the Faithful. *Hispanic,* November: 18–20
  Yolanda Tarango. 1990. Hispanic Woman and Her Role in the Church. *New Theology Review,* Vol. 3 (4): 56–61.
  Gloria Anzaldúa. 1987. La Conciencia de la Mestiza. In *Borderlands: La Frontera.* San Francisco: Spinsters/Aunt Lute.

• On Reserve

Jeanette Rodriguez. 2002. Latina Activists: Toward an Inclusive Spirituality of Being in the World. In *A Reader in Latina Feminist Theology*, eds.
María Pilar Aquino, Daisy Machado, and Jeanette Rodriguez, pp. 114–
130. Austin: University of Texas Press.

Ana Adams. 2002. Perception Matters: Pentecostal Latinas in Allentown,
Pennsylvania. In *A Reader in Latina Feminist Theology*, eds. María Pilar
Aquino, Daisy Machado, and Jeanette Rodriguez, pp. 98–113. Austin:
University of Texas Press.

Tomas Bamat. 1992. Will Latin America Become Protestant? *Maryknoll*
(July): 10–17

Film: *Mexican Americans*

WEEK 3: CHICANO/A RELIGIOUS EXPERIENCES AND IDENTITIES

• On Reserve

Nora O. Lozano-Díaz. 2002. Ignored Virgen or Unaware Woman: A
Mexican American Protestant Reflection on the Virgen of Guadalupe.
In *A Reader in Latina Feminist Theology*, ed. María Pilar Aquino, Daisy
Machado, and Jeanette Rodriguez, pp. 204–216. Austin: University of
Texas Press.

Carla Trujillo. 1998. La Virgen de Guadalupe and Her Reconstruction in
Chicana Lesbian Desire. In *Living Chicana Theory*, ed. Carla Trujillo,
pp. 214–231. Berkeley: Third Woman Press.

WEEK 4: CHICANA/O INDIGEOUS ROOTS

• Readings/Films

David Carrasco. 1990. History and Cosmovision in Mesoamerican Religions. In *Religions of Mesoamerica*. Prospect Heights, Ill: Waveland.

Sylvia Marcos. 1995. The Sacred Earth. *Concilium: Third World Theology*,
eds. Leonardo Boff and Virgilio Elizondo (October): 27–37.

Miguel León-Portilla. 1993. Those Made Worthy by Divine Sacrifice: The
Faith of Ancient Mexico. In *South and Mesoamerican Native Spirituality*, ed. Gary H. Gossen, pp. 41–64. New York: Crossroad.

Film: *The Aztecs*

WEEK 5: CONQUEST/CONTACT AND ADAPTATION

• Readings/Films

David Carrasco. 1995. Jaguar Christians in the Contact Zone. In *Enig-
matic Powers: Syncretism with African and Indigenous Peoples' Religions
among Latinos*, eds. Anthony M. Stevens-Arroyo and Andres I. Pérez y

Mena, pp. 69–79. New York: Bildner Center for Western Hemisphere
Studies.

David Carrasco. 1990. Mesoamerica as a New World. In *Religions of Me-*
soamerica. Prospect Heights, IL: Waveland.

Yolanda Broyles-Gonzalez. 2002. Indigenizing Catholicism: Chicana/In-
dia/Mexicana Indigenous Spiritual Practices in Our Image. In *Chi-*
cana Traditions; Continuity and Change, eds. Norma E. Cantú and Olga
Nájera-Ramírez, pp. 15–33. Urbana: University of Illinois Press.

Film: *El Santuario*

WEEK 6: OUR LADY OF GUADALUPE/TONANZTIN

- On Reserve

Jeanette Rodriguez. 1994. *Our Lady of Guadalupe: Faith and Empower-*
ment among Mexican-American Women, pp. 1–46. Austin: University of
Texas.

Timothy Matovina. 2002. Companion in Exile. In *Horizons of the Sacred:*
Mexican Traditions in U.S. Catholicism, ed. Timothy Matovina and
Gary Riebe-Estrella, pp. 17–40. Ithaca, NY: Cornell University Press.

Film: *Flores Para Guadalupe*.

WEEK 7: RELIGION AND SEXUALITY

- On Reserve

Karen Torjesen. 1995. *When Women Were Priests*, pp. 203–223. San Francisco: Harper and Row.

Virginia Marie Bouvier. 2001. *Women and the Conquest of California, 1542–*
1840, pp. 108–139. Tucson: University of Arizona Press.

Fabiola Santiago. 2003. Our Legacy of Silence. *Latina* (February): 102–
106.

Sandra Cisneros. 1996. Guadalupe the Sex Goddess. In *Goddess of the*
Americas, ed. Ana Castillo, pp. 46–51. New York: Riverhead.

WEEK 8: CHICANO CATHOLIC AND PROTESTANT HISTORY

- Reading

Roberto R. Treviño. 2002. *The Handbook of Texas Online*. Retrieved July
23, 2002. Available at http://www.tsha.utexas.edu/handbook/online/
articles/view/MM/pqmcf.html

Cesar Chavez. 1968. The Mexican-American and the Church. *El Grito* 1
(summer): 9–12.

Gastón Espinosa. 1999. El Azteca: Francisco Olazábal and Latino Pentecostal Charisma, Power, and Faith Healing in the Borderlands. *Journal*
of the American Academy of Religion 67 (September): 597–616.

Paul Barton. Mexican-American Methodists Involvement in the Chicano/a and Farm Worker Movements. Unpublished paper.

WEEK 9: POPULAR RELIGIOSITY

• Readings/Films

Kay Turner. 1982. Mexican American Home Altars: Towards Their Interpretation. *Aztlán* 13 (spring/fall): 309–326.
Karen Mary Davalos. 2002. "The Real Way of Praying": The Via Crucis, *Mexicano* Sacred Space, and the Architecture of Domination. In *Horizons of the Sacred: Mexican Traditions in U.S. Catholicism*. eds. Timothy Matovina and Gary Riebe-Estrella, 41–68. Ithaca, NY: Cornell University Press.
Film: *The Soul of the City*

WEEK 10: *DÍAS DE LOS MUERTOS* OR DAYS OF THE DEAD

• Readings/Films

Lara Medina and Gilbert R. Cadena. 2002. Días de los muertos: Public Ritual, Community Renewal, and Popular Religion in Los Angeles. In *Horizons of the Sacred: Mexican Traditions in U.S. Catholicism,* eds. Timothy Matovina and Gary Riebe-Estrella, 69–94. Ithaca, NY: Cornell University Press.
Slides on Days of the Dead in Los Angeles
Film: *La Ofrenda* by Lourdes Portillo

Midterm: Take home

WEEK 11: *DÍAS DE LOS MUERTOS* OR DAYS OF THE DEAD CONTINUED

Construct *ofrenda* for Class Presentation. Attend Day of the Dead Event on Nov. 1 or Nov. 2.

WEEK 12 CURANDERISMO

• Reading

Robert T. Trotter II and Juan Antonio Chavira. 1997. *Curanderismo.* Athens: University of Georgia Press.

WEEK 13 CURANDERISMO: HISTORICAL AND CONTEMPORARY HEALERS

• Reading

Luis León. 2002. Soy una Curandera y Soy una Católica. In *Horizons of the Sacred.*

WEEKS 14 AND 15: PRESENTATION OF OFRENDA PROJECTS

Final Exam

ADDITIONAL BIBLIOGRAPHY

Alcalá, Kathleen. 1998. *The flower in the skull*. San Francisco: Chronicle Books.
Allen, Paula Gunn. 1992. *The sacred hoop: Recovering the feminine in American Indian traditions*. Boston: Beacon.
Anaya, Rudolfo A. 1994. *Bless me, Ultima*. New York: Warner.
Burkhart, Louise. 1993. The Cult of the Virgin of Guadalupe in Mexico. In *South and Meso-American Native spirituality: From the cult of the feathered serpent to the theology of liberation*, ed. Gary H. Gossen, in collaboration with Miguel Léon Portilla, 197–228. New York: Crossroad.
Castillo, Ana. 1993. *So far from God: A novel*. New York: W.W. Norton.
Comstock, Gary David, and Susan E. Henking, eds. 1997. *Que(e)rying religion*. New York: Continuum.
Dolan, Jay P., and Gilberto M. Hinojosa, eds. 1994. *Mexican Americans and the Catholic Church, 1900–1965*. Notre Dame, IN.: University of Notre Dame.
Elizondo, Virgilio P. 1997. *Guadalupe, mother of the new creation*. Maryknoll: Orbis.
Lafaye, Jacques. 1976. *Quetzalcóatl and Guadalupe: The formation of Mexican national consciousness, 1531–1813*. Chicago: University of Chicago Press.
Medina, Lara. 2004. *Las Hermanas: Chicana/Latina religious-political activism in the U.S. Catholic Church*. Philadelphia: Temple University Press.
Moraga, Cherríe. 1993. *The last generation: Prose and poetry*. Boston: South End.
Poole, Stafford. 1995. *Our Lady of Guadalupe: The origins and sources of a Mexican national symbol, 1531–1797*. Tucson: University of Arizona Press.
Portillo, Lourdes and Susana Muñoz. 1988. "La Ofrenda: days of the dead," video. Santa Monica, CA.
Rechy, John. 1991. *The miraculous day of Amalia Gómez: A novel*. New York: Arcade.
Sánchez Walsh, Arlene M. 2003. *Latino Pentecostal identity: evangelical faith, self, and society*. New York: Columbia University Press.
Véa, Alfredo Jr. 1993. *La maravilla*. New York: Dutton.
Villaseñor, Victor. 2001. *Thirteen senses: A memoir*. New York: Rayo.

PART IV

Through the Study
of Shamanisms

9

Shamanism as a Point of Departure: Two Courses on Christianity and Healing

Amanda Porterfield

My two courses on religious healing begin with discussions of shamanism, presented as a type of ritual practice. In the subsequent sections of both courses, we explore historical changes in beliefs and practices associated with Christian healing. We focus on Christianity because my particular research interests prepare me to direct discussion of the role of healing in the historical development of that tradition more effectively than in the history of other religions. But other religious traditions would work just as well in this section of the course devoted to historical study, and instructors with other areas of expertise might revise this section of the course accordingly.

I define shamans as performers who interact with spirits, and who attempt to manage the influence that people believe spirits have in their lives and environments.[1] Defined broadly, shamanism can be found in many different cultures and historical periods, and it can be considered one of the most long-lasting and widespread types of religious practice. The term "shaman" first appeared in English at the end of the seventeenth century as a name for religious specialists, or "priest-doctors," among Asian tribes. In the eighteenth and nineteenth centuries, Western ethnographers extended the term to include the medicine men observed among North American Indian tribes. Some scholars have cited similarities between Siberian and North American healers as evidence of the Asian origin of American Indians.[2] Others have broadened the term to include all kinds of healers, prophets, and mediums who diagnosed ills and prescribed remedies by embodying and interacting with spirits. Some scholars have focused on the ecstatic trance states experienced by shamans, and yet others have tried to describe the social functions of shamanism. In recent years, the terms "shaman" and "shamanism" have come to be used by some practitioners of religious healing themselves. No longer exclusive to the parlance of outside observers, these terms have been taken up by New Age practitioners and other revivalists of tribal art eager to emulate indigenous healers and their mastery of spiritual power.

Shamanism's appeal can be explained, at least in part, by its effectiveness in promoting human strength and healing. Shamanic performances stimulate feelings of confidence, physical vitality, and relief from stress. While often concentrated on an individual patient, the benefits of shamanic performance also extend to a larger community. Onlookers get caught up in the drama of shamanic performances, and in the feelings of communal bonding they elicit. Shamanic activity contributes to the construction and support of cultures that hold people together in social groups. Thus, in addition to the immediate effects of increasing people's sense of control over their bodies and environments, shamanic performances help sustain loyalty to the spirits represented in sacred stories and ritual practices, and to the social groups associated with those spirits, stories, and practices.

Shamanism, Stress, and Social Order

Shamanism is a good place to begin a course on religious healing because it serves as a useful model for conceptualizing the general phenomenon of religious healing and for comparing different instances of religious healing with one another. Defined as a ritual practice that represents the hidden forces influencing human life and material reality, shamanism helps us discern elements of ritual practice and dramatic performance in many instances of healing. Thus appeal to shamanism as a conceptual model calls attention to the ritual performance involved in Pentecostalism and other forms of modern faith healing and even in medical procedures in which the symbolic and dramatic dimensions of healing often go unnoted. White coats, stethoscopes, medical jargon, and antiseptic smells may not represent "spirits" in any customary religious sense, but they are manifestations of otherwise invisible power, and they can function much like the symbols of social authority and individual transformation wielded by shamans.

At the University of Wyoming, I developed an upper-division undergraduate course on religious healing using a lecture-discussion format. Later, at Florida State University, I developed a graduate course on the same topic, but in the format of a research seminar. In both courses, shamanism served as the point of departure for comparative analysis of a variety of different forms of religious healing and for discussion of how symbolism and ritual practice can contribute to biological processes of healing. Though these general lines of investigation are common to both the undergraduate course and the graduate seminar, the kinds of interests and questions that undergraduates bring to a course on religious healing differ in important ways from the kinds of interests and questions that pre-professional students bring to a graduate seminar. Likewise, my goals as instructor in the undergraduate course differ in equally important ways from those as leader of a graduate seminar.

In many cases, undergraduates bring expectations for resolving personal questions about religious healing to the course. As their instructor, I do my best to help them think through these questions, even as I focus more systematically on helping them develop skills in critical thinking that they can build on in other academic courses and in their intellectual lives. I don't ask them to leave their religious concerns at the classroom door, but I do try to make it clear that our primary job, as a class, is to study a list of readings on the topic of religious healing, develop some understanding of the cognitive, emotional, biological, and social aspects of religious healing, and become familiar with specific characteristics of religious healing in a number of different cultural settings. When students introduce personal events and questions into discussion, I try to address them in the same spirit of intellectual curiosity and fair-minded inquiry that I hope students are learning to bring to the study of religious healing in other cultures and in the lives of other people. For undergraduates, then, the course offers an intellectual approach they might use in exploring their own personal questions about religion, sickness, and suffering. But more fundamentally, it is designed to help them develop an intellectual understanding of religious healing through a combination of academic approaches—comparative, historical, sociological, psychological, and biological.

Graduate students may also have personal questions about religion, suffering, and healing, but they tend to be more accustomed to thinking about religions as cultural symbol systems than are undergraduates, and they are more invested in mastering a range of interpretive approaches that involve scrutiny of historical and scientific evidence that can be employed in systematic analyses of religious phenomena. Graduate students are more self-conscious (and should be) about the obligations involved in joining a field of study constructed and sustained by a community of scholars. Their investment in training for membership in that community carries expectations of contributing to a larger enterprise of learning. They understand that, even though personal religious questions may help motivate an individual to become such a contributor, the larger enterprise of academic work addresses topics of more general interest and aims to discover findings useful to other scholars.

Though using the concept of shamanism as a point of departure for critical inquiry into religious healing in both courses, I expect graduate students to investigate that concept more strenuously On the assumption that graduate students like the idea that everything is open to inquiry, I begin their seminar with a critical investigation of the implications involved in using shamanism as the conceptual point of departure for the course. This investigation sends a message about my respect for critical inquiry and makes clear at the outset that I am just as interested in lively discussion of the methods of investigating religious healing as I am about their mastery of information on the topic.

In the undergraduate course, on the other hand, I ask students to take the usefulness of shamanism as a conceptual model for religious healing somewhat on faith. My methods and model for conceptualizing religious healing are a fundamental part of the course content I expect undergraduates to learn. I don't expect them to investigate the conceptual underpinnings of the course, as I do graduate students, as a way of getting the course started. I want to build on the momentum generated by the interests that led them to enroll in the course, and do not want to frustrate and lose them at the outset. If we get around to interrogating the course's conceptual structure later, I will be pleased, but that is not the first priority. Of course, overlap between advanced undergraduates and beginning graduate students is often considerable, and the lengths to which any particular class can go in investigating the methodologies relevant to the study of religious healing, while at the same time accumulating knowledge about cultures and histories of the topic, will depend, as so much does, on the students and their interests, talents, and previous education.

In both classes, as we work toward a shared understanding of what shamanism means, we move further into the analysis of religious healing by exploring both the biological and social effects of shamanic performance. We consider the role that symbolic procedures can play in stimulating cognitive, emotional, and biological processes that alleviate stress, make people feel stronger, and even slow or reverse the progress of disease. We consider literature on the placebo effect, looking at theories that explain religious healing, and shamanism in particular, in terms of symbols, and symbolic procedures, that generate expectations of power, healing, and health. We also discuss the meaning of the term "placebo" as it has changed over time, and consider recent arguments challenging the viability and usefulness of the term.

We also look more closely at the social settings in which shamanic performances occur, focusing on the role that such performances play in constructing communities, and on the role these communities play in shaping expectations, moods, and behavior. In the performances they conduct, shamans expel malevolent spirits from suffering individuals and invite beneficent spirits to extend their powers to relieve sickness and misfortune. The spirits that shamans invoke represent the vitalities of particular communities and the strength of ancestral taboos, totems, and kinship structures. For individuals whose bodies and life stories become centers of social attention in shamanic performance, engagement with these symbols of communal life can generate extraordinary feelings of power and determination.

Though uplifting in many cases, this engagement with the symbols of communal life can have coercive effects. Religious healing works as much to strengthen a group as it does to relieve individual suffering, and conformity to collective rules of feeling and behavior has often been part of the social responsibility entailed in religious healing. The strengthening or restoration of group integrity is such a powerful feature of shamanism that shamanic techniques have sometimes been employed to scapegoat individuals rather than heal them. For example, the early-twentieth-century Danish ethnographer Rasmussen reported that Inuit shamans attempted to reverse bad luck in hunting

by pressuring women to confess to—and presumably accept punishment for—
secret miscarriages.[3]

Healing in the History of Christianity

In the second sections of both courses, as noted earlier, we explore historical
changes in beliefs and practices associated with Christian healing. To apply
some of what we learned in the first section, I begin the second one by asking
students to explore the implications of considering Jesus as a shaman. In the
undergraduate course especially, where I am introducing most students to
historical literature about the ministry of Jesus for the first time, I spend a
good deal of time developing the distinction between Jesus the historical person
in first-century Galilee and Jesus Christ as an object of faith for twenty centuries. I ask students to look at New Testament accounts of the exorcisms and
other healings conducted by Jesus as historians do, and I invite them to explore
theories about these healings that historians and textual critics have developed
in sorting through the numerous layers of historical evidence in New Testament accounts. I focus on theories that help us weigh the pros and cons of
conceptualizing Jesus as a shaman.

This historical discussion of the healing ministry of Jesus sets the stage
for moving forward in time to consider some of the ways in which Jesus as
Christ has functioned as an object of faith and agent of healing for countless
believers. In shifting attention from consideration of the historical ministry of
Jesus to his presence as Christ in the minds and hearts of believers, we enter
into vast terrains of Christian history characterized by a multitude of images,
ideas, and ritual practices across many centuries and in many different places,
all of which are associated with the person of Christ, and with his different
understanding of healing and saving power.

In working through some of the major turning points of this history, we
consider, in sequence, some of the ways Christian healing changed under the
influence of Neo-Platonic philosophies; with the spread of Christianity into
Europe and Asia, in relation to differences between Eastern and Western
churches; as a result of various reform movements in the early modern period;
as a result of the impact of modern science; and through the more recent
modern expansion of Christianity in Africa, Asia, and the Americas. We build
upon a lesson from the first section of the course, that performances of religious healing often have a social function, by looking for changes in Christian
belief and practice that reflect larger currents of social unrest and development.
We look, in particular, for ways that Christians have utilized religious healing
to negotiate social unrest, initiate social reform, and develop new strategies for
constructing community. For example, in examining the popularity of new
forms of Christian healing in southern Africa during the nineteenth and twentieth centuries, we focus on the infusion of traditional practices into Christian
healing. New combinations of Christian and indigenous forms of healing not

only represented the suffering and injustice of colonialist and apartheid situ-ations, but also contributed to social reform and to the development of political leadership in Africa.

Native Americans have also combined traditional healing practices with Christianity, and interpreted the healing messages of Christianity in light of sufferings endured as result of colonization. Although in many cases, conver-sion to Christianity coincided with missionary efforts to undermine Native cultures and force Western culture upon Native Americans, Native people de-veloped interpretations of Christianity that strengthened traditional commu-nity life, promoted individual vitality, and combated the social ills resulting from the imposition of Western culture.[4] To cite just one example from a mul-titude of Native American interpretations of Christianity, for participants in the Native American Church, Christian belief combines with traditional commit-ment to visionary experience in devotion to Jesus as the spirit of healing man-ifest in visions.

We also consider the historical interplay between Christianity and bio-medicine in world history. Conflicted at times, but often highly cooperative, this interplay has figured importantly in both traditions. For example, the or-igins, expansions, retractions, and transformations of hospitals contributed to the historical development of both medicine and Christianity. Beliefs about Christ as the Great Physician contributed to respect for physicians, as well as to the popularity and success of healing practices within Christianity. New developments in science often found their way into the language Christians used to describe their healing experiences and expectations, as in the case of modern Pentecostals, who often describe the healing work of the Holy Spirit as an invisible force or current not unlike electricity.

Pedagogical Strategies and Challenges

My goal as a teacher is to enable students to develop a combination of intel-lectual mastery and passionate curiosity that enables them to become clear thinkers and skilled investigators in their own right. A course is succeeding when students can summarize information and construct questions and ar-guments, with more confidence and skill than before the class. A course is succeeding when students are contributing to its momentum, and when there is a sense of discovery in the air. Thus in every class session, I give students some responsibility for defining issues and questions, and I make speak-ing up and speaking out as natural and easy as possible. At the same time, I work to keep us all focused on assigned readings and predefined topics, and I constantly press for insightful thinking, clear argument, and sound ev-idence.

In graduate seminars and in undergraduate classes with fewer than twenty students, two students start off discussion at the beginning of each class with short presentations that formulate questions for discussion based on the as-signed reading. We spend the rest of the class building on those questions in ways that connect to the points I bring for the class to consider, usually through a couple of mini-lectures introduced at appropriate junctures in the discussion. In larger undergraduate classes, I begin class with a mini-lecture that lays out the main point to be covered that day, and then ask students to respond, orally, to a series of questions designed to develop the implications of that point. In all classes, I aim to create an intellectual climate in which everyone in class is actively engaged in thinking and in taking ideas from one point to the next together as a class. When this happens, students leave class feeling, and rightly so, that they accomplished something.

With respect to the topic of religious healing, the main pedagogical challenge is to keep skeptics and true believers in conversation with each other in ways that advance the thinking of everyone in class. Some students are constantly drawn to the manipulative aspects of religious healing, and they see religious leaders as enhancing their own power by exploiting desires for healing among vulnerable people. Other students are drawn, with equal constancy, to the intense emotional dramas involved in religious healing, and they identify with the transformational power of healing stories and liturgies. Everybody learns when students on both sides express themselves clearly and forcefully, and when the class engages in comparative discussion of the merits of the two perspectives.

For students and for me, the most exciting aspect of the study of religious healing is the way the topic draws us into the nature of religious experience and practice. To take religious healing seriously, we have to think deeply and systematically about how religious experience and practice actually work. This effort requires a combination of empathic imagination and critical analysis that, to me, epitomizes the academic study of religion at its best.

Religion and Healing: Undergraduate Syllabus

Religious healing is a major topic of interest today. Religious people representing many faith traditions in many different parts of the world turn to prayer and other religious practices in the hope of finding healing for themselves and their loved ones. At the same time, a growing number of physicians and other health care professionals are taking seriously the positive effects that religious faith and practice can have in recovery and illness prevention, and in promoting relief from suffering, pain, and stress. This course will help you explore the implications of these current interests in religious healing through a wide-ranging survey of religious healing in a variety of different cultures and historical time periods.

The course begins with discussion of shamanism, a type of religious healing characterized by performances conducted by ritual specialists who interact with spirits, and manage spiritual power in order to stimulate health and well-being, and dispel sickness and misfortune. Shamanism serves as a point of departure for consideration of the social and biological aspects of religious healing, as well as for some of the many different cultural contexts in which religious healing occurs. The course investigates possible shamanic elements in modern medicine, surveys the role of healing in the history of Christianity, and explores the interplay between the history of Christianity and the history of medicine.

Course Objectives

Students who successfully complete this course will be able to:

- describe and compare several different forms of religious healing in particular cultural and historical contexts;
- explain some of the ways that religious belief and practice can reduce stress and stimulate the body's natural processes of healing;
- identify and describe several important developments in the history of Christian healing; and explain how religious healing can be understood in terms of religious experience and practice.

Required Readings

David R. Kinsley. 1995. *Health, Healing and Religion: A Cross Cultural Perspective*. Upper Saddle River, NJ: Prentice Hall.

Amanda Porterfield. 2005. *Healing in the History of Christianity*. New York: Oxford University Press.

Carol Laderman and Marina Roseman, ed. 1996. *The Performance of Healing*. New York: Routledge.

Schedule of Assignments

Week 1: Introduction and Overview

Weeks 2 and 3: Kinsley, *Health, Healing, and Religion*

Week 4: First paper due. Papers should compare and contrast shamanism with modern medicine, distinguishing those aspects of modern medicine that correspond with shamanism from other aspects of modern medicine that differ from shamanism.

Weeks 5—8: Porterfield, *Healing in the History of Christianity*

Week 9: Review and Essay Exam on *Healing in the History of Christianity*

Weeks 10—12: *Performance of Healing*, ed. Laderman and Roseman

Week 13: Second paper due. Papers should use one of the theoretical arguments about religious healing in the Laderman and Roseman anthology to develop a thesis explaining a particular expression of healing in the history of Christianity.

Week 14: Course wrap-up and review

Week 15: Comprehensive final exam

Religion and Healing: Graduate Seminar Syllabus

I ask graduate students to choose a topic for independent research at the beginning of the semester, and I work with them over the course of the semester as they develop individual research programs and papers. We reserve several sessions at the end of the seminar so that students can report on their research. I encourage topics that enable graduate students to explore healing in the context of religious traditions they are familiar with through previous academic coursework, especially if those traditions have not been covered in much depth during the main part of the seminar. A list of suggested research topics can be found in the graduate syllabus below

Course Description

Healing is an important area of research in religion. As an old and still almost universal phenomenon, religious healing is an ideal topic for comparative, cross-cultural analysis. It is also a useful focus for historians interested in religious belief and practice as a means of communal bonding and a means of negotiating social change. As a phenomenon that often interplays with medicine, healing is a good way to approach questions about the relation between religion and science, as well as questions about the role of religion in particular cultures. And as a topic that is currently receiving a good deal of attention from researchers interested in promoting religion as an aid to health care, healing offers an excellent focus for discussing therapeutic expectations of religion in American society and for discussing changing attitudes toward religion and spirituality in health care professions.

The seminar begins with discussion of shamanism as a type of religious healing, using shamanism as a model for thinking about the social, cognitive, and biological changes that healing can entail. Following discussion of shamanism in a variety of cultural contexts, we examine several theories about ritual practice that contribute to understanding how religious healing can work. We also spend considerable time thinking about healing in the history of Christianity, focusing on changing beliefs and practices within the history of Christian healing, the influence of indigenous cultures and other religious traditions on Christian healing, and the long history of interplay between Christianity and medicine.

In addition to common readings and class discussions, the seminar includes independent research. Each student will select a research topic at the beginning of the semester, present his or her research findings to the seminar toward the end of the semester, and submit a research paper.

Common Readings

David R. Kinsley. 1995. *Health, Healing, and Religion: A Cross-Cultural Perspective*. Upper Saddle River, NJ: Prentice-Hall.

Jerome D. Frank. 1961 (1993). *Persuasion and Healing: A Comparative Study of Psychotherapy*. Baltimore: Johns Hopkins University Press.

Carol Laderman and Marina Roseman, eds. 1996. *The Performance of Healing*. New York: Routledge.

Amanda Porterfield. 2005. *Healing in the History of Christianity*. New York: Oxford University Press.

Catherine Bell. 1992. *Ritual Theory, Ritual Practice*. New York: Oxford University Press.

Robert A. Orsi. 1996. *Thank You, St. Jude: Women's Devotion to the Patron Saint of Hopeless Causes*. New Haven, CT: Yale University Press.

Philip Jenkins. 2002. *The Next Christendom: The Coming of Global Christianity*. New York: Oxford University Press

Examples of Research Topics

- History of healing beliefs and practices among Latter Day Saints
- Therapeutic practices among American Buddhists in the Vipassana tradition
- Healing pilgrimages to shrines of Islamic saints in medieval India
- Competition among healing centers in the ancient Mediterranean world
- Disputes over the healing powers of religious icons in Greek Orthodoxy
- Christian hospitals in China
- Indigenous forms of healing within African Christianity
- Healing and communal bonding in the Lakota Sun Dance
- Comparative implications of Catholic, Pentecostal, and indigenous healing in Brazil

Class Schedule

Week 1: Introduction and Overview
Week 2: Kinsley, *Health, Healing and Religion*
Week 3: Frank, *Persuasion and Healing*
Weeks 4–5: Laderman and Roseman, *The Performance of Healing*
Weeks 6–8: Porterfield, *Healing in the History of Christianity*
Week 9: Bell, *Ritual Theory, Ritual Practice*
Week 10: Orsi, *Thank You, St. Jude*
Week 11: Jenkins, *The Next Christendom*
Week 12: Research presentations
Week 13: Research presentations
Week 14: Research presentations
Week 15: Research presentations
Research papers due in the week following the last seminar class.

ENDNOTES

1. I use the term *shaman* as an instance of what the sociologist Max Weber called an "ideal type." In other words, I use shaman and shamanism as generic categories covering many different cultural and historical instances. My purpose in using the term this way is to call attention to elements of ritual performance in religious healing, and to underlying similarities in the operations and effects of many different instances of religious healing.

2. For more detailed discussions of shamanism, see *Shamanism: A Reader*, ed. Graham Harvey (London: Routledge, 2003). Also see Daniel Merkur, *Becoming Half Hidden: Shamanism and Initiation among the Inuit* (Stockholm: Almqvist and Wiskell, 1985); Ake Hultkrantz, "Introduction: Ecological and Phenomenological Aspects of Shamanism," in *Studies in Lapp Shamanism*, ed. L. Backman (Stockholm: Almqvist and Wiksell, 1978); and Mircea Eliade, *Shamanism: Archaic Techniques of Ecstasy* (orig. 1954), trans. Willard R. Trask (New York: Harper & Row, 1959).

3. Knud Rasmussen, *Intellectual Culture of the Hudson Bay Eskimos: Report of the Fifth Thule Expedition, 1921–4* (Copenhagen: Gyldendals Forlagstrykkeri, 1930), 123–129.

4. See George E. Tinker, *Missionary Conquest: The Gospel and Native American Cultural Genocide* (Minneapolis: Fortress, 1993); Christopher Vecsey, *American Indian Catholics*, Vol. 1, *On the Padre's Trail*, and Vol. 2, *The Path of Kateri's Kin* (Notre Dame, IN: University of Notre Dame Press, 1996 and 1997).

10

Teaching about Shamanism and Religious Healing: A Cross-Cultural, Biosocial-Spiritual Approach

Michael Winkelman and Christopher Carr

This course addresses the healing and spiritual practices of shamans in the broader context of their roles as diviners, psychopomps, charismatic leaders, public ceremonial specialists, war leaders, intergroup mediators, and material and spiritual ecologists. As two anthropologists, our approach borrows from the classic perspectives of Eliade (1964) on shamanism, as well as Harner's (1990) concept of "core" shamanism. We distinguish (core) shamans from a universal manifestation of shamanistic healers—practitioners who use altered states of consciousness (ASC) to interact with the spirit world in order to heal and divine on behalf of their communities (Winkelman 1986a, 1990, 1992; see also Carr and Case 2005). Two basic approaches guide our pedagogy: one is cross-cultural and comparative; the other is interdisciplinary, specifically biopsychosocial. The cross-cultural, comparative approach involves examining shamanism in multiple traditional cultures and relative to other magicoreligious healing practices. Similarities and differences among various shamanistic traditions are identified, and the social conditions that are associated with them and that shape their particular forms are elucidated. The interdisciplinary, biopsychosocial approach attempts to understand universal aspects of shamanism from perspectives provided by biological, psychological, clinical, and spiritual models, and their relationships to social, cognitive, and ecological processes. This view helps to illustrate shamanistic healing as a part of the human heritage.

Process of Teaching the Course

Our process of teaching about shamanism has evolved over time, but it has always included a mixture of academic presentations and experiential activities:

Setting and Students. Our shamanism course is taught in academic settings, in the regular classroom, with largely academic content and by primarily academic methods. However, we also have presented similar concepts and materials in nonacademic contexts as "experiential seminars" or short courses. In both cases, we include activities designed to produce personal experiences of the shamanic worldview routinely produced in the context of shamanic practices. We use rituals to take students into experiential realms not customarily addressed in academia, guiding students in examination of their personal, subjective experiences. In this regard, our course pushes the edge of ordinary academic content and methods. Our students come from a nonprofessional and nonmedical audience, representing a broad spectrum of undergraduate academic disciplines. These students often seek shamanism as an aspect of their personal growth, and they include a somewhat disproportionate number who are unconventional in their lifestyles.

Pedagogies. We use a cross-cultural, comparative approach to foster understanding of the similarities underlying diverse manifestations of shamanic potentials. This approach provides a basis for etic, cross-culturally shared concepts of shamans, and illustrates the social and cultural factors responsible for producing the differences found around the world among shamanistic healers. Students read material about classic shamanic healers (e.g., ¡Kung Bushman n/um masters) and contemporary shamanistic healers (e.g., Mazatec *sabias* like Maria Sabina) to grasp the similarities and differences. A radical aspect of our pedagogy involves experiential activities and approaches, using participation in ritual to help students understand directly and in depth the cosmological, philosophical, religious, and spiritual concepts associated with shamanism. Since ritual is a manifestation of religion and worldview, engaging in ritual is a tangible way to learn the worldviews of non-Western cultures. Rituals potentially provide a way of learning how members of those other cultures learn those viewpoints. These experiential activities provide primary personal data for relating to readings, which include case studies of individual cultural traditions and individual healers. Together, the experiential activities and readings help the students cognitively grasp and directly experience shamanic concepts about the nature of mind, its structure and content, mind-body interactions, and spirit.

Learning Goals of the Course. We have a number of more traditional academic goals: (1) providing an understanding of the empirical basis for the concept of the shaman and the richness of individual shamanic traditions; (2) exploring cross-cultural diversity in shamanistic thought and practices, and the social factors producing differences in shamanistic activities; and (3) explaining the factors that have produced a worldwide manifestation of shamanistic phenomena. We want students to understand the cross-cultural similarities in core shamanism around the world, the socially patterned differences in manifestations of shamanistic healers, and the biological bases of shamanism. An equally primary course objective is to provide opportunities for directly experiencing shamanic realities and ASC; we see this as broadening student appreciation of and respect for non-Western cultures, as well as inducing an expanded view of the nature of the self.

Nontextual Resources. The course relies on a variety of nontextual resources, the most important being the shamanic experiences induced in experiential activities. Also, practitioners of different contemporary healing traditions with shamanistic influences are invited to speak to the class and are featured in videos. Other nontextual resources that reveal information about shamanism include a variety of shamanic paraphernalia (e.g., drums, smudge sticks, stones, sucking tubes) and artistic representations of shamans, their paraphernalia, and their cosmological formulations.

Regional Resources. We help illustrate the continuing importance of shamanistic healing traditions through local healers whom we invite as guest speakers. These include Native American healers, road men (Peyote Religion), and a variety of eclectic and cosmopolitan traditions that utilize ASC and other shamanistic practices.

Theoretical Issues in Course Design

Our approach explicitly draws on cross-cultural, biopsychosocial, evolutionary, interdisciplinary, social, and cultural perspectives. To illustrate:

1. We use ethnological research to establish both the universals of shamanism and the cultural differences in shamanistic practices (Winkelman 1986a, 1990, 1992). This cross-cultural approach provides a basis for examining social and cultural influences on shamanic practices and developing theoretical models of psychological healing needs embedded in a social-evolutionary framework.

2. The psychobiological bases of ASC provide a framework for understanding similarities in diverse shamanistic practices and the bases for healing and divination processes (Winkelman 1986b, 1996, 1997, 2000). This perspective places the experience and effects of shamanism in the context of ordinary biological processes and integrative psychobiological processes.

3. We use perspectives of physical and sociocultural evolution to provide an understanding of adaptive aspects of shamanic practices. Biological approaches reveal the roles of shamanism in human social and cognitive evolution and in terms of an evolved psychology, innate human dispositions used in shamanic practices (Winkelman 2002a, 2002b). A social evolutionary approach identifies subsistence influences and social processes transforming "core shamanism" of hunter-gatherer cultures into the varied shamanistic practices found world-

wide. This social evolutionary perspective illustrates that shamanic practices are not primitive in some absolute sense, but rather are the particular form in which human potentials adapted to the conditions of simpler subsistence practices and small-scale communities.

4. An interdisciplinary approach integrates nonanthropological perspectives to understanding the manifestations of the psyche in shamanistic practices. We particularly use perspectives from psychology, especially transpersonal, depth, Jungian, Buddhist, and consciousness theory, that enable an understanding of the phenomena of spirits and spiritual practices in terms of natural structures of human consciousness (Winkelman 2004) and neurotheology (Winkelman 2003). We maintain a neutral stance on the ontological reality of spirits, while emphasizing their empirical reality in human experience.

5. A cultural and social approach emphasizes understanding the interactions of cultural, social, biopsychological, and spiritual mechanisms in healing. Especially important are the dynamics of body-mind interactions that produce healing outcomes. We identify symbolic effects upon the body, psychosomatic reactions, and unifying psychosociobiological effects of metaphor as significant shamanistic healing processes.

Content about Shamanism. Our teaching about shamanism combines cross-cultural frameworks that reveal the structural constants of shamanism and other forms of shamanic healing with culture-specific information that provides richer descriptions of the practices in cultural context. We address the universal principles of shamanistic practices from the perspective of human biology, medicine, and psychology, illustrating the natural and empirical basis of these healing traditions.

Concepts of Healing. We emphasize shamanic healing as simultaneously biopsychosocial spiritual, addressing many levels of human well-being. This perspective is illustrated through a focus on classic concepts of healing. Such concepts reflect spiritual and physical conceptualizations that are social contexts with psychological and physical modalities that link the individual, community, and cosmos. Core shamanic concepts of disease, illness, and healing that we address include: soul loss/retrieval, power animal loss/retrieval, object intrusion/extraction, and possession/depossession. We explore these forms of illness and healing at the intersection of classic and modern conceptualizations of shamanism.

A primary shamanic illness concept is soul loss, which is the loss or injury of the personal essence of an individual. It is manifested in disharmony in life and feelings of disconnectedness from others. Soul recovery restores a sense of identity and emotional well-being through therapeutic processes involving the participation of the entire community, providing healing through enhanced social bonding. Loss of one's power animal, or animal spirit guardian, produces symptoms similar to soul loss, can lead to it, and is treated in similar ways.

An object intrusion is an energy or object that is sent to or "blown into" a person purposefully by an enemy or by a dark shaman hired by an enemy, or that is released upon another unconsciously by an angry person. Object intrusion becomes possible when one has lost one's power animal guardian. Intrusions are commonly removed by sucking, scooping, or pulling them out of the body.

Possession is the control of a person by spirits that produce changes in personality, consciousness, or awareness. In its negative guise, shamans treat possession as an illness. In its positive guise, possession is a quality of some shamanistic healers, particularly the mediums of more complex societies. There, possession is used to engage spirits in diagnosis, healing, self-development, personal expression, intragroup mediation, and professional empowerment.

Cosmology and Epistemology. We characterize shamanic cosmology and epistemology through a variety of approaches, an especially important one being direct experience based on drumming and shamanic journeying. Although the common cross-cultural elements of shamanic cosmologies can be described to students, an equally compelling and complementary approach is to allow students to experience these elements directly for themselves. Art is another medium for exemplifying shamanic cosmologies and includes various representations of the three levels of the shamans' worlds, the four directions, the world axis in its many forms, and the many beings that inhabit the shamans' worlds. A fundamental shamanic epistemology that differs from that of modern science has been characterized as the "spirit hypothesis." We emphasize accepting the empirical reality of spirit experience while maintaining a critical attitude about their ontological reality. We directly address questions about the nature and realities of spirits from a number of perspectives, including an approach that naturalizes spirits as normal phenomena of human consciousness. This involves the necessary and inevitable projection of the human self and cognitive and emotional capacities into the unknown (Winkelman 2004). Addressing spirits from this perspective provides a framework for understanding spirits as representations of human psychological dynamics—sometimes repressed complexes of the unconscious that represent important information for psychological integration and healing.

Gender. We address the role of gender in shamanism from the perspectives provided by systematic cross-cultural research. This reveals that although core shamans are primarily males, females are generally allowed to practice prior to and following childbearing years. This restriction is viewed in light of the potential damage to the fetus that could result from the nature of the ASCs induced. We also address the contrast of shamans and mediums, the latter being primarily females. The cross-gendered status often ascribed to shamans is challenged, with the male transgendered activities being more likely associated with mediums.

Pluralism. We embrace both restrictive and pluralistic concepts of shamanism within the context provided by systematic cross-cultural research and the social factors associated with different forms of shamanistic healers (core shamans, shaman/healers, mediums, and healers). This provides a useful ped-

agogical function in distinguishing core shamans from a variety of other shamanistic healers to whom the term shaman has been overextended. By re-
vealing the socioeconomic determinants of the different forms of shamanistic
healers, factors producing variation in shamanistic practices can be examined
and analyzed. Within this context of the socioeconomic differences in practices,
we address issues of structural violence and the destruction of shamanic practices through political integration, class warfare, colonialism, and other forms
of repression associated with the development of state political organizations.

Interaction between Traditions. Our course examines a number of interactions of modern Western traditions with the shamanic traditions. We explore
recent trends in integrative medicine that combine traditional shamanic practices with biomedicine, particularly research on alternative and complementary
medicine, which helps illuminate the physiological and neurobiological basis
for the efficacy of shamanic healing. Another integration we consider involves
historical and contemporary relations of Buddhist psychology with shamanism. In general, we examine contemporary healing practices that, through
elucidating the dimensions common between them and shamanistic healing,
help one understand both.

Distinctive Features That Could Be Adapted to Other Contexts. We teach students specific tools that derive from shamanism and related psychotherapeutic
methods with the intent that students might apply them in their own lives for
self-help, personal growth, and intellectual growth. (1) Guided imagery is used
to simulate shamanic journeying and to create and explore nonordinary realms
where the student can reduce stress, gain insight into and solve problems,
resolve conflicts with others, consult with personal teachers, and connect with
sources of power and well-being. (2) Music is used to stimulate visualizations
of realms where the above work can take place and to simulate soul flight
without an out-of-body component. Richard Wagner's *Lohengrin* has worked
well to produce an empowering place, as has Ralph Vaughn Williams's *The
Lark Ascending* for simulating soul flight. (3) Spiritual dimensions of nature
are explored by helping students learn to quiet and center their minds and
focus on communicating with trees, rocks, animals, and other elements of
nature. (4) The Lakota Sioux method of rock reading is used to develop personal
intuition and to gain insights useful in solving problems.

Unique Problematic Issues

We have discovered two general aspects of the course that are problematic, one
related to what some Native Americans view as appropriation of their exclusive
cultural rights to shamanism. The other concerns the nature of the students
attracted to the course.

Some Native Americans perceive shamanistic practices as Native American cultural property and feel that "white" people (European Americans) do
not have a right to engage in such activities. The popular perception that sha-

manism is a Native American religion presents problems for those who wish to practice and teach *core* shamanism. We want to be clear that we are not advocating appropriation of Native American practices. Where there are such sensitivities among local groups, it is advisable to avoid using Native American materials to exemplify shamanistic practices. A focus on core shamanic activities, with examples from different traditions, helps distinguish core shamanism from contemporary Native American spiritual practices. Cross-cultural approaches and a focus on core shamanism help establish that certain fundamental shamanistic practices are not the property of any particular tradition, but rather are universal activities that have been particularized by different premodern societies.

The questions about cultural appropriation can additionally be addressed by presenting information about the ancient roots of shamanism and its remnants in one's own culture and by using cross-cultural perspectives that avoid cultural particulars. The universality of shamanic practices means that just about every religion will recognize something of "their traditions" in shamanism. To counter the accusations that "white" people who practice core shamanism are engaged in cultural appropriation of Native American religion, it may be useful to trace the remnants of shamanism in European cultures. This would include the rock art traditions, reinterpretations of ancient witchcraft, and modern reconstructions of Celtic shamanism.

Some critics may ask what gives young and middle-age faculty the right to practice shamanism, pointing to their own traditions where the elders control access to the practice. Our response is that, in most societies, the traditional concepts of shamanism emphasized that the right came from the spirits and was validated by the community. Other critics have objected to shamanism being taught in the university, stating that although it is appropriate to teach *about* religions, students should not have spiritual experiences induced in classroom settings. Our colleagues may express similar attitudes. We would respond that many aspects of academics—music appreciation, music therapy, cross-cultural training, psychiatry, and geology—all induce natural experiences directly related to the fields they study.

Sometimes another objection is that introducing students to shamanism exposes them to powerful forces that they are not prepared to manage. They may not have a support system for follow-up on their experiences, and may not have adequate preparation, protection, and long-term guidance to deal with great powers beyond their control, placing them at risk of psychological and/ or spiritual harm. We advise students who are invited to engage in experiential shamanic activities about these potential difficulties, but we also tell them that shamanic practitioners have always faced this risk of entering into a world of powers beyond their control.

We have noted that the course topic tends to draw a disproportionate number of students who may already need counseling care. These needs are beyond the capacity of the instructors and ordinary classroom contact. We make it clear that personal issues raised by the course's experiential activities cannot be adequately addressed within its context. Sensitivity, time issues, and professional qualification preclude addressing problems that may emerge in student's visionary experiences, some of which could include disturbing psychological material. In the context of teaching the experiential class, we made arrangements to have a counseling co-faculty in the class (when possible). If a problem emerges, we contact the student counseling center for referral assistance. We emphasize that, with this experiential focus, students should self-screen, to dissuade those with psychological and emotional disturbances from taking the course.

Summary: Shamanism in the Context of Religion and Healing

Our courses on shamanism have a particularly powerful potential for addressing religion and healing. In illustrating "humanity's original neurotheology"— a biologically based spiritual practice that had healing as a principal focus— we are able to demonstrate in a powerful way the linkages of religion and healing. This shamanic approach illustrates healing as a spiritual process, and healing and religion as having a common basis in human psychobiology. We also allow students to see religious healing in action, especially through the experiential activities provided.

Syllabus: ASB355 Shamanism, Healing and Consciousness

Course Description and Rationale

This course introduces the traditional shaman as a healer, therapist, philosopher, mythologist, political leader, diviner, psychopomp and ecosystem regulator. Shamans' worldviews, arts, and practices are examined cross-culturally, with an emphasis on the universals of shamanism and cultural differences in shamanic practices. The nature of shamanic practices are examined in light of theories of mind, consciousness, altered states of consciousness, and healing processes, particularly from perspectives that link their biological and psychological bases. A variety of traditional shamanic healing methods and their biopsychosocial bases are presented.

- • Texts Used

Doore, G., ed. 1988. *Shaman's path*. Boston: Shambhala.
Halifax, Joan. 1979. *Shamanic voices*. New York: Dutton.
Harner, Michael. 1990. *The way of the shaman*. San Francisco: Harper.
Mails, Thomas. 1991. *Fools Crow: Wisdom and power*. Tulsa, OK: Council Oak.
Nicholson, Shirley, ed. 1988. *Shamanism*. Wheaton, IL: Theosophical Publishing.

Vitebsky, Piers. 2001. *Shamanism*. Norman: University of Oklahoma Press.

Walsh, Roger. 1990. *The spirit of shamanism*. Los Angeles: Tarcher.

• Reading Packets

Readings in the reading packets are listed in the bibliography, below, for Topics 1 through 28.

• Advanced Readings

d'Aquili, E. and A. Newburg. 1999. *The mystical mind: probing the biology of religious experience*. Minneapolis: Fortress.

Laughlin, C., J. McManus, and E. d'Aquili. 1992. *Brain, symbol and experience: Toward a neurophenomenology of consciousness*. New York: Columbia University Press.

Winkelman, M. 1992. *Shamans, priests and witches: A cross-cultural study of magico-religious practitioners*. Anthropological Research Papers #44. Tempe: Arizona State University Press.

Winkelman, M. 2000. *Shamanism: the neural ecology of consciousness and healing*. Westport, CT: Bergin and Garvey.

Assessments

This semester-long course is typically evaluated on the basis of exams, short experiential papers, and a research paper. Exams cover readings, lectures, and films. The short papers have students write about their phenomenological experiences from participating in a shamanic activity (soul journey, lower world journey, "talking to rocks," and so on). The research paper is an expansion on some topic of shamanism covered in the course through outside library-based research.

Lecture Topics

SECTION I: CROSS-CULTURAL OVERVIEW OF SHAMANISM

1. Introduction to Shamanism: Core Shamanism and Four Paths to Wholeness
2. Characteristics and Roles of the Shaman
3. The Shamanic Soul Journey
4. The Shamanic State of Consciousness
5. Shamans' Relations to Nature and Power Animals
6. Shamanic Relations with Plant Helpers
7. Shamanic Material Culture: Paraphernalia and Imagery
8. Forms of Recruitment and Training of Shamans
9. Cross-cultural Classifications: Shamans, Shamanic Healers, and Other Magico-Religious Practitioners

10. Case Studies of Shamanic Practices
11. History of Shamanic Studies

SECTION II: EMIC THEORETICAL PERSPECTIVES ON SHAMANISM

12. Universal World Views of Shamanism
13. Universal Cosmology and Symbols of Shamanism
14. Case Studies in Shamanic Cosmology and Symbolism

Native American Shamanic Cosmology and Medicine Wheels
Celtic Shamanism
Shamanic Imagery in the Archaeological Record, I: Rock Art
Shamanic Imagery in the Archaeological Record, II: Hopewell Art

SECTION III: ETIC THEORETICAL PERSPECTIVES ON SHAMANISM

15. Models of the Psyche, Self, Consciousness, and Reality

Shamanic Psychology, Therapeutics, and Worldview
Depth Psychology and Jungian Psychology
Transpersonal Psychology: Stanislav Grof and Ken Wilber

16. The Biopsychological Bases of Shamanic Journeys and Altered States of Consciousness
17. Psychological Dissociation and Possession
18. The Health of Shamans: Shamanic Journey Compared to Schizophrenia, Possession and Mystical States
19. Cross-Cultural Comparison of Shamanic and ASC Experiences

SECTION IV: SHAMANIC HEALING AND OTHER PRACTICES

20. Shamanic Concepts of Illness and Healing: Object/Spirit Extraction and Soul Retrieval
21. Case Studies: iKung Bushman Healing, Sucking Doctors, Maria Sabina
22. The Western Medical Model and Shamanic Healing Compared
23. The Biopsychology of Shamanic Healing and the Role of Imagery
24. Contemporary Therapies with Shamanic Concepts of Healing

Energy Body, Dreamwork, Therapeutic Touch, Acupuncture, Jin Shin Jyutsu
Music and Dance Therapy, Holotropic Breathwork

25. Shaman as Diviner: Cross-Cultural Examples
26. Shaman as Sociopolitical and Ecosystemic Regulator
27. Shaman as Psychopomp: Death and Dying
28. Conclusions: Shamanism in Ancient and Contemporary Society

Bibliography

TOPIC I. INTRODUCTION TO SHAMANISM: CORE SHAMANISM AND
FOUR PATHS TO WHOLENESS

Halifax, Joan. *Shamanic voices*, 1–34.
Harner, Michael, and Gary Doore. 1988. The ancient wisdom in shamanic cultures. In Nicholson, *Shamanism*, 3–16.
Swan, Jim. 1988. Rolling Thunder at work. In Nicholson, *Shamanism*,
149–157.
Townsend, J. 1997. Shamanism. In *Anthropology of religion: A handbook
of method and theory*, ed. S. Glazier, 429–469. Westport, CT: Greenwood.
Walsh, Roger. *The spirit of shamanism*, chaps. 1 and 2.

TOPIC 2. CHARACTERISTICS AND ROLES OF THE SHAMAN

Harner, Michael. 1988. What is a shaman? In Doore, *Shaman's path*,
7–15.
Hultkrantz, Ake. 1988. Shamanism: A religious phenomenon. In Doore,
Shaman's path, 33–41.
Noll, Richard. 1988. The presence of spirits in magic and madness. In
Nicholson, *Shamanism*, 47–61
Pattee, Rowena. 1988. Ecstasy and sacrifice. In Doore, *Shaman's path*,
17–31.

TOPIC 3. THE SHAMANIC SOUL JOURNEY

Halifax, Joan. *Shamanic voices*, chap. 2, 37–49, 54–62, 164–169.
Harner, Michael. *The way of the shaman*, chap. 2, 20–39.
Pattee, Rowena. 1988. Ecstasy and sacrifice. In Doore, *Shaman's path*,
17–31.
Walsh, Roger. *The spirit of shamanism*, 141–158.

TOPIC 4. THE SHAMANIC STATE OF CONSCIOUSNESS

Harner, Michael. *The way of the shaman*, 40–56.
Winkelman, M. Trance states.

TOPIC 5. SHAMANS' RELATIONS TO NATURE AND POWER ANIMALS

Halifax, Joan. *Shamanic voices*, chap. 6, 157–191.
Harner, Michael. *The way of the shaman*, 57–65, 69–94, 101–103, 95–112.
Mails, Thomas. *Fools Crow*, 9–17.
Swan, Jim. 1988. Sacred places in nature: One tool in the shaman's
medicine bag. In Doore, *Shaman's path*, 151–159.

TOPIC 6. SHAMANIC RELATIONS WITH PLANT HELPERS

Harner, Michael, ed. 1973. *Hallucinogens and shamanism*. New York: Oxford University Press.

La Barre, W. 1972. Hallucinogens and the shamanic origins of religion. In. *Flesh of the gods*, ed. P. Furst. New York: Praeger.

Macy, Joanna. 1990. The greening of the self. *Common boundary* (July/August): 22–25.

Winkelman, M., and W. Andritzky, eds. 1996. Introduction to *Sacred plants, consciousness, and healing. Yearbook of cross-cultural medicine and psychotherapy, Volume 6*. Berlin: Springer-Verlag.

TOPIC 7. SHAMANIC MATERIAL CULTURE: PARAPHERNALIA AND IMAGERY

Artscanada. 1974. *Stones, bones, and skin: Ritual and shamanic art*. Thirtieth anniversary issue of *Artscanada*. December/January. Toronto, Canada.

Bostwick, Todd. 2002. *Landscape of the spirits Hohokam rock art at South Mountain*. Tucson: University of Arizona Press.

Reichel-Dolmatoff, Gerardo. 1987. *Shamanism and the art of the Eastern Tukanoan Indians*. Leiden: Brill.

Harner, Michael. 1990. *The way of the shaman*. San Francisco: Harper and Row, 22–30.

Carr, Christopher, and D. Troy case. 2005. The nature of leadership in Ohio Hopewellian societies: Role segregation and the transformation from shamanism. In *Gathering Hopewell: Society, ritual, and ritual interaction*, ed. C. Carr and D. T. Case. New York: Kluwer.

Price, Neil S. 2001. *The archaeology of shamanism*. London: Routledge.

TOPIC 8. FORMS OF RECRUITMENT AND TRAINING OF SHAMANS

Halifax, Joan. *Shamanic voices*, 49–52, 65–75, 140–156, 180–183.

Harner, Michael. *The way of the shaman*, 1–19.

Walsh, Roger. *The spirit of shamanism*, 21–33, 34–41, 42–55, 56–69, 70–88, 89–100.

TOPIC 9. CROSS-CULTURAL CLASSIFICATIONS: SHAMANS, SHAMANISIC HEALERS AND OTHER MAGICO-RELIGIOUS PRACTITIONERS

Siikala, A. 1978. The rite technique of Siberian shaman. *Folklore Fellows Communication* 220. Helsinki: Soumalainen Tiedeskaremia Academia.

Winkelman, Michael. 1986a.

Winkelman, Michael. 1989. Shamans and other "magico-religious" healers: A cross-cultural study of their origins, nature, and social transformation. *Ethos* 18: 308–362. Read only pp. 325–349.

TOPIC 10. CASE STUDIES OF SHAMANIC PRACTICES

Halifax, Joan. *Shamanic voices*, 65–75, 95–110, 129–148, 159–171, 195–213, 249–252.

TOPIC 11. HISTORY OF SHAMANIC STUDIES

De Rios, Marlene Dobkin, and Michael Winkelman. 1989. Shamanism and altered states of consciousness: An introduction. *Journal of psychoactive drugs* 21(1): 1–7.

Flagherty, G. 1992. *Shamanism and the eighteenth century*. Princeton, NJ: Princeton University Press.

TOPIC 12. UNIVERSAL WORLDVIEWS OF SHAMANISM

King, Serge. 1988. Seeing is believing: The four worlds of a shaman. In Doore, *Shaman's path*, 43–52.

Mails, Thomas. *Fools Crow*, 30–73.

Medicine Eagle, Brooke. 1988. To paint ourselves red. In Doore, *Shaman's path*, 209–216.

TOPIC 13. UNIVERSAL COSMOLOGY AND SYMBOLS OF SHAMANISM

Eliade, Mircea. 1964. *Shamanism*, chap. 8 (259–279 only); chap. 13 (466–494 only). Princeton, NJ: Princeton University Press.

TOPIC 14. CASE STUDIES IN SHAMANIC COSMOLOGY AND SYMBOLISM

Harner, Michael. 1992. A possible survival of Celtic shamanism in Ireland. *Shamanism* 5(1): 1–9.

Matthews, John. 1991. *The Celtic shaman*, 35–43, 58–64, 66–68, 75–78, 80–82, 92–97 only. Rockport, MA: Longmead, Shaftsbury, and Dorset.

Vitebsky, Piers. *Shamanism*.

TOPIC 15. MODELS OF THE PSYCHE, SELF, CONSCIOUSNESS, AND REALITY

Doore, Gary. 1988. Shamans, yogis, and bodhisattvas. In Doore, *Shaman's path*, 217–225.

Grof, Stanislov. 1988. The shamanic journey: observations from holotropic therapy. In Doore, *Shaman's path*, 161–175.

Hunt, H. 1995. *On the nature of consciousness*. New Haven, CT: Yale University Press.

Jung, Carl G. 1971. The structure of the psyche. In *The portable Jung*, 23–46. New York: Penguin.

———. 1971. The concept of the collective unconscious. In *The portable Jung*, 59–67. New York: Penguin.

O'Connor, Peter. 1985. *Understanding Jung, understanding yourself*, 12–23. New York: Paulist.

Starhawk. 1992. The heritage of Salem. *Common Boundary* (July/August): 17–21.

Swanson, G. 1963. The search for a guardian spirit: The process of empowerment in simpler societies. *Ethnology* 12: 359–378.

von Franz, Maria L. 1971. The process of individuation. In *Man and his symbols*, ed. C.G. Jung, 160–211 only. New York: Doubleday.

Walsh, Roger. *The spirit of shamanism*, 215–222, 223–232, 233–241, 242–250.

Wilber, Ken. 1980. *No boundary*, chap. 1 (1–14). Los Angeles: Center.

———. 1986. The spectrum of development. In *Transformations of consciousness*, ed. K. Wilber, J. Engler, and D. P. Brown, 65–105.

TOPIC 16. THE BIOPSYCHOLOGICAL BASES OF SHAMANIC JOURNEYS AND ALTERED STATES OF CONSCIOUSNESS

Goodman, Felicitas. 1988. Shamanic trance postures. In Doore, *Shaman's path*, 53–61.

Hughes, Dureen. 1991. Blending with an other: An analysis of trance channeling in the United States. *Ethos* 19(2): 161–184.

Hughes, Dureen J., and Norbert T. Melville. 1990. Changes in brainwave activity during trance channeling: A pilot study. *Journal of transpersonal psychology* 22(2): 175–190.

Leary, Timothy. 1964. The religious experience: Its production and interpretation. *Psychedelic Review* 1(3): 324–346.

Lewis-Williams, J. D., and T. A. Dowson. 1988. The signs of all times. *Current anthropology* 29(2): 201–217. Read pp. 201–213 only.

Mandell, A. 1980. Toward a psychobiology of transcendence: God in the brain. In *The Psychobiology of consciousness*, ed. D. Davidson and R. Davidson, 379–464. New York: Plenum.

Noll, Richard. 1983. Shamanism and schizophrenia: A state-specific approach to the "schizophrenia metaphor" of shamanic states. *American ethnologist* 10: 443–459.

Reichel-Dolmatoff, G. 1987. *Shamanism and art of the Eastern Tukanoan Indians*, 1–3, 12–18 only. Leiden: Brill.

Sanders, Joanne. 1989. Standing up for ecstasy. *Common boundary* 7(3): 14–19, 38–39.

Walsh, Roger. *The spirit of shamanism*, 70–88, 89–100, 159–177, 215–222, 223–232, 242–250.

Winkelman, Michael. 1986b. Trance states.

———. 1997. Altered states of consciousness and religious behavior. In *Anthropology of religion: A handbook of method and theory*, ed. S. Glazier, 393–428.

TOPIC 17. PSYCHOLOGICAL DISSOCIATION AND POSSESSION

Lewis, I. 1988. *Ecstatic religion: An anthropological study of spirit possession and shamanism*. London: Routledge.

Winkelman, Michael. *Shamanism: The neural ecology*, chap. 3.

TOPIC 18. THE HEALTH OF SHAMANS: SHAMANIC JOURNEY COMPARED TO
SCHIZOPHRENIA, POSSESSION, AND MYSTICAL STATES

Noll, Richard. Shamanism and schizophrenia.
Walsh, Roger. *The spirit of shamanism,* 70–88, 89–100.

TOPIC 19. CROSS-CULTURAL COMPARISON OF SHAMANIC AND ASC
EXPERIENCES

Peters, L., and D. Price-Williams. 1981. Towards an experiential analysis
of shamanism. *American ethnologist* 7: 398–418.

TOPIC 20. SHAMANIC CONCEPTS OF ILLNESS AND HEALING: OBJECT/SPIRIT
EXTRACTION AND SOUL RETRIEVAL

Achterberg, Jeanne. 1985. *Imagery in healing, shamanism in modern medi-
cine.* Boston: New Science Library/Shambhala.
Donovan, Bill. 1994. Navajo "hand tremblers" have gift for "seeing." *Ari-
zona republic,* February 28, B1, B3.
Harner, Michael. *The way of the shaman,* 91–94, 101–103, 113–134.
Harner, M., and S. Harner. 2001. Core practices in the shamanic treat-
ment of illness. *Shamanism* 3(1, 2): 19–30.
Ingerman, S. 1991. *Soul retrieval,* 10–24, 36–45, 68–76, 78–82.
Krippner, Stanley. 1988. Shamans: The first healers. In Doore, *Shaman's
path,* 101–114.
Mails, Thomas. *Fools Crow,* 136–150, 151–168, 169–178.
Pert, Candace B. 1986. The wisdom of the receptors: Neuropeptides, the
emotions, and bodymind. *Advances* 3(3): 5–13. Institute for the Ad-
vancement of Health.
Wilbur, Ken, and Treya Wilber. 1988. Do we make ourselves sick? *New
age journal* (September/October): 50–54, 85–91.

TOPIC 21. CASE STUDIES: ¡KUNG BUSHMAN HEALING, SUCKING DOCTORS,
MARIA SABINA

Andritzky, Walter. 1989. Sociopsychotherapeutic functions of ayahuasca
healing in Amazonia. *Journal of psychoactive drugs* 21(1): 77–89.
De Rios, Marlene D. 1989. A modern-day shamanistic healer in the Pe-
ruvian Amazon: Pharmacopoeia and trance. *Journal of psychoactive
drugs* 21(1): 91–99.
Halifax, Joan. *Shamanic voices,* 129–137, 159–162, 169–173, 183–191, 195–
213.
Paul, Benjamine D. 1976. The Maya bonesetter as sacred specialist. *Ethnology* 15(1): 77–81.
Winkelman, Michael. *Shamanisms and survival.*

TOPIC 22. THE WESTERN MEDICAL MODEL AND SHAMANIC HEALING
COMPARED

Achterberg, Jeanne. 1988. The wounded healer: Transformational journeys in modern medicine. In Doore, *Shaman's path*, 115–125.

Dossey, Larry. 1988. The inner life of the healer: The importance of shamanism in modern medicine. In Doore, *Shaman's path*, 89–99.

————. 1993. *Healing words*, 169–195, 211–235. San Francisco: Harper.

Krippner, Stanley. 1988. Shamans: The first healers. In Doore, *Shaman's
path*, 89–98.

Krippner, Stanley, and Patrick Welsch. 1992. *Spiritual dimensions of healing*, 39–75. New York: Irvington.

Lawlis, Frank. 1988. Shamanic approaches in a hospital pain clinic. In
Doore, *Shaman's path*, 139–149.

Levine, Stephen. 1987. *Healing into life and death*, 1–16 only. New York:
Doubleday.

Mehl, Lewis E. 1988. Modern shamanism: Integration of biomedicine
with traditional world views. In Doore, *Shaman's path*, 127–138.

Pert, Candace B. The wisdom of the receptors.

Walsh, Roger. *The spirit of shamanism*, 178–182, 183–193, 194–204.

TOPIC 23. THE BIOPSYCHOLOGY OF SHAMANIC HEALING AND THE ROLE OF
IMAGERY

Achterberg, Jeanne. 1988. The shaman: Master healer in the imaginary
realm. In Nicholson, *Shamanism*, 103–124.

Bravo, Gary, and Charles Grob. 1989. Shamans, sacraments, and psychi-
atrists. *Journal of psychoactive drugs*, 21(1): 123–129.

Dow, J. 1986. Universal aspects of symbolic healing: A theoretical synthesis. *American anthropologist* 88: 56–69.

Noll, R. 1985. Mental imagery cultivation as a cultural phenomenon:
The role of visions in shamanism. *Current anthropology* 26: 443–451.

Walsh, Roger. *The spirit of shamanism*, 101–109,178–182, 183–193, 194–
204.

TOPIC 24. CONTEMPORARY THERAPIES WITH SHAMANIC CONCEPTS OF
HEALING

Brennan, Barbara Ann. 1987. *Hands of light*, 41–56, 81–88 only. Toronto:
Bantam.

Burmeister, Mar. 1981. *Introducing Jim Shin Jyutsu Is, Book 2*. J.S.J. Dis-
tributors.

Crowe, Barbara. 1989. Music therapy and shamanism. *Music therapy perspectives* (fall). National Association for Music Therapy.

Groff, Stanislav. 1988. The shamanic journey: Observations from holotropic therapy. In Doore, *Shaman's path*, 161–175.

Higgins, Melisa. 1988. Mary Burmeister, master of Jim Shin Jyutsu.
Yoga journal (March/April).

Jung, Carl G. 1964. Approaching the unconscious. In *Man and his symbols*, 18–49, and 67–82 only. New York: Doubleday.

Leviton, Richard. 1994. The art of dreaming. *Yoga Journal* (March/April): 50–57, 131–132.

Williams, Strephon K. 1985–1986. *The Jungian-Senoi dreamwork manual*, 28–37, 84–93. Berkeley, CA: Journey.

Winn, Thomas, Barbara Crowe, and Joseph J. Moreno. 1989. Shamanism and music therapy. *Music Therapy Perspectives* (fall): 67–71.

TOPIC 25. SHAMAN AS DIVINER: CROSS-CULTURAL EXAMPLES

Dillard, Annie. 1982. Teaching a stone to talk. In *Teaching a stone to talk: Expeditions and encounters*, 67–76. New York: Harper and Row.

Harner, M. *The way of the shaman*, 97 103–108.

Mails, Thomas. *Fools Crow*, 123–135, 179–185.

Matthews, John. 1991.*The Celtic shaman*, 153–166 only. Rockport, MA: Longmead, Shaftsbury, and Dorset.

Walsh, Roger. *The spirit of shamanism*, 178–182.

TOPIC 26. SHAMAN AS SOCIOPOLITICAL AND ECOSYSTEMIC REGULATOR

Andritzky, Walter. Sociopsychotherapeutic functions of ayahuasca healing in Amazonia. *Journal of Psychoactive Drugs* 21(1): 77–89.

Netting, Robert McC. 1972. Sacred power and centralization: Aspects of political adaptation in Africa. In *Population growth: Anthropological implications*, ed. B. Spooner, 219–242. Cambridge, MA: MIT Press.

TOPIC 27. SHAMAN AS PSYCHOPOMP: DEATH AND DYING

Huntington, Richard, and Peter Metcalf. 1980. *Celebrations of death*, 175–183 only. Cambridge: Cambridge University Press.

Rosenberg, K. 1990. Musically midwifing death. *Common Boundary* 8(5): 9–12.

TOPIC 28. CONCLUSIONS: SHAMANISM IN ANCIENT AND CONTEMPORARY SOCIETY

De Rios, Marlene. 2002. What we can learn from shamanic healing: Brief psychotherapy with Latino immigrant clients. *American Journal of Public Health* 92: 1576–1578.

Gagan, Jeannette. 1998. *Journeying where shamanism and psychology meet*. Santa Fe: Rio Chama.

Grof, S., and C. Grof. 1989. *Spiritual emergency: When personal transformation becomes a crises*. New York: G. P. Putnam.

Harner, Michael. 1988. Shamanic counseling. In Doore, *Shaman's path*, 179–187.

Jakobsen, M. 1999. *Shamanism: Traditional and contemporary approaches to the mastery of spirits and healing*. New York: Berghahn.

Lawlis, Frank. 1988. Shamanic approaches in a hospital pain clinic. In Doore, *Shaman's path*, 139–149.

Lyon, William. 1988. Black Elk: then and now. In Nicholson, *Shamanism*, 285–295.

Perkins, John. 1997. *Shapeshifting shamanic techniques for global and personal transformation*. Rochester, VT: Destiny.

Townsend, Joan B. 1988. Neo-shamanism and the modern mystical movement. In Doore, *Shaman's path*, 73–83.

Walsh, Roger. *The spirit of shamanism*, 264–268.

Syllabus: ASB191 Freshman Seminar: Shamanism:
An Experiential Introduction

Shamanism is an ancient healing practice that has recently undergone a modern resurgence. Shamanic practices are found in the traditions of many different indigenous cultures and do not represent any particular spirituality or religion. This seminar provides an experiential introduction to shamanic practices, including shamanic journeying, the use of intuition, discovering power animals, and shamanic healing. These activities are presented from a "neurotheology" perspective that emphasizes the psychobiological foundations of these experiences. Students who will enjoy the class are open to many points of view and are comfortable with trying out-of-the-ordinary psychological experiences. The class is not intended to provide counseling or therapy. Class members are expected to respect each other's privacy and to use personal discretion in deciding to participate in any of its experiential activities.

This course provides an experiential introduction to core shamanism, focusing upon activities involving "shamanic journeying" and the experience of "non-ordinary realities." This course is based in a "neurophenomenological" perspective, accepting the phenomenal reality of the experiences and assuming that they reflect basic operations of the brain. This course is not based upon any particular religious system but reflects a cross-cultural perspective on the universals of shamanic practice. You are not required to believe anything in particular to benefit from this class; you may however, need to suspend some of your prior beliefs to accept and understand the experiences you encounter.

This class is not a "healing program" or counseling class. However, because of the unusual nature of the experiences induced through shamanic activities, you may encounter your own unconscious conflicts, repressed dynamics, dissociated complexes, and shadow aspects of the self. If you encounter disturbing material as a consequence of these activities, please document them (see below) and bring them to the attention of the instructors. If you feel in need of assistance with the psychological effects of these experiences, please see the staff at the ASU counseling center (tel. 480 965-6146). If you consider yourself to be psychologically unstable, this class is not recommended for you.

Course Requirements

Attendance: If you miss more than 3 sessions you will not receive a passing grade.

Participation: You are required to be in class but are not required to participate in any activities that you do not feel comfortable with. Participation may include presentations about your experiences, but this is not required.

Respect: Information divulged in this class should not be disclosed to other people. Please respect the privacy and confidentiality of other class members.

Documentation: You are required to maintain a notebook and log of your experiences in this class. You will bring your notebook to class to take brief notes and type up fuller versions of your experiences on the computer. These notebooks will be reviewed and may be used for research purposes. You may maintain your anonymity by placing only the last four digits of your ASUID# on your notebook.

TEXT

Vitebsky, Piers. 2001 *Shamanism.* Norman: University of Oklahoma Press.

ADDITIONAL READING

Harner, Michael. 1990. *The Way of the Shaman.* New York: Bantam.

Basic Course Activities

Introduction to Concepts of Shamanism
Soul Journey/Flight to a Place in Nature
Journey to Lower World
Journey to Find Power Animal
Divinatory Journey
Recovering Power Animals
Soul Loss Recovery

Additional Topics

Circles of Power	World View/Middle and Upper World Journey
Mutual Journeys	Stone Divination
Divining for Others	Emotional Healing
Extraction	De-Possession
Personal Power	Power Animals, Guardian Spirits and Spirit Allies
Death and Rebirth	Nature Activities
Vision Questing/Fasting	Visions and Seeing
Sorcery and Sucking	Knowledge and Shamanic Powers
States of Consciousness	Dancing

REFERENCES

Carr, Christopher, and D. Troy Case. Forthcoming. The nature of leadership in Ohio Hopewellian societies: Role segregation and the transformation from shamanism. In *Gathering Hopewell: Society, ritual, and ritual interaction,* ed. C. Carr and D. T. Case. New York: Kluwer-Plenum.

Eliade, M. 1964. *Shamanism: Archaic techniques of ecstasy.* New York: Pantheon.

Harner, M. 1990. *The way of the shaman.* San Francisco: Harper and Row.

Winkelman, Michael. 1986a. Magico-religious practitioner types and socioeconomic analysis. *Behavior Science Research* 20(1–4): 17–46.

———. 1986b. Trance states: A theoretical model and cross-cultural analysis. *Ethos* 14: 76–105.

———. 1990. Shaman and other "magico-religious healers": A cross-cultural study of their origins, nature, and social transformation. *Ethos* 18(3): 308–352.

———. 1992. Shamans, priests, and witches. A cross-cultural study of magico-religious practitioners. *Anthropological Research Papers #44.* Tempe: Arizona State University.

———. 1996. Psychointegrator plants: Their roles in human culture and health. In *Sacred plants, consciousness and healing cross-cultural and interdisciplinary perspectives. Yearbook of Cross-cultural Medicine and Psychotherapy, Volume 6,* ed. M. Winkelman and W. Andritzky, 9–53. Berlin: Springer-Verlag.

———. 1997. Altered states of consciousness and religious behavior. In *Anthropology of religion: A handbook of method and theory,* ed. S. Glazier, 393–428. Westport, CT: Greenwood.

———. 2000. *Shamanism: The neural ecology of consciousness and healing.* Westport, CT: Bergin and Garvey.

———. 2002. Shamanism and cognitive evolution. *Cambridge Archaeological Journal* 12(1): 71–101.

———. 2002a. Shamanic universals and evolutionary psychology. *Journal of Ritual Studies* 16(2): 63–76.

———. 2004. Spirits as human nature and the fundamental structures of consciousness. In *From shaman to scientist: Essays on humanity's search for spirits,* ed. J. Houran, Lanham, Md.: Scarecrow.

———, ed. 2003. *Shamanisms and Survival. Cultural Survival Quarterly* (Guest-edited special issue, summer 2003).

PART V

Experiential Pedagogies

II

The Anthropology of Experience: The Way to Teach Religion and Healing

Edith Turner

It was clear to William James in 1901 that religious experience was a major force among humankind. But in the century that followed, the discipline of religious studies seemed limited to textual investigation, philosophy, and theology, and little notice was given to religious experience. With a few exceptions this is still the case, and, even with attempts to explain religion psychologically, religious studies seem at a dead end, afraid to say anything about experience. However, we now find in the sister discipline of anthropology the dawning realization that the personal experience of spiritual things is at the origin of ritual and religion and that the actual experiencing of religion may also be the necessary entry point for its anthropological investigation. As a result, an array of truly experiential studies of ritual and healing events in various cultures have appeared in which the investigator bonds herself or himself with the religious community in question in order to learn on the pulses what religion really is in its source and outpouring. Religion is being considered in its own right, in its own peculiar living context in each case, and experienced personally in its full power.

To save religious studies from near death (just as it has been necessary to save anthropology from a similar death resulting from postmodernism), it appears to be necessary to get back to basics and *reteach* students from scratch, showing them new vistas of exploration that lie ahead of them in experiential religious studies. This chapter lays out the pretraining phase for this new approach, consisting of vivid close-up stories of healing in different societies, then the fieldwork, or work in the world, without which the student is likely to miss a major faculty for gathering this kind of knowledge—that is, the inner sense of religion. Suggestions for fieldwork are supplied—even for undergraduate courses—concerned with the subfields of healing, music, shamanism, the *unio mystica*, the origins of morality, and an understanding of the nature of spirit figures and power, and followed by the feedback or debriefing stage of the student fieldwork.

Throughout the course and at all stages I emphasize spirituality and drop the prohibitions against taking spirituality seriously. Particularly in the area of religious healing, the sense and experience of the religious event taking place has primacy over descriptions and texts divorced from the living human contemporary context. Here the teaching of the *reality* of the religion, of whatever kind—as demonstrated by experiential fieldwork—is a sine qua non.

When I teach about healing, I draw attention to the agency from which it derives, whether from energy, power, or spirits, sources beyond the mundane. "Spirit" and "power" here seem to be different. A spirit has the form of a living being, human or animal. It is something that is there, and does things. Power is a force; it is the means by which one does things. This is like the way physicists describe light. Light can be either a particle, called a "photon," or it can be a "wave," depending on the viewpoint and context. Light is known to travel in a straight line, much like a beam of particles. But if a ray is passed through a minute hole and falls on a screen, diffusion rings are obtained, much like the rings on a still pond when a stone is thrown in. These rings are waves, movement itself, energy. A spirit, too, is that which moves, very like ourselves. Healing *power* is like a wave, a strong force or a vibration, and one feels it as an overpowering effect setting one ashiver. People call it "energy" or "vibrations."

Many things in nature have ways of switching their existence, such as the way a chrysalis turns into a butterfly, or the way two quiescent bodily cells, once united, become an embryo that suddenly takes on food, having been nothing before but a couple of blueprints of genes. Energy can quiver into particularity and become a person, or a person, when fully attentive, can flow into pure energy and then heal.

The terms themselves are interesting. A word that translates as "spirit" is used in most cultures. Many Native Americans refer to power. The Lakota call it *wakan*. "Energy" is known as *chi, qi,* or *ki* in China and Japan, and this term has caught on among Western healers. What we know here as "energy" is the right term for what people often experience in healing across the globe. Each of them has words for it.

Thus the learning goal of the students in such a class is to resensitize themselves to these forces that have been in play for many ages and that are known across the world. The students do begin to recognize them as they arise in subtle forms during the course, and may then relate them to a real and spiritual dimension of human nature. The reading list consists of anthropological research that relates the experiencing of these original sources of religion in present-day cultures, particularly in healing. The writers of the stories are mostly looking from the point of view of the inhabitants of the field. Particularly telling are the transcriptions of what healers themselves say about their work and about their initial call to the craft. Along with the storytelling phase the class does personal fieldwork in ordinary life, in the local area, any-where. Experience of shamanism and healing being the actual life of healing, the class further learns how to approximate the sense of shamanism and heal-ing by literally enacting it. Experience, as Victor Turner said, is anthropology's truest material.

My most recent experience of teaching healing and shamanism, in the fall term of 2003, has been like this. To begin with, students jostled to get into my class, which ended up with a ratio of about six to one in favor of women—a significant and hopeful indication, because the mood of women today is both firm and adventurous, not held back by the "objectivism" and rule of nonin-volvement of the old sciences. The new popularity of religious healing gives some idea of how the young intelligentsia is viewing what used to be a largely tabooed field. Nowadays it is hard to envisage that old era when any instruction that positively endorsed healing was considered to be bowing to superstition and magic. At all events, we had to change our venue to a larger classroom, out of the Arts and Sciences block altogether. We went—significantly—to the Nursing School, in a room with an inbuilt video system and screen.

Anthropology, my own discipline, is changing across most of its fronts, even though in some sectors there remains a well-nigh superstitious taboo against any such participation. At the 2003 annual meetings of the American Anthropological Association in a session called "Practice, Performance, and Participation," several papers were given by anthropologists who had them-selves learned and taken up the work of the religious healing practiced by their people of study. These scholars healed. They had become practitioners. They knew the truth of religious healing (Knab 2003; Earle 2003).

It is on foundations like this, confirmed by my own experience, that the philosophy behind my own course on shamanism and healing is based. An-thropologists have now experienced the power of spirits and energy and have been grateful to access the ability to use the power themselves. Obviously the peoples studied have always done so. I have done it. It is for this reason that I teach that these entities exist. In one form or another the powers are known by all the world's peoples. Therefore my course material is linked to the dif-ferent religions of the world, and much of it is also linked to the ancient shamanisms that still exist in more peripheral places—practices that are be-coming accepted as the primal root of religion.

What then is religious healing? It is almost beyond words and definitions. I tell the students, "when you can't put it into words, you're on to it." They soon understand what I mean. One could characterize it with long words, such as "ineffable," but this leads to the swamps of jargon, which are not what healing is about. Healing is known *in* the experience of the healer and of being healed. The easiest way to put it is that you're no longer in pain. The way opens up more or less quickly to the betterment of the body, soul, and mind, in that order. (We put mind last because it may become a distraction.) Healing is done by a spirit or spiritual power coming through a willing person (made willing by the gift from the spirit or power), which works on the sufferer and takes away pain and the source of the trouble.

Healing is *central at the depth of human consciousness*—at the depth of its human pole; and healing can happen just where that consciousness latches onto the powers or conscious spirits that dwell around and through a person. Healing, along with the loss of self in sex, is the best physical act a human being can do. Of all religious acts, healing is the most innocent, the most often miraculous, the most often desired.

How to teach this sort of thing in class? From long experience I have concluded there are no better means than, first, the storytelling method and, second, enabling students to have the experience, and where possible, have a healer come in and show them how. Other methods also work quite well

Storytelling. The telling of the story of a spiritual experience—transmitted by speech or even print—is the means whereby a spiritual fact can be conveyed to another person whole and entire, and can be received by the other person as an actual experience and be counted as such in the memory. A trip to Africa of my own showed me that there were such things as spirits, for I saw one at the height of an Ihamba healing ritual. My curiosity was hooked. I wrote about it, told the story, then realized how much the story—the remembered facts—of such an event mattered. The story, the awareness of it by the teller as the teller speaks, is the second gift, *after* the experience. True storytelling is the opening, the breath, the connection of the soul with others. The human being with its soul can reach another. This is part of the connectedness that runs through the universe. As an example I give my first words of teaching in the first class, after the students give their names and interests. It is the story of a healing in Nepal, told by Robert Desjarlais (1992), and which I paraphrase:

> *The Nepali shaman's eagle flight.* An elderly woman had three sudden losses in her family and fell ill with what we would call post-traumatic depression. She tried to bear her losses silently as her people were supposed to do, but a further fear assaulted her. One day, when she was crossing a wild Himalayan stream on her way to attend the funeral of her uncle, she missed her footing and very nearly fell to her death in the raging rapids. She was terribly shaken up. After that her soul left her body. She began to suffer from fever, swollen glands in her neck, and a heavy body. She had bad dreams of police and ghosts, and did not want to walk, eat, or work.
>
> Her spirit began to wander hither and thither, near the forest, stream, or cremation grounds, a prey to ghosts or witches. Her spirit had left her body, and she could do nothing about it. She remained withdrawn, numb, reticent, out of it. She sat on her porch with her eyes downcast and her hair unkempt.
>
> What she needed was healing. The old shaman (*bombo*) gathered the people in her house and set up an altar with rice cakes as an offering to the gods. His aim was to retrieve the woman's spirit. He began by playing his drum. Energy built up in him in the crowded room; he started to shake like the wind until the movement climaxed in a controlled ecstatic frenzy. Soft whistles pierced the

bombo's clenched teeth as the god's breath stormed through his body. Soon the god spoke. The staccato breath of words came quickly, without too much effort, the first syllable of each breath matching the force and volume of the drum beat. The people all around him prayed to the god for help. The very corners of the house became fused with the four sacred directions. The central pillar of the house, heavy with coats and oil lamps, stood for the *axis mundi*, the hub of the universe, leading to the central heavens. The cosmos became further merged with the shaman's altar and body. East, south, west, north, center; the ritual altar, embodied, was a material thing; the human body, enshrined, was a sacred thing. The *bombo* was facing east. Ghosts were exiled from the house and life forces were able to start returning to the flesh.

In this way the *bombo* meshed his body with supernatural forces to create an impenetrable shell around his form. "It's like putting up fences," he said. "Just as the police live with their weapons on them, so we need to tie our bodies, tie the four directions, to protect ourselves from witches and ghosts."

He now called the fierce Buddhist eagle god to his assistance. This is how he described what happened The eagle responded to his call and his spirit left his body with a joyful ecstatic shout and glided through space, clinging to the bird's chest as it escorted him in the search for the lost spirit.

All was silent as the *bombo's* spirit searched above. The *bombo* traveled through the air, scavenging like a hawk in search of the displaced spirit. From time to time he confronted evil spirits—a witch, a ghost, an angry god. In a struggle to escape their clutches, his body shook, causing the bells strapped around his chest to ring out. "We had to go like thieves without evil spirits knowing of our presence," said the *bombo*. "Otherwise they would attack. We went like a hawk hunting a chicken, looking from a long distance, then coming close to snatch it away. A tiger came to attack us. We were startled. We looked inside a house, we looked in the jungle, in the land of the dead, above, below. We roamed and roamed for a long time. There were other vagrant spirits around, so I had to look carefully to recognize the face of the right spirit. Suddenly the right spirit was there before us! The eagle immediately hooked it with his claws. Even so, something else was pulling the spirit away from us so it was difficult to drag it free. I was scared. At last we shook it free and flew back to the earth with it."

Meanwhile the neighbors in the room saw the *bombo* start to shake and chant fiercely, his head thrown back and brows raised in trance even while he was playing the drum. His body was struggling with something. Then he hooked the spirit and returned with it, with everyone shouting in celebration. When the *bombo* came to himself, the spirit of the woman fell onto the drum surface in the image of three white snow-flowers the size of specks of dust. The *bombo* dropped these specks into the food and gave it to the sufferer to eat.

Afterward the sufferer described what she felt. "While participating in the rite I was in pain. But when the spirit returned it felt like a jolt of electricity to the body. At 7 that night the rite ended. By 9 I was asleep. Now I want to eat and walk and sleep again. I don't have bad dreams anymore." Her body lightened up and her eyes and consciousness brightened. The pain left her little by little, and she made a full recovery. The turning point was when her soul was given back to her.

Commenting on this story to the students, I emphasized that this cure worked because the *bombo* and the others were not playing a part, nor were they *imagining* a soul and its loss. People *feel* soul loss. "Depression" is a banal description of it. Those experiencing it know it because it is a positive fact. They can often perceive the soul when it is there. It is not found written in an array of symbols, and its loss is not cured by symbolic tricks. The rites are deadly serious, and they cost the old *bombo* much trouble and fear.

Thus the syllabus consists of the laying out of people's own experience, in case after case, in their different contexts, with the energy-type cases gathered and discussed, the power cases similarly gathered, and also the spirit-derived cases.

Stories Given during the Course

(A Syllabus in Storytelling Form. See Turner, 2005)

Energy Healing

Energy healing among anthropologists at the San Francisco Hilton
A personal experience of acupuncture and the meridians, America
David Eisenberg's account of *Qi* energy in China
The "Inner Wind" that yearns for release: Malay healing
"Electricity" in the hands of an Irish Celtic healer
Num, "boiling energy": healing among the Kalahari Kung
"Radio" in the East African sense: "Divination is like radio, you open up the wavelength and you get through to the spirits"
"You can feel it in your hands" in suburban America: gifting the sick body with energy from a cloud
Conclusions, energy healing

The Experience of Power

Shakti, power and goddess: Hindu spiritual healing
The charismatics and the power of God: resting in the spirit

The Presence of Spirits in Healing

The Power of the Group in Healing: Communitas and Music

The Fruits of the Exploration: The Nature of Spiritual Healing

> Energy, power, and spirits
> The place of healing in the sum of things
> The soul
> The natural organic compound, spirit-and-world
> Trance
> The "opening" phenomenon
> The Call

May We Heal Too? Seven Practicum Sessions

> How to experience *qi*: finding out through Therapeutic Touch
> Iñupiat hands-on healing
> Praying in a circle of trust
> Singing for healing—from the forests of Congo
> Finding a sufferer's signature tune
> Shamanism: finding a spirit helper
> For those who cannot journey, sing, pray, or sense with their hands

The students enjoy the continual contrasting of societies and ways of life. The story method, bringing them right into the middle of some healing or rescue of the soul, opens them up to a wider reality. In the middle of the healing narrative they can feel the energy going over, know that something has passed. These are not stories in the words of an analyst who attributes the experiences of those healed to a theory of psychological phenomenology or argues that they happened merely in people's heads. The stories are by the experiencers. They are about *surprise*, the encounter with a force beyond them, the "I know" flash. They come from the best anthropology on religion and ritual—but from passages that are often hidden in obscure language. Yet this "story" material retains more power than the endless tomes of moral instruction written by sages in the various "great" religions.

Experience and Fieldwork

The students are involved in a personal and practical manner. On the strength of their new knowledge, they have to keep notes of their own experiences and those of friends. They note when "everything comes together" for them; when music, performed or heard by themselves, is "just right"; when they have cold chills; when they get into the "flow" of an activity; when writing, and the words write themselves; when a bright idea comes to them or a problem is solved; when they are tired and experience an unusual access to strength; when they experience a strong sense of unity in a group, however ephemeral; or when they experience communication with animals, a sense of a spirit or God speaking or touching or pushing them, answers to prayer, a sense of having lived before, déjà vu, an out-of-the-body or near-death-experience, a strong sense of place, sudden memories of persons they have not seen for a long time or who have died, a sense of a helper, or seeing ghosts. They learn that special or predictive dreams are significant, as are synchronicities, turnaround or "now-I-see-it" situations, sudden vivid memories, awareness of spirit friends, old spirit playmates, helpers, or angels, experiences of light or sudden high consciousness, or the sense that their spirit is absent from the body on some shaman journey. Also there may be negative examples, like fright, soul loss, and premonitions of danger. Any of these may be material for the students' own probings expressed in a term paper or discussion.

When the class is a two-and-a-half-hour seminar, the students may make longer presentations on their own fieldwork. This is how I advise them on fieldwork: first in importance are the situations that people take most seriously—a visit to the doctor, emergency room, or intensive care waiting room; hospice work; or any experience of extreme danger or major life change or bereavement. Students are to note what happens to the consciousness and how the human being obtains help. Now they may seek out different kinds of hands-on healing, learning them and performing them. They can investigate places and situations with power or energy, such as peace parades, times of celebration, music sessions, or places notably without them, the way certain rooms feel, and so on. They may note their dreams and pay attention to the people and animals in them, and also respond. They may sometimes sing in a round or "canon," like "Frére Jacque" or "Row, Row, Row Your Boat," listening to each other as they sing, or sing or play contrapuntal music with others. They may particularly play in jam sessions, even attend "raves" or diving into the "mosh" pit. They may elicit someone else's personal signature tune, then sing or play it with vigor for them—and discover what this act of sympathy and charity can do. In all these they become alive to the *communitas* of working with people for the good of the community.

They may happen across the sense of a spirit or power in shrines, temples, or churches, and I encourage them to go along with the sense—to totally worship with the people, never minding any rules of exclusivity. The Pentecostals, the great "feeling" people, might well liven up those students who have deadened souls. There are the great ritualizing religions, Catholicism, the Greek Orthodox Church, and Judaism. Then there are those that meditate or chant—Muslims, Hindus, Buddhists, and Quakers—and there are the rites of passage in the great and little traditions, into which (if possible) one might enter personally.

I point out how different this fieldwork is from that of the sociologists. (The sociologists themselves might become interested in this "qualitative," not "quantitative" approach. The most dramatic healing I ever experienced was performed by a sociology professor.) These student investigators of religious social processes do not use notebooks, tape recorders, or "instruments" and questionnaires; they act without formality and only in the spirit of ordinary, real friendship and interest. This is no science; it is an actual sacred activity.

What the explorer in this matter needs to keep in mind and in memory—until there is peace and quiet to take notes—are the circumstances, the place itself, name of place, its history, the geography, date, time, conditions; the people involved, their names, ages, type of person, role in present situation, job if possible, and background. Furthermore they will have to grasp the story of the activity, ritual, or experience, always in detail, plus the style of the affair. What is *said* is needed, word for word, as are style and manner, the student's own words, the other person's feelings, and the student's own feelings. The difference from the work of the regular sociologist is obvious. Subjectivity is highly valued, while old-style scientific objectivity is not. Yet, curiously, a participant in religion may be overcome with the magnificent sense that the religion is *objectively* true. The spirit is "out there," real, and not a subjective construction of the mind. The faculty for religion has been broadened and can recognize and deal with far more of what is outside, and in the process, the gift becomes interiorized, within a person. Thus this stretching process gives a person a different life. Some anthropologists have been specially bidden *by their hosts* to go into training to be healers. They have done so, with startling revelations of the truth of what passes through their healing hands.

In obtaining another person's story, students ought to follow the person's predilections and not "steer" him or her into the students' own topics. The person knows what he or she is doing. Students should follow up on how the people concerned *feel*, and get interested in the stories they have to tell. Above all, students need to forget the interview and questionnaire styles. Much the best way to learn about healing is to relate one's own experiences, modest though they may be. Others invariably butt in with theirs, and one's questions can come up in the natural course of things. Thus it is essential for students to train their memories. This whole style of training is for the purpose of obtaining live ethnographies, avoiding generalities and the watered-down descriptions found in endless books of good thoughts. Especially, our disciplines need to develop beyond theologies, beyond one-sided and partisan histories, and beyond abstractions that are of no concern to human beings.

In addition to the immediate role of fieldwork in waking up the students' religious sense comes the galvanizing effect of a good ethnographic film on ritual or religion. We use *N/um Tchai, the Ceremonial Dance of the iKung,* on the healing dance in the Kalahari desert; also *Pomo Shaman,* an old film showing a healing by the sucking shaman Essie Parrish. The gradual accumulation of energy in this film, even coming over in black and white, is magical. A film I have, obtainable only in the Arctic, *Traditional Iñupiat Healing,* shows native healers at work. Laurel Kendall's superb film of the training of a Korean woman shaman, titled *An Initiation "Kut" of a Korean Shaman,* directed by Diana S. Lee, is more readily obtainable. Then there is a great movie about the power of the god Skanda in Sri Lanka called *Kataragama, a God for All Seasons,* directed by Charlie Nairn; and a movie from Lisa Mertz called *Sister's Ghost,* in which a Native American woman tells the story of a child killed by accident who came back to the desolated family and comforted them.

Most important of all are the practicum sessions. The first one takes place in the second week of the course, when we all practice feeling energy with our hands. Straightaway, in the fall of 2003, one of the students, J, discovered the power in her hands—more of which I describe below. Most of them feel it to a greater or lesser extent, just in their own hands or around the bodies of others. In this way the group becomes aware that their ordinary skins are not the boundary of their souls, that it is possible to find the soul or psyche four inches out, and that the soul is permeable in an interesting way. Further into the course we try the Iñupiat's healing, with the hands actually on the body, removing pain and stiffness. At the class session following this first practicum, a student came in limping after a karate dislocation. I asked J, the student with the hand energy, to work on the student with the dislocation, and she healed her then and there. A week later we made the shamans' journey, lying on the floor with drumming going on in that wonderfully soundproof classroom. Though the students found their attempt at "journeying" to be rather hard, the second try was more successful, and they came up with some wonderful stories of where they went while lying on the classroom floor. When this experience works, it is gentle but hard to gainsay. You never know where you may find yourself and with what animal spirit. Toward the end of the semester we all tried singing a round, listening to each other and to the different, blending ups and downs of the music—which always produces an effect full of *communitas*, fellow feeling. Finally, we heard at the end that our hand-healing student and four others were holding their own drumming sessions in their own time and were busy healing various other students.

Of course there were drawbacks. The New Age advocates, for example, did not want to deviate from their own patterns of healing nor to consider those of societies different from the ones from which their own healing was derived. They had no comparative sense. Ironically, they resembled the anthropology graduate students in this narrowness, the latter being already indoctrinated with Marxist materialism and equally hard to shift. However, I believe the New Age types will find themselves going from one to the other of the alternative healing methods and will gradually find what truly suits them. This may take a lifetime. Such fruitful wandering and searching cannot be put into one term's course. Neither was I emphasizing the contrast between religious healing and ordinary medical treatment. It was the students who drew negative conclusions about biomedicine—but we tried to see ways to combine both.

The success of a course such as this depends more on imponderables than do courses dealing with the externals of religious healing. Some students did wonderfully because they had few predecided "isms" and still lived with an awareness of spirituality. A Russian woman student, T, did best of all, with a masterly, personal, and sensitive account of Tarot divination, showing what it does to the mind of the diviner. Only she, not I, could put such matters into words.

Closing Thoughts

As regards the problem of violence in the world, the purpose of my course was to allow the students to do something positive, to experience for themselves something of the incoming powers available to healers and to all of us. This was a yea-saying purpose. We did not dwell on the prevalence of violence in the world but turned our attention to reviving interest in positive powers in the world. Social justice can happen when the nature of things is put right. The material and stories show, for example, how successful women are as healers and as allies of spiritual forces. When knowledge of the facts of healing and spirituality gains precedence in people's minds, justice and morality have something on which to feed, whereas morality as a teaching by itself has no hope—unless backed by force and revolution. With a sense of the power of healing, the balance of attention changes, and the breaking-down-and-elimination aspects of our society take a more minor place, just as a living body's life and energy is not focused all the time on its elimination processes but on the natural positive activity of its species.

In conclusion, in several ways this is a different kind of course. It positively *teaches* religion, covering all the religions, and therefore does not transgress the rule against proselytizing any particular one of them. What it does transgress is the limitation of the activity of academics to acts of the mind. Rather like music or athletics, the course seeks to awaken a sleeping faculty, in this case, that of connection to spirit, a faculty that I think is held in readiness in a human being as a biological predisposition, like the inborn propensity of a child to learn to talk. At present the course is more successful among undergraduates and non-Westerners because of the way graduates have previously been trained. The study of the anthropology of religion needs to make a breakthrough so that students can have the chance to understand in reality what they read about or encounter in fieldwork.

RECOMMENDED BOOKS

Boddy, Janice. 1989. *Wombs and Alien Spirits: Women, Men, and the Zār Cult in Northern Sudan*. Madison: University of Wisconsin Press.
Desjarlais, Robert. 1992. *Body and Emotion: The Aesthetics of Illness and Healing in the Nepal Himalayas*. Philadelphia: University of Pennsylvania Press.
Earle, Duncan. 2003. The Imaginary Self on the Borders of Distinctions: Dog Days. Paper read at the Society for Humanistic Anthropology Invited Session, "Practice, Performance, and Participation," at the Annual Meetings of the American Anthropological Association, Chicago, November.
Friedson, Stephen. 1996. *Dancing Prophets: Musical Experiences in Tumbuka Healing*. Chicago: University of Chicago Press.
James, William. 1958 [1902]. *The Varieties of Religious Experience*. New York: Mentor.
Knab, Timothy. 2003. Practice and Participation: Serving the Most Holy Earth. Paper read at the Society for Humanistic Anthropology Invited Session, "Practice, Per-

formance, and Participation," at the Annual Meetings of the American Anthropological Association, Chicago, November.

Krieger, Dolores. 1979. *Therapeutic Touch: How to Use Your Hands to Help or to Heal.* New York: Prentice Hall.

Laderman, Carol. 1991. *Taming the Winds of Desire: Psychology, Medicine, and Aesthetics in Malay Shamanistic Performance.* Berkeley: University of California Press.

Neihardt, John G. 1988. *Black Elk Speaks: Being the Life Story of a Holy Man of the Oglala Sioux.* Lincoln: University of Nebraska Press.

Samanta, Suchitra. 1998. The Powers of the Guru: Sakti, "Mind," and Miracle in Narratives of Bengali Religious Experience. *Anthropology and Humanism* 23(1):30–50.

Saris, Greg. 1994. *Mabel McKay: Weaving the Dream.* Berkeley: University of California Press.

Turnbull, Colin. 1990. Liminality: A Synthesis of Subjective and Objective Experience. In *By Means of Performance,* ed. Richard Schechner and Willa Appel, pp. 50–81. Cambridge: Cambridge University Press.

Turner, Edith. 1996. *The Hands Feel It: Healing and Spirit Presence among a Northern Alaskan People.* DeKalb: Northern Illinois University Press.

————. 2005. *Among the Healers: Stories of Spiritual and Ritual Healing around the World.* Westport, CT: Praeger.

I2

Medicine, Healing, and Spirituality: A Cross-Cultural Exploration

Paula K. R. Arai

An Overview

The perspectives of modern Western scientific (allopathic) medicine and several Asian healing and spiritual practices are the focus of a course I teach, titled "Medicine, Healing, and Spirituality." Analysis of cultural and religious influences on the concepts of illness and health and the relationship of body and mind directs the inquiry. Linda Barnes's "Integrated Model of Affliction and Healing" promotes cross-cultural understandings and discussions. The list of questions that constitute the model draw out core concepts that enable one to compare divergent views. It helps one find clarity about specific differences and similarities and yet see them in their own context, and it infuses some precision into discussions of cosmologies and epistemologies. It also helps students gain insight into the ramifications of differences. It makes it easy to see that deeming something to be "sound knowledge," "New Age nonsense," or "primitive" turns upon one's concepts of knowledge and self. Concepts of knowledge also define the contours of what is evaluated and how it is evaluated. Whether one's concept of self is a bifurcated mind and body or an inextricably integrated mind and body makes a difference in what one considers possible and realistic.

I organize the course around having students develop a field research project investigating the relationship between healing and spirituality. The questions that guide the quest include: How do attitude and belief influence health and illness? What difference does culture make to your health? Each student must talk with a collaborator for at least three two-hour sessions. At the end, they must write a paper analyzing just what "the healing process" of their collaborator *is*. There are many steps before this, and I have designed the class to provide various conceptual issues and field research skills needed to be successful in this project.

Awakening students' understanding of the different assumptions and concepts that guide our thoughts, emotions, and expectations—particularly in relation to a topic of inquiry—is the core objective of the course. Cultivating critical consciousness is the basis for learning a multitude of ways in which peoples around the world and through history have understood and practiced medicine, healing, and spirituality. Although these terms are not necessarily used by all peoples, one can see how each culture includes something akin to these by transposing what these terms might mean in each context. This requires refined analysis in a cross-cultural mode, which is dependent upon an interpreter first having keen insight into his or her own assumptions.

Skills, Methods, and Design

We begin this journey by encouraging students to become conscious of their biases and assumptions. To this end, I first articulate biases and assumptions relevant to the course material that I have come to be aware of in myself. I should make clear here that class policy is that no one has to reveal any information that he or she does not want to. Full disclosure is not as important as establishing respect and trust for each other in the classroom.

Brainstorming on the board is how we launch into a discussion on the meaning of the three main concepts of the course: medicine, healing, and spirituality. As words go up on the board, students immediately see how their ideas are not always shared by their peers. We then probe to find what root assumptions of self, death, body, mind, and so on are implicit in their concepts of medicine, healing, and spirituality. They must analyze themselves and find a coherent way to explain their thinking to their classmates. I often analyze my own concepts to model how to do this exercise. For example, I think healing is the result of accepting life as it is and not rejecting parts of it. This is based on my view that everything in the world is interrelated. Within this view, one cannot be whole if one does not embrace all events as part of oneself. This classroom exercise is intentionally designed to trigger students' gut ideas. I point out that time for careful reflection is a detriment here, because the goal is to get at core concepts before they have been filtered through sophisticated reasoning. Students have commented how this exercise makes it apparent that their views are distinctive, and they begin to see how experience and background are strong forces that shape their understandings of the world.

They then try to observe how their assumptions affect their perception of events and, hence, their actions. This task requires more careful reflection. To facilitate such focused reflection and analysis, the first formal assignment of the course is to answer the question "What kind of a researcher am I?" The response includes explication of one's race, gender, sexual orientation, age, educational background, concentration of study, social class, language(s), health/illness experiences, and anything else that a student thinks relevant to becoming conscious of their assumptions and to gain insights into the context in which they are doing this work. The assignment has either been a one-page paper or a five-minute oral presentation. The students reported that doing several of these types of exercises in oral form, rather than written, helped them more, as it allowed them to benefit from the views and insights of others. It also fostered tighter bonds of trust, which enabled them to deal with some difficult issues in a nonthreatening environment. This is essential to entering into the heart of the material, because painful experiences and intense sadness often emerge, especially as students delve into the field project. This work becomes the foundation upon which to proceed with a nuanced study of the sundry worldviews that inform the various concepts of medicine, healing, and spirituality.

In order to be successful in collaborating with someone to learn about their healing system and process, one must have various skills. Therefore, the course seeks to foster three kinds of intelligence, as defined by Howard Gardner (1991):

1. *linguistic intelligence*: the ability to use written and oral language flexibly and productively;
2. *interpersonal intelligence*: the capacity to understand other individuals, to work well with them, to motivate them; and
3. *intrapersonal intelligence*: a correlative understanding of oneself: one's strengths, weaknesses, desires, fears and the capacity to use this knowledge to make judicious decisions about how to lead one's life.

The writing assignments, oral reports, and formal presentation cultivate linguistic intelligence. Designing the collaboration, the actual collaborating process, and in-class discussions promote interpersonal intelligence. One oral report is explicitly about the collaborators' relationship. Indeed, all the oral work in the class requires interpersonal intelligence. The more cultivated the intelligence in this area, the higher the quality of communication. The self-reflexive questions discussed in class, and most pointedly in the oral report on "What kind of a researcher am I?" nurture intrapersonal intelligence. Journaling and the report on journaling also require intrapersonal intelligence.

I find anthropological approaches most helpful in advancing inquiry into the three foci of the course, medicine, healing, and spirituality. I also think that learning through firsthand discovery is effective, which is why the field research project drives the course. The rhythm of reading and writing assignments, the order of the class materials, and the inclusion of oral reports all grew out of the needs of field research. I assign more reading and writing in the beginning of the course, as we learn various theories and study different understandings and orientations in medicine, healing, and spirituality. The middle of the course does not have much writing, so that students can spend time collaborating, journaling, and transcribing. The oral reports also help students learn from one another. When I had students write short papers on the same content, I was the only one to benefit from the diverse issues, concerns, and insights of the class as a whole. Students also did not seem to gain more from writing about their material than from doing oral reports. So we all agreed that oral reports were best for everyone.

The main class projects result from the collaborations with other persons in relation to their healing process, for which oral data is the basis for analysis. Supplementing the original oral material, several commercially produced videos provide visual and audio dimensions to our study of Tibetan medicine, Chinese medicine, facing death, and meditation used in allopathic clinics and hospitals. My own research footage has been helpful for explaining rituals used in Japanese Buddhist healing. These different media also enable students with various learning styles to access the material. We also use Barnes's integrative model with each tradition and each person, listing its seven categories (see Barnes, introduction) on the board to get clarity about each tradition insofar as it makes similarities and differences across traditions visible.

I have found that an effective way to launch the course into the crux of the issues is to start with the book *Speak the Language of Healing: Living with Breast Cancer without Going to War*, written by four women, each at a different stage of breast cancer. The authors are personal and intimate with the readers, so in addition to providing useful information about talking with someone diagnosed with breast cancer, it prepares students for collaborating with someone who has gone or is going through a health crisis. Students have commented that the book sensitized them to the need to think about the words and metaphors they use. They learn that assumptions about self and body inherent in the words we choose to discuss issues of health and illness have power to shape experience.

The course is designed as a seminar, its enrollment capped at fifteen. The intensity of the self-reflexivity inherent in the field research project requires each person to have time to engage actively with the material during class time. Initially, I had reservations that the self-reflexivity I wanted to cultivate might not go well because undergraduates may not have encountered enough tragedy in their lives to address the issues that might come up in their collaborations. Unfortunately, I was wrong. They had an abundance of suffering experience. I had also begun by encouraging them to find older collaborators (in their forties through seventies), thinking that they might yield richer material to analyze. I was wrong again. Many collaborated with fellow undergraduate students and received more than enough tragedy, trauma, and illness to work with. I did teach the course once as a first-year seminar. Even then, with students fresh out of high school, we were able to make deep strides in wrestling with the issues. Still, when there are more juniors and seniors, the level of engagement is correspondingly more sophisticated in terms of critical analysis of reading material and nuance in reflexive analysis of their work.

Each student is responsible for collaborating with another person in relation to his or her "healing process." Usually the collaborations are conducted over three sessions for about two hours each time. This enables the relationship between the collaborators to develop, and it allows both of them to address issues raised in between the collaboration sessions. After the first session, the students must also write or present a report on their working relationship with their collaborator, flagging likely bias (positive or negative) and noting issues of communication (similar styles, distance, etc.). As the collaboration process proceeds, they must also give a report on their field journal. They offer excerpts with notations on the significance of events and ideas in the process of ascertaining the healing process of their collaborator. At the end of the class, each student gives an oral presentation (more formal than a report, because it is timed, and students polish their wording and organization), addressing their own process of doing the research. The final paper focuses on their analysis of their collaborator's healing process. I place the needs of the project above the other lesson plans. So if students want more time to discuss collaboration questions or how to analyze, I devote class time to it.

So far I have been fortunate that most students have been able to find collaborators without my assistance. It is always an anxious time until everyone is settled. I have found some collaborators, but it is a delicate issue. Being hooked up to a network of people would be ideal, but I have yet to establish that. Most students collaborate with people from the local community. Some, however, have done telephone collaborations with people in various parts of the country.

When teaching the course in Nashville, I drew on regional resources in addition to local collaborators by including three guest speakers, who helped make some class sessions particularly compelling. One was surgeon John Tarpley of Vanderbilt Medical Center, who directs a "Medicine and Spirituality" program at Vanderbilt's Medical School. A punctual person, he once came running in, remarking that the surgery he had just performed had gone a little longer than anticipated. He was confident that his assistant could finish up alone. At that moment, the rest of us in the room felt the gravity of his occupation, the power of a surgeon entirely palpable. I am sure that I was not the only one whose breath momentarily froze as the image of Dr. Tarpley working over a person cut open on the operating table—utterly dependent on his skill and care—flashed across my mind's eye. To be so close to someone with the power to affect people's health in such dramatic ways inspired awe.

So was being in the presence of another guest, Dr. Susan Kuner, one of the coauthors of *Speak the Language of Healing*. Living with a breast cancer diagnosis, she describes her journey with an animation that can emerge only out of a well of wisdom and suffering. Our third guest was an Alive Hospice grief counselor, John Baker. His gentle demeanor and kind voice modeled for us just what he came to explain: how to be with a person who is grieving. Students deeply benefited from his experience, because some had felt uncertain about how to respond to a person who cries or clearly aches during conversations with their collaborators. They wanted to do the "right" thing but did not always know what that might be. Having a quarter system schedule, as I do at Carleton, makes it more difficult to bring in outside speakers, but having had the same speakers for three runs of the class, I am able to convey some of their contributions myself. In the future, I hope to include guest speakers somewhere in the quarter schedule, because it is a richer experience for the students. It is one thing to talk *about* people who have experienced cancer; it is another to speak openly *with* someone with these experiences.

I present my own work on Japanese Buddhist women's rituals of healing as a model of the field research techniques being cultivated, as well as an example of how to assess a healing process in relation to cultural and religious contexts. For example, my research led me to make explicit decisions about the collaborating relationship and about strategic self-disclosure due to the Japanese concept of a "relational self." I discovered that the Japanese Buddhist women I collaborated with grounded their healing process in the Buddhist-based assumption that we are born with a longing for good things to be permanent and for the fulfillment of our desires. This is the condition from which we must be healed. Healing is not about finding a cure. Nor is it framed as a direct cause-and-effect relationship. Rather, it is a worldview, or way of living and facing all kinds of challenges of the nonbifurcated body and mind. For these women, healing involves transformation of habitually deluded ways of looking at the world through the lenses of desire and aversion. Therefore, for them, all of life is a process of healing, of transforming the way life is viewed and experienced.

In Japanese culture, *tatemae* (public face) and *honne* (private face) are clearly delineated, especially among the generation of women with whom I was collaborating. In this cultural context, people are adept at sincerely expressing their public face, making it difficult to discern how much their public and private faces might differ. Moreover, it is considered improper to express your private face or *honne* to someone with whom you have only a public relationship. The standard collaborators' relationship falls into the "public" category. Therefore, it is difficult to access the "private face" (*honne*) of a person.

Since the information I sought lies deep in a person's heart, mind, and body, I decided that keeping an objective observer's distance would yield little about the highly personal and private dimensions of these women's lives. In the Japanese context, it was only fair that I make myself vulnerable before expecting others to open up about their most intimate and often painful experiences. Consequently, I made the carefully considered and deliberate decision to disclose my own personal emotions and experiences to each of the women. In return for having exposed my shortcomings and difficulties, I received not only valuable and helpful advice, but also a treasure trove of details essential to understanding their concepts, experiences, and feelings, especially about the role of the deceased in their rituals of healing. As we cultivated intimate relationships, we broke through the socially scripted façade of efficient tidiness and impeccable self-control, and delved into the excruciating, infuriating, and terrifying realms where healing and transformation take place.

Ancestors, or dead "Buddhas," play a vital role in Japanese Buddhism, and are foci for healing power. Therefore, there is often no clear boundary between the therapeutic and the religious. The identity of the dead in the construction of the self and how it bears upon the healing process are key factors in the analysis of this phenomenon.

I have used Barnes's integrated model to help clarify how the dead are part of the healing process of Japanese Buddhists. Of its seven foci, the first is "understandings of ultimate human possibility." In the case of these Japanese Buddhist women, ultimate human possibility involves not only the potential of enlightenment in daily life, but its guarantee in death. Second, affliction and suffering in general are understood as relatives, not enemies. They are part of one's life with which, no matter what, one must interact. *How* one interacts is the key. Third, the self is understood to be interrelated with everything in the universe, and not bifurcated as "mind" and "body." This interrelatedness means that the realms of life and death can interact. Fourth, in understanding illness/sickness in particular, the women see themselves as having the power to respond positively or negatively. Positive and negative here do not refer to valuations of good and evil, but rather to weaving the illness into living, versus trying to reject it. Weaving leads to healing, while rejecting leads to greater suffering.

Fifth, while the women consider allopathic doctors and acupuncturists to be healers, they also stress how they see Zen Buddhist nuns as fulfilling this role. The nuns guide them in how to have better relationships with their illnesses. The most intimate healers, however, are their dead loved ones, the Buddhas who know them best and who are with them everywhere all the time, no longer restricted by the forces of gravity or the limitations of space and time. Sixth, beyond medical treatments, the nature of the care to which these women turn is a transformation of their own perspective. Whether it lies in healing from the loss of a loved one or dealing with the residence of cancer in one's body, the awareness of how one is internally related to everything else is what helps. The intervention sought involves learning to cut out the delusion that one is an isolated, independent entity. Finally, efficacy or healing is oftentimes not addressed directly. Instead, experiencing and expressing gratitude becomes one of the key components of healing and its expressions. After all, if one is *related to* everything, then the only reasonable response is gratitude for everything as an aspect or expression of that relatedness. The gratitude may or may not help arrest the development of cancer cells, but it makes each breath of air sweeter, every load of laundry lighter, and every committee meeting feel like a slice of heaven. Like scholarly inquiry, the art of healing is a creative process of transformation, leading one to see everything interrelated in a perpetual dance of change. Women use Buddhist rituals in this art, to promote a direct experience of interrelatedness that gives rise to their gratitude—a place where they can feel at peace and intimately connected to family and friends, to the living and the dead, to nature, and to the cosmos.

In addition to the cross-cultural discussions that hopefully arise out of a focus on methodological considerations, employing this interpretive model fosters a rich cross-cultural reflection on the role of the deceased in healing rituals, allowing the class to compare the case of Japanese Buddhist ancestor rituals with those of other cultures. For example, with comparing understandings of ultimate human possibility, do other cultures view death as the moment when someone can attain the highest potential, as in the Japanese Buddhist case when one can become a Buddha? Are these more powerful beings then understood to be the source of affliction and suffering, the reason one is healed and protected, or both?

Conclusions

Focusing on religion and healing exposes students to the ramifications of religion on how people perceive and experience life and death. Examining fundamental concepts that make up a worldview, such as self, body, world, and meanings of life and death, helps them to see differences between religious traditions. The implications of those differences also become easier to identify. Once students learn that they need to be clear about the assumptions at work in any given activity or concept, they can then analyze an event or idea while being less likely to project their own worldview inadvertently onto someone else. This analytical skill and its attendant awareness are at the roots of the academic study of religion.

Highlighting the theme of healing is particularly fruitful because it goes beyond theoretical concerns and requires attention to what people *do*. Environment, diet, rituals, human relations, gender-specific roles and activities all come into focus. It is in the messy details that one can broach accuracy. With a view to the details and an open mind, one begins to see things from different perspectives. Students then start to realize that a tight definition of "religion" is neither possible nor desirable. So much depends on the details of the specific context that generalizations can simply be misleading or, as students have observed, even imperialistic arrogance at work. They discover that misunderstanding and poor communication often result from trying to understand "religion" with a generalized definition. What I hope the students learn about religion through this study of healing is that any topic must be pursued first with questions and a careful examination of one's own assumptions and those of others, through which a more nuanced understanding may develop and distinct perspectives emerge.

By focusing on the fundamental assumptions of a religious tradition, my own understanding of healing has changed. I have found that studying religion opens a vista onto the details of a culture and era. It brings into high relief particular concepts like life and death, body and mind. In my experience, this is an essential foundation from which to understand and appreciate what healing means in any given context. Without it, insight can easily be lost in unexamined assumptions and uninformed concepts. With it, however, one can see what and why people value what they do. What might look like irrational superstition from one set of assumptions can look like powerful healing from another. My goal is to understand both *why* people experience healing—so I examine their worldview—and *how* healing occurs, leading me to study their practices and rituals. The study of religion is a cornerstone of the study of healing, and, one could argue, the reverse holds true as well.

Course Syllabus: "Medicine, Healing and Spirituality"

Course Requirements

Assignment	Due Date	% of grade
Course engagement:	Ongoing	25%
Attendance, participation in discussions, oral reports in class		
6-page essay on cultural perspectives of healing	May 1	25%
Presentation of research findings	June 3	15%
10-page final essay	June 9	35%

All reading assignments are to be prepared for the class date under which they are listed. Since this course runs as a workshop and discussion section, individual preparation and participation are crucial to group success. If you are not ready to speak, listen, disagree, and argue when you come to class on any given day, then you are not prepared for class. The success of the class depends on the enthusiastic participation of each and every member.

Course Schedule

WEEK 1

Introduction to course (field project)

Integrative Model for Discourse on Medicine, Healing, and Spirituality

> Susan Kuner, Carol Orsborn, Linda Quigley, Karen Stroup. 1999. *Speak the Language of Healing: Living With Breast Cancer Without Going to War.* Berkeley, CA: Conari.

WEEK 2

Allopathic Medicine—Before and Beyond—Herbert Benson, MD (Part 1)

> Herbert Benson, M.D. 1997. *Timeless Healing: The Power and Biology of Belief,* pp. 151–168; 171–191. New York: Simon & Schuster.

Allopathic Medicine—Before and Beyond—Herbert Benson, MD (Part 2)

> Benson, *Timeless Healing: The Power and Biology of Belief,* pp. 193–219; 265–281; 290–304.

WEEK 3

Field Project Plan: Collaborations, Privacy, Journals

> Paula Arai. 1993. "Methodology" from *Zen Nuns: Living Treasures of Japanese Buddhism,* unpublished Ph.D. dissertation, Harvard University, pp. 34–53 (on closed reserve).

Dalai Lama. 1991. *MindScience: An East-West Dialogue*. Boston: Wisdom.

What Kind of a Researcher Am I?

Student Oral Reports
Designing the Collaboration

WEEK 4

Healing in Cross-Cultural Perspectives

David Kinsley. 1996. *Health, Healing and Religion: A Cross-Cultural Perspective*, pp. 1–83. Upper Saddle River, NJ: Prentice Hall.

Modern Medicine as Secular Religion

David Kinsley, *Health, Healing, and Religion: A Cross-Cultural Perspective*, pp. 139–198.

WEEK 5

What Is the Relationship between Myself and My Collaborator?

Student Reports on How It Is Going and Discussion of Salient Issues

Buddhist Concept of Self and Ultimate Reality

Thich Nhat Hanh. 1988. *The Heart of Understanding*. Berkeley, CA: Parallax.
Japanese Buddhist artist, Tsuneo Iwasaki (slides)

WEEK 6

Japanese Buddhist Healing Process: Arai's Research (I)

David Crow. 2000. *In Search of the Medicine Buddha: A Himalayan Journey*. New York: Penguin Putnam.
Japanese Buddhist Healing Process: Arai's Research (II)

WEEK 7

Japanese Esoteric and Everyday Healing Rituals: Arai Field Research Footage
Discuss Collaborations

Student Oral Reports on Collaborations and Discussion
David B. Morris. 1998. *Illness and Culture in the Postmodern Age*. Berkeley: University of California Press.

WEEK 8

Tibetan Medicine

> John F. Avedon. 1984. "Tibetan Medicine: The Science of Healing." In *In Exile from the Land of Snows*, pp. 137–156. New York: Vintage.

Discuss Field Journals

> Student oral report on field journals. Bring in excerpts to share. We will address concerns and begin to analyze the data.

WEEK 9

Chinese Medicine

> Maoshing Ni. 1995. *The Yellow Emperor's Classic of Medicine*. Boston: Shambhala.

Living With Loss

> "Living Fully until Death." 1995. Dartmouth-Hitchcock Medical Center Production. 29 min. video in class

WEEK 10

Presentations of Research

Course Assignments

I. FIRST WRITING ASSIGNMENT

Six-page essay on cultural perspectives of healing (25%).

Create a dialogue between at least two people. At least one person is a medical doctor in the modern Western biomedical system. Another person is from a "traditional healing tradition" (a figure who would fit the criteria explicated in chapter 1 of Kinsley). Have each person discuss the meaning of illness and its relation to his or her religious orientation or worldview. What are their concepts of the body and mind? What are their concepts of healing? What assumptions do they make that enable them to think the methods they employ are effective? Make sure they reflect upon their similarities, differences, and what they can learn from each other.

Either at logical intervals in the conversation or at the end, write some paragraphs from your perspective as a student of these matters, that analyze why they say what they do.

II. ORAL REPORTS

All oral reports are to be about 4–5 minutes long.

Oral Assignment #1: "What kind of a researcher am I?"

Oral Assignment #2: Report on the collaborator relationship.

Oral Assignment #3: Report on salient issues and questions that have arisen in the collaborations.

Oral Assignment #4: Report on journal excerpts. Select passages that demonstrate your:

- insights into the nature of field research, if they occur;
- insights into the healing process, if they occur;
- insights into cultural context, if they occur; and
- awareness of the complexities of the issues

III. ORAL PRESENTATION

In class

This assignment is more formal than the oral reports. Please rehearse and time your presentation carefully—(15%).

The presentation should focus on the methodological aspect of the project. Fundamental to that is self-reflexive analysis of the research. In addition to the methodological issues, salient features of the collaborator's healing process are appropriate to include.

IV. FINAL WRITING ASSIGNMENT

In 10 pages, explicate an answer to the question: What is the healing process of my collaborator? Use the "Integrated Model" as the basis of the analysis.

Additional Resources

Howard Gardner. 1991. Cognition: A Western Perspective. In *Mind-Science: an East-West dialogue*, ed. Daniel Goleman and Robert A. F. Thurman, pp. 82–84. Boston: Wisdom.

Susan Kuner, Carol Orsborn, Linda Quigley, and Karen Stroup. 1999. *Speak the Language of Healing: Living with Breast Cancer without Going to War*. Berkley, CA: Conari.

13

Religious Healing as Pedagogical Performance

Stephanie Y. Mitchem

Teaching an undergraduate course in the anthropology of religion provided an initial context in which I included religious healing content. I had expected that the topic would serve as a theme demonstrating the dynamics of anthropology of religion. Instead, healing rapidly came to hold the center of students' attention. I also tried to incorporate some foci on religious anthropology—that is, how different religions have operative anthropologies—because American politics were focused on the possibility of war with Iraq. Again, healing proved to be the window into these differences. My assumptions in structuring the course were, as usual, complicated by encounters with students and university climate. Both I, as the instructor, and my students became caught up in pedagogical performances that encompassed nation, race, gender, and class. This essay discusses some of the dynamics of teaching religious healing in one anthropology of religion course. Within the context of the classroom and university setting and my initial assumptions, I began by constructing a course that seemed to only use religious healing as an example. However, as this essay explains, discussions of religious healing became increasingly central to the students' experiences of the course and raised more attendant issues than I expected.

Context and Structure

Teaching anthropology of religion at University of Detroit Mercy required special consideration of the students and institutional setting. Few students are religion majors, and there is no anthropology major or minor. Therefore, the undergraduate student population is primarily driven to take the course to fulfill the religion objective in the core requirements. These groups of students, primarily from the Detroit area, are also encouraged by peers, family, and often the surrounding culture, to consider economic success—defined as making a great deal of money—as the primary indicator of a successful college education. Such thinking makes sense in this region: metropolitan Detroit, like many urban areas, is continually struggling to overcome the effects of population shifts away from the city, based on income (most often the wealthiest) and race (most often white) during the 1960s and 1970s. Race becomes a subtext to almost any discussion about the city, considered by some as a shining example of contemporary segregation. Detroit is 88 percent African American and is surrounded by suburbs with their own interesting race stories: Livonia has a nearly all-white population, and Southfield has a significant high-income black population. But in Detroit, the bleeding out of the business base accelerated the weakening of the city as lowered tax revenues shorted out the city's ability to support the material infrastructure, such as sewage, and left long-standing institutions like hospitals struggling for survival.

Though the city has claimed to be on a comeback track for the past twenty years, institutions like the University of Detroit Mercy continue to exist in survival mode. Of prime consideration is a simple question: What should the relationship of the college be with the poor, black neighborhood where it is located? The response to that question has been occasional lip service to "Catholic social justice," even as fences are constructed to keep the neighbors out. This thinking has led to an administrative preferencing of the white traditional-age student (based on an erroneous belief that all white students are rich and all black students are poor), leading to additional tensions in a class where cultures are analyzed. African American and white American students, often living in different relationships with the city, populated the Anthropology of Religion class.

Also, a range of ages attends my classes, including both traditional-age as well as returning adult students. Conversations across ages often added richness to our discussions. Regardless of age, however, each group shared a trait important to an anthropology of religion course: students regularly struggle to grasp concepts and tolerate ambiguity, hoping that life can be drawn in sharp definition, black and white with no shades of gray. With this general mind-set, an emphasis on religious healing presents a special challenge because it introduces so many shades of gray.

However, when I initially structured this course, I was thinking of none of these perspectives. Instead, I was focusing on two other issues. First, the practice of thinking about human beings demands more than a text. A strictly text-based course seemed the least interesting path to engaging students in religious anthropology; and documentaries, no matter how well done, are too distant from the grit of understanding humans. Second, as a sign of our times, society frequently labels the liberal arts as "fluff" and glorifies the vocational areas as "solid." By incorporating a thematic study of religious healing into a course on the anthropology of religion, I hoped to help students realize that the "fluff" designation was patently false.

My original objective for including discussions of religious healing was simple: I wanted to foster undergraduates' learning about anthropology of religion and its work without taking them directly into the field. As a faculty member in a school that does not honor the liberal arts, I perceive a critical need to act upon theories of anthropology of religion while considering religious anthropology—performance in itself—as a learning methodology. But the real performance ensued from a post-9/11 world, one in which we necessarily held discussions across races and cultures. I offered this anthropology of religious course at a challenging time in the politics of the United States, as the decision to invade Iraq was becoming an unavoidable visitor in classroom discussion. It surfaced a number of typically ugly-American attitudes toward anyone not white, Western, male, middle class, or Christian. All these became part of overlapping performances of nations, races, and cultures.

Religious Healing in the Classroom

The class began with discussions of "religious healing" that immediately challenged students' thinking about bodies and healing. How were bodies defined in different cultures? What were different meanings of healing? Were such definitions of bodies or healing always limited to the physical? This beginning point led to the related discussion of the possibilities of being healed through religion. Each student brought some definition of religion that played into thinking patterns about healing and bodies and with this, some view of the Divinity. For instance, when a student understood religion as limited to an hour-a-week event, the imagination was stretched beyond hospitals and clinics in the process of connecting healing, medicine, the body, everyday life, and culture. This was the beginning point of performance, which I did not yet recognize. Although students were also being introduced to concepts of anthropology, religion, culture, and interrelationships between them, religious healing swiftly became the center of our focus.

I led students into that focus using an approach that could be described as "folkloric." My frame of reference was Zora Neale Hurston, who wrote that folklore "is the boiled-down juice of human living. It does not belong in any special time, place, nor people. No country is so primitive that it has no lore, and no country has yet become so civilized that no folklore is being made within its boundaries" (1999:69). With this in mind, I invited students to locate forms of religious healing in their lives and experiences. My assumption was that religious healing has meaning in the everyday lives of many students, so I asked them to tap into their own knowledge base. Students had three related tasks, for which excerpts from Eric J. Bailey's work (2002) proved particularly helpful. In addition to his discussions of understanding African American folk healing, Bailey includes a chapter on methodology in medical anthropology that presents a brief outline of research rules and roles. Students used this chapter in their own research as they entered their modified fieldwork assignment.

Their first task was to engage in a process of discovery and find something that connected religion and healing. This opening assignment invited them to recognize—to "find"—some evidence of religious healing in their everyday lives. I expected that they would pick up information on a faith healer, such as a televangelist or information from a website. Instead, the research quickly became personal for some of them. For instance, a second-generation Italian student discussed his grandmother's role as the family healer, primarily through the use of prayer. He knew that she prayed for ill family members, but did not know what she said: he no longer understood Italian. He also knew that she was reputed to be able to pray someone to death: her prayers were so powerful that God would answer by killing the offending person. This student had a certain distance from this presentation; although his grandmother was involved, he claimed no direct healing experience for himself. He did, however, find this practice related to the larger issue of religious healing and, I stressed to the class, worthy of study.

This opening assignment surfaced several tensions that continually played out around the theme of religious healing during the class. The fault lines became obvious as the presentations continued. In one example, an older African American female student brought in a handkerchief reputed to have healing power, having been blessed by a faith healer. She believed in the cloth's power and discussed how she had lent it to family and friends. As she continued her presentation, she blurred the lines of researcher and informant, creating some discomfort for other students, who were unsure how to respond. In particular, disbelief could be seen in the smirks on the faces of some of the younger white male students.

I gradually became aware that something else at play. Whenever a student presentation raised the question of belief in religious healing, some students gravitated to what Parker Palmer terms "objectivism," which

> portrays truth as something we can achieve only by disconnecting ourselves, physically and emotionally, from the thing we want to know . . . *Any way of knowing that requires subjective involvement between the knower and the known is regarded as primitive, unreliable, and even dangerous.* The intuitive is derided as irrational, true feeling is dismissed as sentimental, the imagination is seen as chaotic and unruly, and storytelling is labeled as personal and pointless. (1998:51–52, emphasis mine)

Palmer contends that this objectivism is at the heart of a fearful way of knowing. The younger white male students were from the "practical and rational" colleges of engineering and business; their responses to any believer in religious healing particularly reflected the fear of which Palmer writes. They often challenged and argued against the "primitive" or "uneducated" conviction that religious healing is possible. Why don't these people know better? When they get better educated and know about hospitals, they won't use this strange stuff anymore, will they? The intellectual differences between these young white male students and the other students (primarily women of all colors and men of color), in relation to what counted as knowledge, became increasingly clear.

Another level of performance also became clear to me: the younger white students expected that their ways of thinking were privileged, and they expected me, as a faculty member, to uphold their views of the world. Instead, I challenged their views of universals, of objectivity, and of the rightness of the Western world, and invited them to recognize the validity of *both* the world of Western science *and* what Paolo Freire refers to as "local knowledge" (1995:85). Whether I succeeded is questionable—after all, the educational climate of the university frequently minimized the significance of worlds beyond their grasp. Still, the alternative was raised.

Each of the three assignments to locate religious healing aroused some of the same tension. Over the weeks, I attempted to engage all the students in reflection and analysis of their beliefs. On what grounds do we determine that one system is "better" than another? Why do some people try to claim superiority over others? What is really helpful in order to achieve dialogues between people of different cultures? How do we *know*? What is truth? But by the end of the course, the fault lines had become even more sharply drawn, as the younger white males began to wave American flags with underlying Western cultural biases in the face of each ambiguity. This nationalistic performance was directly related to the buildup toward war on Iraq; the fervor with which these young men mouthed slogans was alarming. I persisted in pushing the conversations. By the end of the course, several students commented that they appreciated the space to have calm and reasoned exchanges with people of different opinions about the war. I, however, had not felt that calm and reason; instead, I repeatedly felt as though I was performing on a high wire.

As students continued to bring in materials related to religious healing, their analyses grew more sophisticated. One student completed the assignment to bring in an example of the notion of a "faith or belief that supports religious healing" by discussing a prayer formula in her church which, she contended, supports psychological healing. The prayer formula—ACTS—calls on the petitioner to praise God (Adoration); acknowledge human weakness (in Confession); recognize the blessings already received (Thanksgiving); and ask for the next gifts, especially praying for others, not oneself (Supplication). When asked why she believed that this formula indicated psychological healing, she argued that the impact of recognizing human limits and God's power while praying for others healed the petitioner by freeing her or his mind from limited thinking. An extended class discussion followed her presentation.

Such student assignments produced another kind of pedagogical performance, balancing certainty on the part of some students with uncertainty and ambivalence on the part of others. The roles shifted, depending on the context. The experience demonstrated that fieldwork and scholarly thinking do not necessarily lead to the safety the objectivist desires. As Thomas Tweed has noted about his own research, "We are obliged in all our work, ethnographic and historical, to be as clear as possible about our confused location, to be as attentive as possible to our continually shifting position. And in that reflexivity is all the comfort available to interpreters" (2002:73).

An additional approach to religious healing I used throughout the course involved engaging students' imaginations through the living narratives of three guest speakers. Rather than providing folkloric material, these speakers, all employed at University of Detroit Mercy, presented information about formalized systems of healing. Each speaker discussed traditional healing and healers with the students, focusing on a particular culture. Cornelius Sikawa spoke from within the culture of the Masai of Kenya, and Donna Roe, from a Native American frame of reference. The third speaker, Gail Presbey, was a researcher who encountered traditional healers in her work among the Masai in Kenya.

The two speakers about Kenya's religious healing, Sikawa and Presbey, provided unique perspectives for students through contrasts in their views on the same topic. Sikawa spoke from within Masai culture, while Presbey was clearly an outsider. Despite the amount of time she had spent in Kenya, it was clear that she could resonate with some of the issues of believability raised by students. Students, in turn, asked each speaker the question that guided many of their discussions: Do you *believe* that such healing can take place? Presbey shrugged, became somewhat apologetic, and launched into a discussion of a taking a nonjudgmental approach to her work. The Masai speaker, Sikawa, laughed, shrugged, and stated, "It worked." He also turned the tables, at times destabilizing an American view of the world. In discussing a cultural difference in dress between American and Masai women, he laughed off critiques of Masai women going topless. "Yes, breasts! Who cares? We know you have them."

Besides the culturally derived differences in understandings the body, Sikawa pointed to health practices that differed from those of the West. For example, the Masai in the Kenyan countryside live on an arid land, herding cattle and growing some crops. Their diets include fat, milk, and blood. However, during pregnancy, Masai women eat less than they ordinarily do. Sikawa also pointed out how traditional healing and related culture are endangered by the imposition of various Western values, including those of biomedicine. It was important for students to engage in questions and answers with all the speakers, but especially with one like Sikawa, whose culture so radically differs from their own. A human person can enter into exchanges with students that the in-class film documentary cannot.

The Native American speaker, Donna Roe, brought the greatest richness to the discussion of religious healing, perhaps because, as an Other from within the American cultural framework, she speaks directly to American-style concerns. She has been involved in different tribes because of her parents, and she now participates in another tribal council. Additionally, she studies First Peoples extensively. Thus she brought a panoptic view of Native Americans to the classroom, contextualizing their varieties, defining ways of life and thought, in which religious healing made sense, and contrasting "Western" or scientific thinking with that of First Peoples. Western thinking, she suggested, often separates and controls mind, spirit, and body. The laws of state govern health care, and healers are accountable to the government. Health care is a business supported by the government and taxpayers, creating dependency on the part of the person who seeks healing. In contrast, the First People view the body, mind, and spirit holistically, working in an integrated unity. The laws of nature control healing, and the healers are accountable to the creators and to creation. Healing is not for profit, it is supported by the earth, and the one seeking healing is assisted toward greater self-sufficiency.

Several important lessons grew out of all the speakers' presentations, each of which became other performances that we later explored in the class, sometimes painfully. Growing from the presentations by Sikawa, we as Americans learned that we needed to recognize the political, national, and cultural power of the United States, especially when relating to other nations. This discussion entered the students' analysis of relations with Iraq.

In a related discovery, students felt that there is a need to find a balance between one's own cultural perspective and other people's, which requires the vision to understand oneself. Through the presentations, I was able to emphasize that scholars must, at all costs, avoid romanticizing or exoticizing other cultures. With that in mind, not *all* of the Western views or *all* Iraq or *all* of anything is bad; to think thusly is a kind of reverse romanticizing that creates some ultimate, comic-book style of evil. Most important, the students discovered that there is a critical need for dialogue among cultures and that these intercultural dialogues can be quite rich. The most important lesson for many of them was that religions—especially through anthropological studies—provide important doorways to appreciation of cultures.

Conclusion

Focusing on religious healing in a single anthropology of religion course generated experiences of pedagogical performances on multiple levels. The students' assignments to locate different types of religious healing in their world led to insights beyond any textbook. The guest speakers represented another level of performance of religious healing. Through it all, the students and I learned and relearned the potential performance of a university as limits of each person's understanding were challenged. Latin American scholar Alberto Moreiras has written about the relationships between the university and processes of globalization:

> Western universities are not just purveyors of globalization at the
> technical level, but also significant sites of theorization for nonglobal
> practices and experiences. . . . The Western university is an over-
> whelming machine for the colonizing and dismantling of singular
> practices. . . . At the same time, the university is also the theoretical
> site of enunciation for any number of singularizing practices: of
> feminist practices, of gay and lesbian practices, of calls for the cul-
> tural survival of threatened or disappearing human communities

and calls for solidarity for the poor, of theories of racial consciousness, of resistance to colonial discourse, and of a certain enactment
of postcolonial discourse. (1998:81–82)

It was when poised between dismantling and enunciating singular practices, supporting and confronting objectivist thinking, that the class underwent
its most significant performances. The question "How does anyone believe in
religious healing?" highlighted this interesting position. By the end of the
course, most students could distinguish these tensions, even if they did not
have Moreiras's language. Most of them became more comfortable with ambiguity than they had been when they entered the class. This comfort level
included a willingness to be more than tolerant toward other cultures and to
try to expand their understanding beyond their own boundaries, the most important pedagogical performance of religious healing.

Syllabus: Anthropology of Religions

Winter 2003 Thursdays, 4 P.M.

Course Overview

The study of anthropology has special applications in researching religions,
both as a methodology and a field in itself. This course will provide the student
a basic introduction to anthropology of religion, covering basic terminology,
significant historical thinkers, and important contemporary questions. As a
focus for our study, we will consider religious healing. Healing provides a
thematic application to consider each of the sections of the text: controversies,
body, identity, gender, culture, ritual, and shamanism. Study of religious healing will also give the student an opportunity to be the researcher.

Text

> Fiona Bowie. 2000. *The Anthropology of Religion: An Introduction*. Oxford:
>   Blackwell
> Eric J. Bailey. 2002. *African American Alternative Medicine: Using Alterna-
>   tive Medicine to Prevent and Control Chronic Diseases*. Westport, CT:
>   Bergin and Garvey.

Process, Assignments, and Grading

In this anthropology of religion course, multiple methods will be used to introduce students to the material. Participation is a key component of student
success in this class. Grading is based on the following three sections:

1. *Participation*: The material of anthropology of religion is beyond the classroom, text, and readings. Guest speakers and videos will expand our view beyond the classroom walls. Several in-class exercises (interview techniques and observation/description) sharpen the focus on anthropological methods. Contemporary issues shape the ways disciplines are viewed. One important current issue that takes many shapes is the interaction(s) of culture(s). Keeping current with world events will assist students in these discussions. All these are participatory works. While no specific points are assigned to this section, your participation will be noted in the final grading process.

2. *Research*: Religious healing provides the lens to understand many of the dynamics of religious anthropology. You become the researcher in this portion of the class. In your study of religion and healing, locate the following:

   • A "find:" The process of discovery means seeing things with new eyes. At some point, you should "see" something differently and recognize it as a religion and healing connection—15 points.
   • Identify a faith belief (any denomination) that supports religious healing—10 points.
   • Bring in a photo or artwork that depicts religious healing—15 points. These will be discussed in class. If necessary, make copies for the rest of the members.

3. *Tests*: Three tests will be given through the term. These tests will focus primarily on the text, but if material of note is covered in that section, it will be included. Tests are not cumulative, but focus on the identified section. Each test will definitely include vocabulary (words in bold through text) and discussion of key theorists. (Study suggestions: work with your group for study and begin to use the vocabulary in our class discussions.)

The date of each test is listed in the final section of this syllabus.
Each test will be worth 20 points of the grade.

Class Process

In order to engage this course in the most exciting way, we will operate occasionally as a seminar, with a few lectures in between. It is expected that each student will come to class with any assignments or readings of the day completed, prepared to participate in the discussions. To this end, the student prompt will assist us. We may employ a variety of scholarly methods through the course, including group work and student reports.
Starting Norms for the class (initial list; more to be added the first day):

   • We will fully listen to and respect the experiences and feelings of others.

- We will work together as co-learners.
- We will take care not to impose our views on one another.

Nonnegotiable

You will not succeed in this class if you do not do the reading or writing on time; if you never participate and are regularly tardy; or if you miss more than three hours of class.

The importance of your presence: There will be a variety of ways to participate, including small-group and in-class discussions. For the sake of establishing communication lines, students will select small groups for the entire term the first day of class. Language is powerful, and our verbal expressions are another form of the usage of language we wish to explore. Your presence also speaks. As noted elsewhere in this syllabus, if you miss more than three hours of classes or are regularly tardy, expect a much lower grade.

Total points = 100

BIBLIOGRAPHY

Bailey, Eric J. 2002. *African American Alternative Medicine: Using Alternative Medicine to Prevent and Control Chronic Diseases.* Westport, CT: Bergin and Garvey.

Freire, Paulo. 1995. *Pedagogy of Hope: Reliving Pedagogy of the Oppressed* New York: Continuum.

Hurston, Zora Neale. 1999. *Go Gator and Muddy the Waters: Writings from the Federal Writers' Project,* ed. Pamela Bordelon. New York: W. W. Norton.

Moreiras, Alberto. 1998. "Global Fragments: A Second Latinamericanism." In *The Cultures of Globalization,* ed. Fredric Jameson and Masao Miyoshi, 81–102. Durham, NC: Duke University Press.

Palmer, Parker J. 1998. *The Courage to Teach: Exploring the Inner Landscape of a Teacher's Life.* San Francisco: Jossey-Bass.

Tweed, Thomas A. 2002. "Between the Living and the Dead: Fieldwork, History, and the Interpreter's Position." In *Personal Knowledge and Beyond: Reshaping the Ethnography of Religion,* ed. James V. Spickard, J. Shawn Landres, and Meredith B. McGuire, 63–74. New York: New York University Press.

14

Magic, Witchcraft, and Healing

Arvilla Payne-Jackson

I teach the course *Magic, Witchcraft, and Healing* to both undergraduate and graduate students at Howard University, a historically black university that has a large, international student body. Class discussions revolve around multiple worldviews, bringing to light the many ways in which the supernatural effects the way we live, as well as the similarities and differences across cultures. Students from different cultures, religious backgrounds, and persuasions disclose their beliefs and practices. Most of them begin the course with a general conception of religion as a structured/organized institution or system of faith, in which a Supreme Being or deities merit obedience, reverence, and worship; of magic as illusion and deception performed by a magician on stage; of witchcraft as the practice of people who cast evil spells and participate in strange rituals; and of healing only as curing a disease or restoring health. Students usually see each of these as a separate entity.

This course challenges them to examine their own belief systems. They learn to explore the interrelationships among these four domains as well as others: to see religion as more than a building or formal institution—as an attitude, a state of life, devotion, and conscience; to see magic as it manifests in religious practices *and* beliefs across cultures and in health practices; to distinguish between sorcery (a learned art) and witchcraft (an inherited characteristic or a religion, as in the United States); and to view healing as more than healing a wound or disease, as a means of making whole through reconciliation, purification or cleansing—restoring to wholeness. The learning goals of the course are to stimulate students to explore their own beliefs about the supernatural and how those beliefs affect the ways in which they relate to others, how they live their daily lives and how they interact with the environment. As we cover different topics in the course, I encourage them to disclose to others their beliefs, experiences, and questions that they are otherwise hesitant to discuss because of the stigma attached to belief in the supernatural and paranormal.

The course begins with an exploration of "centrisms"—ideocentrism, egocentrism, ethnocentrism, sociocentrism, and geocentrism. I use this discussion to bring students into an awareness of some of their own biases and beliefs. A discussion of great and little traditions follows, which allows for the exploration of the many ways in which the dogma of a belief system translates into practical religion and praxis. Within the context of these traditions, we examine the roles of rituals as the storehouses of cultural values, and myth as the cultural histories and explanations for who, what, where and how we are, together with their relationship to each other. This section sets the background for the ritual report assignment and introduces them to the importance of understanding the symbols used during rituals.

We then discuss *mana* and *tabu* in relation to both the sacred and the profane. The greater the power, the more the tabus needed for protection. We follow with the supernatural forces associated with sacred powers, images, locations, and objects, and the tabus that surround them as a means of protection (e.g., the Arc of the Covenant, Mecca, the Ganges River). We also talk about the profane in relation to a variety of cultural forms, ranging from political power (including charisma) to individual power using objects with special mana (e.g., a lucky rabbit's foot, or a special tennis racket).

The next topic is "death and dying," often a tabu area in our death-denying society. Discussion of funeral rites, afterlife, and the relationship between the living and dead is, in the beginning, often tenuous. I have students write a "funeral report" to examine their personal philosophy concerning death and the afterlife, the context of designing a ritual that affirms their concept of life and the afterlife, and the symbols needed to affirm their philosophy. The section on the occult (magic, sorcery, witchcraft, Satanism) and demons provides a mechanism by which students can discuss many of the things they have heard of and/or experienced. The power struggle between good and evil as it relates to the individual and to the political arena opens the door to reviewing events in history from a new perspective (e.g., the Inquisition). Various forms of occult practice are discussed, such as "rooting," "hexing," "ju-ju," "voodoo" (or in layman's terms, witchcraft), as are the various types of practitioners.

The discussion of disease and illness grows out of the question of the role of the occult in disease etiology. A discussion about the biomedical and various ethnic or folk medical explanatory models of disease opens the door to the question of who has the power to make medical decisions and set medical policies. The power assigned by the lay public to medical practitioners brings to light the hidden dynamics linked to cultural morals and values. For example, medical insurance provides less coverage for psychiatric disorders than for physical ones. The final section of the course addresses divination, that deep human desire to be able to foretell or unlock the mysteries of the future. Divination can be related to all aspects of individuals seeking control over of their lives, and is often related to different systems of healing.

Students are challenged with several different kinds of learning experiences—lectures, discussions, videos, assigned readings, and assignments that involve self-evaluation, research, and some fieldwork. The course uses a variety of media to enhance students' awareness of the topics covered in class. Lectures provide the basic concepts and foundation for the topics covered in the course. A historical overview, along with definitions and theoretical perspectives concerning each topic, are covered. I provide cross-cultural examples and draw comparisons that highlight how different cultures in different parts of the world frequently have similar traditions. One example is the dwarfs or little people who assume the role of teachers of healers, as in the spirit people who train the fetish priests in Ghana, the little people who teach the Tuscarora medicine men in the northern United States, and those who teach the *curanderos* in Mexico. There are similarities in some of the treatment styles of spiritual healers and psychologists: the one may dress in robes, the other in suits, but both may use reality therapy to drive out the "devils" haunting their clients. We talk about the manifestation of mana in American culture, whether in the political arena (the charisma of politicians vs. the mana of pharaohs) or the modern use of astrology to decipher the future (in the political arena—the College of Augers in ancient days, Hitler during WWII, Nancy Reagan in the White House, the more recent work on recondite Bible codes, or individuals having their astrology charts read).

During class, I encourage the disclosure of personal experiences. I sometimes use my own experiences as a starting point for a discussion, then ask students to talk about their own. It is important to recognize and validate a person's experiences and maintain a nonjudgmental environment in the classroom. One way to build an environment in which students can engage in such discussions is to begin with happenings that most people have experienced: thinking about someone and having them phone; having premonitions or dreams, followed by the event actually taking place; or using a particular object imbued with mana to ensure success (such as always using a particular tennis racket in competition). One can also explore cultural beliefs on a broader scale, as in illness seen as resulting from the breaking of tabus, as is sometimes held in relation to sexually transmitted diseases.

I use videos to demonstrate cultural variations of the topic under discussion. For example, the first video, *The Spiritual World*, contrasts the great and little traditions of the Roman and Mayan civilizations and illustrates how political leaders used their religious cosmologies in similar ways to build and manipulate the power base and political structure of their governments. We compare these cases with the role of religious beliefs and cosmologies in today's political arena. The retention of African religious beliefs and practices and the influence of European traditions in relation to "syncretic" religions is demonstrated in the video *Bahia: Africa in America*, which explores the roles of Catholicism and African traditional religions in the practice of Bahia in

Brazil. *Hopi: Songs of the Fourth World*, demonstrates the power of symbols, and it explores the relationship between the Hopi's environment and belief system through a focus on corn, which is central to their life and belief system. *The Plain Pine Box* describes the impact on a Jewish community in Minneapolis, Minnesota, of returning to the traditional burial practices given in the Torah. The resulting demystification of death is important for students accustomed to a death-denying society like the United States. *Magical Curing* and the *20/20 Exorcism* provide examples of similarities and differences in the role of exorcism in curing illness among the Wape people and in the United States. *African Roots to American Roots: A Story of Folk Medicine in America* describes the influence of European and American Indian traditions on African American folk medical practices. Our fascination with discovering the unknown takes a new twist with the documentary *Bible Codes*, which exhibits a modern-day attempt at divination using computer technology to divine scripture. The documentary *Shroud of Turin* demonstrates the use of modern technology and science to resolve a religious mystery of history. Television documentaries add a rich resource that can be used in the classroom.

Assignments and Requirements

I place all course information, quizzes, and announcements on the course Web site. The study guideline consists of a summary of the main points of the lectures given in class. This frees students up to participate in class discussions and not have to concentrate on taking down every word. Students are assigned readings from the text and are required to do an oral report and a written critique of the reading. Guidelines for the critical reviews of articles/readings are provided in the syllabus. When doing the review, students are reminded that, since they are to use examples from their readings, lectures and films to support their answers on the final exam, their reviews should highlight the important points and relevant examples.

Students undertake two basic assignments: a ritual report (15–20 pages) and a funeral report (5–8 pages). The ritual report requires them to attend a ritual (secular or religious) of their choice as participants-observers (with permission of the instructor), that they have not attended before. This allows them to explore other belief systems about which they may have been curious but had not had the opportunity to attend. Obtaining the instructor's approval in advance is a safeguard against students attending a ritual that could be harmful or dangerous. The ritual report engages them in participant observation, which allows them to move beyond reading examples and stories in a textbook. Over the years, students have participated in a variety of rituals, including calendrical rituals of various faiths—Buddhist, Catholic, Russian Orthodox, Greek Orthodox, Baptist, Pentecostal, Santería, Vodun (what students often think of as "voodoo"), and Wiccan—as well as critical rituals such as spiritual healings, weddings, baptisms, naming ceremonies, funerals, and many others.

After deciding which ritual to attend, students select a definition of ritual to use as a framework for analyzing their event—either one given on a handout in class or one they choose. Next, they write a paragraph on their preconceptions about the event—what they actually expect to see happen, and what they expect the fieldwork experience to be like. This should be submitted before attending the ritual and included in their discussion of what they have learned. The most difficult part of the ritual report is learning how to observe and report on what is observed; therefore, I provide the following guidelines:

Ritual Guidelines

DEFINITION

Choose a definition of ritual. Write about your preconceptions of what you expect to see and what you expect doing fieldwork to be like.

PREPARATION

Think about, and make notes to yourself, about the following:

- How and why did you choose this ritual?
- How did you prepare to attend (e.g., read some related literature; ask a friend what to expect or how to dress)?
- If you consulted references, be sure to note them in the footnotes and bibliography when applicable.
- What were some of the preconceptions you had concerning both the ritual itself and the field experience?

ENTRANCE

- How did you obtain permission to attend (e.g., did you call individuals associated with the ritual)?
- Were you invited?
- Did someone else obtain the permission for you?

METHODOLOGY

- How did you record your observations?
- Did you use a key consultant or interview people there?
- Was any information available at the site of the ritual (e.g., pamphlets) that the student found useful and could use as a reference? (If the student thinks that a tape recorder, videotape, or other audiovisual aids would be particularly useful, he or she must be certain to first obtain permission from the organizers of and/or the participants in the ritual.)
- Have you addressed the time required to prepare for, attend, and write up your report.

DESCRIPTION OF RITUAL

- Location: Where was the ritual held (any locational symbolism)? Describe the exterior and interior, date, time, days of the week of the ritual, and their significance.
- Personnel involved: Describe the practitioners and participants (type, number, gender, roles, statuses, etc.).
- Physical objects: Describe the nature, composition, type, color, and symbolism used by both the practitioner(s) and participants.
- Form of ritual: Divide (if applicable) into specific parts and tell how this was done; describe prayers; chants; hymns; offerings; dances; key words or actions.
- Symbolism evoked: Describe the symbolism of words, actions, objects, garments worn, sacrificial aspects (if any).
- Nonverbal communication: Describe the interaction of participants with one another and with the practitioner—the spacing; significant gestures or actions, and so on.
- Functions (latent and manifest): Determine the functions of the ritual itself as it relates to sociological and psychological effects on the individual and on the group. For example, does the ritual reinforce social ties between individuals? Strengthen or perpetuate the social structure of the group? How does it satisfy the individual and his psychological needs? Or rather than preserving structure, does the ritual reflect and/ or induce social change?

ANALYSIS

- Compare your observations with your original definition of ritual.
- Indicate what you feel you learned from this experience.

Participation in such a ritual provides a mechanism by which students can explore their own centrisms and learn the importance of honing their observation skills. Reading about a ritual or seeing one in a video leaves them with an abridged and edited experience from the perspective of the writer or producer. Participation-observation in a ritual allows students to develop not only important observational skills, but also critical skills they can bring to bear when reading works by others. Rituals provide a direct window into a society's cultural values and significant symbols. They enable students to become more aware of the power structure that exists between the supernatural and the natural world by asking questions such as who has access to the power and how is it controlled (for example, either directly or through patronage). They learn to *think* about the symbolism in artifacts, such as colors (red for Pentecost in Christian religion, red to ward off "duppies"—ghosts—in Jamaica) or sacred symbols such as the cross, pentagram, Star of David, Crescent Moon, and so on. They gain insight, too, into how the underlying beliefs and tenets of a religion translate into practice. As a result, they gain a new appreciation for their own beliefs, and a greater awareness of the importance ritual plays in their own lives and well-being. Many students report an intensification of their spirituality and, most frequently, an opening of doors to exploring other cultures and belief systems with a more open mind. Student reflections repeatedly include an appreciation for how sharpening their observation skills assists them in becoming more aware of their surroundings, of the significance of the roles played by different individuals, and of how symbols are a conscious means by which to reinforce basic cultural values.

Funeral Report

The object of the funeral report is to make students more conscious of the central importance of the funeral ritual. Some students are leery of writing about their own death; therefore, it is important to offer the option of writing the report for a fictitious person of the same ethnic and social background. The purpose of this exercise is to allow students a way to explore their feelings about death and afterlife and to demystify death. This exercise also leads to discussions about experiences with visions, dreams, and encounters with those who have died, both at the time of death and during life crises. This helps bring to light the reasoning behind customs practiced around the world that honor the dead so as to avoid their sanctioning them as violators of community and family well-being, bringing illness, death, and destruction. A practical benefit reported by a number of students is that they knew what to do when one of their family members died, making it easier for their families. The following guidelines are provided:

Introduction: You are required to design a realistic funeral that could be conducted at the present time in the United States or your country of origin. In a complex society, funeral behavior is limited by legal restrictions, health codes, and business procedures. The funeral ritual is shaped by religious and philosophical concerns and by ethnic customs. Your funeral format should fulfill the psychological and spiritual needs of the participants while operating within the limits imposed. You may compose your own funeral; or, if you wish, you may arrange one for a more general group, reflecting your own economic and social status. Give explicit treatment to each of the stages below, whether you follow a traditional pattern of funeral behavior or create an innovative plan.

PHILOSOPHICAL FRAMEWORK

Give the religious context or philosophical framework. State the purpose and values that shape the following funeral arrangements:

- Obituary notice/death notice (write each);
- Manner of disposition of the body (e.g., taking the body from home or hospital to funeral home; transferring the body direct from home or hospital to crematorium, if allowed by law; donating the body to medical school; burying at sea);

- Observances—describe:

    Wake or visitation including viewing (or not) of the deceased
    Funeral service or memorial service including order of events and
        symbols used (e.g., religious ritual; reading of poetry or literary pas-
        sages; procession [music/ flowers]; symbolic objects);
    Observances at the cemetery or crematorium, or during the scattering
        of the ashes (or on private property if allowed by law);

- Postcommittal gathering of friends and relatives (e.g., location, activi-
    ties, provision of food; state in detail relationships of the participants
    to the deceased).

MEMORIAL INSCRIPTION

- Memorial parks restrict certain kinds of inscriptions that can be used
    for brass grave markers.
- Stonecutters provide more variation in the traditional stone cemetery
    marker.

ITEMIZED COSTS

- Costs for all items should be computed, including coffin/container, fu-
    neral home services, transportation, clergy, flowers, opening and clos-
    ing of grave/grave marker, and so on.

SOURCES OF INFORMATION

- List all sources consulted, including funeral directors, state, county or
    city personnel, clergy, books, articles.
- Provide definitions in a handout for funeral, funeral service, memorial
    service, committal, traditional "stone" cemetery, and memorial park.

Service Learning

More recently, I have added a service-learning component to the course, to
combine service to the community with addressing and learning ways to improve the quality of life for people and their communities. Students work as
interns with Solutions VII, a faith-based organization started by ex-offenders,
to help restore community wellness by addressing the needs of ex-offenders,
at-risk families, and youth in the metropolitan community. Violence and its
associated sense of power are glorified in American culture, from the ritual of
TV wrestling, to MTV, to relationship violence, and the extremes of murder
and mayhem. Violence in the family becomes translated into violence on the
street. By engaging students in hands-on community work to bring about a
change in the balance of power, they learn that one individual can make a
difference, and that helps them to think about healing on a social level. Projects
they have worked on have included:

- an all-day workshop on domestic violence;
- annual consortium breakfasts bringing the community, government, and academe together to build partnerships, to find new solutions to the havoc and devastation wreaked by violence in communities and on families;
- building a database of resources for distribution to faith communities and the public in general;
- conducting interviews with individuals, as part of a project to identify what community members think needs to be done to resolve the issue of violence as they experience it;
- doing a photographic history of graffiti in Lorton Prison, to understand the spiritual and physical sense of place that offenders experience;
- organizing the "Race Against Violence," held in the fall of 2005.

The result of this work is that students gain new insight into the power of faith in action, and of an individual's ability to make change happen.

Students are given the final essay-exam questions at the beginning of the semester. The exam is due the last day of classes. They are required to discuss relationships among the different concepts and topics covered during the course of the semester, and must include references (properly cited) from their readings, the videos, and their own research, observations, and discussions, to support their observations and findings. Bimonthly quizzes on the readings and films are on *Blackboard*. Students are given a set time to take each quiz, along with the date by which it must be taken, or it becomes unavailable.

Challenges

A few challenges have occurred in relation to this course. Occasionally a concerned parent will call to find out what the content of the course is about and to make sure that their child is not being taught "how to do" witchcraft. This response is mostly a reaction to the title of the course. My response to this query is that the course does not teach students how to do witchcraft, but rather that students learn about different traditions from around the world that help them better understand their own beliefs. A second problem is that most students have not done field research. Nor have they had to analyze data collected firsthand. Therefore, I allow them to rewrite their assignments, in order to develop their skills of observation and writing. However, to improve the grade the rewrite must fully address all inadequacies in the first report, and this often requires a second or even third visit to a ritual.

In summary, this course allows students to expand their understanding of their own worldviews, as well as to gain an appreciation and understanding for others. They also learn that religion, magic, witchcraft, and healing do not exist separate and apart from each other. The course gives them the opportunity to explore their own perceptions of what magic, witchcraft, religion, and healing are, without feeling overwhelmed or judged. Classroom discussions provide a format for them to come together as a group and to talk openly about their experiences and beliefs. Students leave the semester with a better understanding of how to view a culture holistically, exploring similarities and appreciating the wealth of diversity. Students learn to examine beliefs within the context of experience and strip away the labeling of others' beliefs and cultures as *exotic*.

Syllabus: Magic, Witchcraft, and Healing

Name: _____
Office: _____
Phone: Main Office _____   Direct Line: _____
Office Hours: E-mail

This course analyzes the relationship among magic, witchcraft, religion, and healing and the significance of each for an understanding of our own cultures as well as other societies. The underlying theme (leitmotif) and organizational concept is power, the seeking and manipulation of it. Topics to be covered include ritual, myth, symbols, mana, tabu, cults, witchcraft, demons, and death and dying among others. You will be challenged with four kinds of learning experiences—lectures, assigned readings, discussions and assignments (which involve self-evaluation, research, and some fieldwork). Yours is the responsibility to integrate and apply these materials.

Required Text

Lehman, Arthur and James Myers eds. *Magic, Witchcraft and Religion: An Anthropological Study of the Supernatural.* 6th ed. 2004. Mountain View, CA: Mayfield.

Course Requirements

Undergraduate students are responsible for completing the following assignments:

Ritual Report
Funeral Report
Consortium Breakfast
Assigned Reading—Written Review (750 words) and Oral Presentation
Essay Exam
Readings Exam

Graduate students are responsible for completing the following assignments:

Research Paper (3,000 words)
Ritual Report
Funeral Report
Assigned Reading
Two Book/Article Reviews (750 words)
Essay Exam
Readings Exam

Students may participate in helping put on the Consortium Breakfast to be held in November. The class will have two tasks to perform:

Assess what activities different departments and programs on Howard's campus do to help the community

Call the local faith-based organizations in the district to see what programs are offered for TANF (Temporary Assistance for Needy Families) families and youth. This will be added to the information gathered by the class last year on services for ex-offenders.

A short report of the findings will be prepared and distributed at the breakfast, and a summary of the findings will be presented by students.

Guidelines for Review of Assigned Reading (Undergraduate Written Review) and Article Reviews (Graduates)

Part One: Begin with a complete citation. Then objectively and carefully report in *summary* the relevant key points, findings and arguments of the reading. *Do not* give more than one or two quotations (if any), and keep them short. *Do not* simply paraphrase the author. *Use your own words.* In this part, do not give opinions or criticize: just state the facts.

Part Two: Do a *critical* review of the reading selection. This does not mean finding fault but rather shows that you think actively for yourself. Use your critical faculties to evaluate the author's claims, findings, achievement, the data, the argumentation, the significance of the results. You may briefly relate it to one or two other works (How similar are their methods? Assumptions? Goals? Do they share a framework?). If you do compare with other sources give a *full citation* of each at the end. Focus on the reading's content more than its presentation, and take into account the historical context of when the work was written. The review should be 750 words, +/− 10%. Give the word count at the end of the paper. Use the word count feature to get this. (Submit the review in hard copy and on disk)

Part Three: (Undergraduates) An *oral presentation* of the review of *assigned reading* will be presented to the class. The typed review is due on the day it is given in class.

Research Paper (Graduate Students)

The topic for your research paper must be approved prior to beginning work. The length of the research paper is 3,000 words plus/minus 10%. You will be penalized if you write too much or too little. Please indicate the length of your assignment at the end of the main text (for the number of words, use the word count feature to get this). Submit the paper in hard copy and on disk. Please feel free to consult me at any time during the semester if you have any questions or problems with your reading or other assignments. Details of and guidelines for assignments—exams, field reports, research reports, and term papers (graduates)—are coordinated with the instructor. The choice is wide, and you are encouraged to develop your scholarly interests.

Grading

All students are encouraged to actively participate during classes and/or discussion sessions and to offer their own perceptions of or questions about the subject matter. Each assignment will be graded for *content, grammar, spelling, organization,* and *composition.* You are responsible for correcting typos. Each student is responsible for *all* materials covered in class, *all* readings and assignments. If a student is absent from class for *whatever* reason, he or she is responsible for obtaining the material covered during that time from other students—with no exceptions. All assignments should be typed, double-spaced, spell checked. Follow standard requirements for margins, footnotes, and bibliography! Use Times New Roman, 12-point type.

Please note: Any time you refer to or explicitly use the work of a scholar, you must cite the surname, year of publication, and page number of any reference in a body note and then give full reference in the bibliography. Whenever you use someone else's words (five words or more), they must be enclosed in quotation marks and clearly identified. You will be penalized for poorly structured work and inadequate bibliographical referencing!

Written work that is inadequately referenced, quotes without attribution, or copies from someone else's work that presents material as if it were your own, falls under the heading of plagiarism (this includes self-plagiarism). This will result in your failing the assignment with no possibility of rewrite and also subjects you to penalties including expulsion.

Do not come in at the end of the term and try to bargain for a grade. If you need to improve your grade, come in during the semester and make arrangements to earn extra credit.

GRADE POINTS

UNDERGRADUATES

Ritual Report	25%
Funeral Report	15%
Consortium Breakfast of Funeral Report	10%
Essay Exam	25%
Readings Exam	15%

Oral Presentation   5%
Attendance   5%

GRADUATES

Research Paper (3000 words)   25%
Ritual Report   25%
Funeral Report   15%
Two Book/Article Reviews   10% (5% each)
Essay Exam   20%
Attendance   5%

Due Dates

QUIZZES

The four quizzes are put on *Blackboard* and cover the assigned readings and
films seen in class.

REPORTS

October 29   Ritual Report
November 19   Funeral Report

EXAMS

The final exam is given out at the beginning of the semester. It is an essay
exam that will require you to use the materials from your readings, films, class
discussions, and personal experiences to answer the questions. The final exam
should run between 15 and 20 pages in length. It is due the last day of class.

Films

A total of nine films will be shown during the course of the semester. Periodic
quizzes on the films are given in class.

The Spiritual World	September 12
Bahia: Africa to America	September 19
Hopi: Songs of the Fourth World	October 3
Plain Pine Box	October 24
Magical Curing/20-20 Exorcism	November 12 and 17
African Roots to American Roots	November 21
The Bible Codes	December 1

Discussions

Once a week the class will discuss the assigned readings. Students will give
oral presentations on their assigned readings from the text. The rest of the

class is responsible for discussing the concepts and ideas presented in the readings.

Tentative Schedule

WEEK 1

> Anthropological Approach
> Introduction
> Terms and Concepts

WEEK 2

> Centrisms
> Little and Great Traditions

WEEK 3

> Ritual
> Discussion of Readings
> Film: *The Spiritual World*

WEEK 4

> Ritual (Cont.)
> Discussion of Readings
> Film: *Bahia: Africa to America*

WEEK 5

> Symbolism: Symbols and Culture
> Discussion of Readings
> Film: *Hopi: Songs of The Fourth World*

WEEK 6

> Mana and Tabu
> Discussion of Readings

WEEK 7

> Power of Ritual and Myth
> Rites of Passage
> Discussion of Readings

WEEK 8

> Ritual and Myth
> Discussion of Readings
> Film: *Plain Pine Box*

WEEK 9

Ritual and Myth (Cont.)
Discussion of Readings

WEEK 10

Death and Dying
Discussion of Readings
Ritual Reports Due

WEEK 11

Death and Dying (Cont.)
Witchcraft and The Occult
Discussion of Readings

WEEK 12

The Occult and Demonism
Discussion of Readings
Film: *Magical Curing/20-20 Exorcism*

WEEK 13

Illness and Curing
Discussion of Readings
Film: *African Roots to American Roots*
Funeral Report Due

WEEK 14

Illness and Curing (Cont.)
Discussion of Readings

WEEK 15

Divination
Film: The Bible Codes
Final Exam Due

(Acknowledgment: This course is an adaptation of the one taught by the late
Dr. Michael Kenny at Catholic University.)

PART VI

Courses for Caregivers

15

Spirituality of Healing

Kwok Pui-lan

During the orientation period at the beginning of the semester, I tell students that if they want to train not just the mind but also the body, they might consider taking the course Spirituality of Healing. In the field of spirituality, while some teachers emphasize that it is an academic discipline with its own systems of knowledge and methods of study, others see spirituality as having more to do with practice and the spiritual formation of the students, especially if the students are pursuing professional or ministerial training (see Schneiders 1993: 207–218). Teaching at a divinity school in which the majority of the students are preparing for ordained ministry, I have adopted a "both-and" approach. Otherwise it would be like teaching the students to swim without ever asking them to touch the water.

Most people taking the course are second-career students who regard healing as a significant component of their future vocation and ministry, whether in religious or secular settings. Over the years, the course has attracted students from diverse backgrounds and walks of life: health care professionals, priests and members of religious orders, cancer survivors, musicians, artists, poets, social workers, teachers, and businesspeople. The majority are Christians, and a few are Jewish, Buddhist, or Goddess worshipers. Many have had hands-on experience in various dimensions of the healing ministry: visiting the sick, counseling the family, empowering the community, assisting in sacraments, accompanying bereavement, and preparing for funeral services. Some have taken or will soon take the course on clinical pastoral education, in which they will work in a hospital under the supervision of the chaplain or other certified personnel. While they have opportunities to learn about pastoral counseling and liturgics in other courses, they want to explore the spiritual foundation of healing and the connection between the body, the mind, and the spirit.

As a professor who is from Hong Kong, I want to introduce a cross-cultural perspective of healing, drawing insights from Chinese and Christian traditions. I have decided to focus on these two very broad traditions instead of sampling additional religious traditions, such as Hinduism, Islam, and Native traditions, because I know them best in terms of both theory and practice, and I have consulted Chinese and Western medicine throughout my life. Given the relatively short duration of a semester, I believe that if students can learn to appreciate Eastern and Western ways of healing as cultural counterpoints, they will develop a broadened understanding of healing and acquire the tools needed to learn from traditions other than their own. The term "cultural counterpoints" is from Tan Dun, the Oscar award-winning Chinese composer, whose music combines both Chinese and Western, classical and vernacular musical motifs and techniques, and breaks the boundaries between classical and vernacular, Eastern and Western art forms. His compositions sometimes highlight the contrast and sometimes assimilate different rhythms, tonal qualities, silences, and harmonies, thereby creating a new context for the audience to understand different musical traditions anew. (He is best known for winning the Oscar for original score for the film *Crouching Tiger, Hidden Dragon*.)

In the beginning of the class, I emphasize that healing is an open book and that no one has all the answers. Instead of using a banking model, I encourage students to speak of what they know about the subject and participate actively in class so that they will feel a sense of ownership of the learning process. I tell them about my own insights gleaned from reading Jane Tompkins's extraordinarily candid and compelling book, *A Life in School: What the Teacher Learned*. Tompkins, a professor of English literature in a prestigious university, laments that nowadays literature is often taught in such a dry and abstruse way that students may acquire all the latest jargon in literary criticism yet lose the passion that drew them to literature in the first place. She says, "My chief concern is that our educational system does not focus on the inner lives of students or help them to acquire the self-understanding that is the basis for a satisfying life. Nor, by and large, does it provide the safe and nurturing environment that people need in order to grow" (Tomkins 1996: xii). Tompkins experimented with a new way of teaching *Moby-Dick* by taking students on a field trip to the sea and asking them to take an active part in designing the course. The result was amazing: she was not just teaching literature, she was teaching about life as well. Like Tompkins, I want my class to nurture and sustain students' interest in the spirituality of healing and to integrate classroom learning with their daily lives.

To respect the diverse spiritual traditions of the students and to broaden their horizons, I introduce in the first class more than fifteen definitions of spirituality of healing from spiritual teachers, medical doctors, poets, and writers. These range from the Dalai Lama's teaching that the ultimate aim of all human beings is to obtain happiness, to Dr. Christiane Northrup's delineation of the difference between healing and curing. I will describe several important features and characteristics of the course below.

Engaging the Body

Healing has so much to do with the body. In Chinese philosophy and medicine, the human body is often seen as a microcosm of the universe; the life force *qi* runs through the human body as well as enlivens and animates every sentient being in the cosmos. Chinese traditional medicine treats the body as a complex and integrated organism and not as a machine with separate parts to be fixed. Christianity emerged from the Hebraic and the Hellenistic cultures and inherited very divergent views of the body. On the one hand, the Hebrew tradition has a more holistic view of the body and sees sexuality as a blessing of God. On the other hand, many of the early Christian writers were influenced by Gnosticism and neo-Platonism and espoused a hierarchical view of the spirit over the flesh. The Augustinian understanding of sexuality and original sin and the long ascetic tradition within monasticism contributed to a negative view of the body, the separation between spirituality and sexuality, and the repression of desire in the Western tradition. This cultural baggage has caused a lot of anxiety, guilt, and self-alienation, leading to all kinds of neuroses and diseases, as Freud and his followers have long pointed out.

One of the important goals I have in designing the course is to recover the body as a locus of spiritual wisdom. Sandra Schneiders defines spirituality as "that dimension of the human subject in virtue of which the person is capable of self-transcending integration in relation to the Ultimate, whatever the Ultimate is for the person in question" (Schneiders 1993: 210). The advantages of her definition are that it is comprehensive and does not name God or any other supreme beings as the Ultimate. The disadvantage is that the language of self-transcending is too closely linked to the Christian tradition and Western epistemology since Descartes. Why does the self need to be transcended in order to reach integration, and what part of the self needs to be transcended? Sadly, it has been the body in much of the Christian tradition. Therefore, I want to offer a more body-friendly definition: spirituality is that dimension of the human subject by virtue of which the person is capable of integrating the body, mind, and spirit, of maintaining just and right relationships with other human beings, and of communion with the divine and the whole cosmos.

Such a definition requires us to engage the body, mind, and spirit in the class. In our academic training, as we are required only to bring our brains, we often check out the rest of our body when entering the classroom. This poisonous pedagogy is hazardous to students' health and counterproductive in a course on spirituality of healing. Currently the body has become a fashionable topic, treated as a sign or debated as a site of contestation in gender, cultural, and queer theories. But the concern has been in the erotic body, and not the body that actually eats or breathes (Eagleton 2003: 2). To counteract the prevalent body and mind split in higher education and to recover the ancient spiritual wisdom by which the body provides insights to the spirit, I want the course to engage the body and respect the different ways of knowing and multiple intelligences of the students.

We begin each class with a short meditation guided by a chant introduced by Thich Nhat Hanh: "Breathing in, breathing out. I am blooming like a flower. I am fresh as the dew." I explain that meditation has a long tradition both in the East and the West, and that Thomas Merton, the well-known Trappist monk, traveled to Asia to converse with the Buddhist and Hindu leaders on meditation, mysticism, and monastic renewal. I introduce sitting postures, different breathing techniques, and guided meditation gradually during the course. Since some students find sitting still and clearing their minds a challenge, I encourage them to think that meditation is a spiritual practice and that it takes time and patience to learn. I also introduce Herbert Benson's finding that the "relaxation response" is helpful in maintaining optimal health.

In addition to sitting meditation, I teach simple movements of *taiqi* in class and sometimes invite a *taiqi* instructor to offer a short course when we discuss the Chinese healing system. The movements of *taiqi* enact the interplay between yin and yang, and amply illustrate the principles of balance and transformation in Chinese medicine. I also invite a guest lecturer who practices Chinese traditional medicine and acupuncture to speak and demonstrate in class. In one class, seven students who volunteered had needles sticking out from their toe, knee, or the center of their skull as they spoke animatedly with the acupuncturist and other students.

For each class, I ask a volunteer to create a centerpiece as a visual focus for the topic discussed and another to select a poem or an invocation to read. In the classroom we debate about truth and discuss virtue, but we seldom attend to beauty and imagination. The creation of the centerpiece—which I had not expected—became an important channel for students to bring what they were learning into dialogue with their own spiritual journey and a means for community building. Students bring something from their personal belongings or their cultures, and explain what those objects and artifacts mean to them. One student from Albuquerque brought a rich collection of objects from the Southwest; another brought the icon she was writing about; still another brought momentos as a Latina lesbian fighting for justice. The reading of poetry in class had the unintended effect of encouraging students to write their own poetry. Poetry fires the imagination, touches our emotions and longings, and captures the minute details of life. In *The Witness of Poetry* (1983), Czeslaw Milosz writes: "A poet stands before reality that is every day new, miraculously complex, inexhaustible, and tries to enclose as much of it as possible in words. That elementary contact, verifiable by the five senses, is more important than any mental construction" (56).

We concluded each class with a short ritual led by me for the first few times, and then by student volunteers. I stated at the beginning that participation in the rituals was voluntary, so that nobody would feel coerced, and that the rituals would be clearly explained beforehand. I talked to students who needed some assistance in planning rituals, and I asked them to take into consideration the diversity of the participants. The closing rituals included symbolic actions, songs, prayers, lighting candles and incense, blessings; we concluded the course with the Holy Eucharist. These rituals not only strengthened the bonds between the participants but also provided a liturgical framework to enact and hold together what we had learned in that particular class. Over the course of the term, the centerpieces and the closing rituals created a rich visual memory, much like a mosaic of contrasting colors, shapes, and sizes. Students enthusiastically took turns contributing to the class, and appreciated what their classmates had offered to enrich the learning process The other course assignments included a weekly spiritual journal in which they could express themselves through poetry and prose, painting, collage, photography, or other media, and a final project that discussed the collective dimension of healing. To allow creativity to flow and to foster a noncompetitive learning atmosphere, students were encouraged to take the course for pass or fail rather than for a grade.

The Personal and Systemic Dimensions of Healing

Because American culture is highly individualistic, many of the popular self-help books on healing focus primarily on the personal dimension: dieting, personal health, overcoming aging, coping with pain and depression, and promoting a sense of wellness. Such a personalistic approach fails to address the larger social and political issues that make people and the society sick, such as racism, poverty, pollution, homophobia, and patriarchy. Students who have a more individualistic understanding of both healing and spirituality expect the course to provide help for their own healing and nourish their spirit. But they soon find out the course challenges them to think outside these narrow parameters.

To prepare students to discuss the wider contexts of both personal and communal healing, I begin the course with a session on cross-cultural understanding of healing. I discuss different images and metaphors used to describe the body, the diagnostic process, and the roles of the healer in Chinese and Western healing systems. Students find it intriguing that the diagnosis in traditional Chinese medicine is more like a weather report; illness and healing are related to the elements of wind, water, metal, and so forth Drawing upon the work of Robert C. Fuller (2001), I introduce the historical roots of alternative forms of healing in America. A scholar who has published several volumes on "unchurched America," Fuller argues that from the mid-1880s until 1910, new religious philosophies and movements mushroomed in America, influenced by Transcendentalism, Swedenborgianism, Theosophy, spiritualism, and Eastern religions. People alienated from the church found in alternative medical practices such as homeopathy, chiropractic, and mesmerism some avenues to explore alternative spiritual frameworks for the body and the psyche. William James, author of *The Varieties of Religious Experience*, was interested in expanded states of consciousness, mysticism, and other psychic phenomena such as telepathy. Some of these trends, Fuller points out, are reemerging in the contemporary spiritual quest. For example, many are attracted to alternative medical systems offered by Asian traditions including yoga, *taiqi*, acupuncture, and herbal medicine. Techniques that seek to integrate the body, mind, and spirit, including holistic healing, reiki, therapeutic touch, massage, and aromatherapy have a large following and consumer base.

As students begin to see that healing has personal, interpersonal, cultural, institutional, and spiritual dimensions, they are more open to discussing the difficult issues of racism, homophobia, and gender discrimination in society. Since students in the school have taken a required course on social analysis and theological praxis, I have opted to use personal narratives to discuss the multiple levels of racism and internalized oppression. James Baldwin's enthralling account of living as a stranger in a Swiss village illustrates the daily challenges and injuries of a black person in a white society. Andrew Hollaren's and Carter Heyward's stories of facing homophobia with integrity and courage have a quality in their writing that is sublime. I enlist the help of both white students and students of color to share their reflections on these soul-searching readings, and take care to ensure that students of color not feel that we are dealing with "their problems" or that their lived experience is being put under microscopic scrutiny. Racism affects both white people and people of color because it distributes rights and privileges in an unjust way, causing indifference or guilt on one side, and anger and bitterness on the other. Racism is difficult to discuss openly in class because there is so much historical baggage, tainted with hurt, shame, and guilt. I try to create an atmosphere that promotes active listening, compassionate understanding, and a willingness to hold different realities together.

As I taught the course in the fall of 2003, the Massachusetts Supreme Judicial Court ruled that gays and lesbians have the legal right to marry under the Massachusetts Constitution. This momentous decision provided a changing context for discussing human sexuality and homophobia; it shifted the discourse from whether homosexuality should be tolerated to whether gay and lesbian couples have the same rights and protections in relation to the institution of marriage. The issue of sexuality has direct bearings on spirituality because it touches on the desire and longing for intimacy, the seeking of fulfillment in erotic relationship, and the risk and vulnerability in opening oneself and loving others. We began the discussion with sexual identity development, so that both gay and straight students had to reflect on their journey of coming to know their own sexuality. Just as white people are seldom called upon to examine whiteness, heterosexual people are seldom asked to "come out" and examine what it means to be heterosexual. We discussed how sexuality is socially constructed and different cultures have diverse expressions of the sexual self. It was important to explore biblical teachings on sexuality, since the Bible has selectively been used to legitimate discrimination against gays and lesbians. We moved on to discuss how gay and lesbian theologians have worked toward reconstructing the Christian tradition, helping to rediscover the profound connection between sexuality and spirituality, and between human eros and the love of God. We challenged each other to think how an expansive understanding of human sexuality and love of God would influence our sexual expression and bodily practices as gay and straight people. The closing ritual of the class was led by a student who created a wonderful ceremony of blessing our bodies.

To help students understand the deeper connection between the personal and systemic dimensions of healing, I invited as guest lecturer Miriam Greenspan, a psychotherapist who has explored the healing power of grief, fear, and despair in what she has called "the alchemy of dark emotions." Greenspan has offered an impassioned discussion of "emotional ecology" in her book *Healing through the Dark Emotions* (2003), arguing that our heartfelt personal sorrows connect us to the brokenhearted world. While she provides a step-by-step guide to befriend our dark emotions, she convincingly argues that personal healing and global healing are one integrated process When Greenspan came to class, she not only discussed the major tenets of her book, but also led exercises to get to know, name, and befriend one's emotions. Even in a divinity school, we rarely have the opportunity to learn about and discuss the emotional contours of spiritual life. Students listened attentively, engaged actively in the exercises she led, and said they wished they had learned about living through the dark emotions a long time ago.

I conclude the class with a section on healing and social transformation because I want to include some practical suggestions and strategies of how we can bring what we have learned into congregations and workplaces. Since most students belong to a congregation, we diagnose the problems facing their congregations and explore avenues and opportunities for renewal. Students also learn about the different organizational structures of congregations and how they could be made more relevant to social life. The literature on spirituality of the workplace has increased dramatically in recent years. For many people, work gives them a sense of identity, security, and purpose of life, but in the past it has been an area often left out of talk about spirituality or healing. Because of the privatization of religion in America, many people think the spiritual life has more to do with the personal dimension and less with the corporate sphere. Thus churches in America have been preoccupied with sexuality and less so with economic justice. But a holistic understanding of healing must take into consideration the whole person and not separate life into compartments. In the class discussion, students have astutely observed that much of the discussion on spirituality in the workplace has a middle-class bias and does not touch on the lives of the working classes. They debated how an inward-looking and self-reflective approach to spirituality would benefit the working people who do menial labor or work two jobs to feed the household.

Success and Evaluation

How do we evaluate the effectiveness of a course that includes meditation, music, poetry, lecture, discussion, centerpieces, and ritual? With a banking model of education, we assess knowledge by gauging how much knowledge has trickled down to the students at the end of the course. In contrast, we measure the success of student-centered learning by the degree that students have taken charge of their own learning and show evidence of their ability to apply what they have learned to their life circumstances. How and by what means, though, do we measure the success or limitation of a course on the spirituality of healing?

After teaching the course several times, I began to discover some indicators that the teacher may use to see how the class is going. The most important one, by far, is the level of participation of the students, because the course is designed in such a way that collaborative learning is key to its success. The enthusiasm shown by students in taking turns to create an aesthetic and communal learning environment, and their engagement with the readings and discussion indicate the degree to which they embrace this pedagogy, which does not involve their brains alone. In the beginning, some students may need time to adjust, since the lecture format is still the predominant mode of academic instruction. Once they understand healing in a broader context, they gradually see that meditation and ritualistic action are integral parts of the learning process.

Through reading their weekly journals, I am able to have a broader picture of how each individual is learning in class. I discuss different genres of journal writing at the beginning, citing the works of Henri Nouwen (1996) and Dorothy Day (1972), and have students try free writing in class. I try to persuade them to think of writing as a spiritual discipline, for it demands us to pause and be mindful of things happening in our lives. As the course proceeds, I notice that many students enter into deeper dialogues with themselves in their journals, and I have been honored to witness their spiritual development. In the middle of the semester, I check with them to see if they want to change anything about the class, and reflect back to them what I have learned from their journals.

The course works best when it has fewer than 20 students, so that each will have ample opportunity to share and participate. I understand that a course like this one is not for everybody, and I take time in the beginning to explain the rationale and the pedagogy. It has been helpful to ask students at that point to name their fears and vulnerabilities in taking this course, and to suggest ways to overcome such challenges. Students have also met in small groups of three to five outside the class to discuss further the issues raised. As usual, some groups function more actively than others, depending on personalities and the level of engagement of group members.

The success of the course also hinges and is dependent upon the general learning atmosphere of the school. Otherwise this type of learning will be labeled as "soft" or "nonacademic." In its mission statement, my school has stressed the goal of embracing diversity and multiculturalism in our curriculum and pedagogy. In addition, the denomination of the school (Episcopalian) has always underscored the use of music, arts, poetry, and symbolic action in face of the mystery in its liturgy and devotional life. Thus, the students are not uninitiated. Still, they are challenged to integrate their own spiritual pursuit with what is happening in the classroom, which does not always occur even in a divinity school. They are also challenged to get outside the box to see the congruencies and differences between the Christian and Eastern forms of spirituality. I say repeatedly in class, "When the student is ready, the teacher will come." I expect and have the patience that some students are more ready than others.

Learning to Teach

In *The Courage to Teach* (1998), Parker Palmer explores the inner spiritual landscape of the teacher and emphasizes that we teach who we are and that the identity and integrity of the teacher matter. Confucius could not have agreed more, for he also saw the personal integrity and quality of life of the teacher as paramount. In the course on the spirituality of healing, I have experienced a dynamic and intimate interplay between my knowledge and passion for the subject, my embodiment of the values taught in the course, and my role as a model for the students. Students are not just looking for knowledge; they are searching for wisdom to be healers and to be healed.

Throughout my graduate training, I did not participate in a class that involved the body, which means I have had to acquire a new set of skills and expand my teaching repertoire. During a sabbatical, I applied for a grant to go to Italy to learn about religious arts, sacred sites, and pilgrimage in Christian spirituality, and to visit Thich Nhat Hanh's Plum Village in southern France and the Taizé community to observe spiritual formation in Buddhist and Catholic traditions. I talked with colleagues in theological schools about teaching spirituality and spiritual formation, and I exchanged syllabi with them. I practice *taiqi* and yoga and have observed reiki, *qigong*, foot massage, and demonstrations of healing touch. Located in Boston, my students and I have had the opportunities to attend workshops offered by the Mind/Body Medical Institute of Harvard Medical School, visit a Chinese medicine shop in Chinatown, and attend lectures by Thich Nhat Hanh and other spiritual teachers. I have also been invited to lead a workshop for the faculty and students of the New England School of Acupuncture.

What is rewarding about teaching a course like this? What makes it possible for a teacher to overcome the fear that he or she may have little to teach when standing before the class, knowing that the subject matter of healing is so immense? I think it is seeing your students changed by what they are learning and yourself transformed in the process. It is walking the fine line of challenging the students and providing them with necessary support at the same time. It is in the deep respect that students are different, learning at their own pace and in their own ways, and knowing that you are a catalyst at best. It is in the realization that teaching is an art and that, as Julia Cameron says, "art is a spiritual transaction." She goes on: "Making our art, we make artful lives. Making our art, we meet firsthand the hand of our Creator" (Cameron 2002: xiii, xix).

Syllabus: Spirituality of Healing

I. Course Description

This course explores the spiritual foundations of healing, including the mind and body connection, breaking the cycle of violence, and developing life-affirming spiritual practices. Particular emphasis will be on healing from internalized racism, homophobia, and other forms of structural oppression. There will be opportunities to study Chinese approaches to healing.

II. Specific Goals

This course is designed to:

- introduce ancient Eastern medicine and healing as resources for celebrating mind and body connection, living in balance, and developing earth-based spirituality;
- make connections between personal and corporate dimensions of healing. Healing takes place through personal and communal transformation; and
- explore strategies to enliven and rejuvenate the workplace, faith communities, and liturgies so that they can be vehicles of healing and instruments of grace.

Healing takes place in a context that celebrates differences and inclusivity. This course will be taught with a commitment to antiracism, diversity, and multiculturalism.

III. Course Requirements

- Participate in class discussion and complete assigned readings.
- Prepare an introductory statement of 2–3 pages. Introduce yourself to the instructor, briefly describe your spiritual practice (if any) and experience in healing and your expectations for the course.
- Form a small group to meet regularly to discuss the readings and issues of healing.
- Keep a journal on the "spirituality of healing," including reflections, artworks, images, music, poetry, photographs, and other creative

forms. Each entry should be about 2–3 pages to be handed in each week.
- A final individual or group project on the corporate dimension of spirituality of healing.

Participants are strongly encouraged to take this course for pass/fail.

IV. *Course Schedule*

I. INTRODUCTION AND EASTERN APPROACHES TO HEALING

Week 1: Introduction
Week 2: Cross-Cultural Understanding of Healing
Week 3: Writing Your Own Spiritual Journal
Week 4: Journey between the East and the West
Week 5: Chinese Herbal Medicine and Acupuncture

2. HEALING: PERSONAL AND SYSTEMIC LEVELS

Week 6: Overcoming Internalized Oppression
Week 7: Healing the Dark Emotions (guest speaker: Miriam Greenspan)
Week 8: Healing, Homophobia, and Abuses

3. HEALING AND SOCIAL TRANSFORMATION

Week 9: Congregational Spirituality
Week 10: Reinvention of the Workplace
Week 11: Healing for the Long Haul
Week 12: Conclusion

Required Texts

Bolker, Joan, ed. 1997. *A Writer's Home Companion: An Anthology of the World's Best Writing Advice, from Keats to Kunitz*. New York: Henry Holt.

Fox, Matthew. 1995. *The Reinvention of Work: A New Vision of Livelihood for Our Time*. San Francisco: Harper San Francisco.

Greenspan, Miriam. 2003. *Healing through the Dark Emotions: The Wisdom of Grief, Fear, and Despair*. Boston: Shambhala.

Reid, Daniel. 1996. *The Shambhala Guide to Traditional Chinese Medicine*. Boston: Shambhala.

Tessier, L. J. 1997. *Dancing after the Whirlwind: Feminist Reflections on Sex, Denial, and Spiritual Transformation*. Boston: Beacon.

Other articles on reserve.

Weekly Readings

WEEK 2: CROSS-CULTURAL UNDERSTANDING OF HEALING

Andrew Weil. 1995. An Eight-Week Program for Optimal Healing Power. In *Spontaneous Healing*. New York: Ballantine, pp. 262–70.

Nhat Hanh, Thich. 1993. *The Blooming of a Lotus: Guided Meditation Exercises for Healing and Transformation*. Boston: Beacon, pp. 1–11, 17–20.

Freeman, David L. 2001. Illness and Healing in Jewish Thought and Practice: Mapping the Interface of Medicine and Religion. Paper presented in February 2001 at Episcopal Divinity School, Cambridge, MA.

Kelsey, Morton T. 1973. What, How, and Why Did Jesus Heal? In *Healing and Christianity: In Ancient Thought and Modern Times*. New York: Harper and Row, pp. 69–103.

Reid, Daniel. *The Shambhala Guide*, introduction and chap. 3.

WEEK 3: WRITING YOUR OWN SPIRITUAL JOURNAL

Bolker, Joan. *The Writer's Home Companion*, 4–14, 67–73, 76–91, 101–16, 14–53, 154–63, 174–77, 183–99, 230–33.

Paulsell, Stephanie. 2002. Writing as a Spiritual Discipline. In *The Scope of Our Art: The Vocation of the Theological Teacher*, ed. L. Gregory Jones and Stephanie Paulsell. Grand Rapids, MI: Eerdmans, pp. 17–31.

WEEK 4: JOURNEY BETWEEN THE EAST AND THE WEST

Tu, Weiming. 1998. Beyond the Enlightenment Mentality. In *Confucianism and Ecology: The Interrelation of Heaven, Earth, and Human*, ed. Mary Evelyn Tucker and John Berthrong. Cambridge, MA: Harvard University Center for the Study of World Religions, pp. 3–21.

Fuller, Robert C. "Alternative Medicines, Alternative Worldviews" In *Spiritual, but Not Religious*. New York: Oxford University Press, pp. 101–21.

Ornish, Dean. 2001. *Eat More, Weigh Less* New York: HarperTorch, pp. 90–105.

Ching, Julia. 1999. The House of Self. In *Journeys at the Margin: Toward an Autobiographical Theology in American-Asian Perspective*, ed. Peter C. Phan and Jung Young Lee. Collegeville: Liturgical Press, pp. 41–61. (See also her memoir *The Butterfly Healing: A Life between East and West*.)

Gottlieb, Roger. 1999. The Transcendence of Justice and the Justice of Transcendence: Mysticism, Deep Ecology, and Political Life. *Journal of the American Academy of Religion* 67: 149–66.

WEEK 5 CHINESE HERBAL MEDICINE AND ACUPUNCTURE

Reid, Daniel. *The Shambhala Guide*, chaps. 4–10.

Choy, Virstan. 1995. From Surgery to Acupuncture: An Alternative Approach to Managing Church Conflict from an Asian American Perspective. *Congregations* (November-December): 16–19, and responses.

WEEK 6 OVERCOMING INTERNALIZED OPPRESSION

Baldwin, James. 1997. Stranger in the Village. In *The Norton Book of Personal Essays*, ed. Joseph Epstein. New York: Norton, pp. 263–75.

Rodriguez, Richard. 1997. Going Home Again. In *The Norton Book of Personal Essays*, ed. Joseph Epstein. New York: Norton, pp. 408–21.

Eng, Phoebe. 1999. She Takes Back Desire. In *Warrior Lessons: An Asian American Woman's Journey into Power*. New York: Pocket Books, pp. 117–41.

Walker, Alice. 2001. Metta to Muriel and Other Marvels: A Poet's Experience of Meditation. In *Writers on Writing: Collected Essays from the New York Times*. New York: Time Books, pp. 246–50.

Bullitt-Jonas, Margaret. 1999. *Holy Hunger: A Memoir of Desire*. New York: Alfred A. Knopf, pp. 240–50.

Holleran, Andrew. 1995. The Sense of Sin. In *Wrestling with the Angel: Faith and Religion in the Lives of Gay Men*, ed. Brian Bouldrey. New York: Riverhead, pp. 83–96.

Heyward, Carter. 1992. Healing Addiction and Homophobia: Reflections on Empowerment and Liberation. In *Lesbians and Gay Men: Chemical Dependency Treatment Issues*, ed. Dava L. Weinstein. New York: Haworth, pp. 5–18.

WEEK 7 HEALING THE DARK EMOTIONS

Greenspan, Miriam. *Healing through the Dark Emotions*, Parts 2, 3, and 4.

WEEK 8 HEALING, HOMOPHOBIA, AND ABUSES

Tessier, L. J. *Dancing after the Whirlwind*, chaps. 2, 3, and 4.

WEEK 9 CONGREGATIONAL SPIRITUALITY

Koenig, John. 1997. Healing. In *Practicing Our Faith*, ed. Dorothy Bass. San Francisco: Jossey-Bass, pp. 149–62.

Kujawa-Holbrook, Sheryl A. 2002. *A House of Prayer for All Peoples*. Bethesda, MD: Alban Institute, pp. 12–25.

Stebinger, Peter A. R. 1998. Two Paths to Congregational Holiness or Why Do Some Congregations Grow in a Time of Denominational Contraction. *Occasional Papers from the Cathedral* (winter): 1–6.

Thomas, Owen. 1997. Parish Ministry: A Theologian's Perspective. *Sewanee Theological Review* 4: 444–56.

Moore, Paul, Jr. 1985. A Pastoral Spirituality. *Ministry Development Journal* 6: 14–17.

Wentz, Cynthia Carsten. 1995. Martin Luther King, Jr., and the American Mystical Tradition. *Sewanee Theological Review* 38: 105–13.

Parks, Sharon Daloz. 1989. Home and Pilgrimage: Companion Metaphors for Personal and Social Transformation. *Soundings* 72: 2–3: 297–
315.
Talvacchia, Kathleen. 1993. Learning to Stand with Others through Compassionate Solidarity. *Union Seminary Quarterly Review* 47 (3–4): 177–
94.

WEEK 10 REINVENTION OF THE WORKPLACE

Fox, Matthew. *The Reinvention of Work*, chaps. 1, 4, 6–9.

WEEK 11 HEALING FOR THE LONG HAUL

Heschel, Abraham Joshua. 1983. Prayer. In *I Asked for Wonder: A Spiri-
tual Anthology*. New York: Crossroad, pp. 20–33.
Welch, Sharon D. 1999. *Sweet Dreams in America: Making Ethics and
Spirituality Work*. New York: Routledge, pp. 119–36.
Martin, Joan M. 1999. A Sacred Hope and Social Goal: Womanist Es-
chatology. In *Liberating Eschatology*, ed. Margaret A. Farley and Serene
Jones. Louisville, KY: Westminster, pp. 209–26.
Spencer, Daniel T. 1994. Shattering the Image, Restoring the Body: To-
ward Constructing a Liberating Lesbian and Gay Ecclesiology. In *Spiri-
tuality and Community: Diversity in Lesbian and Gay Experience*, ed. J.
Michael Clark and Michael L. Stemmeler. Las Collinas: Monument
Press, pp. 83–107.
Eugene Toinette M., and James Newton Poling. 1998. *Balm for Gilead:
Pastoral Care for African American Families Experiencing Abuse*. Nash-
ville, TN: Abingdon Press, pp. 154–81.

WORKS CITED

Cameron, Julia. 2002. *The Artist's Way: A Spiritual Path to Higher Creativity*, 10th an-
niv. ed. New York: Tarcher/Putnam.
Day, Dorothy. 1972. *On Pilgrimage: The Sixties*. New York: Curtis Books.
Eagleton, Terry. 2003. *After Theory*. New York: Basic Books.
Fuller, Robert C. 2001. *Spiritual, but Not Religious: Understanding Unchurched America*.
New York: Oxford University Press.
Greenspan, Miriam, 2003. *Healing through the Dark Emotions: The Wisdom of Grief,
Fear, and Despair*. Boston: Shambhala.
Milosz, Czeslaw. 1983. *The Witness of Poetry*. Cambridge: Harvard University Press.
Nouwen, Henri J. M. 1996. *The Inner Voice of Love: A Journey through Anguish to Free-
dom*. New York: Doubleday.
Palmer, Parker. 1998. *The Courage to Teach: Exploring the Inner Landscape of a
Teacher's Life*. San Francisco: Jossey-Bass.
Schneiders, Sandra M. 1993. Spirituality as an Academic Discipline: Reflections from
Experience. In *Broken and Whole: Essays on Religion and the Body*, ed. Maureen A.
Tilley and Susan A. Ross. Lanham, MD: University Press of America.
Tompkins, Jane. 1996. *A Life in School: What the Teacher Learned*. Reading, MA: Addison-
Wesley.

16

The Worldviews Seminar: An Intensive Survey of American Urban Religious Diversity

Lucinda A. Mosher and Claude Jacobs

After the attacks of September 11, 2001, a statement commonly heard from New York City's caregivers was, "We are working to heal this city, one person at a time." Clearly, improved interreligious understanding would be an important component of this healing; furthermore, the need to heal breaches of interreligious understanding certainly was not peculiar to New York City: it was an imperative for the nation as a whole. The Worldviews Seminar was inaugurated in the aftermath of the events of 9/11/01 to be a mechanism for healing and a vehicle for teaching about how healing is understood and effected by America's many religions. Our own objective was to equip "healers" (health care professionals, religious leaders, educators) with the cultural awareness and sensitivity needed to go about their work.

An innovative and collaborative enterprise, the Worldviews Seminar's founding was motivated by a desire to broaden people's knowledge of America's increasingly diverse religious landscape and deepen their comfort level with it. The initial proposal for the one-week seminar came from the leaders of the Interfaith Educational Initiative—a joint project of Episcopal Research and Development (an agency of the Episcopal Church, USA) and the national Episcopal Church's Office of Ecumenical and Interfaith Relations. Although a venue for the seminar was unspecified, a location in the Midwest, easily accessible to all parts of the country, had high priority. After careful consideration, the choice was Metropolitan Detroit.

A number of factors led to this decision: the area's religious diversity; the presence of the University of Michigan-Dearborn and its commitment to documenting local religious centers; and the leadership of the Reverend Daniel Appleyard, rector of Christ Church

(Dearborn), whose personal enthusiasm for the project, long involvement in interfaith relations locally and beyond, and extensive network of relationships with Metropolitan Detroit's religious leaders ensured solid community support for such an undertaking. The Worldviews Seminar's subsequent development was assisted (and continues to be aided) by the Rev. Appleyard and a regional planning team of concerned religious leaders, educators, and UM-Dearborn staff, and a teaching team comprising a Christian moral-theologian with deep experience in teaching about the world's religions and the practice of interreligious dialogue (Lucinda Mosher), and an anthropologist with a background in medical anthropology and ongoing research on religion and health and the changing religious landscape of Metropolitan Detroit (Claude Jacobs).

The course now enjoys official sponsorship by the University of Michigan-Dearborn's Center for the Study of Religion and Society and the Pluralism Project at the University of Michigan-Dearborn, yet continues to receive degrees of support from the Episcopal Church at several levels, including a local parish with considerable interest in interfaith activities (Dearborn's Christ Church), the Diocese of Michigan, and the Episcopal Church's national Office of Ecumenical and Interfaith Relations. Attempts to include a wider range of religious institutions and interfaith organizations in the base of support are ongoing—both in an effort to broaden the seminar's appeal and to maintain the nonsectarian character of the university. This is seen in the added support now coming from the Detroit office of the National Conference of Community and Justice and the Metropolitan Detroit Chapter of the American Jewish Committee, as well as the participation on the planning committee by Muslim and Unitarian Universalist laypersons. The discussion to follow will describe this course's design, with particular attention to the theoretical, pedagogical, and logistical considerations informing it; explain the place of healing as a topic in the overall scheme of the course; and, reflect upon its successfulness and considerations for transplanting it to other settings.

Design

Theoretical Issues

In its first year, the Worldviews Seminar was strictly a continuing-education offering, with 27 participants drawn primarily from Metropolitan Detroit (the inaugural class had participants from Hawaii and Texas as well). Some participants took the course as interested members and leaders of specific religious congregations. Others were professionals (including teachers, hospice workers, and hospital chaplains), who saw the seminar as a way to enhance their training. This format of continuing education proved highly successful. Once the university assumed sponsorship of the Worldviews Seminar, however, the possibility arose of offering it to students enrolled in degree programs at the University of Michigan-Dearborn and elsewhere. Though continuing education units are still awarded, the university now grants academic (graduate or undergraduate) credit equal to a semester-long course. The Worldviews Seminar is thereby able to accommodate a variety of students: traditional undergraduates, graduate students, and community residents with personal interest in religion, religious leaders, and professionals who need or desire a continuing education course to inform their work in settings (such as education or health care) in which knowledge of and sensitivity to ethnic and religious difference are important.

The overarching rationale for the Worldviews Seminar is that people in contemporary America ought to have foundational information about beliefs and practices of several of the religions they now encounter in the country's multireligious landscape, sufficient to engage in interreligious dialogue, and to be more sensitive to beliefs and practices of others. Metropolitan Detroit is an exciting locus for this program. With 5.2 million residents, concentrated largely in Wayne, Oakland, and Macomb Counties, and a history of religious centers dating from 1701, it is one of the most ethnically and religiously diverse regions in the nation. Since the establishment of its first place of worship, Ste. Anne de Detroit Roman Catholic Church, Southeast Michigan has become home to people of many faiths: a wide array of Christians, Jews, Muslims, Sikhs, Jains, Buddhists, and Baha'is, plus many others. In other ways, however, Metropolitan Detroit is characteristic of contemporary urban America, with extremes of wealth and poverty, wide disparities in educational opportunities, ethnic and racial separation, and unequal access to health care.

Methodologically, we embrace the notion of "the city as text."[1] Most of our students have been living in a parallel, rather than an intersecting, relationship with their neighbors from other religions. We treat Metropolitan Detroit as an excellent religions-of-the-world "textbook"—which we invite our students to "read" afresh under our guidance. We give special emphasis to changes in the American religious landscape after 1965 with the passage of new immigration laws, and to the history of Metropolitan Detroit's religious diversity.

We encounter a unique theoretical challenge insofar as most decisions about classroom content are in the hands of a Christian moral theologian, while most decisions about site-visit venues are made by a professor of anthropology. This unusual form of team teaching is both exciting and problematic. One of the first questions we had to resolve was whether a theologian and an anthropologist could indeed teach together with integrity—and if so, then how. Our training and academic experience contrast boldly, with anthropology's focus on religion as a social construction and a part of culture, and theology's focus on the development of integrated "insider language" for a particular religion. Nevertheless, we work together successfully, each of us operating from our strengths: the anthropologist's experience in fieldwork and participant observation in a variety of the area's religious centers; and the theologian's considerable teaching experience in departments of religious studies (which share more in terms of methodologies and concerns with departments of anthropology than do departments of theology per se), coupled with her sensitivity to the degree to which the intricacies of each worldview are informed by *conviction* (defined by James McClendon and James Martin as so persistent a belief that it will not easily be relinquished—and indeed cannot be, without making the person or community significantly different from what it was before) (McClendon and Martin 1994).

In terms of our approach to the study of religion, we agree on a phenomenological methodology. We employ a working definition of religion as that constellation of beliefs, practices, institutions, literature, and so forth, which—as Byron Earhart puts it—helps a community "establish, maintain, and celebrate a meaningful world" (1992). This is not unlike the definition of religion put forth by anthropologist Morton Klass as an "instituted process of interaction among members of [a] society—and between them and the universe at large as they conceive it to be constituted—which provides them with meaning, coherence, direction, unity, easement, and whatever degree of control over events they perceive as possible" (Klass 1995: 38).

Religion, for Klass is that part of culture which orders a people's universe, "thereby eliminating (or at least walling off) chaos, meaninglessness, and human helplessness" (Klass 1995:38, 3). His notion of an "ordered universe" coincides nicely with our notion of "worldview" (a term we have appropriated with gratitude from Ninian Smart (2000), and on whose insights we rely heavily). A community's "worldview" comprises all those elements that enable it to make meaning of the world; it is that which helps it find fresh answers to "worldview questions"—questions such as, "How did the cosmos come to be, and how does it work?"; "What is the nature of humanity?"; "Is there a God? If so, what is God's nature?"; "What's wrong, and how can it be fixed?"; "What are we doing here?"; "What happens when we die?" Cosmology, thus, is a religion's explanation of how the world came to be and how it works. The worldview question, "What is wrong, and how can it be fixed?" leads us into the realm of a religion's understanding of health and healing; the worldview questions, "What happens when we die?" and "What is the nature of humanity?" lead us to consideration of a religion's rituals and customs when bad things (illness and suffering) happen to good people or a member of the community dies.

When worldview questions inform our syllabus, we necessarily must address issues of gender roles and relations, structural violence, and health and healing. We approach gender in three ways. First, we are careful to include the role of women as well as men in each religion. Second, our team of presenters is gender-balanced fairly well over the course of the week, and our preference is that our participants meet women as well as men on every site visit (although we cannot guarantee this). Third, the site visits provide students an opportunity to see clearly how each religion handles gender in terms of clothing requirements for males and females, seating arrangements in ritual spaces, and role allocation and status (ritual and organizational). Gender issues are not unrelated to issues of structural violence. To the extent that time allows, we bring up the ways in which activists within each religion are taking on issues such as racism, classism, sexism, and homophobia, as well as the ways in which past experience of colonialism and imperialism inform today's interreligious tensions and religions' present self-understandings. (These latter issues are most likely to come up vis-à-vis Islam and Native American spirituality.) However, this is necessarily cursory, given our focus on basic, more normative beliefs and practices.

In addressing issues of pluralism (within a tradition, between traditions, and involving different cultural, racial/ethnic, and socioeconomic groups), we have adopted "No religion is a monolith" as our mantra for the week! In the introductory lectures, we try our best to indicate the major streams within each tradition, something which is reiterated in the handouts included in the course notebook that participants receive. Though we can visit only one example of each religion we highlight, we remind our participants that, had we taken them to a different exemplary site, they might well have gotten very different answers to their questions.

Pedagogical Issues

We employ an experiential, phenomenological, interactive methodology by which we encourage seminar participants to become "empathetic visitors" who stand "imaginatively within" the various worldviews we explore during the week. We attempt to balance delivery of factual and theoretical information, exploration, conversation, and reflection. Many voices are heard during the course of the week, but we maintain continuity through our own daily opening presentations and our daylong availability to the group.

Our learning goal for Worldviews Seminar participants is that they finish the week with broader awareness of six things: (1) the nature and value of appreciating their own religion and the religions of others in terms of "worldview"; (2) the degree to which religious diversity has always been a part of American culture; (3) the elements of America's present religious diversity— that is, the various categories of religions (Judaism, Islam, Buddhism, and Native American spirituality, for example); the variety of expressions within each category (e.g., Orthodox vs. Conservative; Theravada vs. Pure Land; Sunni vs. Shi'a); the basic vocabulary and concepts appropriate to each; (4) the nature and value of the notion of "empathetic visitation," thus how to be a sensitive conversation partner with—and visitor to the "home turf" of—various religious communities; (5) implications of the First Amendment to the United States Constitution; and, (6) awareness of how each tradition defines health and handles illness and end-of-life issues.

Each time we have taught this course, we have been fortunate to have a group of students who themselves represent a wide variety of cultural, racial/ethnic, and socioeconomic groups, as well as age and formal education. With only one week to work with a diverse group of people with equally diverse personal goals for participating in the Worldviews Seminar, mastery of vocabulary and concepts cannot be our goal, nor can depth of understanding. Nevertheless, we believe that our participants finish the week better equipped to engage in intelligent interreligious dialogue and better informed to visit other people's religious spaces; they also leave with many suggestions and some resources for continuing study of America's religious diversity at their own pace. Throughout the week, we must keep in mind the wide range of expectations and experiences before us, as well as participants' range of comfort levels with covering the head or taking off shoes, and the range of their ability to see and hear easily, to sit on the floor, to climb on and off the bus to visit religious centers, and so on.

We employ a variety of teaching methods each day, but our emphasis is on the experiential. Through classroom presentations and many religious field trips, this seminar places an emphasis on what people believe and do—and how that informs the meaning they make of the world. Our selection of film resources favors the experiential as well. We choose film projects and documentaries informed by a phenomenological rather than a history-of-religions methodology. Whenever possible, we opt for audiovisual aids in which adherents of the religion in question speak for themselves (as opposed to those in which an unseen narrator describes them). The order in which the religions are covered may pose a pedagogical challenge, since what is presented in the classroom needs to be coordinated with the site visits. The visits have to be set up well in advance of the seminar, and a particular religious center may or may not be able to accommodate the group on a given day. The result is that the historical development of religions and their exact relationship to each other may not always be reflected in the syllabus. In essence, the scheduling of the site visits in many ways determines the organization of the course, and this can change each time the seminar is offered. As a consequence, it is the instructor who must weave all of the experiences (classroom and site visits) together in a meaningful way.

In the opening lecture, we begin with optical illusions, by which we make the point that two people or groups can observe or experience the exact same thing but make quite different meaning of it. We move to a series of maps to illustrate the many ways cartographers help us visualize our world. We introduce the notion of religion as worldview, and the notion of "worldview questions"—questions for which religions offer answers. We introduce Alan Race's (1983) notion that theoretical attitudes toward those outside one's worldview fall into three overarching categories: exclusivist, inclusivist, and pluralist.[2] We also offer David Lochhead's (1988) paradigm of concrete relationships between religious communities: a relationship will be primarily one of isolation, or hostility, or competition, or partnership. We commend the notion of the "empathetic visitor," which Ninian Smart (2002) describes as an openhearted visitor from another tradition—one who is able to stand imaginatively within someone else's worldview; comparisons may be drawn, but for the purpose of clarity rather than apology, and certainly not polemic. We argue that the notion of empathetic visitation can be embraced by inclusivists as well as pluralists. We present several late-twentieth-century definitions of pluralism, and embrace that of Diana Eck. For her, pluralism is not simply relativism, nor is it the displacement or elimination of deep religious or secular commitments. Rather, Eck employs the term to name an "encounter of commitments," which "goes beyond mere plurality to active engagement with that plurality." Pluralism thus is "a dynamic process through which we engage with one another in and through our very deepest differences" (Eck 2001).

Pluralism for hospital chaplains in the seminar has an added dimension. In addition to working within the arena of religious pluralism, they also work within a plural health-care system. Though biomedicine dominates the institutions in which chaplains work, their patients are often members of a particular religion and bring to their illness a host of meanings that might not be familiar to physicians. Even when patients are not associated with a religious tradition, they are still faced with the fundamental questions that a worldview attempts to answer. Patients may move from one understanding of their illness and correspondingly of themselves to another (religious to biomedical, or in the opposite direction), or hold to both understandings simultaneously, arriving at a synthesis that is either cultural or unique. Questions of cosmology for the hospital chaplain, therefore, become more complex, and often have to be addressed in times of crisis for the patient and family.

Because time is so tightly scheduled, we favor lecture, followed by Q&A, over more interactive teaching methods. Because information—much of it incorporating foreign words—is delivered quickly, we make liberal use of PowerPoint as a means of anticipating requests for spelling, repetition, and definition. Rather than show entire films, we show excerpts, and provide ordering information for those who wish to see the piece in its entirety. We do not log on to the Internet during class time. However, the Web has proved invaluable in locating resources on each religion, some of which we include in the course notebook (with permission where necessary). We have considered creating a Web site for the course, but have not done so because the week's schedule is too tight to allow time to use it during the actual course. We do provide Web addresses for suppliers of the unusual teaching aids we use and for good sources of supplemental information.

The course notebook (which contains a plethora of supplementary materials) is an important adjunct to the course. We provide one for each participant upon arrival on the first morning. Distribution of a loose-leaf notebook which we have loaded in advance allows us to encourage study and review without demanding that everyone read a religions survey textbook. It provides an efficient way to distribute handouts and folios we have created to underscore the particular topics and concepts we cover, and it allows us to integrate materials provided by other agencies with materials we generate ourselves. We code the course notebooks with colored tabs: everything relevant to Tuesday's topics can be found behind the brown tab, Wednesday's behind the red one (and so on). The color tabs accomplish two things: anyone with the heart and time for preparing for the next day (which we do not expect, but are pleased when it happens) can find what he or she needs; during class, we are able to call attention to particular resources with minimal disruption.

Primary among our nontextual teaching materials is Metropolitan Detroit itself—its history, its demography, its religious institutions and their spokespersons. Most of the site visits engage the senses: participants hear prayers, musical instruments, and chants and sometimes are even invited to join the singing; they smell incense, taste food, examine two- and three-dimensional objects. Back in our classroom, "artifacts" (statuary, beads, and so on) may be handled, and posters, photos, and maps are made available for study before class and during breaks (in addition to whatever role these objects play in formal presentations). And, as we have said, we make liberal use of videos, DVDs, slides, and the like to prepare for and supplement site visits.

We encourage all Worldviews participants to read Diana Eck's *A New Religious America* before the course begins. We insist upon this for those wishing academic credit, and we also require them to read an undergraduate introductory text on the world's religions, which can be quite helpful in filling in gaps of information on each religion necessarily created by the pace of the week.[3]

This pace is not conducive to nightly preparation. Nevertheless, our seminar notebook appears to be sufficiently enticing that students report having read much of it as the course progressed—in spite of our 12-hour-daily contact time! Participants wishing academic credit toward bachelor's or master's degrees are assigned a research project and receive several hours of mentoring beyond the 50 hours of contact time during the seminar week itself. Final projects are submitted electronically or by post. Both professors read all papers, and determine grades collaboratively.

Logistical issues

Logistical issues fall into several categories: planning, scheduling, transportation, meals, and set-up.

PLANNING

The planning team comes entirely from the Metropolitan Detroit area, but the lead teacher (Mosher) lives in New York City. The team "meets" by e-mail frequently during the academic year preceding each Worldviews Seminar. Several face-to-face meetings are held at the university or Christ Church, with Mosher staying in touch by e-mail and telephone. The planning team takes care of all arrangements for food, transportation, fund-raising, Mosher's housing and transportation for the week, advertising, registration of participants, scholarships, and a plethora of last-minute details. Jacobs makes arrangements for site visits and is the advisor to all students who take the course for credit. Mosher does all planning of course content, and takes responsibility for providing audiovisual aids and other "show-and-tell" items. She plans and assembles the model course notebook; duplication and collation takes place at the university just before the seminar convenes.

SCHEDULING

The course meets for five and a half days—essentially, Monday through Friday, 9 AM until 7:30 PM, and 9 until noon on Saturday. Our one-week format is convenient for health care professionals, hospice workers, and religious leaders who are able to take time away from work for intensive study, and for teachers who come during their vacation. Given our single-week format, the vagaries of Metropolitan Detroit's traffic patterns and the need to arrange all site visits at the convenience of the institutions we visit, logistical concerns may trump pedagogical considerations in overall scheduling. This is mitigated in part by provision of time each day for debriefing from site visits. The shared-sponsorship arrangement has us spending most mornings in an auditorium on a university campus, and our noon meal and early-afternoon sessions at nearby Christ Church. We must allow time for participants to make the short drive from university to church, and for getting everyone on and off the bus during our multiple field trips.

A typical day begins with continental breakfast in the atrium of the College of Arts, Sciences, and Letters at the University of Michigan-Dearborn. A recording of music, chants, recitations, and prayers associated with the day's religious focus is playing as participants enter the auditorium. After any necessary debriefing, we launch into the day's content. Formal presentations combine lectures, Q&A, slides, short excerpts from films, music, "show and tell" (maps, posters, books, artifacts, and the like), and the occasional guest speaker. At noon, the group adjourns to Christ Church for lunch and more content lessons using the same variety of methods and materials enjoyed in the morning session. The group then boards an air-conditioned bus for visits to various Metropolitan Detroit religious centers—Hindu, Buddhist, Jain, Sikh, Jewish, Christian, Muslim, and Native American—for conversations (and sometimes a meal) with leaders and members of those religious communities. The group returns by bus to the university or church parking lot by 9 PM each evening. One evening (usually Tuesday) is kept free for rest and reflection.

TRANSPORTATION, FOOD, AND SET-UP

Participants commute or stay in a motel near the university. Thus they arrive on campus by car each morning. By choosing to teach this course in one of America's most intensely religiously diverse cities, we are faced with an amazing palate of choices for site visits and guest speakers. This wealth is problematic: we cannot incorporate all of it into the syllabus. Obviously, however, this is a delightful problem to have. We can be selective within a tradition; the multiple examples of each tradition make it easier to map our travel in a way that avoids rush-hour traffic as much as possible. Sites are selected for location and are heavily weighted to the west side of Metropolitan Detroit, where the university and Christ Church are located, even though there are interesting sites elsewhere in the area. Our goal is to minimize the amount of time spent on the bus. Nevertheless, students often use this time effectively, reading course material or talking with each other The bus microphone allows the instructor to clear up unanswered questions related to course material or to a site visit itself. The above-mentioned traffic vagaries, geographic constraints, the real possibility of getting lost on the way to a site visit, and our contention that the dynamics of the group as a whole are affected by traveling in multiple vehicles inform our decision to limit participation in the seminar to the seating capacity of a single motor coach and our policy of discouraging participants from following the bus in their private cars.

All lunches and snacks, and most dinners, are provided. This helps us keep a large group on a tight schedule. It also encourages conversation within the group. Usually, one day's schedule will demand that boxed suppers be eaten on the bus. As noted, some of our site visits include a meal served by that religious community.

At the university, we use a "smart auditorium," which means that all audiovisual equipment is set up and ready to go at all times. However, our access to the equipment before class each day depends on the arrival of the university audiovisual staff. Thus it is crucial to have everything as bug-free as possible before the week begins. Christ Church provides us with audiovisual equipment similar to what we enjoy at the university, which allows us maximum flexibility in presentation scheduling. A few of our site-visit venues are also equipped to show videos and DVDs or to play audiotapes or CDs.

Worldviews and Healing

Theologically, we use the term "healing" to denote restoration of wholeness, the return of well-being—physically, mentally, or spiritually. We acknowledge that "healing" and "curing an illness" are not necessarily equivalent. Phenomenologically, we emphasize that the definition of "healing" may differ in each worldview we visit, and that within a worldview there may be more than one operative definition. Pedagogically, we meld consideration of healing in each religion with our consideration of health care, death, and grieving issues. We recognize that, in the face of life-threatening illnesses, chaplains will frequently have to help a patient with questions of ultimate cause: "Am I at fault for my condition, through sin or failure to fulfill my religious obligations?" "Is my suffering a punishment from God?" In keeping with our definition of religion as that which helps a community answer (or, at least, ponder) worldview questions, we see teaching about health and healing as intrinsic to our consideration of such questions (as explained in our discussion above of theoretical issues).

We introduce attitudes and customs relevant to health, healing, and death in our introductions to each religion in its turn. In addition, students are made aware of the way each religion constructs the body, in terms of its corporeal and incorporeal dimensions and the relationship between the two, especially in healing and at death. More important, however, on each of our site visits, our participants have the opportunity to hear about these issues from an adherent. Thus, when we visit Detroit's American Indian Health Center, we listen to an explanation of the health-giving properties of each traditional item in the delicious lunch we are served. We learn as well about the sweat lodge, puberty rituals, and how traditional indigenous healing methods are used in combination with biomedicine and to address contemporary problems like stress, addictive behaviors, and teenage sexual activity. When we visit the Theravada Buddhist monastery, we experience a guided meditation and learn how the value of this discipline is understood to benefit mind and body. When we visit the Jain Center, we learn about *ahimsa* (nonharming), and its implications for health and wholeness. At the Antiochian Orthodox Church, we learn about care for the dying and for the bereaved. At the synagogue, we learn about the Jewish notion of *Tikkun Olam*—healing the world. At the Hindu temple, we hear how cosmic influences affect a person's destiny (thus one's health) and lead one to make particular decisions. From the Sikhs, we receive guidelines for what to do when a child is bullied; at the *gurdwara*, we experience the wholesome generosity of the *langar*—the common meal at which all are welcome and equal. At the mosque, students not only observe the way Muslims pray, but are made aware of ideas related to the body: ritual cleansing and purification during life, and ritual washing and wrapping at death.

Because our time at each site is limited, notions of healing within that tradition cannot be addressed exhaustively. Rather, we receive only a glimpse, and *what* we glimpse may be a different node on the spectrum of healing issues at each stop on our itinerary. Thus at one site, the role of diet in healing is emphasized; in another, a cross-cultural critical-care nurse explains the relationship between her work and her spiritual life; at a third, the emphasis is on healing the grieving community after the death of a loved one; at a fourth, it is on the health of the mind as crucial to the health of the body.

Were this a traditionally scheduled, semester-long (or yearlong) course meeting once or twice per week, homework and field research could encourage consideration of a more consistent list of topics and issues in each tradition. However, given the intensive approach, and our desire for breadth of exposure more than depth of engagement, we compensate in several ways. We suggest materials for further reading. We provide pamphlets on health care issues from the vantage point of each religion included in the syllabus. These materials have been developed or approved by adherents of the religion in question, specifically for the purpose of encouraging chaplains and health care providers to deal more sensitively with the religious concerns of their patients. Some of these materials include prayers at time of illness and death, and rules for handling the body of the deceased. The difficult health-related issues raised by modern society are not overlooked, including abortion, autopsies, blood transfusion, life support, assisted suicide, organ transplantation, artificial reproductive technology, and contraception. The course notebook includes brief discussions of each religion's position on these topics. Students may raise further questions about them during site visits. Case studies are sometimes incorporated into the summary session on healing and health care and the religions we have considered during the week. Our resource table provides examples of other useful books and materials on these subjects.

Reflections

One testimony to the success of the Worldviews Seminar is that several participants have enrolled in it repeatedly. Students' evaluations indicate that it has been an extremely positive learning experience. The site visits are highly valued, according to the comments we receive in our course evaluations. However, little in these visits would have much meaning without adequate classroom preparation.

Despite their praise for the site visits, some participants question the site selections. Why did we go to one place and not another? Were particular groups of people ignored completely? Hispanics? African American Christians? Why did we hear from a recent convert instead of someone who has grown up in this religion? Breadth of representation is a problem we simply cannot solve in a one-week course. For all the diversity to which we do expose our students, there will always be omissions. Problems of representation can be mitigated over time by changing which sites are selected and visited each subsequent summer. However, to do this would presume we wish to encourage repeat participants—something the constraint of our decision to use a single motor coach makes us reluctant to do.

The more familiar our students are with a particular tradition, the more they are liable to question our choice of a particular site to visit. They may wonder if we are ignoring a center associated with their tradition, or (more positively) wish that we would give it some exposure. With regard to Christianity, we have decided that to do justice to the diversity of expressions of this religion in Metropolitan Detroit would necessitate a separate course. We opt to represent Christianity in the Worldviews Seminar syllabus by lecturing on Orthodox belief and practice and by visiting a Middle Eastern church rich in symbolism and visual appeal, consonant with our commitment to explore what is generally unfamiliar to most participants.

That this course is designed to take full advantage of a Southeast Michigan context is indeed distinctive. Can the Worldviews Seminar then be taught somewhere other than Metropolitan Detroit? Certainly. In fact, it was intended from its inception to be translatable to any number of settings. Most major American cities are multireligious "texts" waiting to be read, and indeed other approaches to intensive immersion courses in the world's religions are known to us. However, the Worldviews Seminar's blend of anthropological, religious studies, and theological concerns, team planning and team-teaching, and site-visit-driven syllabus and schedule differentiates it from other such courses. Anyone wishing to replicate the Worldviews Seminar would do well not only to read Diana Eck's *A New Religious America*, but also Ninian Smart's *Worldviews: Crosscultural Explorations of Human Beliefs*. The Matlins and Magida opus, *How to Be a Perfect Stranger: A Guide to Etiquette in Other People's Religious Ceremonies* (2002), can be quite helpful in planning and preparing for site visits. Our course notebook includes suggestions (some of them annotated) for further reading on every major topic on the syllabus. These items would, of course, be useful to someone wishing to teach a seminar such as ours.

We view ideas of health, illness, and healing as embedded in particular worldviews, or in the ways that specific religious traditions conceptualize the world and give life meaning. Our focus, therefore, is not on health and illness per se or on various traditions' prayers and rituals at times of crisis. Instead, our emphasis is on broader issues: conceptualizations of divinity, ideas about the meaning of life and death, views of the body, and actions (prayer, sacrifice, fasting, or pilgrimage) to affect or influence divinity—and thereby life on earth. Though we frame our course in terms of worldviews and religions, we fully realize that worldviews and religions do not become ill, suffer, and die—people do. And at these times people turn to sacred symbols, texts, and rituals that sustain life, day by day and at its most difficult moments of disruption and potential meaninglessness. What is it like to be surrounded by sacred things? What does one feel, hear, taste, or touch? What is the body's response? To these questions, our emphasis on experiential learning—by which we invite our students to become "empathetic visitors" and give them the opportunity to stand "imaginatively within" the variety of religious traditions that are a part of the changing American landscape—seeks to help participants not only to understand worldviews, but especially to understand the relationship between religion and healing wherever it is needed: for suffering bodies, communities, or nation-states.

Sample Syllabus

Course Objective

The purpose of this course is to broaden participants' knowledge of America's increasingly diverse religious landscape and deepen their comfort level with it by acquainting them with foundational information about beliefs and practices of some of the many religions of Metropolitan Detroit sufficient to engage in interreligious dialogue and other positive interreligious interaction.

Rationale

The relationship between religion and ethnicity has been a feature of American culture from the colonial period to the present. During the twentieth century, the relationship not only remained intact but was reinforced as new waves of immigrants to the United States arrived from Asia, Latin America, Africa, the Caribbean, and the Middle East. As this increasing ethnic and religious diversity became a part of the existing pattern, it reshaped local communities and presented ever more complex opportunities and challenges.

Metropolitan Detroit, consisting of 5.2 million residents, concentrated largely in Wayne, Oakland, and Macomb counties, is one of the most ethnically and religiously diverse regions in the nation and has a history of religious centers dating to 1701. Since the establishment of this first place of worship, Ste. Anne de Detroit Roman Catholic Church, southeastern Michigan has become home to people of many faiths, including a wide array of Christians, Jews, Muslims, Sikhs, Jains, Buddhists, and Baha'is.

A fresh (or first-time) look at the beliefs, practices, literature, and institutions comprising the worldviews of their neighbors can benefit traditional undergraduates, graduate students, and community residents who have a personal interest in religion or need continuing education credit to work in settings such as education, health care, or community services where knowledge of and sensitivity to ethnic and religious difference is important.

Methodology

The methodology informing the Worldviews Seminar is experiential, phenomenological, and interactive. The course will combine lectures and other formal presentations with visits to many Metropolitan Detroit religious centers. Participants take breakfasts, lunches, and many dinners together, and they travel to sites together via motor coach—all of which provides additional opportunity for discussion.

Materials Required for Students Desiring Academic Credit (and recommended for all)

Course Pack (distributed on the first morning of the seminar).

> Mary Pat Fisher, *Living Religions*, 5th ed. Upper Saddle River, NJ: Prentice Hall, 2003.
>
> Diana L. Eck, *A New Religious America: How a "Christian Country" Has Become the World's Most Religiously Diverse Nation*. San Francisco: Harper, 2001.

Recommended Reading

> *CrossCurrents*: all articles, 2001, 51(1).
>
> Byran Earhart, *Religious Traditions of the World*. New York: HarperCollins, 1992.
>
> Morton Klass, *Ordered Universes: Approaches to the Anthropology of Religion*. Boulder, CO: Westview Press, 1995.
>
> Lowell W. Livezey, ed., *Public Religion and Urban Transformation: Faith in the City*. New York: NYU Press, 2000.
>
> David Lochhead, *The Dialogical Imperative: A Christian on Interfaith Encounter*. Maryknoll, NY: Orbis, 1988.
>
> James Wm. McClendon Jr. and James M. Smith, *Convictions: Diffusing Religious Relativism*. Harrisburg, PA: Trinity Press International, 1994.
>
> Jacob Neusner, ed. *World Religions in America: An Introduction*, revised. Louisville, KY: Westminster John Knox, 2000.
>
> Robert Orsi, *Gods of the City: Religion and the American Urban Landscape*. Bloomington: Indiana University Press, 1999.
>
> C. C. Pecknold, "The Readable City and the Rhetoric of Excess," in *CrossCurrents* 2003, 53(4):516–520.
>
> Alan Race, *Christians and Religious Pluralism: Patterns in the Christian Theology of Religions*. London: SCM Press, 1983.

Ninian Smart, *Worldviews: Crosscultural Explorations of Human Beliefs*, 3rd ed. Upper Saddle River, NJ: Prentice Hall, 2000.

Stuart M. Matlins and Arthur J. Magida, eds., *How to Be a Perfect Stranger: The Essential Religious Etiquette Handbook*, 3rd ed. Woodstock, VT: Skylight Paths, 2002.

NOTES

1. The term "the city as text" was integral to the syllabus developed by Professor Thomas Breidenthal for the Tutorial Seminar Program of The General Theological Seminary of the Episcopal Church (NYC) during the three years he chaired its teaching team (1998–2001)—on which Mosher served. See also Robert Orsi (1999), C. C. Pecknold (2003), the entire spring 2001 issue of *CrossCurrents*, and Livezey (2000) for other examples of this concept at work.

2. While the paradigm emerged from, and continues to be prominent in, Christian theological discussions, we see evidence of these three stances in many other worldviews, and thus define them more generally. Briefly, an *exclusivist* asserts that his/her own religion is the only source of authentic truth, the only vehicle to salvation (i.e., positive outcome); the multiplicity of religions on the world stage is contrary to the way things are meant to be (i.e., contrary to God's will). An *inclusivist* sees only his/her own religion as true, but can be generous to adherents of other religions and respectful of their desire to hold fast to their worldview. An inclusivist concedes that other religions may embody partial or complementary truth: while his/her own religion is the only valid vehicle to salvation, it is not necessary for everyone to adhere to (convert to) it, because adherents of other religions are included in (or, will benefit from) the economy of salvation (or, the vehicle to a positive outcome) the inclusivist's own religion provides. Pluralism is defined variously. A *pluralist* may assert that paths to salvation/positive outcome/God are many and equally true and valid; similarly, that truth is absolute, but humans perceive it variously in different times and places; or that to eliminate the multiplicity of religions in the world (in favor of a single, "true" path) is as undesirable as it is unfeasible; or that multiplicity of religions is the way things are supposed to be (i.e., God's will). As noted in the text above, we embrace the Eck definition of pluralism, which emphasizes delight in difference.

3. We recommend Mary Pat Fisher, *Living Religions*. However, we acknowledge other fine introductory survey textbooks that would serve this encyclopedic function well. One interesting example, which we include on our "recommended reading" list, is the anthology *World Religions in America: An Introduction*, edited by Jacob Neusner.

17

Teaching Religion and Healing: Spirituality and Aging in the San Francisco Japanese Community

Ronald Y. Nakasone

All cultures are involved with each other. None is single and pure. All are hybrid, heterogeneous, extraordinarily differentiated, and un-monolithic.

> Edward Said (1936–2003), *Culture and Imperialism*, p. xxv.

"I look forward to growing old."
"But, why?"
"I want to see how my art will deepen and change."

> Morita Shiryū (1912–1998) to a surprised student

In an attempt to reconcile their traditional culture with their modern American experience, the Japanese American community of San Francisco initiated a unique experiment in community-based education for eldercare in planning for the newly built Kokoro Assisted Living Facility. Envisioning a seamless blend of modern medicine with culturally and spiritually competent care for Japanese American elders in a multicultural and multifaith setting, the Japanese America Religious Federation of San Francisco (JARF)[1] commissioned the design and implementation of "Spirituality and Aging in the Japanese Experience." This yearlong, six-unit graduate course would serve as a blueprint for a comprehensive and continuous in-service training strategy for a health care team that would include, in addition to medical professionals and social service providers, elders themselves, their families, volunteers, community leaders, clergy, and others in need of or wanting information and training in geriatrics. It was offered through the Graduate Theological Union in Berkeley, California, in partnership with Sanford Geriatric Education Center of Palo Alto, California. The syllabus below details the content, movement, and mechanics of the course. This essay highlights the conceptual framework, implementation, outcomes, and concludes with an assessment. I begin with the context and motivation for the course.

JARF's interfaith consortium of 11 Buddhist, Christian, and Shintō-based congregations is an outgrowth of the Shūkyōka konwakai (Gathering of religious persons) that coordinated the temporary housing needs of Japanese nationals and Japanese American internees who were released from U.S. Department of War concentration camps at the conclusion of World War II. Though the Shūkyōka konwakai closed its last hostel in 1954, changing housing needs prompted the creation of JARF as a nonprofit entity in 1968, which in turned incorporated the Japanese American Religious Federation Housing (JARF Housing) to build and manage Nihonmachi Terrace, a 245-unit low income and affordable senior housing complex. Though Nihonmachi Terrace has been operating successfully, it is unable to serve elders who no longer meet its ambulatory and safety requirements. Responding to this need, JARF and JARF Housing created the Japanese American Religious Federation Assisted Living Facility in 1997 to build Kokoro Assisted Living, Inc., a 54-unit building located within the San Francisco Japantown district. The clerical and lay leadership of the respective JARF congregations insisted that spiritual and cultural components be integral parts—not an afterthought—of the design of the building, staff training, services, and administrative policy. Years of experience with the American health care system impressed the community with the need for cultural and spiritually sensitive eldercare. Anecdotal evidence and systematic research support such a need (Smedley, Stith, and Nelson 2002; Ellor, McFadden, and Sapp 1999).

The Course

The course was listed in the Graduate Theological Union's 1999–2000 catalog of offerings as "Spirituality and Aging in the Japanese Experience, an interdisciplinary, multifaith, and cross-cultural exploration of the spiritual/cultural needs of older persons within a living community." The two-semester course consisted of six daylong (six hours) weekend modules. Offered on Friday and Saturday, one weekend a month, the course was divided into two sections: Medical Perspectives on Health and Aging, and Religious Perspectives on Health and Spirituality. The former familiarized the student with the physical, medical, ethical, and legal issues, focusing on culturally appropriate geriatric care, assessment, health care interventions, access, and utilization. It focused on the needs of Japanese elders. Religious Perspectives on Health and Spirituality explored Japanese Buddhist, Christian, Confucian, and Shintō reflections on aging and the human spirit, and it discussed the Japanese and Japanese American notions of self, family, community, health, dying, and death.

Rituals and ceremonies were also part of the content. The course set aside the last hour of each day for instruction and practice of calligraphy, massage, tea ceremony, storytelling, folk songs, and hand dance, all of which provided a window into Japanese life. In addition to graduate credits, continuing education in nursing and social work were offered through Stanford University. Nursing home administrator continuing education credits were also available.

"Spirituality" and "aging" were understood to be aspects of an ever-changing personal and community reality that engages health care teams with cultural and spiritual traditions in concrete and pressing ways. "Spirituality and aging" is an age-specific experience. For the purposes of the course, "aging" signified individuals 65 and older. "Spirituality" referred to experiences that touch on and emerge from humanity's deepest core, where a person is open to or touches the transcendent and/or immanent. For the most part, "spiritual experience" is inseparable from the story—the historical and cultural backdrop, and current context—of the elder person. Thus, the course applied narrative whenever possible on the assumption that we are the stories we tell. The diaspora, discrimination, folk practices, organized beliefs, and the massive displacement during World War II are part of the Japanese American experience. Finally, "health" was understood to mean personal and community well-being. "Healing" meant to recover, develop, and maintain the mutual concern and responsibility among elders, their families, and the community that have been diminished by modernization and urbanization.

The interdisciplinary, multifaith and cross-cultural pedagogy was informed by spiritual pluralism and filial reverence. The belief that elder care is a community-wide effort entailed on-site instruction and the utilizing of the wisdom and experience embedded within the community.

Spiritual Pluralism

Cognizant of the plurality of faith traditions and diversity of cultures, the course understood Japanese and Japanese American cultural and spiritual experiences to be "porously laminated."[2] Namely, they are informed by the indigenous Shintō, Chinese Confucian and Taoist, and Indian and Chinese Buddhist, and Christian traditions, as well as by folk beliefs and practices. Modernization, American values, and varying degrees of enculturation and acculturation are also part of the community's ethos. Enculturation, the process by which individuals and the community learn the content, practices, and values of their new home, are evident in the evolving images of caring for the elderly. My family experience is an example. My grandmother was cared for by her children until a perforated stomach forced her hospitalization, and she died a week later. My grandfather died at home. My parents passed away in a hospital. We, their children living in different cities, were unable to care for them in their home. Although they never spoke about it, I believe they expected to be taken care of and to die with their children at their side. My spouse and I have no illusions about the burdens of old age. We have invested in long-term insurance to lessen the burden on our daughter. Such shifting attitudes are also evident in our institutions. Acculturation, the process of mutual borrowing between cultures that result in new blended patterns, is evident in Buddhist mortuary and memorial observations. A sermon, a standard feature of Christian worship and never a part of traditional Buddhist ritual, has been integrated into the service. The once obvious "living truths" of the faith need to be articulated.

Though spiritual and cultural syncretism is seamlessly integrated, diversity is also a source of confusion and conflict. Response to a request by a woman who lost her adult son to have a *tamautushi* ritual performed at the Christ United Presbyterian Church (formerly the Japanese Church of Christ) is instructive of the challenges of spiritual pluralism. *Tamautushi* is a Shintō ritual that transfers the "spirit" from one being to another. Within the animist Shintō context, the "spirit" does not need to be transferred to another person, but to an appropriate tree or a stone. The church board refused the request of the longtime member. Wishing to accommodate the mother's wishes and to mitigate her grief, Rev. Donald Drummond consulted with Rev. Masato Kawahatsu of the Shintō based Konkōkyō Church, who advised him that the *tamautushi* ritual is performed before the funeral rite. Though the mother was satisfied with this solution, this incident illustrates the personal and institutional conflicts that arise from the "laminated" nature of the Japanese spiritual experience. Notwithstanding the divergent views of the respective faith traditions, filial piety and reverence for the ancestors are sentiments shared by the JARF congregations.

Filiality

Filial piety, a fundamental tenet in Confucian thinking, reinforces indigenous Japanese notions of ancestral venerations. Filial piety places certain obligations and responsibilities on parents and children. Parents normally love, provide for, and protect their children, without any expectation of being repaid. Nurtured and cared for, children respond with sentiments of gratitude, respect, reverence, and affection; later they come to understand that they owe their very existence to their parents and to a long line of ancestors. The parent-child relationship is nonegalitarian, and the indebtedness and responsibility associated with this relationship are asymmetrical. It is not a debt that the child incurs voluntarily, and it is one that the child can never fully repay (McLaren, 1990).

The importance of filiality is epitomized in the complex and long memorial cycle developed by the Chinese Buddhists. Seamlessly blending Indian Buddhist notions of karma, Chinese Confucian thinking on filial piety, and Japanese Shintō ideas of personhood, the memorial ritual cycle observed by the Japanese and Japanese Americans begins immediately after death and continues for thirty-three or more years. Traditionally, after the funeral rites the family observes a memorial service every seventh day until the forty-ninth day; subsequently, special observances are called for on days marking the hundredth day, the first year, and then the third, seventh, thirteenth, seventeenth, twenty-fifth, thirty-third, and forty-ninth years. Each of these calls for special observances. This long memorial cycle crystallizes the dynamic and evolving roles of an individual in life and in death, and it highlights the importance of family lineage and cohesion, the reciprocity between the living and dead, and the nature of our memories (Nakasone 2000). The centrality of filiality is evident in the discussion that followed Module Three: Rituals and ceremonials. Our exercise began with reflections on "The Story of a Pheasant," a folktale popular with Buddhist, Konkōkyō, and Christian clerics.

In the story, a one-eyed pheasant fleeing from the local magistrate's hunting party takes refuge in a farmhouse. Believing the pheasant to be the incarnation of her father-in-law, the woman who lives in the farmhouse hides the bird in a large empty rice pot and rescues it. When her husband returns from laboring in the fields, she relates the incident and shows him the pheasant. Like his father, the pheasant is blind in the right eye and with its good eye scrutinizes the son in the same manner that the father often had. The son is convinced that the pheasant is indeed Father. "Poor Father must have thought to himself, 'now that I am a bird, better to give my body to my children for food than to let the hunters have it.' " Thereupon the farmer snatches the pheasant from his wife and wrings its neck. Outraged and terrified, the woman immediately flees and reports the incident to the magistrate. The woman is appropriately rewarded by the authorities, but the farmer is banished from the village (Hearn 1958).

As a Buddhist cleric, I understood the tale as a lesson in karmic responsibility. Clearly the son deserved to be run out of town for his outrageous behavior. For her righteousness, the wife reaped an appropriate reward. As a law of karmic retribution, karma simply states: one reaps what one sows. Ted Thompson, an Episcopalian priest spoke of the father's sacrifice for his son as a lesson of love and divine grace, reminding Christians of the need to be open to the unusual ways grace manifests itself. The story is illustrative of humanity's breaking its covenant with God and the expulsion from the kingdom of heaven. Rev. Masato Kawahatsu, noting that Konkōkyō believe *Tenchi Kane no Kami* is present in all things and all beings, faults the son for failing to understand *aiyo-kakeyo* (mutuality between *Tenchi no Kami* and human beings).[3] Unaware of this truth, the son unhesitating dispatches his father-pheasant, causing distress to himself, his wife, and *Kami* who agonize over human suffering.

In the discussion that followed, regardless of their faith, the Japanese American participants recoiled at the son's lack of gratitude and reverence toward his father, who gave abundantly of himself for the sake of his son. In addition to being the progenitor, the father provided for, protected, and no doubt found a suitable wife for his son. The son did not respond with gratitude and affection, but wrung his father's neck to satisfy his hunger—a most unfilial act. Such disrespect is a violation of the most fundamental obligation of the child toward a parent.

Community Wisdom

Based on the assumption that elder care is a communitywide concern, classes were held on site. Nihonmachi Terrace was our principal instruction venue, and it proved to be ideal for a number of reasons. Its centralized location in Japantown allowed for easy access to additional venues. Thus, for example, instruction on Buddhism was given at the San Francisco Buddhist Church, two blocks away. Our discussion of caregiving and caring included a visit to Kimochi Home, a 20-bed board and care facility owned and operated by Kimochi Senior Services two doors away. The last discussion of Model Programs and Future Projects, was held in Berkeley at Strawberry Creek Lodge, a senior housing facility and Chaparral House, a skilled nursing facility. Alternating instruction sites aimed to engage and impress civic leaders with the personal and community benefits of the project. Instruction was coupled with advocacy. An anticipated bonus, the senior residents at Nihonmachi Terrace provided lunch at nominal cost, and they donated their profits to the Kokoro building fund. The course evolved into a community event. Instruction on site merged theory with practice, impressing upon the seminarians the daily reality of elder care and offering the community information on geriatrics.

The importance of on-site instruction was further reinforced by tapping the wisdom of the community. Though Marita Grudzen, assistant director of the Sanford Geriatric Education Center, and I were the primary instructors, wherever and whenever possible we enlisted the expertise of instructors who worked and lived in the community. This pedagogical strategy was based on the assumption that the people who were known and loved by the community would be the best teachers. Moreover, since eldercare is a community effort, it was important to utilize the wisdom embedded in organizations and individuals committed to providing geriatric care. The course would end, and the instructors would leave, but the community organizations and individuals would continue their work. Thus, Sanjo Hiromi, a social worker from Kimochi Senior Services, shared his insights on family dynamics; Rev. William Masuda, a Buddhist cleric and licensed family therapist, lectured on traditional Japanese and current counseling theories and methods; Steve Nakajo, executive director of Kimochi Senior Services, spoke on the community resources dedicated to senior services; John I. Umekubo, a geriatrician who practices in San Francisco, Japantown, offered insightful observations on the particular health concerns of elders in the community; Rev. Don Drummond of the First Christ Presbyterian Church spoke on folk beliefs and rituals, and their presence in current rituals in all faith traditions; and John Grossberg, Ph.D. a bilingual therapist in private practice, led a discussion on images of aging.

Finally, based on the assumption that elders should be actively involved in their care and that they are also our teachers, Module One, Aging in America, brought in Gwen Yeo of the Sanford Geriatric Education Center to introduce the course with a historical overview of cohort experiences that affected Japanese elders' health and well-being. This cohort experience was recounted by five elders, who had been displaced from their homes during World War II. They were invited to address the questions, "To what do you attribute your health and longevity?" and "What is the role of spirituality in your life?" Their cohort experiences were instructive and inspiring, and they set the tone for subsequent modules. All of the elders—two Christians, two Buddhists, and a Konkōkyō devotee—credited their respective faith traditions with giving them the courage to live through their concentration camp experiences and the indignities of racial prejudice. In addition to sharing their years of experience, elders were inspirational. This was most evident in our lesson on Japanese Tea Ceremony, held at the Nichibei Kai's tearoom and led by 88-year-old (now 91-year-old) Kikuyo Sekino, who highlighted the importance of teaching by, and learning through, example.

Since no texts or reference books dealt specifically with much of the course content, each instructor assembled source materials for distribution. By the end of the academic year, we managed to assemble a three-inch loose-leaf binder. In addition to academic articles, relevant magazine and newspaper articles were also distributed.

During the fall 1999 academic semester, six seminarians from the Graduate Theological Union enrolled in the class for academic credit. Six health care professionals enrolled for continuing education units in nursing and nursing home administrator. In the spring 2000 semester, seven seminarians and five health care professionals enrolled. Various individuals from the community, JARF clergy and lay leaders, and seniors who resided in Nihonmachi Terrace often drifted in to attend specific modules. At times, more than 30 participants shared their experiences and expertise.

This mix of students posed some challenges. Health care professionals complained that the material related to Diseases of the Older Adult, and other Track A medical and scientific modules were too rudimentary; they desired more in-depth information. This concern was partially offset by providing current materials. Seminarians and other nonmedical professionals, on the other hand, found the information most useful. In contrast, health care professionals found practical content of such Track B modules as Folk Beliefs, Rituals and Ceremonies, and Therapies useful.

An Assessment

The key features of this community-based "Spirituality and Aging in the Japanese Experience" are its modular design, on-site instruction, and utilization of community expertise. The modular structure allowed health care providers, graduate students, families, clerics, and community volunteers who might need additional training or an upgrade of their skills to receive advanced professional training in spirituality and cultural competency in the care of elders. The format permitted full-time professionals and community volunteers to enroll in specific modules. As evident in the appended syllabus, the course was designed to accommodate working professionals who are unable to commit themselves to weekly academic sessions. Chaparral House, a skilled nursing home located in Berkeley, California, sent six staff members and the daughter of a resident for all six modules. A Cantonese-speaking social worker working in Oakland's Chinatown attended just one Saturday session to fulfill her required continuing education units to maintain her license. The thirty-nine hours of instruction fulfilled the requirements for graduate course accreditation.

The module structure allows for additional and/or new modules in the series as the need arises to address other issues and/or for other cultural- or faith-specific populations. Please note, for example, that each full-day session in the syllabus is divided into interrelated but separate morning and afternoon sessions. Thus, for example, Module Two in the Religious and Cultural component was divided into Images of Aging and Expectations of the Elderly, both of which focused on the Japanese context. I reworked the content of this module to reflect the Chinese experience when "Spirituality and Aging in the Chinese Experience" was subsequently offered.[4] The content for Module Two under Scientific and Medical sessions, Diseases of the Older Adult and Health Promotion and Disease Prevention can be similarly modified. One participant wanted more information on the pathology of vitamin B12 deficiencies that commonly affect older Japanese women. The module format can easily accommodate requests of this sort.

The inclusion of working professionals, volunteers, and family, and on-site instruction replicated—and introduced seminarians to—the multidisciplinary team approach to elder care (Klein 1996: 57; Smedley et al. 2002). In addition to the most up-to-date medical information and practical instruction from the religious leaders, we benefited from the wisdom of the community, especially the elders, who related their life stories and the importance of their faith and culture as they approach the end of life. The student participants also shared their expertise, as did the staff of Chaparral House, most notably in Module Five, Health Care Services, and Module Six, Community Resources.

Shifting to off-site venues brought the resources of working professionals to the community, and the benefits were immediately apparent. Seminarians were able to see firsthand the dynamics of a community and ongoing services, and to speak to and hear from service providers and elders—features difficult to replicate in the classroom. The on-site and multidisciplinary instruction created a unique setting for practical and theoretical study.

Final Remarks

It is difficult to evaluate the outcome of the course, since it was designed to be an integral part of Kokoro Assisted Living's in-service training for staff and for professionals, families, and volunteers who will be part of the care team. Kokoro began operations in October 2003, and its successful operation will ultimately determine the validity of original vision of this project. However, in the meantime, the course evaluation sheets have been overwhelmingly positive.

The success of the course is reflected in anecdotal evidence from former students, who report that they have been sensitized to the needs of peoples of other ethnic and spiritual traditions. Jim Johnson, administrator of the Chaparral House, who attended the modules with five of his staff, remarked that quite apart from conveying practical information, the yearlong learning experience broadened his and his staff's personal growth.

Finally, Spirituality and Aging in the Japanese Experience was conceived and designed for a specific community and would not be entirely applicable to others. However, some insights are worthy of consideration. First, tapping the professional resources embedded in the community merged theory with practice, thus greatly enriching the learning experience. This effort required an intimate knowledge of, and detailed coordination with, medical professionals, social service providers, clergy, family, and volunteers who served the community of elders. A similar effort in a more ethnically and culturally diverse community would surely encounter additional challenges. Second, opening the course to the "caregiving community" approximated the reality of eldercare and reinforced the importance of community involvement. Third, the yearlong course provided ample opportunity to explore and reflect in depth a number of issues related to eldercare. Fourth, the voices of the elders were especially rewarding. Mrs. Misako (Mary) Misaki, a deeply devout Buddhist, remarked, "Spiritual care is especially important at the end of life."

Syllabus Movement and Course Modules

Spirituality and Aging in the Japanese Experience integrates medical/scientific understanding of aging and the experiences of a living community, with the express goal of providing a multidisciplinary, cross-cultural, and team approach to attending to geriatric clients' spiritual and cultural needs.

Curriculum: Objective and Approaches: The overarching cognitive/affective aim is to help students to acquire a richer, more complex understanding of spirituality, aging, and the respective religious traditions, and to give them information that can help them to deal with elder needs, end-of-life issues, and family concerns. The lectures, readings, and site visits are designed for seminary students, social workers, and health care professionals who will be or are already working with Asian American—specifically Japanese—elders.

Cognitive aims: (1) The course will promote understanding of spirituality and complexity of culture in eldercare. (2) The course seeks to assist service providers, and clergy in identifying questions that address the cultural and spiritual needs of elders. (3) The ultimate aim of this course is to improve cultural literacy in a variety of religious traditions so that students, family members, clergy, and volunteer and professional caregivers will be able to provide spiritual care in routine and emergency situations, will be aware of issues in end-of-life decision making, and will be sensitive to cultural issues in family dynamics.

Affective aims: The course will enhance the students' appreciation of other religious traditions and will foster an enlarged consciousness of spiritual experience as being embodied in the life of the individual and the world at large.

Outcomes: The course will have immediate and long-term effects. The student will be able to immediately apply the insights from the course in the care of elders. Seminarians will be able to recognize health, psychological, and social pathologies of the older adult as they go about their ministry. Health care professionals will be sensitive to the spiritual and social needs of the older adult. In the long term, the course will contribute to changing society's perception of elders and will include volunteers, clerics, and families as part of the health care team.

Requirements: Each student will produce a handbook with information about each of the three faith traditions (Buddhist, Christian, and Shintō) studied. Each section will sketch the history, doctrines, rituals, and specific rituals and images that are meaningful for elder care, and their importance with respect to end-of-life decision making, grief counseling, and other topics may be of use to caregivers. The student will assemble "an interfaith emergency kit" that includes ritual implements, prayers, and liturgy needed for emergency situations in the absence of a proper clergy person.

Student Assessment: Evaluation and successful completion of the course will be based on mastery of the lectures and readings and on class participation. Objective tests (true/false, multiple-choice), essay questions, assigned papers, especially those that reflect increased self-knowledge of students' own cultural attitudes and values, research papers (on such issues as medicine and health, religion and spirituality, interdisciplinary care teams), case studies, reports from individual or group projects, community-workshop design and presentation, and student performance at the public forum will also be assessed through an evaluation from the people who attend. Students who elect to fulfill their internship requirements will negotiate directly with an approved supervising clergy or health care administrator their particular project and requirements, and evaluation. The six-unit, two-semester course (3 units per semester) can be taken for a letter grade or pass/fail. Stanford University Medical School offered nursing and social work continuing education units and applied for Nursing Home Administrator continuing education units.

Track A: Medical and Scientific

MODULE I: AGING IN AMERICA

Aging in America is devoted to the demographic characteristics, acculturation, and health status of elders. It includes a review of the theories, images of aging, and myths and realities of aging. Special attention is devoted to Asian and Asian Americans, especially Japanese and Japanese American elders. Students are also introduced to the discipline of *ethnogeriatrics*, which assesses the needs for and develops training and programs in culturally appropriate geriatric care, client assessment, health care interventions, and client utilizations of long-term-care services and senior centers.

MODULE 2: HEALTH CARE

Diseases of the older adult introduces common maladies of the older adult: Alzheimer's, arthritis, dementia, mental health, motor control, osteoporosis, and stroke. Particular attention is devoted to the epidemiology of Asian and Asian American populations. *Health promotion and disease prevention* reviews the biological changes in aging, the pathology of disease, and strategies to promote health and well-being, and it outlines the psychological issues involved in memory, learning, mental health, and personality in the older adult, especially as they occur in Asians and the Asian-American community.

MODULE 3: CAREGIVING AND CARING

The health care team describes the role of the physician, nurse, nursing assistants, medical social worker, the nursing home administrator, volunteers, and family in the care of the older adult; discusses the importance of continuum and interdisciplinary care; reviews current models of care, levels of care, and Asian models. *Physical needs and aids/drugs and other therapies* introduces common drugs and therapies, their uses and dangers, and the place of culture-specific therapies and herbal remedies.

MODULE 4: ELDER CONCERNS

Illness and disability explores the needs and concerns of the older adult. Though safety is a prime concern of caregivers, this is the least of the older adult's concerns. Illness and disability are frequently amplified or mistakenly diagnosed because of cultural and religious misunderstandings and differing images of health and well-being. *Dying, death, and bereavement* explore pain and palliative care, thirst and hydration at the end of life. The older adult is often concerned with pain control and hospice care. Drugs, alternative therapies, and grief support groups are important to combat depression and loneliness in the older adult, especially after the death of a lifelong partner.

MODULE 5: HEALTH CARE SERVICES

Health Care Services outlines the kinds of health care and services that are currently available—care facility categories (life care, assisted living, skilled nursing, etc.) and their levels of care and pricing structures—and reviews issues of access and utilization by Asians and Asian-Americans. *Aging and spirituality: Insights and clinical applications* explores spiritual issues that arise during the process of aging; introduces findings from the empirical literature concerning the relationship between spirituality or religiosity and physical and mental health in the aging person; identifies ways spiritual resources can enhance the mental and physical health of elders; and outlines ways that spiritual resources can help staff enhance the quality of care they provide.

MODULE 6: OLDER PERSONS AND THE LAW

Public policies, professional practices, and polity reviews government policies and professional practices that relate to elders; outlines Medicare/Medi-Cal and managed care guidelines; government oversight agencies; and care facility categories (life care, assisted living, skilled nursing, etc.) and their levels of care and pricing structures. Ministers, caregivers, and elders must be informed consumers and advocates for change. *Ethics* introduces critical ethical issues, such as competing needs and the allocation of competing resources, elder abuse, pain management and assisted suicide; introduces decision making and end-of-life issues; reviews patient rights; and outlines duties and responsibilities of institutions and of physicians, nurses, and other health care professionals.

Track B: Religious and Cultural

MODULE 1: THEORY: CONTEXT/SPIRITUAL

Cross-cultural communications describes and contrasts values, customs, mores, language, and communication styles of cultural groups, with an emphasis on their implications for working with elders. It focuses on how to interpret the communication behavior of elders from various ethnic groups with a focus on Asians and Asian-Americans, how to overcome barriers when the culture patterns are different from one's own, and how to understand that the norms of appropriate conversation and caregiving differ from culture to culture. *Spirituality and faith* surveys the history and classical doctrines of Buddhism, Christianity, and Shintō, the three representative organized faith traditions in the Japanese American community, with an emphasis on their respective places in the cultural and community continuum and personal and family life.

MODULE 2: PRACTICAL: FOLK BELIEFS/CULTURAL CONTEXT

Images of aging reviews Japanese and Japanese American images of health and well-being. Issues to be addressed include attitudes toward growing old, response to the elderly and their care, the role of elders in the community and the home, and paradigms of loss and grief. *Expectations of the elderly* focuses on social attitudes toward aging, especially on the psychological, social, and spiritual aspects of elders as they relate to the realities of their own aging. These issues will be discussed from the Buddhist, Christian, and Shintō traditions. This segment also addresses issues of intergenerational and age-cohort differences.

MODULE 3: FAMILY

Family introduces a range of effective cross-cultural techniques and strategies for working with Japanese cultural patterns in families that include elderly parents, adult children, and the youngest generation; considers the "total family," including members of the family born in the United States as well as those who have immigrated and those who may remain in Japan; explores creative methods of therapeutic and social interventions as well as our own biases and prejudices in working with Japanese residents. *Rituals and ceremonials* discusses rituals marking important life transitions (late life, funerals, memorials) and their significance; examines customs that are common to the Japanese community and those that are special to Buddhist, Christian, and Shintō traditions.

MODULE 4: THERAPIES

Counseling presents basic concepts and techniques of communicating with and counseling elders and their families, surveys traditional Japanese methods of counseling (*naikan*, Morita, *shadan*, *seiza* and *zazen*), and explores the healing arts that are currently practiced with great effectiveness by new faith traditions such as Konkokyō and Tenrikyō. *Folk practices, alternative beliefs and other coping therapies* explore folk practices and beliefs that affect day-to-day life including shamanic and animistic beliefs and herbal and folk remedies. We will also introduce the Taoist influence on Japanese spiritual life, describing key concepts of luck and misfortune, signs and portents, filial gratitude and restitution.

MODULE 5: COMMUNITY

Role of family and community introduces cultural and religious dimensions of aging among Japanese Americans. The module describes the Japanese American immigration experience and the dynamics of intergenerational and age-cohort issues. Instruction highlights the Confucian values and attitudes that permeate the life of the Japanese family and society. Interfaith and interracial marriages, personal and vocational lifestyle choices, approaches to child rearing, and funerals and the passing of generations raise many issues that affect the care of elders. *Family and minister on the health care team* explores the roles of family members and spiritual counselors in the care of elders and examines issues that they need to be aware of to be effective members of the caregiving team. This session also explores the need for support and counseling for families who admit elders to nursing homes.

MODULE 6: COMMUNITY RESOURCES

Community Resources identifies the agencies within federal, state, and local governments and the private, volunteer, and religious organizations that are devoted to elder issues; and examines the role of local congregations in accessing services (advocacy, education, referral, and follow-up). *Model programs and future projects* discusses model programs, identifies community and congregational needs, and suggests solutions to meeting the needs of older adults. The module explores the need for elder ministry in the churches, hospitals, and senior center, and the future role of congregations, interfaith organizations, and seminaries in multifaith and interdisciplinary studies on aging.

NOTES

1. The founding congregations were the Buddhist Church of San Francisco, Christ Episcopal Church, Gedatsu Buddhist Church of America, Japanese Church of Christ (Christ United Presbyterian Church), Konkōkyō Church of San Francisco, Nichiren Buddhist Church of America, Pine United Methodist Church, St. Francis Xavier Catholic Church, San Francisco Independent Church, Seventh-Day Adventist Japanese Church, and Sōtō Zen Mission (Sōkōji Temple of San Francisco). The Gedatsu Buddhist Church, Seventh-Day Adventist Church, and the San Francisco Independent Church have been replaced by Hokkeshū Hon'nōji Buddhist Temple, Risshō Kōsei Kai Buddhist Church and Tenrikyō—America West.

2. Watsuji Tetsurō (1889–1960) coined the expression *jūsōsei* (the quality of being stratified or laminated) to describe the various traditions and cultures (Shintōism, Confucianism, Christianity, Taoism, Chinese and Indian Buddhism, Neo-Confucianism), and a variety of influences in Western thought and culture that inform the Japanese experience.

3. Konkōkyō was established by Ikigami Konkō-Daijin in 1859. The Konkō faith holds that the universe is the Grand Shrine of the *Tenchi Kane no Kami*, the Principal Parent of the universe. Human beings owe their existence and being to its infinite benevolence. Since the Divine is present in all things, daily life is the setting for spiritual training. By earnestly practicing a life of sincere faith based on the principle of *aiyo-kakeyo*, the devotees are able to realize a good life for themselves and their families, which is Divine fulfillment.

4. Impressed with the JARF program, some leaders of the Chinese community encouraged the design and implementation of "Spirituality and Aging in the Chinese Experience." A three-unit course was offered through the Graduate Theological Union during the spring 2001 semester. The primary venue was the Chinese Hospital in the heart of San Francisco Chinatown. Twenty seminarians and eight staff nurses from the hospital enrolled for the various modules. The experience gained from these efforts was the basis for the long-term grant submitted by the Sanford Geriatric Education Center to the Bureau of Health Professions of the Health Resources and Services Administration in the U.S. Department of Health and Human Services. The proposal asked that funds be allocated to develop training modules for underserved communities. The proposal, submitted at the end of 2000, has been funded.

REFERENCES

Ellor, James, Susan McFadden, and Stephen Sapp. 1999. *Aging and spirituality, the first decade.* San Francisco: American Society on Aging.

Hearn, Lafcadio. 1958. The one-eyed pheasant. In *Kōtō*, 33–36. Tokyo: Dai'ichi gakushū sha.

Klein, Susan M., ed. 1996. *A National agenda for geriatric education: White papers,* Vol. 1. Washington, DC: Bureau of Health Professions, Heath Resources, and Services Administration.

McLaren, Ronald. [1984] 1990. Kawaiso, justice, and reciprocity: themes in Japanese and Western ethics. In *Aesthetic and ethical values in Japanese culture,* ed. Jackson H. Bailey. Richmond, IN: Earlham College Press.

Nakasone, Ronald Y. 2000. Buddhist issues in end-of-life decision making. In *Cultural issues in end-of-life decision making,* eds. Kathryn L. Braun, James H. Pietsch, and Patricia L. Blanchette, 213–228. Thousand Oaks, CA: Sage.

Smedley, Brian D., Adrienne Y. Stith, and Alan R. Nelson, eds. (2002). *Unequal treatment, confronting racial and ethnic disparities in healthcare.* Washington, DC: National Academy Press.

18

Religion and Healing for Physician's Assistants

Fred Glennon

The Context and the Students

This course on religion and healing came about in response to Le Moyne College's efforts to develop a Physician's Assistants (PA) program. The originators wanted the program to have a Le Moyne stamp, which meant that it needed to add some key humanistic disciplines, especially philosophy, literature, and religion. Le Moyne is a Jesuit college in Syracuse, New York, and a central part of our mission is to develop whole persons who appreciate diversity and are committed to service and justice regardless of their chosen professions. A PA program that only prepared students for the scientific and practical aspects of the profession was unacceptable. That is why the school wanted to be sure to add courses in the humanities, especially religion and ethics, to prepare students for the broader human context into which their practice would take them.

Yet because the program was a professional one, there was a desire on the part of the directors to shape the courses in ways that focused on the professional lives of the students. Thus, instead of an introduction to philosophical ethics, PA students took medical ethics; instead of literature came the cultural foundations of medicine; and instead of an introduction to the study of religion, our department developed a course on religion and healing. In many ways, this infusion of humanistic disciplines into the program is what makes it unique among PA programs.

The recent hire of a new director has generated changes. First, the PA program is moving from a certificate to a master's program. The intent is to incorporate the three separate humanities courses into a yearlong medical humanities seminar that will illustrate the interdisciplinary nature of the material presently covered separately. In addition, the new director is implementing a more problem-based, case-oriented approach to the clinical medicine aspects to push students to take more responsibility for their learning. Both developments have implications for the content and pedagogy of my course.

Currently, however, the course I teach has evolved in response to student needs and interests. The majority of PA students already have undergraduate degrees, except for those who are in the combined BS/PA program. Students are, on average, thirty years old, with some in their early twenties and late fifties. The classes reflect the gender balance of Le Moyne College—approximately 60 percent female to 40 percent male. They are overwhelmingly white, Christian, and middle class. All have working experience beyond college in some type of medical setting; it is a requirement for admission into the program. They come to Le Moyne seeking a professional degree and expect that their courses—including those in the humanities—will enable them to become better professionals.

Early on, most students had had no courses in the study of religion as undergraduates. That is why my predecessor had moved the Religion and Healing course in the direction of being an introduction to the study of religion, with some attention to how religious traditions incorporated healing. Her rationale was that many PA students had little understanding of the nature of religion. By the time I started teaching the course four years ago, however, the student body had changed some, and this approach no longer worked. Many more came from religiously affiliated colleges and universities and thus had taken at least one course in religion; a sizeable minority had taken two. Moreover, their interests had changed. Though some enjoyed theoretical discussions of religious issues and ideas, the majority wanted to know how religious beliefs and perspectives would influence their work as a PA.

When I first started teaching it, about one third of the students were hostile to taking such a course. They felt that, in a two-year program, a course in religion meant no course in an area more critical to their practice as PAs, such as radiology. Another third were indifferent, and did only what was needed to pass it and move on. The final third welcomed it—some because their own religious tradition affirmed the role of religion in healing; others because they wanted to understand the beliefs and practices of the patients they would encounter and the effect of these factors on patient care. In the last two years, more students have become interested in the religious grounding of complementary and alternative forms of medicine they see practiced throughout the country. Though most see modern biomedicine and its allopathic focus as the primary and best form of medicine, some realize the limits of such medicine in certain areas, especially chronic forms of illnesses. Thus they seek to understand the many ways homeopathic and holistic forms of medicine can aid in the healing process.

Theoretical Issues That Shape the Course

The context and the students described above shape the theoretical issues that drive the course. The first one to note is the difference between teaching in a pre-professional program and teaching traditional undergraduates. With the latter, a liberal arts education seeks to enable students to develop a good grasp of the religious underpinnings of human experience. A religion and healing course for undergraduates might direct that goal into the ways it plays out in healing traditions. (As I write this essay, I am in the process of developing a similar course for traditional undergraduates. This difference is in the forefront of my mind). In a preprofessional setting, what drives student interest is a course that enables them to become better health care practitioners—the pragmatic, practical side. What I seek to do is to balance their interest with the theoretical underpinnings of the practices that shape the course.

A student focus on the practical side of healing and religion also poses a different theoretical challenge. While my students are quick to acknowledge the religious worldviews, beliefs, and values that underlie traditional religious healing practices, they often fail to see that worldview and ideology are foundational also to medicine and science. They do not recognize the ideological basis of much of biomedicine. They make the simple assumption that their work is based in fact, not belief, as they claim traditional healing practices are. Thus, one of my objectives is to get students to explore the cultural foundations of biomedicine and their effect on the current shape of modern practice.

Related to this issue is my interest in broadening the students' understanding of health, illness, and healing. Their training up to now has taught them to focus on the body (understood anatomically), and perhaps also the emotions, of their patients. While they may pay lip service to the World Health Organization definition of health, which includes spiritual and social aspects of health, they have not fully embraced it. Moreover, they have an allopathic approach to medicine and health care; they define illness narrowly as disease, and equate healing with curing—the elimination of disease with drugs or surgery. They dismiss traditional homeopathic practices; at best, they consider them a placebo, and at worst, a nuisance. By having students attend more fully to the spiritual dimensions of illness and see healing as the ability to restore balance even in the face of disease, I can help them to appreciate the insights that traditional approaches to healing offer them as health care providers, or "HCPs."

A third issue that drives the course revolves around the various ways that faith, religious commitments, and practices influence the behaviors and health care practices of patients and practitioners. This issue includes looking at a broad array of religious orientations they might encounter among their patients and at how these phenomena affect health care decisions. While most of the patients these PA students encounter may be Jewish or Christian, it is important for them to understand the diversity of belief and practice within those traditions. Moreover, as the United States becomes more culturally and religiously pluralistic, students will encounter a more diverse group of religious practitioners in their work than did previous generations. These would include religious traditions that accept modern scientific health care, those that complement it with other health care practices, and even those that reject it. The course addresses this issue also through an exploration of various alternative and complementary health care practices, with a strong focus on their theoretical—spiritual and religious—underpinnings. Further, we look at various ritual practices, such as prayer and religious service participation, which either maintain or restore health. In light of the students' scientific outlook, the course reviews scientific studies on the efficacy of these beliefs and practices.

A final theoretical issue centers on the nature of suffering, dying, and death, and their connection with spirituality and the search for meaning on the part of both patients and practitioners. Suffering and illness, especially when life threatening, not only affect one's body; they affect one's sense of oneself. As the growing number of published patient and practitioner pathographies—written accounts that attempt to document and make sense of serious illness—illustrate, they often call into question one's whole way of life. They push people to think about their lives before, during, and after the illness in attempt to make meaning of the illness in their lives. For practitioners, continued suffering, illness, and death call into question the nature of their role as HCPs. They cannot always cure disease; death is not always an enemy. As a result, practitioners must find additional or broader metaphors for understanding their work and accept the role of enabling patients to find healing and restore balance even in the face of disease and death.

The Teaching-Learning Process

The interplay of context, student resistance and interest, and the issues has led me to shape the course around three active pedagogical models: contract learning, cooperative learning, and experiential learning. Overcoming the resistance of students and incorporating the program's new push to enable students to take more responsibility for their learning fit in well with my own pedagogical commitments to have students take an active role in the shape and direction of their learning. As someone who teaches required courses, I have long seen the importance of getting students to take responsibility if their learning is going to be meaningful. Learning information and skills is more significant when students are able to make important connections with their own goals and interests. This happens best when they become partners, with the freedom and responsibility to determine both the content and the process of the learning that takes place.

One contemporary pedagogy practice that I use effectively in enabling student responsibility for learning in this course is learning covenants. Covenant or contract learning engages students in the learning process by building a program of study upon the compelling interests of each student. Instead of asking, "How can I teach so that you will be motivated to learn?" the teacher asks, "What do you want to learn?" This approach empowers the student by giving over a large measure of control over what learning takes place, thereby providing ownership of that learning. The covenant begins with some assessment of what the student needs to know and what they want to learn (learning objectives). These objectives can be based on the student's own self-assessment, or they can be more institutional or teacher oriented. This course includes both types. On the basis of these objectives, the student then decides on the strategies, activities, and resources he/she will need to meet these objectives (learning resources). The student must also indicate what the outcomes will be, how and by whom those outcomes will be evaluated, and the timetable for their completion.

Ironically, many PAs initially resist taking on such responsibility. All of their classes up to now have dictated what they should learn and when they should learn it, although this has recently changed somewhat. They would rather not take the time to determine what to do on their own. Yet, as end-of-semester student evaluations demonstrate, most students eventually come to appreciate the flexibility and ownership such a pedagogical approach provides. They appreciate being able to focus their learning on specific ideas and issues they want to explore and to apply their creative abilities through artwork, journaling, and other activities to express their learning.

At the same time the covenanting process is going on, I structure the class on a cooperative learning model. Cooperative learning contends that, because humans are social, interdependent beings, we learn best in cooperation with one another. Traditional approaches to learning are based on competitive or individualized models. But these models do not tap the students' potential to contribute to the learning process. This is especially true in the PA program, where students bring diverse experience, backgrounds, and skill levels to the classroom. Students are almost never encouraged, much less rewarded, for helping each other learn. However, when teachers encourage students to work together and provide incentives for them to learn from one another, students learn better in the vast majority of cases. Numerous research studies support this claim (Slavin 1991; Cooper and Mueck 1989). This means that every person in the class has some responsibility for the learning that takes place in class. My goal is to promote cooperative behavior and ultimately cooperative motives—the predisposition to act cooperatively, something essential to their work and success as HCPs, where the team model is the norm.

Using cooperative strategies to teach much of the course content has implications for my role in the classroom. I seek to minimize student perceptions of me as an authority figure and instead enhance their understanding that I am there to promote their learning primarily as a resource person. I attempt to create a context for them to learn together and to assume responsibility for their learning. This role has been far more demanding because, while I must ensure that learning is taking place, I must do so in ways that invite ideas and perspectives different from my own.

A final pedagogical model I use in this course is experiential learning. Experiential learning at its heart draws from John Dewey's contention in *De-*

mocracy and Education, "An ounce of experience is better than a ton of theory simply because it is only in experience that any theory has vital and verifiable significance" (1966:144). All education provides experiences, whether they be experiences with a text or in a classroom setting. Yet for those experiences to be educational, they have to be significant in ways that are fruitful for further learning. They must be relevant, reflective, and connected to previous knowledge and experiences even when they challenge students to rethink or modify their prior knowledge and ideas. If I really want my students to broaden their understanding of healing and learn to appreciate the role that religion can play in the healing process, I must find ways for them to experience those connections firsthand. Developing such quality experiences places tremendous responsibility on the teacher, but the assumption of such responsibility is well worth it.

The theoretical issues and pedagogical approaches that drive the course culminate in cognitive, affective, and behavioral learning goals that address the content and the skills needs of the students. These include:

1. Broadening students understanding of health, illness, and healing beyond the allopathic model;
2. Investigating the cultural and ideological underpinnings of modern medicine;
3. Developing students' sensitivity to and awareness of the religious experiences and convictions that affect the ways that patients and health professionals approach health care decisions and interactions;
4. Researching alternative and complementary healing practices and their theoretical grounding in spiritual and religious worldviews;
5. Developing students' appreciation of the human desire to place suffering, illness, and death into a broader context of meaning;
6. Exploring metaphors for their roles as HCPs that include the broader moral and spiritual aspects of their relationships with patients;
7. Working cooperatively with others on various tasks in a group context; and
8. Taking an active role in and responsibility for their learning.

These goals are met in part through traditional classroom practices, which include some lectures, group discussions and presentations, audiovisual presentations, structured reading and writing assignments, guest presentations, and other media, the particular configuration depending upon student interest and involvement. But the goals are met primarily through the active pedagogical approaches discussed above.

I begin the semester not only with students taking responsibility for individual learning objectives through their covenants, but also by inviting them to develop significant content portions of the syllabus. While most groups of students have some similar interests associated with religion and healing, they also often have particular issues or concerns they would like to address during the semester. Inviting their participation in creating the syllabus furthers their role in the learning process and their ownership of the course.

Group research and presentations have been quite helpful in enabling students to address the goals of working in groups, taking responsibility for their learning, and addressing some of the cognitive goals and content areas of the course. I ask students to research topics of interest to them that connect religion and healing, and to make presentations accordingly. They are free to shape these presentations in whatever ways they desire, but there are evaluation criteria they all must meet, including evidence of appropriate preparation and research, smooth implementation, methods to engage students actively in discussion, and appropriate insights on the subject matter. One of the strengths of student presentations thus far is their use of nontextual resources, including food, video, music, and practical demonstrations of such healing practices as meditation, yoga, and therapeutic oils. One weakness I have had to address in some cases involves emphasizing to students that their role is to present material in the best light. Some students often begin with a negative perception of the traditional healing idea or practice they research. Though providing critiques is certainly appropriate, there have been times when student presentations on such practices as therapeutic touch, aromatherapies, and so on have been done in quite dismissive ways.

Experiential forms of learning have proven successful at enabling students to broaden their views of health, illness, and healing and to learn more about complementary healing practices. One learning activity that I require is for students to become observer/participants in a healing practice/ritual that has its roots in some religious/spiritual tradition. Aside from the observation and participation, they must research the practice/ritual and compare the related notions of healing with their own. The goal of this activity is to have students experience firsthand some healing practices that are not allopathic in focus. Second, I have developed relationships with various practitioners of complementary healing practices, and I invite them to discuss and demonstrate their healing art with my students. For example, an acupuncturist who was trained in traditional Chinese medicine in Beijing lives in my community. When she visits the classroom, she speaks about the foundation of the practice in Chinese religion and philosophy and then demonstrates the use of the needles for various chronic ailments. She never lacks for volunteers. Reiki and other forms of Therapeutic Touch are complementary healing practices that interest my students. I have the fortune of having an alumnus living in the area who is both a biomedical doctor and a certified Reiki master. While he speaks to the class about the religious/theoretical foundations of the practice, members of his clinic walk among the students performing various Reiki techniques. Students are then invited to the clinic to learn more about the practice and/or to engage in further Reiki experiences. They comment that observing/experiencing these practices provides a better understanding of them than any reading alone could do.

I use a variety of textual resources. I have found David Kinsley's essay "The

Ideology of Modern Medical Culture," in *Health, Healing, and Religion* (1996), useful in getting students to discuss the possibility that ideology is foundational for biomedicine as well. I complement this discussion with traditional definitions of culture and the role that worldview, ethos, and social structures play to support a particular way of life and practice. While they read Clifford Geertz's essay "Religion as a Cultural System," from *Interpretation of Cultures* (1976), to see how religion functions in the lives of individuals and communities, I turn the concepts back onto the cultural foundations of biomedicine. The purpose is not to dismiss biomedicine but to surface its theoretical aspects.

The course addresses questions of race, ethnocentricity, gender, and cultural differences through the use of case studies. Galanti's book, *Caring for Patients from Different Cultures* (1997), provides dozens of cases drawn from hospital settings that illustrate practical problems that arise when HCPs overlook these considerations in their treatment of patients. The focus of discussion on these cases moves in both theoretical and practical directions. We look at how race, ethnicity, gender, and cultural differences influence the perspectives and behaviors that patients and practitioners bring to health care decisions. We also look at the processes and procedures that HCPs should incorporate into their treatment of patients to ensure that problems either do not arise or are addressed appropriately.

Another textual resource I have used with some success to develop student sensitivity to, and awareness of, the many implications of religious experiences and convictions is the *Religious Traditions and Health Care Decisions* handbook series (2002). The strength of these short handbooks is that they provide religious/theoretical discussions underlying the particular medical and ethical positions that these traditions have in the clinical setting. Moreover, with examples drawn from a variety of Christian and Jewish traditions as well as from Islam, Buddhism, and Hinduism, these texts illustrate the diversity both within and across traditions that is a part of the religiously pluralistic context into which students will be placed. These texts also address the practical bent of my students. For example, when treating a Jehovah's Witness, students want to know what medical procedures they can or cannot perform and why Witnesses have the positions they do on specific issues, like blood transfusions. These texts focus on such practical questions.

Novels, films, and pathographies are key textual and nontextual materials that enable students to develop an appreciation of the human desire to place suffering, illness, and death into a broader context of meaning. Such films as *Wit* and *The Doctor* are wonderful resources for illustrating how struggling with serious or terminal illness can lead a person to recast one's perspective on life and its meaning (in addition to calling into question an overly allopathic and mechanical approach to disease and healing). I have had students read such books as *A Grief Observed* by C. S. Lewis, *A Leg to Stand On* by Oliver Sachs, and *The Measure of Our Days: A Spiritual Exploration of Illness* by Jerome Groopman, because of the depth with which they explore the spiritual and religious dimensions of illness and death.

I use a variety of Web-based resources for instructional and supplemental purposes. I use Blackboard, a virtual classroom, to organize and structure the class. Aside from providing a place for all course materials, Blackboard's group, communication, and virtual classroom functions allow the class to further the collaborative work within and among groups. The Web provides excellent tools for researching and understanding the religious beliefs and practices of various traditions, through electronic journals, official websites, and other media. The course website I develop provides links to some of the best of these sites, among which are sites that make nontextual materials increasingly available, such as streaming video. For example, *Scientific American Frontiers*, a PBS program, has numerous streaming videos that demonstrate various alternative and complementary medical practices, such as acupuncture, Reiki, and aromatherapy. These provide excellent discussion starters. Students can see a particular practice, such as therapeutic touch, and then hear about the controversy surrounding it. We supplement the video with reading and discussion. Of course, the effective use of these Web-based resources is connected to their quality, availability, and technology. Nothing is more frustrating than when one's plan to use Web-based media for instructional purposes goes awry because of problems at the site or with the technology in the classroom.

Conclusion

In truth, some students have not experienced success in achieving the learning goals for the course. I can think of at least two reasons. Though the course is required of every student in the program, a number of them still see it as secondary, not central, to their education as HCPs. They appreciate my efforts to connect the concepts and practices we explore to their professional lives. But they are often not ready at this stage in their education, with its focus on the science of medicine, to admit any significant role for religion in healing. Another reason is my own lack of expertise. My graduate training is in religious ethics, and I do not bring a strong research background on religion and healing into this course. I have done and continue to do extensive reading on the interrelationship between religion and healing to prepare for this course each year. Yet I need to further my own background in this growing field if I am to enable more of my PA students to be successful at meeting course goals and objectives.

Nevertheless, taking this course has enabled participants to broaden their views of healing and religion, especially those who have actively engaged the course materials and activities. Looking at the ways that religious traditions conceptualize illness and healing helps to enlarge the narrow view of healing so dominant today. Participants, many of whom have been immersed in training that overemphasizes disease and cure, come to appreciate the multifaceted nature of illness and view the possibility for healing even when there is no cure. In an evaluation of the course, one student captures this idea best when she writes: "The focus on religious traditions opens us up to other healing modalities than simply curing the sick."

Moreover, the focus on religion and healing has had significant consequences for our understanding of religion. We often conceptualize religion narrowly as a set of orthodox beliefs and practices that require participants to believe and act in certain ways. By looking at religion's role in healing, restoring balance and finding meaning—in face of the threats to oneself or to one's community, which illness brings—we begin to see the powerful way in which religious belief and practice—especially ritual practice—bring together the spiritual, ethical, and behavioral dimensions of human experience. Religion is no longer simply cognitive assent or institutional participation, but a living tradition that connects human to human and human to transcendent in a web of relationship that can bring wholeness and healing into the lives of its adherents.

Syllabus: Religion and Healing for Physician's Assistants

Course Description and Objectives

This course is an exploration of the plurality of cultural and religious contexts in which healing occurs, with the goal of enabling students to appreciate the overlap between the fields of medicine and religion. We research the understandings that religions and healing systems, both traditional and modern, have of the human condition, of health and illness, and of acceptable ways of maintaining and restoring health. We look at how religious commitments and practices both promote and inhibit processes of healing. Through readings, guest lectures, and field trips, students become exposed to alternative and complementary forms of medicine and healing practices and the religious and spiritual worldviews that give shape to them. Although the course has these theoretical components, how certain worldviews and belief structures shape the various healing systems and practices we explore, it also has a pragmatic edge: to enable students to understand and appreciate the religious and spiritual sensibilities both they and their patients bring with them to the healing interaction in the hope that such awareness and appreciation will lead them to become better health care professionals. This course is exclusively for students in the Physicians' Assistant Program. By participation in and successful completion of this course, students will be able to:

1. Articulate a broader understanding of health, illness, and healing beyond the allopathic model;
2. Discuss clearly the cultural and ideological underpinnings of modern medicine;
3. Demonstrate sensitivity to and awareness of the religious experiences and convictions that affect the ways that patients and health professionals approach health care decisions and interactions;
4. Discuss several alternative and complementary healing practices and their theoretical grounding in spiritual and religious worldviews;

5. State and appreciate reasons for the human desire to place suffering, illness, and death into a broader context of meaning;
6. Discuss intelligently metaphors for their roles as HCPs that include the broader moral and spiritual aspects of their relationships with patients;
7. Develop their research, presentation, observation, analytical, and writing skills;
8. Enhance their skills at working cooperatively with others on various tasks in a group context; and
9. Take an active role in and responsibility for their learning.

Texts and Other Readings

Geri-Ann Galanti. 1997. *Caring for Patients from Different Cultures.* Philadelphia: University of Pennsylvania Press.
Park Ridge Center. 2002. *Religious Traditions and Health Care Decisions.* Chicago: Park Ridge Center for the Study of Health, Faith, and Ethics.
Harold Koenig. 2002. *Spirituality in Patient Care.* Philadelphia: Templeton Foundation Press.
C. S. Lewis. 1976. *A Grief Observed.* New York: Bantam.

Additional readings can be found online or on reserve in the library. Reference is made to these readings in the course schedule.

Student Responsibilities and Rights

Students have responsibility for sharing in and contributing to the learning process. This responsibility includes developing a learning covenant; reading assigned material prior to class; participating actively in group activities, class presentations, and discussions; completing written assignments on time; and evaluating and suggesting positive directions for the class. In fulfilling these responsibilities, the student has certain rights. These include a right to voice an opinion that is based on a self-chosen value system, to dissent or differ from the professor or from others in the class, to have papers and assignments returned within a reasonable amount of time, to talk with the professor at hours other than class time, and to know the grading system.

Evaluation

Student evaluations will be based on successful completion of assigned and self-chosen activities. The assigned activities include group participation (15%), a report on a religious healing ritual (10–25%), and a group presentation and reflection paper (15–25%). The remaining 35–55% of the student's grade will be determined on the basis of the student choosing from a menu of activities (see the learning covenant guidelines and activity options on my Web page:

http://webserver.lemoyne.edu/rel300.htm). Because this class in many re-
spects is a graduate class, I will issue only five letter grades: A, A− B+, B, and
B−. Any activity that is below B− will be returned to the student to be redone
until it meets the level of B− or better.

Tentative Course and Reading Schedule

WEEK 1: INTRODUCTION TO COURSE AND LEARNING COVENANT

See Course Syllabus, Learning Covenant Guidelines, and Activity Options
(http://webserver.lemoyne.edu/~glennon/rel300.htm)

• Reading

Fred Glennon. 1995. The Learning Covenant: Promoting Freedom and
Responsibility in the Religious Studies Classroom. *CSSR Bulletin* 24/2
(April):32–37.

WEEK 2: DEFINING HEALTH, ILLNESS, CULTURE, AND RELIGION

• Reading

Galanti, *Caring for Patients from Different Cultures*, 1–15, 40–55.
Clifford Geertz. 1976. Religion as a Cultural System. Chap. 4 of *Interpretation of Cultures*. New York: Basic Books (on reserve).

WEEK 3: HEALTH, FAITH, MEDICINE, AND MEANING

• Readings

David Kinsley. 1996. The Ideology of Modern Medical Culture. In
Health, Healing, and Religion, 168–184. Upper Saddle River, NJ: Pren-
tice Hall (on reserve).
Harold Koenig, *Spirituality in Patient Care*, 94–104.
Jeff Levin. 2001. The Health Effects of Public Religion. In *God, Faith,
and Health: Exploring the Spirituality-Healing Connection*, 17–69. New
York: John Wiley & Sons (on reserve).
Larry Dossey. 1996. The Importance of Modern Physics for Modern
Medicine In *Healing East and West*, ed. Aneis A. Sheikh, 395–426.
New York: John Wiley & Sons (on reserve).

WEEKS 4 AND 5: RELIGIOUS GROUPS ENCOUNTERED

• Reading

Religious Traditions and Health Care Decisions 2002. Chicago: Park Ridge
Center.

Read the sections on:

Mainline Christian traditions: Roman Catholic, United Methodist Church, Presbyterian Church (USA), Lutheran, Orthodox Christian, Southern Baptist, Episcopal;

Sectarian Christian traditions: Anabaptist, Assemblies of God, Christian Science, Church of God in Christ, Jehovah's Witness, Latter Day Saints, Seventh Day Adventist;

World religions traditions: Judaism, Islam, Buddhism, Hinduism.

Scientology Technology: The Spiritual Factors in Regaining Good Health (http://www.essentialauditing.org/)

WEEK 6: DIETARY PRACTICES, FOLK REMEDIES, AND MEDICAL REJECTIONS OF RITUAL PRACTICE

This is a "show and tell" class. Bring in the homemade remedies for illness— cold, flu, and so on—that your family, nuclear and extended, have used over time.

• Reading

Galanti, *Caring for Patients from Different Cultures*, 56–60, 122–134.

Christine Gudorf. 1999. A Question of Compromise. In *Ethics and World Religions: Cross-Cultural Case Studies*. Maryknoll, NY: Orbis (on reserve).

Cultural and Religious Issues Associated with Circumcision, *Circumcision Information and Resource Pages* (http://www.cirp.org/pages/cultural/).

WEEK 7: SPIRITUALITY, HEALING, AND COMPLEMENTARY HEALING THERAPIES

• Reading

Fred Frohock. 1995. Holistic Medicine. In *Healing Powers*, 173–206. Chicago: University of Chicago Press.

Shamanic Healing. *The Foundation for Shamanic Studies*. (http://www.shamanism.org/articles/857415539.htm).

Ayurvedic Medicine; Traditional Chinese Medicine. *HealthWorld Online*. (http://www.healthy.net/clinic/therapy/ayurv/; http://www.healthy.net/CLINIC/therapy/Chinmed/Index.asp).

Therapeutic Touch; Needles and Nerves. Part of *Scientific American Frontiers* series, *A Different Way to Heal* (http://www.pbs.org/saf/1210/video/watchonline.htm).

Guest speakers: Dr. Powell (Reiki certified master) and Dr. Shu (acupuncturist)

WEEK 8: SPRING BREAK

WEEKS 9–11: FINDING MEANING IN SUFFERING, ILLNESS, AND DEATH

- Readings

Galanti, *Caring for Patients from Different Cultures,* 32–39.

Margaret E. Mohrmann. 1999. Someone Is Always Playing Job. In *Pain Seeking Understanding: Suffering, Medicine, and Faith,* eds. Margaret Mohrmann and Mark Hansen, 62–79. Cleveland, OH: Pilgrim.

Daniel Callahan. 2000. Pursuing a Peaceful Death. In *The Troubled Dream of Life,* 187–219. Washington, DC: Georgetown University Press.

Allen Verhey. 2000. Organ Transplants: Death, Dis-organ-ization, and the Need for Religious Ritual. In *Caring Well,* ed. David Smith, 147–169. Louisville, KY: Westminster John Knox Press.

Lewis, *A Grief Observed.*

David Kinsley. The Search for Meaning in Modern Medicine: The Patient Speaks In *Health, Healing, and Religion,* 185–194 (on reserve).

Jerome Groopman. 1998. Matt. In *The Measure of Our Days: A Spiritual Exploration of Illness,* 88–113. New York: Penguin (on reserve).

Arthur Frank. 1996. The Quest Narrative. In *The Wounded Storyteller: Body, Illness, and Ethics,* 115–136. Chicago: University of Chicago Press (on reserve).

Guest Speaker: Sister Kathleen Rumpf (Francis House for the Terminally Ill)

WEEKS 12–14: STUDENT PRESENTATIONS

WEEK 15: IMAGES OF HEALER FOR HEALTH CARE PRACTITIONERS

- Readings

Koenig, *Spirituality in Patient Care,* 1–87.

The Hippocratic Oath.

The Physician's Assistants Oath.

William May. 2000. *The Physician's Covenant: Images of the Healer in Medical Ethics,* 2nd ed., 112–154 Louisville, KY: Westminster John Knox Press (on reserve).

REFERENCES

Cooper, J. L., and R. Mueck. 1989. Annotated Bibliography of Cooperative/Collaborative Learning Research and Practice (Primarily) at the Collegiate Level. *The Journal of Staff, Program, and Organization Development* 7:143–148.

Dewey, John. 1966. *Democracy and Education.* New York: Free Press.

Slavin, Robert E. 1991. Synthesis of Research on Cooperative Learning. *Education Leadership* 48 (February):71–82.

19

A Medical School Curriculum on Religion and Healing

Linda L. Barnes

I come to this chapter having been, since 1999, on the faculty of Boston University School of Medicine, and after having a visiting appointment at Harvard Medical School. Neither setting would ever have occurred to me during my years of training. Educated in comparative religious studies and medical anthropology, I fully expected to end up on the faculty of a religion department. Who knew! From my current vantage point, however, I have had occasion to think through how to translate some of the objectives of the humanities, and of religious studies in particular, into the training of clinicians.

I am, of course, in no way the first person to teach humanities to students of biomedicine, the biologically based system prevalent in the United States and many other parts of the world. There is a rich legacy of medical humanities that includes literary studies and bioethics. However, little from comparative religious studies has migrated into biomedical education. Indeed, the discussion of religious traditions has generally been marginalized, a legacy of Enlightenment understandings of science in which anatomy, physiology, biochemistry, pathology, and bacteriology were differentiated from religious worldviews. Frequently, the only interaction between the domains has occurred through challenges to clinical benefit by Christian Scientists, Jehovah's Witnesses, and faith healers, particularly in cases involving children. Some clinicians introduce discussions of religion or religiosity with their patients in the face of life-threatening illness, dying, and death. Rarely are they familiar with the multiple ways that religion and spirituality may shape a patient's sense of health over the course of his or her life, or that religion and healing may thrive in their patients' lifeworlds (Barnes 2003).

Yet because religion, spirituality, and medicine all represent responses to suffering, some authors increasingly point to the broader spiritual dimensions of all health care (Schwartz 1991), suggesting that biomedicine's exclusion of these dimensions is anomalous (Sulmasy 1999). The topics of religion and spirituality in relation to medicine have appeared in books, leading medical journals, and major medical conferences. Still, apart from courses that physicians may have taken as undergraduates, most physicians are apt to draw their understanding of religion either from personal experience or from popular culture—making them like many undergraduates. Occasionally, courses in Medicine and Spirituality—many of them funded by the Templeton Foundation and geared toward promoting a generic, ahistorical, popular orientation toward "spirituality"—are offered.

Some medical researchers have attempted to demonstrate that religiosity or religious practices result in quantifiably better health outcomes. The measures used in such studies attempt to quantify specific aspects of inner, personal experience, individual behaviors, and engagement in a faith community. Some measures reflect the orientation of specific traditions and are therefore not useful in addressing the broader religious diversity of the United States. Such questionnaires, for example, focus on institutional factors and practices long contested within comparative religious studies as deriving from a Protestant Christian paradigm, such as (1) membership, synagogue or church attendance, religious preference, and denominational affiliation; (2) belief in God, miracles, life after death, the Bible; and (3) practices such as prayer and Bible reading (Gallup and Lindsay 1999). Some include listening to religious radio shows.

Such studies have been critiqued on two fronts in particular. The first involves the attempt to isolate spirituality or religiosity as the significant variable contributing to a specific health outcome. The second critique questions these studies' claims to present scientific evidence, arguing that the methodologies used are flawed, the findings conflicting, and the evidence lacking in clarity and specificity (Sloane, Bagiella, and Powell 1999). It is argued that correlation between religious behaviors and health outcomes does not necessarily imply causation (Sloane and VandeCreek 2000). I would add that such studies overlook the larger ideas of healing held by many religious traditions, in which healing sometimes does not occur until after death.

In practice, physicians are increasingly called upon to navigate both cultural and religious pluralism in different parts of the United States, and they need training in how to do so. The current frame of reference for such training is "culturally competent care" or "cultural competence"—the ability to serve as a competent provider in response to cultural and religious diversity. Physicians therefore can find themselves in a bind—encouraged to steer away from discussions of religion on the one hand, and to learn about it in relation to multiculturalism on the other. In response, some caregivers reject discussions of "religion" in favor of "spirituality," not unlike sectors of the broader American population. Few sources examine the intersections between religious traditions and related understandings of illness and healing, particularly in connection with cultural versions of religious therapies. Nor are medical educators being trained to address such issues. Conversely, few faculty in the humanities or in religious studies are familiar with the structure, process, and related challenges of medical training. In this chapter, I propose to review these issues and to discuss a curriculum illustrating one approach to teaching biomedical clinicians about religion and healing. It will, I hope, also prove useful to medical faculty interested in building related curricula in their own institutions.

Institutional Setting and Structure of Medical Training

Boston University School of Medicine is one of three medical schools in the Boston area. The school's teaching hospital, Boston Medical Center, is the city's major safety-net health care institution, serving economically disenfranchised communities notable for their cultural, religious, racial, and ethnic pluralism. In this regard, Boston is a microcosm of urban cultural pluralism of the United States. The medical center has developed a range of innovative community services, which include an Interpreter Services program that annually provides more than 100,000 on-site interactions, in 117 languages, 24 hours a day; the Haitian Health Institute, which provides culturally and linguistically sensitive care for Boston's Haitian community; and the Boston Center for Refugee Health and Human Rights, which offers comprehensive care for refugees, coordinated with legal aid and social services for victims of political violence.

Members of the two departments with which I am affiliated—family medicine and pediatrics—have done pioneering work on the needs of disenfranchised communities, particularly in relation to poverty and health, food insecurity, the consequences of poor housing on health, immigrant and refugee health, and the effect of welfare reform on child health. Within the institutional context of both the school and these departments, I have had the latitude and the support to explore the curricular innovations discussed in this chapter.

The Structure of Medical Education—A Primer for Humanities and Social Sciences Faculty

It is, in hindsight, surprising how long it took me to figure out the structure of medical training. Like many faculty schooled in the humanities and social sciences, I had assumed that one simply designed elective courses and introduced them into a medical school curriculum. I knew little to nothing about the relationship between medical students and the other phases of training in a teaching hospital, or about how those other phases can operate to undercut the educational objectives of such electives. For humanities and social sciences faculty, I therefore provide a review. Medical faculty will want to fast-forward.

To elaborate. First- and second-year medical students spend most of their time in the classroom, in addition to taking Gross Anatomy, in which they engage in the dissection of a cadaver. They also begin learning to interview patients, in courses known as "Patient-Doctor." Elective semester-long courses are usually introduced at this level—a process that is not as easy as it sounds. Even when there are a good many options, the number that students can actually fit into their schedules may be low. They may, as at Harvard, have to select just one, for example, to meet the curricular demand of taking a course in the field of social medicine. At Boston University School of Medicine, other curricular demands mean that elective offerings may be minimal or nonexistent. Until recently, there were no electives. Those the school offers now do not appear on a student's transcript, so a faculty member must write a letter for the student's file to provide evidence and evaluation. Electives, therefore, generally reach only small numbers of students.

Third-year students begin what are known as "clerkships" or "rotations." They spend anywhere from four to twelve weeks in both inpatient and outpatient settings in the different disciplinary areas of biomedicine—twelve weeks each, say, in internal medicine and in surgery, and six weeks in pediatrics. During this time, they begin their practical apprenticeship as the low figures on the totem pole who are, paradoxically, often the ones with the most time to spend interacting with patients. They are taught by faculty but more regularly by medical residents, also known as "house staff" or "house officers."

During their fourth year, medical students choose elective blocks that each usually last four weeks. These blocks are intensive tutorials, usually involving no more than a handful of students. In addition to a number of blocks required of all students, there are also those taken in relation to the field one hopes to enter—something like courses in a major. Students usually try to complete these blocks by the end of the fall in preparation for applying to residency programs around the country. During the spring, they continue to take blocks, often in areas that may be of greater personal interest, but that are not necessarily as critical for their acceptance to residencies. To introduce an elective block on religion and healing, therefore, one does better to aim for a spring offering.

Residents—roughly analogous to doctoral students—are themselves both learners and something along the line of teaching fellows. First-year residents are known as interns, second-years as juniors, and third-years as seniors. Interns have just come from medical school, and yet must take on new levels of responsibility for patient care, under the supervision of their faculty preceptors. By their junior year, however, they may be given the responsibility of overseeing specific clinical units. In my department, for example, the juniors manage the newborn nursery.

A typical resident's day might begin with "rounding," visiting inpatients with other members of the medical team, followed by "morning report"—a daily seminar discussion of current, particularly complex cases. Early in the afternoon, there may be a "pre-clinic conference"—a lecture and discussion of core topics lasting from half an hour to 40 minutes. In pediatrics, for example, such topics would include issues to consider during well-child visits at different ages, as well as common illnesses and matters involving more acute care. Residents spend two afternoons a week in clinic, caring for patients under the supervision of faculty preceptors. Residents may end up being on call overnight about every third night, leaving them chronically exhausted.

Somewhat analogous to third-year medical students, they rotate from one division in their field to another in order to develop greater familiarity with their discipline as a whole. For example, a resident in pediatrics rotates every few months from ambulatory care to inpatient, to emergency care, and so on. As they move toward their senior year, they assume increasing clinical and teaching responsibilities. Once a week, residents are required to attend Grand Rounds—a departmental lecture presentation—and the Case of the Week. Indeed, it is often the residents who are expected to develop the Case of the Week presentation.

Following graduation from residency, a select few individuals—usually two—will be asked to stay on as chief residents. The chiefs are largely responsible for scheduling, leading Morning Report, supervising the other residents, and reporting to the faculty directors of the residency program. They therefore assume a more intensive teaching role. To introduce educational initiatives into resident training, it is therefore essential to have the support not only of the program's faculty director, but also of the chief residents. They and a few other residents are the most likely to be invited to stay on as permanent clinicians and junior faculty.

Faculty development and education occurs during biannual retreats for clinic preceptors and, during Grand Rounds and the Case of the Week, physicians are also required to take continuing medical education courses each year, for which they generally attend dedicated conferences. If one can interest faculty in topics involving religious studies issues, one can then teach about religion and healing indirectly, through collaborative research.

Once learners reach the resident and faculty level, they face increasing time constraints imposed by managed care. Even in a setting where free care is provided and covered by the state, reimbursement is well below actual costs, and institutions face untenable choices between solvency and time allotted to patients. Outpatient clinic visits range from fifteen to twenty minutes, during which the physician must secure an updated medical history and make related preventative and therapeutic recommendations. Newer residents take longer because they have to review each case with a preceptor before being able to recommend any therapeutic interventions to the patient. This factor routinely leads to appointment delays, and even experienced clinicians run late if they choose to focus on more detailed discussions with patients. Inpatient care involves not only a growing patient load, but also much sicker patients, requiring one to balance the management of complex cases and teaching medical students. The pressure to become highly efficient is acute, often at the expense of the kind of listening and attention most clinicians want to devote to their patients.

When these more senior members of the medical team do not understand

312   COURSES FOR CAREGIVERS

issues of religion and healing in relation to patient interviewing and care, they are more likely to squelch medical students' attempts to address such issues, in the interest of "getting to the point." In turn, medical students quickly learn to tailor their questions and presentations to what is expected. Therefore, it is not enough to focus one's efforts on medical students; one must include residents and faculty as well. To effect real systemic change, one needs to work across the training pipeline. In some cases one can then anticipate taking part in an individual's training beginning in medical school, and continuing through residency and entry to the faculty. At that point, the different levels become mutually reinforcing.

Another critical consideration is that working clinicians—some of whom acknowledge earlier interests in anthropology, sociology, history, and the study of religion—frequently assume an intensely applied orientation to their training. To maximize interest and engagement, one must be able to show direct clinical relevance, application, and a connection with enhancing patient care. It is not that clinicians are not otherwise interested; rather, in the limited time they have with patients, they need to see direct applications that help them to understand the dynamics of a case better, stretching them to see how more is at stake than they might have realized in patients' various responses.

Pedagogies

As a broad generalization, when teaching physicians-in-training, pedagogies geared for adult learners work best, not only in transforming understanding, but also in changing practice. Lectures are generally the least effective approach; discussion-oriented methods work far better. One of the reasons teaching cases are so widely used is that, when well designed, they approximate the challenges that clinicians face daily.

Humanities faculty are often academically socialized to think of teaching as lecturing, reserving discussions for section meetings or seminars, for which it is assumed that students will have prepared a substantial body of reading. However, medical learners—particularly the more advanced they are in their training—rarely have time to prepare for teaching sessions. At most, one can expect medical students to read from 20 to 30 pages, and residents, nothing. (To put this apparent indifference to learning in perspective, these same residents will have spent hours researching the health conditions affecting their patient instead.) In addition, although one may have an hour or more per session with medical students, one rarely has more than 40 minutes for any given session with residents, and must envision such sessions as one-shot deals—the one occasion, that is, for a focus on a particular topic. These constraints make it even more important to look for as many points of entry as possible across the training spectrum, to generate self-reinforcing messages.

Although some humanities and social sciences programs increasingly expect faculty to formulate precise learning objectives and pedagogical strategies when proposing a new course, I have yet to see such requirements framed in terms that match the demands of medical institutions. Such demands obey two sets of criteria. The first involves the requirement that curriculum specify how it will address *attitudes, knowledge,* and *skills.*

A growing body of literature from academic medicine has shown that clinicians' attitudes play a powerful role in how they deliver care. In particular, different forms of bias such as racism, sexism, classism, and homophobia can undermine equitable treatment, resulting in health disparities for groups targeted by bias. As a profession, the medical community has pledged itself to address such attitudes, and made the demand to do so part of its certification requirements for graduate medical education programs. Course designs must therefore specify how the course will address learner's attitudes, and what changes are to be expected. For example, courses on religion and healing might propose to address learners' possible biases against religious approaches to healing and promote an interest in cultural and religious complexity, rather than an orientation that views it as an obstacle to efficient practice. In this regard, curriculum is expected to address issues of how learners *feel* toward specific topics and types of patients. Feeling, in this case, is understood to involve attitudes.

A related issue involves content and anticipated changes in a knowledge base. What things can participants be expected to *know* by going through the course or curriculum? How have the content and didactic strategies been designed to maximize the transmission of that knowledge? In teaching about religion and healing, one faces the challenge of what counts as knowledge, leading one into comparative questions of efficacy (see below). One also confronts a common tendency to reduce different cultures and traditions to pernicious, essentialized bullet-point summaries. "If a patient is W, then they are X, believe Y, and do Z." Such summaries, in addition to reducing groups to stereotypes, becomes paralyzing, since no one can remember even such minimal compendia of details about multiple groups.

Finally, what skills will learners develop? What will they be able to *do*? In relation to the study of religion and healing, skills prove a crucial countermeasure to narrow conceptualizations of knowledge. Learners who know how to elicit patient narratives—who are able to ask a patient to teach them about how culture or tradition shape that patient's understandings of illness, suffering, and healing—is equipped to utilize broad generalizations as no more than preliminary working hypotheses, particularized through one-on-one discussions with specific persons. Likewise, the learner who develops skills related to locating more complex information about different groups and traditions builds a different kind of knowledge, against which more essentializing approaches can be challenged and contextualized.

The second broad requirement involves how a teacher knows that such objectives have been, in some measure, accomplished. At its narrowest, this requirement leads to mechanistic efforts to quantify often intangible kinds of change. At its best, it leads to reflection on how one can assess one's pedagogical interventions to know whether or not they have effected the kinds of change one hoped for. Such assessment tools must correspond to the different kinds of learning, whether focused on attitudes, knowledge, or skills. In some cases, medical educators use "pre-tests" which they compare with "post-tests." Yet although a knowledge of cultural "facts" can be assessed in this way, there are no standardized measures for the more complex aspects of cross-cultural care. It is difficult, for example, to quantify interpersonal skills. Some methods have been developed for assessing communication-skills courses, but assessment may require additional methods—qualitative reviews; self-evaluation; participant observation; journals and field notes; observation and feedback from community, peer, patient, faculty, and mentor observers; and other key informants. All these forms of evaluation have a place and have, to varying degrees, been employed.

Issues of Efficacy

Even to introduce the broad topic of religion and healing into biomedical training, one must confront one of the most basic questions that routinely arises: "How do we know that it isn't just a placebo effect? Does any of it work?" The operative question is, What does it mean to say that something has "worked"?

The term "biomedicine" was coined by medical anthropologists to counter an earlier habit of referring to it simply as "medicine," suggesting a normative practice. Despite the implication that there are other medicine systems, however, the assumption remains that biomedicine represents the pinnacle. The privileging of this system is a result of its identification with science, accompanied by a conviction that scientific methods govern an objective gathering of evidence through multiple checks and balances, thereby demonstrating their reliability. The notion of "evidence-based" is frequently represented in biomedical literature as placing clinical trial outcomes beyond the taint of the subjective because of placebo controls—even though, as medical historian Ted Kaptchuk notes, "The interaction between data and judgment is often ignored because there is no objective measure for the subjective components of interpretation" (2003: 1453).

Introducing the study of religious healing traditions to biomedical clinicians therefore requires a comparative discussion of healing, through a core concept, "efficacy." Efficacy in any tradition is assessed in relation to how a problem has been defined. In biomedicine, for example, the signs of affliction are organized hierarchically around a "leading sign," or disease. Other signs are assigned to less central categories, such as "subjective" or "nonspecific" (Ots 1991: 44). This arrangement of signs governs the degree of attention paid to the kinds of change resulting from interventions. If marginal signs respond to a therapy, and the leading one does not, the intervention may be viewed as ineffective. Had the signs been organized differently, the judgment of efficacy might have been correspondingly different (Kemper n.d.).

Medical systems structure the experience of affliction by classifying an experience as a particular disease or illness. The very naming and framing of a problem are directly related to how efficacy will be assessed, although they do not necessarily exhaust the potential range of the assessment. Systems also tend to frame problems in relation to the solutions they have to offer (Schön and Rein 1994). In some cases, physiological change may register as the most significant; in others, less tangible change may be what counts. The latter fall under the biomedical heading of "nonspecific effects." This aspect is particularly pertinent in chronic conditions, in which a reorientation to a former self and way of life may be the outcome. "Healing," observes anthropologist James Waldram, "can occur while disease remains; healing can also help the patient deal with the medical problem, even prepare for death. In this sense, healing becomes a means of coping with disease, distress, disability, and recovery" (2000: 606).

Physicians know this, particularly with the more experience they acquire. At the same time, their training orients them to view death as a failure, given biomedicine's lack of soteriological or teleological resources. It can be important to remind them that other systems of healing think in broader terms, as may their patients, and that the role of "healer" remains open to them even when they cannot effect a cure.

A First- and Second-Year Elective: The Cultural Formation of the Clinician—Its Implications for Clinical Practice

One can certainly attempt a structured course in world religions and their approaches to healing, to provide an overview of how pluralism operates between traditions or within a given tradition—a course most likely to be adopted as a first- or second-year elective. Were one to do so, it would be advisable to focus it on local cultural groups and religious communities so that students can see the applicability of what they are learning Such a focus would also allow the instructor to tap related local or regional resources.

Beginning in 1999, I worked with a teaching team based at Harvard Medical School, where we took an approach that grew out of our concern with the role of attitudes in perpetuating health disparities for minority patient groups in the United States.[1] The course that we designed and have taught each year since then also served as the basis for an adapted version that I team-teach at Boston University School of Medicine, where the teaching team includes an internist, a family doctor, a gerontologist, and a medical school graduate who subsequently earned a master's in public health. All of us are present for each class session, resulting in an unusually high faculty-student ratio, given the seminar format of the course.

The course aims to generate a safe context for students to explore and reflect on the culture of biomedicine into which they are being socialized, and to develop their personal resilience and capacity to resist the more dehumanizing dimensions of that training. We hope to help them articulate the values they bring into the profession and how such values influence their personal and professional lives—including their responses to different patient cultures; and their own underlying assumptions about self and other, particularly in relation to matters of difference and power. The course's primary focus is on process rather than content. It does not seek to present a body of factual information organized by disciplinary concepts. Rather, it is designed to model a commitment to self-awareness and introspection, fundamental to the process of developing healing partnerships with patients and colleagues alike.

We work to help students develop an understanding of biomedicine as a cultural, political, economic, and social system, and to recognize the facets of their socialization into this system. We want them to develop a flexible working model that includes an understanding of context and culture, and that enables them to discern the dynamics that generate bias of multiple kinds. This working model must be individually crafted to avoid a "politically correct" agenda. Each person's model should offer a strategy with which to understand how a "different" patient is like all patients, like some patients, and like no other patient. Such understanding requires a negotiation of power in the patient-doctor relationship, enabling patients to teach doctors about their models of illness and healing—including the place of religion. We hope, too, that the models that students develop will allow them to remain conscious of their own cultural responses and will help them develop the skills with which to enlarge their repertoire for negotiating differences and discovering connections with colleagues and with patients and their families.

The framework for the course is the core issue of health disparities. We hold that it is not enough to teach about "diversity" or "multiculturalism," but that such pluralism must be situated in the realities of a post-apartheid state[2] with persisting forms of structural violence, such as institutionalized racism and other forms of privilege enjoyed by dominant groups (Farmer 1997; Singer and Clair 2003). We focus on learning to discern the presence and effects of institutionalized power disparities and their place in one's own experience (Rorie, Payne, and Barger 1996). This social context includes learning how the global environment affects cultures differently (Duffy 2001). When issues of structural violence are not brought to the foreground, students may see Others as the only ones who have culture and may see the Others' differences from themselves as deviations from a norm (Beagan 2003; Wear 2003). They may also not recognize how they themselves partake of certain forms of social power and privilege, and this failure of recognition can lead them to perpetuate health disparities unconsciously. In contrast, recognition and understanding of such factors increase the range of ways in which clinicians can enhance their relationship with patients and support patient empowerment as part of a relational ethics (Rafael 1995).

The course opens by reviewing these objectives and orients students to the concept and theory of structural violence, followed by a week in which each student and faculty member brings in something that symbolizes his or her culture(s). We begin by telling stories about whatever each person has brought. During the following two weeks, each person presents a cultural genogram—a family tree in which various forms of difference are mapped (see Hardy and Laszloffy 1995). Each subsequent week focuses on a particular form of bias, formulated as an experience of power and privilege in contrast with the experience of being targeted. Students prepare small selections of readings, but spend most of their time reviewing their genogram in light of reflection questions related to the week's topic. These topics include gender identity, sexual orientation, racial identity development, social class, body size, religions and spiritualities, immigration, and matters of multiple identities.

We ask students to reflect on how they learned about each of these topics through their family networks and the different communities in which they grew up. What messages did they internalize? How did they learn to assume a privileged or a targeted social location in relation to that particular issue? We emphasize that, when one has a given form of social privilege, there are entitlements that one learns to take for granted to such an extent that they seem "normal." The result can be fundamental blind spots that are all too apparent to those who lack this particular form of social privilege. Our goal is to train students to begin to recognize how blind spots function and to embark on the process of unveiling their own.

For example, in the week dedicated to religion and spirituality, we instruct students to begin by annotating their genograms with the religious background(s) of the different individuals and to try to recall the religious groups present in their communities of origin, with respect to the following reflection questions:

1. What are the stories involving religion in your family of origin/ group(s)?
2. If you think of yourself as American, did religious factors have anything to do with your family's (including earlier generations) coming to the United States?
3. Map the religious/spiritual background(s) of the different members in your extended family.
4. Is there a dominant religious/spiritual tradition in your family background? If so, what is it?
5. What are the ranges of adherence to that tradition? Consequences for deviation? Manifestations?
6. Are there minority orientations (someone, for example, who may have decided to define himself or herself differently)? What have been the effects on, and responses from, the larger family?
7. If there was or is more than one religious/spiritual tradition in your family, how were or are the differences negotiated? What have been/ are the intergenerational consequences? How has this affected you personally?
8. What other tradition(s) was(/were) present in the surrounding community as you were growing up? Which one(s) was(/were) absent?
9. What role did these traditions play for you as a source of meaning and framing values about:

   • work?
   • success?
   • social class?

- gender?
- sexual orientation?

    Were there different messages from different branches of your family about these issues? How did these influences affect your own understanding and experience?

10. How did or does your religious/spiritual formation influence your understanding of the meaning of life and death? Of dying?
11. Does your religious/spiritual orientation shape your feelings about biomedicine, healing, healing practices other than biomedicine? If so, in what ways? Are there aspects of biomedicine that put pressure on your religious/spiritual orientation?
12. Does your religious/spiritual orientation influence your feelings about any of the following areas in which religious traditions and biomedicine are sometimes in tension:

- Abortion?
- Homosexuality?
- Disrobing in front of a doctor?
- Blood transfusions?
- Surgery of any kind?
- Handling of the dead?
- Physician-assisted suicide?

13. Did you come from a religious/spiritual background in which the group had prejudices or stereotypes about itself? What prejudices or stereotypes did this religious/spiritual group have about other groups?
14. Did you come from a religious/spiritual background that shaped your understanding about being sick? About pain? About suffering? If so, in what ways?
15. Over time, have you (choose all to which you would answer yes)

- continued to be part of a tradition of your upbringing?
- rejected a tradition of your upbringing?
- changed your relationship in other ways with a tradition of your upbringing?
- converted to another tradition?
- composed your own private version of spirituality, based on elements drawn from different sources?

16. What have you felt a need to retain from your upbringing? To jettison?

We remind students that, as with all the variables we explore, what may be typical for a family or group does not necessarily predict the orientation of an individual in that family or group. There are wide variations among cultures, within a religious tradition, and among members of a given family and its different generations and genders over time. It is therefore not possible to predict a patient's religious/spiritual worldview or how it will influence his or her understanding of illness and healing. One must, instead, always inquire and listen.

During the actual class session on religion and spirituality, we begin by using the blackboard to generate a group list of the signs of religious privilege in the United States. "If you have religious privilege, you can assume or expect . . ." We discuss the thoughts that people generate, and reflect on how the shadow side of our list illuminates the experience of nondominant and religiously targeted groups We then break into small groups, each with a faculty facilitator, to discuss each person's genogram in light of the topic. We ask, "Which religious traditions were privileged in your background and in what ways?" and "How has the pervasive influence of branches of the Christian tradition in U.S. culture shaped your experience and perceptions?" Each person, whether student or faculty, usually has roughly twenty minutes to talk about his or her background. We conclude by coming back together as a large group to discuss the kinds of issues that people raised. Here, "religion and healing" refers to how religious orientations and differences may inform a clinician's ability to provide healing care.

Interventions for Third-Year Medical Students

The third-year clerkship schedule does not permit medical students to take such an elective. Instead, they are immersed in rotations and finding their feet in constantly changing clinical environments. Two possibilities present themselves. Many clerkships provide a weekly lecture series known as "core conferences," designed to introduce students to the many dimensions of the particular medical field. Different members of a department's faculty offer these talks, usually once per rotation. As minimal as it sounds, one can opt to give such a talk or lead a related discussion. For example, once every six weeks, I give a 50-minute core conference in which I engage students in discussing three issues:

1. If you think of yourself as American, what are the different components of your cultural identity? What are all the hyphenated elements, through which you would say "I am a something-hyphen-something-hyphen-something American." I tell them that I am an English-German-Dutch-Irish American, and that I detail the matter according to show that "European Americans" are often the descendents of multiple cultures. If they think of themselves as coming from another country, are there hyphenated identities that are meaningful to them in that context? (I give them time to think about the question, and then invite volunteers to identify their own backgrounds.)
2. When you were young, and you or someone in your family got sick, did the person or people who took care of you ever do anything in

addition to, or instead of, going to a pharmacy or a doctor? If so, what kinds of things did they do? (I usually suggest that such things could have included foods, herbs, things one had to wear, and so on.)

3. When you were young, and you or someone in your family was seriously ill, to the extent that people may have feared for the person's life, did anyone do anything that you now understand to be religious or spiritual? If so, what kinds of things did they do? (In almost every group, at least someone talks about prayer. In some cases, students talk about other kinds of religious practice.)

Based on the specifics of their comments, I work with them to draw connections between their particular backgrounds, the complementary or alternative therapies used by their families, and the intersections with religion and healing. I observe that if such connections hold true for at least some of them, who are medical students, then how much more likely are they to find analogous connections in the experience of their patients, if they ask. I then open the remaining time (about half an hour) to eliciting examples from their patient experience. Generally, at least several students have had experiences or clinical dilemmas, and these provide the balance of the content and allow us to transition from personal experience to applied dimensions. I make clear that I in no way know all the particulars of any of the patient communities. Instead, I formulate hypotheses, ask others in the group what they think may have been going on in a given situation, and invite them to think about how they might have responded.

Every phase of medical training confronts students with intellectual, emotional, psychological, and spiritual challenges. The third year is particularly demanding because students move from a classroom focus to a clinical one in which they routinely feel as though they don't know the ropes. At worst, they may be subjected to a process known as "pimping," in which the teacher asks one question after another, probing the student's knowledge, until he or she is forced to confess not knowing the answer. Ostensibly aimed at finding out where a student needs to extend his or her knowledge, it can turn into an exercise of ritual humiliation and shaming in front of others, leading students to fear appearing not to know an answer. Although the culture of biomedical education is moving away from the more extreme versions of pimping, some disciplines perpetuate it. At best, of course, the questioning is done in a benign way in which students describe feeling their instructors' sincere commitment to learning and teaching.

Still, providing a forum for students to discuss their enculturation into biomedicine has been shown important in professional development. The "critical incident" group approach developed by William Branch et al (1993) encourages students to talk about experiences in their rotations that affect them. In my department, I co-facilitate such a weekly discussion for those students based at Boston Medical Center (usually about 8 out of the full rotation group of 21, the rest of whom are based in other clinical sites). Students are then required, by the end of the seminar, to write a critical incident.[3] Although not necessarily a part of each week's content, religious/spiritual issues arise quite regularly. This weekly discussion of the interpersonal, cultural, ethical, and spiritual dilemmas that confront third-year medical students allows students to name and explore such challenges, including their own reactions.

Fourth-Year Elective: Cultural Competence and Community-Based Complementary/Alternative Medicine[4]

This course is one of the four-week intensive elective blocks. I usually have from one to three students at a time. Because it is so labor intensive, I offer it only twice a year. It focuses on gaining an understanding of key issues in providing culturally competent care and its relationship with cross-cultural approaches to complementary or alternative therapies and to related religious traditions. Although the block is not a clinical one, it addresses issues that routinely affect the clinical encounter—learning to work across cultural and religious differences and developing the knowledge and skills related to culturally and sometimes religiously based versions of complementary or alternative medicine.

The structured activities include "literature seminars"—weekly sessions in which students are expected to prepare and discuss with me assigned readings providing overviews of (1) complementary or alternative therapies and cultural competence, (2) cross-cultural issues in medical education, (3) models for cross-cultural medical history taking, and (4) related clinical interviewing skills. They also read and discuss sources on different cultural and religious systems of healing (Latino, Haitian, African American, Chinese) and on cases related to culturally complex situations. My colleague Lance Laird, an Islamicist, leads discussions of Islam. They also review selected Web-based resources. Because the block is the only thing students are doing during these four weeks, one can require far more work from them than in any of the other courses described so far.

I take them on site visits to meet with traditional healers in local communities about which they have read. In this case, these healers include a pastor who leads a healing service at a local African Methodist Episcopal church, a Cuban *santero*, a Haitian *Vodou* priest (when he is in town), and a Chinese acupuncturist-herbalist. These meetings give students the opportunity to discuss culturally based understandings of illness and healing, and their relationship with biomedicine. One of the challenges in these meetings is to convince the religious and traditional practitioners that they need not try to appear "scientific" or to look as though they can cure all the ills they see. Advance preparation involves discussions in which I talk with the healers about standing clearly in the domains where they do have authority and speaking from within the meanings of efficacy that characterize their healing practices. (If one were to teach this course in settings where different forms of cultural and religious healing were not present, one could draw on carefully selected practitioner Web sites.)

Students also observe biomedical physicians at work, focusing on the cross-cultural dimensions of the patient-doctor interaction. Through mentored discussions with me, they learn to identify issues in these interactions that are related to cross-cultural care and to locate resources that will help them better understand such issues. Students are also expected to make a research presentation by the end of the block, drawing on their experiences, on a topic developed in consultation with me.

Working with Residents

Of the openings for teaching residents, one has the daily morning report, when one can insert questions and comments relative to the case being discussed. This is not as easy as it sounds, even when other faculty support one's efforts. A case narrative is highly structured, distilled down to the information considered essential for arriving at a diagnosis—a process known as "the differential." The presenter provides minimal details about the patient's gender and age, followed by a description of symptoms. Others in the group—both residents and faculty—then ask questions, probing for potentially relevant additional information. All these details are written on the board, following which everyone engages in building a list of all the possible conditions from which the patient may be suffering. They then discuss which are the likeliest, and they decide which tests will be most useful in differentiating between the actual problem and other prospects. The presenter then provides further information on the medical team's own reasoning about the case, followed by actual test results and discussion of how to manage the case.

As medical anthropologist Arthur Kleinman (1988) has observed, the narrative of suffering, replete with the effects of an illness in the life of a patient, a family, a world, is translated into the clinical narrative, or case. The structure of the latter is formulaic, streamlined to maximize effective diagnosis and therapeutic intervention. As such, it is a powerful tool. At the same time, there is no given place in the formula for inclusion of cultural or religious factors and influences. The matter is complicated by the increased use of computerized medical records, which provide prompts to guide the taking of a medical history. These prompts generally do not include cultural and religious variables or ways in which such factors inform patients' approaches to healing. As a result, residents may not gather related information when meeting with a patient, and are therefore unable to address such issues during the morning report.

There are several ways to respond. One can keep asking pertinent questions about how the patient and family explain what is going on. What else have they done for it? Do any of their explanations or approaches to healing appear to have any specific cultural or religious content? On a more structural level, if one is positioned within the faculty and builds the right alliances, one can work to introduce several strategic questions into the medical-history-taking template, so that physicians are prompted to consider these kinds of issues during the actual clinical encounter. A particularly effective approach involves drawing on cases brought to one's attention by medical students, residents, or faculty, and developing them into teaching narratives.[5]

Conclusion

Humanities and social sciences faculty face several key challenges in developing curriculum for medical trainees. In addition to those I have mentioned, another is that medical schools do not fund the teaching of electives. One must therefore either collaborate with medical faculty to seek funding for course development or figure out a way to develop a course that can be taken by both medical trainees and students whom one *is* funded to teach. In my case, for example, my entire salary comes from grants, which allows me to decide what and when I will teach, if at all. (It also means, however, that I must raise the money to support my own salary every few years.)

A second challenge is a broad lack of familiarity with biomedical culture and, in some cases, a tendency to vilify physicians. I routinely hear unsympathetic references to "the medical establishment" leveled with little understanding of the dynamics of biomedical enculturation, the broader cultural emphasis on commodification, and the pressures imposed by managed care, which have been exacerbated by state and federal funding cuts to public health funding. There is also the power of the biomedical model, which, based as it is on a sophisticated reading of human physiology, can at times appear unassailable. One does better not to argue with it, but instead to complement it with other ways of constructing the body within comparative lifeworlds.

Challenges aside, having taught on a medical faculty, I can now say that it has been a rich and fulfilling experience. Having to learn to teach about religion and healing in a field that styles itself as the pinnacle of therapeutic interventions, I have had to learn complex acts of translation and cross-cultural exchange and negotiation. I do not think that the essential content of what I have to say has changed over these five years, but my understanding of how to present it has. Much of this process has come about as I have become more familiar with the culture of biomedicine, and as I have built collegial relationships over time. It doesn't hurt that some of the individuals now governing schedules and content were at one time medical students and residents in program units of which I was a part. The slow accrual of such individuals in junior faculty roles will, I believe, move over time toward a qualitatively different collective oriented toward the topic of religion and healing, with the authority to relay more effectively a reflective and insightful approach to the topic to both colleagues and patients.

NOTES

1. The coauthors and co-teachers of this course are Drs. Daniel Goodenough, Roxana Llerena-Quinn, Irving Allen and Anne Hallward. At Boston University School

of Medicine, they are Drs. Karen Bryant, Michael Paasche-Orlow, Lana Habash, and Anafidelia Tavares.

2. I owe this formulation to Prof. Allen Callahan.

3. For a description of the assignment, see the section on Religion and Healing on the AAR Syllabus Project Web site.

4. The syllabus and a sample course calendar are posted on the AAR Syllabus Project Web site.

5. For suggested guidelines, see the AAR Syllabus Project Web site.

REFERENCES

Barnard, D, R. Dayringer, and C. K. Cassel. 1995. Toward a Person-Centered Medicine: Religious Studies in the Medical Curriculum. *Academic Medicine* 70(9):806–813.

Barnes, Linda L. 2003. Spirituality and Religion in Health Care. In *Cross-cultural Medicine*, ed. JudyAnn Bigby, pp. 237–267. Philadelphia: American College of Physicians-American Society of Internal Medicine.

Barnes, Linda L., Gregory A. Plotnikoff, Kenneth Fox, and Sara Pendleton. 2000. Religious Traditions, Spirituality and Pediatrics: Intersecting Worlds of Healing: A Review. *Journal of the Ambulatory Pediatric Association* 106(4):899–908.

Beagan, B. L. 2003. Teaching Social and Cultural Awareness to Medical Students: "It's All Very Nice to Talk about It in Theory, But Ultimately It Makes No Difference." *Academic Medicine* 78(6):605–614.

Branch, William, R. J. Pels, R. S. Lawrence, and Ronald Arky. 1993. Becoming a Doctor. Critical-Incident Reports from Third-Year Medical Students. *New England Journal of Medicine.* 329(15):1130–1132.

Daaleman, T. P., and B. Frey. 1998. Association between Spirituality and Health Hard to Measure. *Family Medicine* 30(7):470–471.

Duffy, M. E. 2001. A Critique of Cultural Education in Nursing. *Journal of Advanced Nursing* 36(4):487–495.

Farmer, Paul. 1997. On Suffering and Structural Violence: A View from Below. In *Social Suffering*, eds. A. Kleinman, V. Das, M. Lock, pp. 261–283. Berkeley: University of California Press.

Foglio, J. P., and H. Brody. 1988. Religion, Faith, and Family Medicine. *Journal of Family Practice* 27(5):473–474.

Gallup, George, Jr, and D. M. Lindsay. 1999. *Surveying the Religious Landscape: Trends in U.S. Beliefs.* Harrisburg, PA: Morehouse.

Hardy, K. V., and T. A. Laszloffy. 1995. The Cultural Genogram: Key to Training Culturally Competent Family Therapists. *Journal of Marital and Family Therapy* 21(3): 227–237.

Kaptchuk, Ted J. 2003. Effect of Interpretive Bias on Research Evidence. *British Medical Journal* 326 (June 28):1453–1455.

Kemper, Kathi J. N.d. Clinical Outcomes Research in Complementary and Alternative Medicine: The Glass Slipper and the Princess. Winston-Salem, NC: Wake Forest School of Medicine. Mss. unpublished.

King, D. E. 2000. Faith, Spirituality, and Medicine: Towards the Making of the Healing Practitioner. New York: Haworth Pastoral.

Kleinman, Arthur. 1988. *The Illness Narratives: Suffering, Healing, and the Human Condition.* New York: Basic Books.

Ots, Thomas. 1991. Phenomenology of the Body: The Subject-Object Problem in Psychosomatic Medicine and the Role of Traditional Medical Systems Herein. In *An-*

thropologies of Medicine: A Colloquium on West European and North American Perspectives, eds. Beatrix Pfleiderer and Giles Bibeau, pp. 43–58. Braunschweig: Vieweg.

Rafael, A. R. 1995. Advocacy and Empowerment: Dichotomous or Synchronous Concepts? *Advances in Nursing Science* 18(2):25–32.

Rorie, J. A., L. L. Paine, M. K. Barger. 1996. Primary Care for Women. Cultural Competence in Primary Care Services. *Journal of Nurse-Midwifery* 41(2):92–100.

Schön, Donald, and Martin Rein. 1994. *Frame Reflection: Toward the Resolution of Intractable Policy Controversies.* New York: Harper Collins.

Schwartz, S. G. 1991. Holistic Health: Seeking a Link between Medicine and Metaphysics. *JAMA* 266(21):3064.

Singer, M., and Clair S. 2003. Syndemics and Public Health: Reconceptualizing Disease in Bio-Social Context. *Medical Anthropology Quarterly* 17(4):423–441.

Sloan, Richard P., E. Bagiella, and T. Powell 1999. Religion, Spirituality, and Medicine. *Lancet.* 353:664–667.

Sloan, Richard P., and Larry VandeCreek. 2000. Religion and Medicine: Why Faith Should Not Be Mixed with Science. Available at http//primarycare.medscape.com/Medscape/GeneralMedicine/journal/2000/v02.n04/mgm0804.sloa/mgm0804.sloa.html.

Sulmasy, D. P. 1999. Is Medicine a Spiritual Practice? *Academic Medicine* 74(9):1002–1005.

Waldram, James B. 2000. The Efficacy of Traditional Medicine: Current Theoretical and Methodological Issues. *Medical Anthropology Quarterly* 14(4):603–625.

Wear, D. 2003. Insurgent Multiculturalism: Rethinking How and Why We Teach Culture in Medical Education. *Academic Medicine* 78(6):549–554.

PART VII

Additional Syllabi

20

Religion, Ritual, and Healing in North America

Pamela E. Klassen

Like many professors developing new courses, I began teaching about healing and religion because of my own research interests. At work on a book on mainstream Protestants' relationships to medicine and healing in twentieth-century North America, I developed a seminar as an opportunity to delve into a literature I needed to read. What I found, happily, was that both in my research and my teaching, the study of healing offered an advantageous perspective not only for my own particular questions about Protestant identity, but also for introducing students to critical perspectives on some of the key categories in the study of religion.

My first foray into teaching the graduate and upper-level undergraduate course that I called religion and healing was a fairly straightforward attempt to consider the intersection of religion, medicine, and alternative healing in nineteenth- and twentieth-century North America. Combining a thematic and somewhat chronological approach, I wanted the course to function as an investigation of religion and healing that included critical analysis of wider concerns in religious studies, such as embodiment, gender, and community. Beginning with several theoretical perspectives from medical anthropology, medical sociology, and history of medicine (but as I see now, nothing from within religious studies), the syllabus quickly moved to studies of more specific communities, times, and places. The students read about healing and religion in a wide variety of contexts, including the innovations of nineteenth-century partisans of therapeutic religion such as Christian Science, the struggles of early twentieth-century Jewish doctors within an Anglo-Protestant medical establishment, the devastating treatment of West Coast First Nations peoples at the hands of colonizers both medical and religious in early twentieth-century Canada, and the tragically muddled communication between medical personnel and Hmong immigrants in late-twentieth-century California (see syllabus #1).

This syllabus allowed for both a portrayal and investigation of the diversity of ways religion and healing have intersected in North America, but I found that it did not sufficiently set the grounds for simultaneously interrogating the scholarly categories under which such diversity was catalogued. Especially since the course was a mixture of fourth-year undergraduates and graduate students, it needed a more obvious theoretical underpinning to avoid the case studies becoming just a compendium of interesting stories about people who were not satisfied with taking two aspirin and calling their doctors in the morning. Given the radical difference embedded in the varieties of resistance to biomedicine found in the religious contexts of Christian Scientists, Pentecostals, and Hmong immigrants, the course needed more theoretical ballast spread throughout its 13 weeks to nurture critical comparison and analysis in our conversations.

The next time around, my syllabus did a better job of tying together theory and (at least representations of) reality, but I had to leave North America to do it (see syllabus #2). The heavy reading that resulted may have been hazardous to several students' health, but it was a restorative tonic for others. My approach this second time was to read ethnographic and historical accounts of healing in conjunction with theoretical discussions of ritual and religion. Spreading out the theory and making some unusual pairings prompted insightful and lively discussions in which almost every class member participated. One of the best examples of this came in the section on ritual, exchange, and healing, which combined Marcel Mauss's *The Gift* with Natalie Davis's *The Gift in Seventeenth-Century France,* and with Paul Farmer's essay "Sending Sickness" on understandings of AIDS in Haitian Vodou. A graduate student working on healing rituals in Tibetan Buddhism was struck with the aptness of gift theory for his own work, and was inspired to write his paper using this lens. Another student saw the relevance of both healing and the gift for her work on Baltic folktales. Connections appeared that I had not even imagined when preparing the syllabus, when I had no idea who would be in the course.

Although in some weeks the connections among ritual theory, religion, and healing were more allusive than direct, I found this second syllabus to provide a fruitful challenge both for the students and for myself. The conjunction of texts in the syllabus allowed me to reread classic works in the new context of my present research and the research interests of my students. The always humbling process of reading a text for the second time (or more) and discovering—or being in the position to recognize—something new is especially useful when trying to teach in an empathetic yet rigorous mode, or when trying to write something worth reading. Over time, reading back and forth between the theoretical and the empirical convinced me even further of the virtues of studying healing not only for its own sake, but also for the purchase it affords on wider questions.

Studying healing can focus and enhance the study of religion as a critical practice of interrogating the categories and processes by which human beings give value to some bodies over others. Whether exorcising the possessed body, diagnosing possession as biochemical dysfunction, or transforming the brain dead into victim saints, the confluence of religion, medicine, and healing entails the intersection and collision of categories that are not always mutually decipherable. In my view, the work of scholars and students of religion in this context is not only to document the variety of ways such a confluence occurs, but also to reflect critically on the ways that categories dear to both participants and scholars shape any evaluation of the validity or quackery of religion and healing.

Though these two classes were my most direct theoretical engagement with teaching about religion and healing, perhaps my most personally satisfying experience of teaching this subject has come within the University of Toronto's Research Opportunity Program. In this program, a professor selects students from a pool of applicants to work with her on a particular research project. Given my status as a humanities professor and my subject matter of medicine, my project attracted a great deal of interest from hopeful would-be medical students interested in a humanities credit. Although I learned after the first year that accepting three students was much better than accepting six, both years that I participated in the program I had a group of insightful, hardworking, and diverse students, three of whom have since gone on to medical school.

In this course, second-year students worked directly with me on my research by transcribing and annotating early-twentieth-century church newspaper articles and transcribing taped interviews. During the second year, I had such excellent students that one of them did fieldwork with me while the other two worked in the archives directly with primary sources. This was so successful that I applied for a further research opportunity program that enabled me to take the students with me to Cambridge, Massachusetts, where we made great use of the archives at the newly renovated (and newly opened to scholars) Mary Baker Eddy Library for the Betterment of Humanity. The students also undertook limited fieldwork on their own and together with me. The combination of science students and humanities students in these research-opportunity classes was particularly helpful both for me and for the students, as our assumptions about medicine and religion were continually tested and made apparent as we encountered material new to us all. Although the research orientation lacked the heady theoretical juxtapositions of my graduate courses, the astute critiques of some of the students (including some of the current medical students) were impressive. Given that aspiring pre-meds were usually unlikely to take a fourth-year or graduate course on religion and healing, I was delighted to think that this experience might encourage future physicians to think critically about how they view the significance of religion to healing—if they view it as significant at all.

My approach to teaching religion and healing has evolved over time, shaped both by my own research interests and, as in any course, my sense of what works and does not work in the classroom. If I teach this course again in the future, I will place the word "medicine" in the title to attract graduate students from programs in public and community health, nursing, and medicine, who would bring compelling perspectives to a religious studies-based discussion and who could, in turn, learn much from students of religious studies. In such a mixed class I would probably need to shift yet again, this time away from such a heavily theoretical syllabus to one based more on case studies but still concerned to critically interrogate cultural and scholarly categories. I would measure the success of such a course not only by the engagement of the variety of students, but also by the level to which each participant felt the ability to challenge and be challenged by the ways that discourses and practices of religion and healing categorize human beings in their sickness and in their health as embodied beings living in and through histories not entirely of their own making.

Syllabus: Religion and Healing

Meetings: Thursdays 10–12
Emmanuel College 105
Web site address: www.utoronto.ca/religion

Course description

In this class we will consider the interaction between religion and healing in nineteenth- and twentieth-century North America as a way to investigate "key metaphors" that have guided cultural approaches to themes such as embodiment, gender, eschatology, and community. The antagonistic yet symbiotic relationship between religion and science, the myriad attempts to achieve salvation or fulfillment by transforming or overcoming the physical body, and the negotiation of cultural and religious blending in a multireligious public sphere are all part of the story of religion and healing in North America. This course attends to these issues by considering the intersection of religion and healing in historical and anthropological perspectives. The course is organized thematically, with a focus on questions of method and theory underlying the whole.

Required Texts

Reading Packet, edited by Prof. Klassen, available at Print City, 80 Bloor St. W. or as individual books and articles on reserve at Gerstein Short-Term Loan. (P) indicates a source is in the Reading Packet. (W) indicates the source is available on the course Web site.

Fadiman, Anne. *The Spirit Catches You and You Fall Down: A Hmong Child, Her American Doctors, and the Collision of Two Cultures.* New York: Farrar, Straus, and Giroux, 1997.

Gevitz, Norman, ed. *Other Healers: Unorthodox Medicine in America*. Baltimore: Johns Hopkins University Press, 1988.

Gill, Gillian. *Mary Baker Eddy*. New York: Perseus Books, 1999.

Kelm, Mary-Ellen. *Colonizing Bodies: Aboriginal Health and Healing in British Columbia, 1900–50*. Vancouver: UBC Press, 1998.

Orsi, Robert A. *Thank You St. Jude: Women's Devotion to the Patron Saint of Hopeless Causes*. New Haven, CT: Yale University Press, 1996.

Sontag, Susan. *AIDS and Its Metaphors*. New York: Farrar, Straus, and Giroux, 1989.

Course Requirements

- weekly readings, attendance, and one-page reading reflections
- methods exercise (due February 8, 2001—20%)
- paper proposal (due March 3, 2001—10%)
- final research paper (due on or before April 12, 2001—50%)
- participation (based on class participation and reflections—20%)

Assignments are due in class on the specified due date. The penalty for lateness is 2% per day. Tests can be made up only under very serious circumstances. Essays must be clearly written (laser printers or ink-jet printers are strongly encouraged) and properly referenced. Plagiarism—representing someone else's words as your own—is a serious offence that can result in expulsion. Trust your own ability to think and write, and make use of the various resources available at the university that can help you do so (e.g. professors, teaching assistants, writing centers). My recommendation for a style guide is Kate L. Turabian, *A Manual for Writers of Term Papers, Theses, and Dissertations*, 6th ed. Chicago: University of Chicago Press, 1996. Also, see the University of Toronto writing support Web site: www.utoronto.ca/writing.

Assignments

READING REFLECTIONS

Due each week on the Tuesday before the relevant class, these two- to three-page papers are a chance for you to assimilate the reading and pose critical questions about the texts. Use them to organize your thoughts for class discussion and to summarize the insights of the readings—you may find yourself turning back to them later in the class or even later in your graduate career. You may send them to me via e-mail. Each student will also give a brief presentation of the readings for one of the course meetings.

METHODOLOGICAL EXERCISE (DUE FEBRUARY 8, 2001)

Find a primary source that interests you and that could form the basis of your research paper. Sources may include interviews, participant observation, historical texts (diaries, letters, etc.), philosophical texts, material culture. In four to five pages, answer the following questions about the source: Where and how did you find it? Whose perspective does it reveal? What does it tell you about religion and healing in North America? Did it surprise you in any way? We will discuss how to locate sources in more detail during class time.

PAPER PROPOSAL (DUE MARCH 3, 2001)

This assignment should represent substantial progress toward the completion of your final research essay—that is, it is *not* a chance for you to throw together a few ideas, but an opportunity for you to discuss your *work in progress* with me (and the class). You must discuss your topic with me prior to handing in your paper proposal, and then submit a three-page outline of your essay including the following:

- a thesis statement or organizing question;
- methodology statement (i.e., how you will go about answering your question);
- section headings with brief descriptions of the section contents (showing how you will organize your research into a logical and lucid argument); and
- a briefly annotated bibliography of the primary and secondary sources you've read (or encountered in the case of fieldwork) to date

If time allows, each class member will briefly present his or her paper proposal to the class.

FINAL RESEARCH PAPER

For RLG445S: Write a fifteen-page research essay on a topic relevant to the course.
For RLG2037S: Write a twenty- to twenty-five page research essay on a topic relevant to the course.

In keeping with the goals of the course, your essay must include reflection on the method and theory relevant to your research. Make use of both primary and secondary sources in writing your paper. Primary sources can include interviews and material culture in addition to texts. Your paper must be properly footnoted with a bibliography. Due no later than April 12, 2001.

Course Schedule

WEEK 1: INTRODUCTORY CLASS

WEEK 2: THEORETICAL AND METHODOLOGICAL APPROACHES

- Required Readings

Allan Young. "Anthropologies of Illness and Sickness," (W).
Deborah Gordon. "Tenacious Assumptions in Western Medicine." In *Bi-*

omedicine Examined, eds. M. Lock and D. Gordon, 19–56 Dordrecht: Kluwer Academic, 1988, (P).

Bryan S. Turner. "The Body and Medical Sociology." Chap. 5 in *Regulating Bodies: Essays in Medical Sociology,* 151–174. New York: Routledge, 1992, (P).

David Harley. "Rhetoric and the Social Construction of Sickness and Healing," *Social History of Medicine* 12(3): 407–435, (P).

Marcel Mauss. "Techniques of the Body," *Economy and Society* 2(1): 70–88, 1973, (P).

• Suggested Readings

Nancy Scheper-Hughes and Margaret Lock. "The Mindful Body: A Prolegomenon to Future Work," *Medical Anthropology Quarterly,* N.S. 1(1, 1987):6–41.

Charles Rosenberg. "Framing Disease: Illness, Society, and History." In *Framing Disease: Studies in Cultural History,* ed. Charles E. Rosenberg and Janet Golden, xiii–xxvi. New Brunswick, NJ: Rutgers University Press, 1992.

Michel Foucault. *The Birth of the Clinic: An Archaeology of Medical Perception.* New York: Vintage, 1975.

Pierre Bourdieu. *Outline of a Theory of Practice.* Cambridge: Cambridge University Press, 1977.

Margaret Lock. "Cultivating the Body: Anthropologies and Epistemologies of Bodily Practice and Knowledge," *Annual Review of Anthropology* 22:133–155, 1993, (W).

Phil Brown. "Naming and Framing: The Social Construction of Diagnosis and Illness," (W).

Robert A. Hahn and Arthur Kleinman. "Biomedical Practices and Anthropological Theory," (W).

WEEK 3: NINETEENTH-CENTURY MODELS OF HEALING

• Required Readings

Charles E. Rosenberg. "The Therapeutic Revolution: Medicine, Meaning, and Social Change in Nineteenth Century America." In *Sickness and Health in America,* 2nd ed., eds. Judith Walzer Leavitt and Ronald Numbers, 39–52. Madison: University of Wisconsin Press, 1985, (P).

Catherine Albanese. "Physical Religion." Chap. 4 of *Nature Religion in America.* Chicago: University of Chicago Press, 1990, (P).

R. Laurence Moore. "The Market for Religious Controversy." Chap. 5 of *Selling God.* Oxford: Oxford University Press, 1994, (P).

T. J. Jackson Lears. Preface and "Roots of Antimodernism: The Crisis of Cultural Authority during the Late Nineteenth Century." Chap. 1 of *No Place of Grace: Antimodernism and the Transformation of American Culture, 1880–1920.* Chicago: University of Chicago Press, 1983, (P).

• Suggested Readings

Robert C. Fuller. *Alternative Medicine and American Religious Life*. Chaps.
1–3. New York: Oxford University Press, 1989.

James Whorton. "Patient, Heal Thyself: Popular Health Reform Movements as Unorthodox Medicine." In *Other Healers: Unorthodox Medicine in America*, ed. Norman Gevitz, 52–81. Baltimore: Johns Hopkins
University Press, 1988.

Susan Cayleff. "Gender, Ideology, and the Water-Cure Movement." In
Other Healers: Unorthodox Medicine in America, ed. Norman Gevitz, 82–
98. Baltimore: Johns Hopkins University Press, 1988.

WEEK 4: MIND, BODY, AND MARY BAKER EDDY

• Required Readings

Gillian Gill. *Mary Baker Eddy*. New York: Perseus, 1999.

Rennie B. Schoepflin. "Christian Science Healing in America." In *Other
Healers: Unorthodox Medicine in America*, ed. Norman Gevitz, 192–214.
Baltimore: Johns Hopkins University Press, 1988.

John J. Appel. "Christian Science and the Jews," *Jewish Social Studies*
31(2, 1969): 100–121, (P).

• Suggested Readings

Mary Farrell Bednarowski. *New Religions and the Theological Imagination
in America*. Bloomington: Indiana University Press, 1989.

WEEK 5: RELIGION AND THE RISE OF THE HOSPITAL

• Required Readings

Charles E. Rosenberg. "Expanding a Traditional Institution: Social
Sources of Hospital Growth, 1850–1875." Chap. 4 of *The Care of
Strangers: The Rise of America's Hospital System*. New York: Basic
Books, 1987, (P).

Paul Starr. "The Reconstitution of the Hospital." Chap. 4 of *The Social
Transformation of American Medicine*. New York: Basic Books, 1982,
(P).

Susan M. Reverby. "Character as Skill: The Ideology of Discipline."
Chap. 3 of *Ordered to Care: The Dilemma of American Nursing, 1850–
1945*. Cambridge: Cambridge University Press, 1987, (P).

Ronald L. Numbers. "The Western Health Reform Institute" and part of
"Fighting the Good Fight." Chaps. 5 and 6 of *Prophetess of Health: El-
len G. White and the Origins of Seventh-Day Adventist Health Reform*.
Knoxville: University of Tennessee Press, 1992, (P).

• Suggested Readings

Elaine Showalter. "Florence Nightingale's Feminist Complaint: Women,
Religion, and *Suggestions for Thought*," *Signs*, 6 (spring 1981): 395–412.

Carol K. Coburn and Martha Smith, "Succoring the Needy: Nursing, Hospitals, and Social Services." Chap. 7 of *Spirited Lives: How Nuns Shaped Catholic Culture and American Life*. Chapel Hill: University of North Carolina Press, 1999.

WEEK 6: JEWISH NEGOTIATIONS OF THE MEDICAL MODEL

• Required Readings

Sander Gilman. "The Jewish Body: A Foot-note." In *People of the Body*, ed. Howard Eilberg-Schwartz, 223–241. Albany: SUNY Press, 1992, (P).
Beth S. Wenger. "Mitzvah and Medicine: Gender, Assimilation, and the Scientific Defense of 'Family Purity,' " *Jewish Social Studies* 5(1–2, 1998–99):177–202, (P).
Barry A. Lazarus. "The Practice of Medicine and Prejudice in a New England Town: The Founding of Mount Sinai Hospital, Hartford, Connecticut," *Journal of American Ethnic History* 10(3, 1991):21–41, (P).
Roland Littlewood and Simon Dein. "The Effectiveness of Words: Religion and Healing among the Lubavitch of Stamford Hill," *Culture, Medicine, and Psychiatry* 19 (1995):339–383, (P).

• Suggested Readings

John Efron. *Defenders of the Race: Jewish Doctors and Race Science in Fin-de-siecle Europe*. New Haven, CT: Yale University Press, 1994.
Sander Gilman. *Difference and Pathology: Stereotypes of Sexuality, Race, and Madness*. Ithaca, NY: Cornell University Press, 1985.
Jeanne Abrams. "Chasing the Cure in Colorado." In *Jews of the American West*, eds. Moses Rischin and John Livingston, 92–115. Detroit: Wayne State University Press, 1991.

WEEK 7: DIVINE HEALING AND THE POWER OF RITUAL AND PRAYER

• Required Readings

David Harrell. "Divine Healing in Modern American Protestantism." In *Other Healers: Unorthodox Medicine in America*, ed. Norman Gevitz, 215–227. Baltimore: Johns Hopkins University Press, 1988.
Marie Griffith. *God's Daughters*. Berkeley: University of California Press, 1–23, 80–109, 215–220, 232–234, 1997, (P).
Thomas J. Csordas. "Imaginal Performance and Memory in Ritual Healing." In *The Performance of Healing*, eds. Carol Laderman and Marina Roseman, 91–113. New York: Routledge, 1996, (P).
Mary Abrums. " 'Jesus Will Fix It after Awhile': Meanings and Health," *Social Science and Medicine* 50(1): 89–105, (P).
Karen McCarthy Brown. "The Power to Heal: Reflections on Women, Religion, and Medicine." In *Shaping New Visions*, ed. Clarissa Atkin-

son, Constance Buchanan, and Margaret Miles, 123–141. Ann Arbor: UMI Press, 1987, (P).

• Suggested Readings

David Harrell. *All Things Are Possible: The Healing and Charismatic Revivals in Modern America*. Bloomington: Indiana University Press, 1975.
Margaret Poloma and Lynette F. Hoelter. "The 'Toronto Blessing': A Holistic Model of Healing," *Journal of Scientific Study of Religion* 37 (June 1998): 257–272.
Stephen J. Pullum. *"Foul Demons, Come Out!": The Rhetoric of Twentieth-Century American Folk Healing*. Westport, CT: Praeger, 1999.

WEEK 8: ABORIGINAL HEALING SYSTEMS

• Required Readings

Mary-Ellen Kelm. *Colonizing Bodies: Aboriginal Health and Healing in British Columbia, 1900–50*. Vancouver: UBC Press, 1998.

WEEK 9: CULT OF THE SAINTS

• Required Readings

Robert Orsi. *Thank You St. Jude: Women's Devotion to the Patron Saint of Hopeless Causes*. New Haven, CT: Yale University Press, 1996.

• Suggested Readings

Michael Cuneo. *The Smoke of Satan*. Baltimore: Johns Hopkins University Press, 1997.

WEEK 10: 22/03/01 AIDS AND INTERPRETATION

• Required Readings

Susan Sontag. *AIDS and Its Metaphors*. New York: Farrar, Straus, and Giroux, 1988.
Paul Farmer. "New Disorder, Old Dilemma: AIDS and Anthropology in Haiti." In *The Time of AIDS: Social Analysis, Theory, and Method*, eds. Gilbert Herdt and Shirley Lindenbaum, 287–318. Newbury Park, CA: Sage, 1992, (P).
David Hufford. "Contemporary Folk Medicine." In *Other Healers: Unorthodox Medicine in America*, ed. Norman Gevitz, 228–264. Baltimore: Johns Hopkins University Press, 1988.
Sander Gilman. "Seeing the AIDS Patient." Chap. 14 of *Disease and Representation*. Ithaca, NY: Cornell University Press, 1988, (P).
Julia Epstein. "Explaining AIDS." Chap. 6 of *Altered Conditions: Disease, Medicine, and Storytelling*. New York: Routledge, 1995, (P).

• Suggested Readings

Bonnie Blair O'Connor. "Vernacular Health Care Responses to HIV and AIDS." Chap. 4 of *Healing Traditions: Alternative Medicine and the Health Professions* Philadelphia: University of Pennsylvania Press, 1995.

Paula Treichler. "AIDS, HIV, and the Cultural Construction of Reality." In *The Time of AIDS: Social Analysis, Theory, and Method*, eds. Gilbert Herdt and Shirley Lindenbaum, 65–100. Newbury Park, CA: Sage, 1992.

WEEK 11: 29/03/01 IMMIGRATION AND BIOMEDICINE

• Required Readings

Anne Fadiman. *The Spirit Catches You and You Fall Down: A Hmong Child, Her American Doctors, and the Collision of Two Cultures*. New York: Farrar, Straus, and Giroux, 1997.

Margaret Lock. "Nerves and Nostalgia: Greek-Canadian Immigrants and Medical Care in Quebec." In *Anthropologies of Medicine*, ed. Beatrix Pfleiderer and Gilles Bibeau, 87–104. Braunschweig: Vieweg, 1991, (P).

WEEK 12: 05/04/01 NEW AGE OR OLD?

• Required Readings

Norman Gevitz. "Three Perspectives on Unorthodox Medicine." In *Other Healers: Unorthodox Medicine in America*, ed. Norman Gevitz, 1–28. Baltimore: Johns Hopkins University Press, 1988.

Matthew Ramsey. "Alternative Medicine in Modern France," *Medical History* 43: 286–322, (P).

Mike Saks. "Beyond the Frontiers of Science? Religious Aspects of Alternative Medicine." In *Religion, Health, and Suffering*, eds. John R. Hinnells and Roy Porter, 381–398. London and New York: Kegan Paul, 1999, (P).

Carol P. MacCormack. "Holistic Health and a Changing Western World View." In *Anthropologies of Medicine*, eds. Beatrix Pfleiderer and Gilles Bibeau, 259–273. Braunschweig: Vieweg, 1991, (P).

• Suggested Readings

Robert C. Fuller. *Alternative Medicine and American Religious Life*. Chaps. 5 and 6. New York: Oxford University Press, 1989.

Meredith B. McGuire. *Ritual Healing in Suburban America*. New Brunswick, NJ: Rutgers University Press, 1988.

WEEK 13: 12/04/01 POSTBIOMEDICAL BODIES

• Required Readings

Pamela E. Klassen. "Sacred Maternities and Postbiomedical Bodies," *Signs: A Journal of Women and Culture*, 2001 26(3):775–810, (P).

Richard A. Schweder et al. "The 'Big Three' of Morality (Autonomy, Community, Divinity) and the 'Big Three' Explanations of Suffering." In *Morality and Health*, eds. Allan M. Brandt and Paul Rozin, 119–169. New York: Routledge, 1997.

Emily Martin. "Flexible Bodies: Science and a New Culture of Health in the U.S." In *Health, Medicine, and Society: Key Theories, Future Agendas*, eds. Simon J. Williams, Jonathan Gabe, and Michael Calnan, 123–145. London and New York: Routledge, 2000.

Robert Crawford. "The Ritual of Health Promotion." In *Health, Medicine, and Society: Key Theories, Future Agendas*, eds. Simon J. Williams, Jonathan Gabe, and Michael Calnan, 219–235. London: Routledge, 2000.

• Suggested Readings

David J. Hess. *Science in the New Age: The Paranormal, Its Defenders and Debunkers, and American Culture*. Madison: University of Wisconsin Press, 1993.

R. P. Sloan, E. Bagiella, T. Powell. "Religion, Spirituality, and Medicine," *Lancet* 353 (February 1999): 664–667, (W).

21

World Religions and Healing

Linda L. Barnes

What follows is the syllabus for a thematic—or comparative—lecture course, "World Religions and Healing," which I first taught in 1997 at Harvard University. Since then, I have revised it and offered it through the Religion Department at Boston University, where I serve on the faculty of the School of Medicine. I suggest that composing this kind of course challenges one to think through how, on the one hand, to say enough about the changing constellation of practices associated with a given tradition that students can begin to grasp that tradition's complexity and internal pluralism. On the other hand, one faces the related challenge of illustrating the dynamics of cross-fertilization and ensuing hybridity (see the discussion in the introduction).

Within each of the religious traditions, one finds a spectrum of practices, ranging from the scholarly elite traditions to the popular, and the complex, ongoing cross-fertilizations between the two that complicate such distinctions. The premise of this course is that it is important to begin with a familiarity of what these spectra include in each tradition. I tell my students that the course makes no claim to be exhaustive in what it covers. Rather, it maps parts of the broad terrain for each tradition, suggesting issues that one would need to take into account in claiming familiarity with particular understandings of illness, health, and healing.

Some students come to a course like this expecting it to be a series of hands-on workshops (something akin to the weekend sweatlodge phenomenon) from which they will emerge able to call themselves healers. When I make it clear that the course is something quite different, one contingent never returns. Many come with little or no prior training in the study of world religions. In the best of all worlds, I would require a prior class in world religions. In reality, this course ends up having to fulfill some of that function. In each unit, therefore, I begin with an overview of key elements in the history and worldviews of the given tradition or cultural group(s). I then address a range of ways in which the different practices discussed address the subthemes reviewed above, as illustrations of ways of being Hindu, or Buddhist, or Muslim, and so on. I ask students to try to pull some of these issues together through short writing assignments, in which they have to reflect on what it is that makes certain practices, say, "Hindu," and to think through differences and pluralisms within a given tradition.

I structure each lecture throughout with slides, video clips, and segments of music. It is my conviction that students cannot imagine practices they have never witnessed if they cannot *see* some representation of them. I find that developing an awareness of the local cultural groups present in the area where one teaches is a useful step toward exploring world traditions and related practices in ways that can make the course material more immediate for students. Whenever possible, I photograph such practices or purchase related paraphernalia for use in my teaching. Such examples range from the festival for Our Lady of Soccorso in Boston's North End and the festival for Saints Cosmas and Damian in my hometown of Cambridge (http://www.cosmas-and-damian .com/home.htm) to Chinese medicine practitioners in Boston's Chinatown. When I travel, I look for sites related to healing, such as the church of St. Roch in New Orleans, the Santuario de Chimayo in New Mexico, or pilgrimage sites that often include petitions for healing, such as the Hanuman Temple in Taos, New Mexico.

I implement the course's attendance and participation requirements by having students turn in a signed comment and/or question at the end of each class session. This allows me to track attendance and to get an idea of how students are interacting with the material (attendance and comment together are worth one point per class session of the total grade). I use the questions turned in after the first class session in a given unit to structure the beginning of the following lecture. The six short writing assignments engage students in reflecting on multiple approaches to healing under the rubric of a tradition-based or culturally based grouping, looking specifically at underlying similarities and significant differences. I require a paper proposal in order to ensure that students have formulated a clear research question in relation to the course content and that they have located solid bibliographic resources. It allows students an opportunity to take feedback and incorporate it into a revision.

Syllabus: World Religions and Healing

Prof. Linda L. Barnes
Fall 2005
Tuesdays and Thursdays, 2–3:30
An introduction to approaches to healing integral to Hindu, Buddhist, Jewish,

Christian, Muslim, African, African-descended, Latin American, Chinese, Native American traditions, and to some of the outcomes of their interactions. Through readings and audiovisual materials, we will explore these practices as expressions of some of the ways that people from these traditions understand sacred realities, the meaning and end of human life, the experience of affliction and suffering, the role and authority of the healer or healers, and the nature of the transformations pursued by individuals and communities.

Required Readings

Religion and Healing in America, eds. Linda L. Barnes and Susan S.
    Sered. New York: Oxford University Press, 2004 (RHA).
All articles not in RHA articles available through the CourseInfo Web
    site.

Course Requirements

All written assignments are to be handed in to the Teaching Fellow by the end of the class specified in the assignment or submitted to him electronically no later than by 9 p.m. that same calendar day. Assignments received after that time will not be accepted.

Please note: Students are expected to conduct all work for the course independently. Discussion of assignments with course faculty and peers is encouraged, but any evidence of plagiarism either of source materials or of one's peers—as well as any other suspected academic misconduct—will be referred to the Dean's Office. If work is judged by the Dean to be plagiarized, it will receive a "o" with no opportunity to make up the work. Students are expected to know and understand the provisions of the CAS Academic Conduct Code (copies are available in room CAS 105).

(1) ATTENDANCE AND PARTICIPATION (UP TO 24 GRADE POINTS)

Attendance is expected at all twenty-four class sessions. The class will be conducted in a lecture format on Tuesdays and Thursdays, with time allocated for discussion. I strongly encourage you to interrupt me with questions. Please note that you are responsible for securing any information missed (in the form of announcements, handouts, lecture notes, etc.) from one of your classmates. Failure to do so will not exempt you from any requirements specified in any of those materials.

(2) FOUR 1-2 PAGE WRITING ASSIGNMENTS (UP TO 5 POINTS EACH— POTENTIAL TOTAL OF 20 GRADE POINTS)

Each is a typed assignment on the readings, between 350 and 600 words (not to exceed 600). These response papers are to be turned in by the end of the Thursday class, or electronically no later than 9 p.m. for the specified date. They are to be typed, double-spaced. There are a total of eleven possible topics and related dates. In each of these writing assignments, you are asked to make an argument about the tradition and related practices about which you have read for that week. Your essay should draw on the related readings to make your argument. It should demonstrate that you have done all the week's readings, and should take the grading criteria (below) into account. You are to do a total of four of these assignments. You are free to choose the weeks during which you will and will not turn them in. You may start turning in these assignments beginning with "Hindu Healing Traditions." The last week of class is also included.

Please note: If you wait to begin turning in your assignments, at the very latest you will have to begin doing so on November 10 and not miss any after that. Waiting until this date is *not* at all recommended, as it allows you no room for unpredicted events. Please remember: *no* make-up assignments will be accepted, as there were eleven opportunities to turn them in. If you don't submit the assignment by the deadline for the week during which the readings are assigned, you will *not* be allowed to turn it later. There will be no exceptions.

The papers themselves will be marked on a scale of 1 to 5 (with 5 being the highest possible score). Each assignment will therefore count for *up to* 5 points of your grade. They will be evaluated on the basis of well organized and clearly formulated arguments (see grading criteria, below). They will be handed back by the end of the following week.

(3) TAKE-HOME MIDTERM EXAMINATION (OCTOBER 20): UP TO 20 GRADE POINTS

The midterm will focus on all materials covered through the first seven weeks, including all readings, visual materials, and lecture content. Five essay questions will be provided; the exam will consist of two of these questions, to be chosen by the student. Further evaluation criteria will be handed out and discussed in class.

(4) TERM-PAPER PROPOSAL WITH BIBLIOGRAPHY: UP TO 5 GRADE POINTS

Due at the end of class, Tuesday November 8 (*no* extensions unless substantiated by a note from the Health Services): A 350-to-600 word (not to exceed 600) typed term-paper proposal, including the tradition you plan to discuss, and the particular question/issue on which you will focus your paper. Also provide a bibliography of sources you plan to use (does not have to be included in the word count). We will talk more about these details in class, and more specific instructions will be handed out. The proposals will be handed back by the end of the next week. Mandatory office conferences will be scheduled with me or with the teaching fellow, so that you can discuss your ideas and get feedback. Please feel free to approach us for input before then as well.

Note: You are allowed/encouraged to revise your proposal if you are not satisfied with the points it receives and wish to work to increase them. The revision will be due by Thursday, November 29 (again, *no* extensions).

(5) FINAL TERM PAPER: UP TO 30 GRADE POINTS

A 15-page, double-spaced, typed term paper. Margins may *not* be smaller than 1 inch and font size may *not* be smaller than Times New Roman 11 and not larger than Times New Roman 12. A hard copy of your paper is to be turned in at the Religion Department by 5 P.M., Friday, December 16 (electronic submissions will *not* be accepted for final papers). Papers turned in after this time will be marked down three points per day late. There will be no exceptions to this deadline *unless* accompanied by a medical note from the Health Services, or from your adviser, substantiating a personal emergency. *Note: Always retain a copy of your paper and keep it available until your graded submission is returned.* The especially astute will have noticed that these points add up to 99—for which everyone receives 1 free point!

Grading Criteria

THE UNSATISFACTORY ESSAY OR PAPER

The D or F essay either has no thesis or else makes an argument that is vague, broad, or uninteresting. There is little indication that the writer understands the material being presented or is working closely with it. The paragraphs do not hold together. Ideas do not develop from sentence to sentence. This essay usually repeats the same thoughts again and again, perhaps in slightly different language, but often in the same words. The D or F essay is filled with mechanical faults, errors in grammar, and errors in spelling. More seriously, the use of plagiarized material—material copied without citing the source, or ideas taken from another source without giving the original author credit in an end-note—constitutes an automatic F, and places the student at risk of disciplinary sanctions by the university.

THE C ESSAY OR PAPER

The C essay has a thesis, but it is vague and broad, or else it is uninteresting or obvious. It does not advance an argument that anyone might care enough about to debate: "Modern cities are interesting places." The thesis in a C essay often hangs on some personal opinion. If the writer is a recognized authority, this expression of personal taste might be noteworthy, but writers gain their authority by learning how to justify and give evidence for their opinions. Opinion by itself is never enough. It must be defended. The C essay rarely uses evidence well; sometimes it does not use evidence at all. Even if it has a clear and interesting thesis, an essay with insufficient supporting evidence is a C essay. The C essay often has mechanical faults, errors in grammar and spelling, but please note: a paper without such flaws may still be a C essay.

THE B ESSAY OR PAPER

The reader of a B essay knows exactly what the author wants to say. It is well organized, it presents a strong and interesting idea, and the idea is supported by sound evidence presented in a neat and orderly way. The paragraphs may be awkward now and then, but they are each organized around a main idea, and develop that idea. Some of the sentences may not be elegant, but they are clear, and thought follows naturally on thought. Together, the paragraphs build an argument. The reader does not have to read a paragraph two or three times to get the thought the writer is trying to convey. The B essay is mechanically correct. The spelling is good, and the punctuation is accurate. Above all, the essay makes sense the whole way through. It has a thesis that is not too big, and that is worth arguing. It does not contain unexpected digressions, and it ends by keeping its promise to argue and inform the reader about the issue with which it begins.

THE A ESSAY OR PAPER

The A essay has all the good qualities of the B essay, but in addition it is lively, well paced, interesting, and even exciting. The essay has style. Everything seems to fit and support the argument. It may have a proofreading error or two, or even a misspelled word, but the reader feels that these errors are the result of the normal accidents all good writers encounter. Reading the paper, we feel a mind at work. We are convinced the writer cares about his or her ideas, and about the language that carries them. The sure mark of the A essay is that you find yourself telling someone else about it.
(Lewis Hyde's grading criteria list, edited by Sue Lonoff, with thanks to Richard Marius's handbook.)

Course Outline, Readings, and Assignments

(Schedules and topics are subject to change, in which case, announcements will be made in class as appropriate.)

WEEK 1

Tuesday, September 6: Introduction to the Course and to an Integrative Model for the Study of Religion and Healing

Part One: By Traditions
Thursday, September 8: Orientation to Hindu Traditions

WEEK 2

Tuesday, September 13: Hindu Healing Traditions

- Required Reading (to be completed for September 13th class)

    Margaret Trawick Egnor. 1984. The Changed Mother or What the Small-pox Goddess Did When There Was No More Smallpox. In *Contributions to Asian Studies*, Vol. 18, ed. E. Valentine Daniel and Judy F. Pugh, pp. 24–45. Leiden: E. J. Brill.
    R. Raguram, A. Venkateswaran, Jayashree Ramakrishna, and Mitchell G.

Weiss. 2002. Traditional Community Resources for Mental Health: A Report of Temple Healing from India. *British Medical Journal* 325;38–40.

Alison M. Spiro. 2005. Najar or Bhut—Evil Eye or Ghost Affliction: Gujarati Views about Illness Causation. *Anthropology & Medicine* 12(1): 61–73.

David M. Knipe. 1989. Hinduism and the Tradition of Ayurveda. In *Healing and Restoring: Health and Medicine in the World's Religious Traditions*, ed. Lawrence E. Sullivan, pp. 89–109. New York: Macmillan.

Prakash N. Desai. 2005. Health, Faith Traditions, and South Asian Indians in North America. In *RHA*, pp. 423–437.

Thursday, September 15: Orientations to Buddhist Traditions
Response papers on Hindu Traditions due (for those writing them).

Tuesday, September 20: Buddhist Healing Traditions

• Required Readings (to be completed for September 20th class)

Phyllis Granoff. 1998. Cures and Karma II: Some Miraculous Healings in the Indian Buddhist Story Tradition. *Bulletin, École française d'extrème-orient* 85:285–304.

Nirmala S. Salgado. 1997. Sickness, Healing, and Religious Vocation: Alternative Choices at a Theravada Buddhist Nunnery. *Ethnology* 36(3): 213–226.

Venerable Mettananda Bikkhu. 1991. Buddhist Ethics in the Practice of Medicine. *Buddhist Ethics and Modern Society: An International Symposium*, ed. Charles Wei-hsun Fu and Sandra A. Wawrytko, pp. 195–213. New York: Greenwood.

Daniel Goleman, ed. 2003. *Healing Emotions: Conversations with the Dalai Lama on Mindfulness, Emotions, and Health*, pp. 243–250. Boston: Shambhala.

Paul Numrich. 2005. Complementary and Alternative Medicine in America's "Two Buddhisms." In *RHA*, pp. 343–357.

Thursday, September 22: Orientation to Jewish Traditions
Response papers on Buddhist Traditions due (for those writing them)

Tuesday, September 27: Jewish Traditions

• Required Readings (prepare for September 27th class)

Laura J. Praglin. 1999. The Jewish Healing Tradition in Historical Perspective. *Reconstructionist* 63(2):6–15.

Ronald H. Isaacs. 1998. *Judaism, Medicine, and Healing*, pp. 135–164. Northvale, NJ: Jason Aronson.

Fred Rosner. 2000. Payment for Healing on the Sabbath. *Journal of Halacha and Contemporary Society* 40:59–67.

Howard Schwartz. 1994. Spirit Possession in Judaism. *Parabola* Winter: 72–76.

Eduardo Rauch. 1994. Redeeming the Holy Sparks: Evil, Healing, and the Soul of the World. In *The Parabola Book of Healing*, pp. 37–44. New York: Continuum Publishing Company.

Susan S. Sered. Healing as Resistance: Reflections upon New Forms of American Jewish Healing. In *RHA*, 231–252.

Thursday, September 29: Orientation to Christian Traditions
Response papers on Jewish Traditions due (for those writing them).

WEEK 5

Tuesday, October 4—Rosh Hashanah and 1st day of Ramadan: No class.

Thursday, October 6: Christian Traditions

- Required Readings (prepare for October 6)

Darrel W. Amundsen and Gary B. Ferngren. 1986. The Early Christian Tradition. In *Caring and Curing: Health and Medicine in the Western Religious Traditions*, ed. Ronald L. Numbers and Darrel W. Amundson, pp. 40–64. New York: Macmillan.

Robert A. Orsi. 2005. The Cult of the Saints and the Reimagination of the Space and Time of Sickness in Twentieth-Century American Catholicism. In *RHA*, pp. 29–47.

Mary Bednarowski. 2005. "Our Work is Change for the Sake of Justice": Hope Community, Minneapolis, Minnesota. In *RHA*, 195–204.

Theodore G. Stylianopoulos. 2001. Discernment and Diagnosis in Human Development: An Orthodox Theological Perspective. In *Sickness or Sin? Spiritual Discernment and Differential Diagnosis*, ed. John T. Chirban, pp. 47–60. Brookline, MA: Holy Cross Orthodox Press.

Jennifer L. Hollis. 2005. Healing in Wholeness in the Episcopal Church. In *RHA*, pp. 89–101.

Bobbie McKay and Lewis Musil. 2005. Spiritual Healing in the United Church of Christ. In *RHA*, pp. 49–57.

WEEK 6

Tuesday, October 11: Orientation to Islamic Traditions: Guest Speaker, Dr. Lance Laird
Response papers on Christian Traditions due (for those writing them).

- Required Readings (to be completed for October 11th class)

Frederick Denny. 1987. The Structures of Muslim Life. In *Islam and the Muslim Community*. San Francisco: HarperSanFrancisco, pp. 40–76.

Thursday, October 13: Yom Kippur: No class.

WEEK 7

Tuesday, October 18: Islamic Healing Traditions: Guest Speaker, Dr. Lance Laird

- Required Readings (to be completed for October 18th class)

J. E. Brockop. 2002. Islamic Ethics of Saving Life: A Comparative Perspective. *Medicine & Law* 21(2):225–41.

Marcia Hermansen. 2004. Dimensions of Islamic Religious Healing in America. In *RHA*, pp. 407–422.

S. Beckerleg. 1994. Medical Pluralism and Islam in Swahili Communities in Kenya. *Medical Anthropology Quarterly* 8(3):299–313.

J. Nourse. 1996. The Voice of the Winds versus the Masters of Cure: Contested Notions of Spirit Possession among the Lauje of Sulawesi. *Journal of the Royal Anthropological Institute* 2(3 Sept):425–442.

Part Two: By Cultural Groups
Thursday, October 20: Orientations to African Traditions
Note: Mid-term exam due
Response papers on Islamic Traditions due (for those writing them)

WEEK 8

Tuesday, October 25: African Healing Traditions: Guest Speaker, Onaje X. Woodbine

- Required Readings (to be completed for October 25th class)

Douglas E. Thomas. 2005. *African Traditional Religion in the Modern World*, pp. 83–94. Jefferson, NC: McFarland & Company.

Jacob Olupona. 2001. To Praise and to Reprimand: Ancestors and Spirituality in African Society and Culture. In *Ancestors in Post-Contact Religion: Roots, Ruptures, and Modernity's Memory*, ed. Steven J. Friesen, pp. 49–63. Cambridge, MA: Distributed by Harvard University Press for the Center for the Study of World Religions, Harvard Divinity School.

Wande Abimbola. 1997. *Ifá Will Mend Our Broken World*, pp. 1–23. Roxbury, MA: AIM Books.

Judith Gleason, with Awotunde Aworinde and John Olaniyi Ogundipe.

1973. *A Recitation of Ifa, Oracle of the Yoruba*, pp. 9–44. New York: Grossman Publishers.

John Janzen, Adrien Ngudiankama, and Melissa Filippi-Franz. 2005. Religious Healing among War Traumatized African Immigrants. In *RHA*, pp. 159–172.

Thursday, October 27: Orientation to African American Traditions
Response papers on African Traditions due (for those writing them).

WEEK 9

Tuesday, November 1: African American Traditions of Healing

- Required Readings (to be completed for November 1st class)

Albert J. Raboteau. 1998. The Afro-American Traditions. In *Caring and Curing: Health and Medicine in the Western Religious Traditions*, ed. Ronald L. Numbers, and Darrel W. Amundson, pp. 539–562. New York: Macmillan.

Patricia Guthrie. 1995. Mother Mary Ann Wright: African-American Women, Spirituality, and Social Activism. *Women & Therapy* 16(2/3): 161–173.

Stephanie Mitchem. 2005. "Jesus Is My Doctor": Healing and Religion in African American Women's Lives. In *RHA*, pp. 281–290.

Toinette M. Eugene. 1995. There Is a Balm in Gilead: Black Women and the Black Church as Agents of a Therapeutic Community. *Women & Therapy* 16(2–3): 55–71.

Rachel Elizabeth Harding. 2001. "What Part of the River You're In": African American Women in Devotion to Òsun. In *Osun Across the Waters: A Yoruba Goddess in Africa and the Americas*, ed. Joseph M. Murphy and Mei-Mei Sanford, pp. 165–188. Bloomington: Indiana University.

Claude Jacobs. 2005. Rituals of Healing in African American Spiritual Churches. In *RHA*, pp. 333–341.

Thursday, November 3: Orientation to Latino/a Traditions

WEEK 10

Tuesday, November 8: Latino/a Healing Traditions
Note: Term-paper proposal due, to be turned in by the end of class on November 8, or electronically by 9 p.m. that night

- Required Readings (to be completed for November 8th class)

Gastón Espinosa. 2005. "God Made a Miracle in My Life": Latino Pentecostal Healing in the Borderlands. In *RHA*, pp. 123–138.

Patrick Polk, Michael Owen Jones, Claudia J. Hernández, and Reyna C. Ronella. 2005. Miraculous Migrants to the City of Angels: Perceptions

of El Santo Niño de Atocha and San Simón as Sources of Health and
Healing. In *RHA*, pp. 103–120.

Inés Hernández-Ávila. 2005. La Mesa del Santo Niño de Atocha: The
Conchero Dance Tradition of Mexico-Tenochtitlan: Religious Healing
in Urban Mexico and the U.S. In *RHA*, pp. 359–374.

Lara Medina. 2005. Communing with The Dead: Spiritual and Cultural
Healing in Chicano/a Communities. In *RHA*, pp. 205–215.

Mario A. Núñez Molina. 2001. Community Healing Among Puerto Ricans: *Espiritismo* as a Therapy for the Soul. In *Healing Cultures: Art
and Religion as Curative Practices in the Caribbean and Its Diaspora*, ed.
Margarite Fernández Olmos and Lizabeth Paravisini-Gebert, pp. 115–
227. New York: Palgrave.

Thursday, November 10: Orientation to Chinese Traditions
Response papers on Latino/a Traditions due (for those writing them).

WEEK II

Tuesday, November 15: Chinese Healing Traditions
Required Readings (to be compared for November 15th class)

Ted J. Kaptchuk. 2000. *The Web That Has No Weaver*, (rev. edition),
pp. 41–74. Chicago: Contemporary Books.

Linda L. Barnes. 2005. Multiple Meanings of Chinese Healing in the
United States. In *RHA*, pp. 307–331.

Linda L. Barnes. 1998. The Psychologizing of Chinese Healing Practices
in the United States. *Culture, Medicine and Psychiatry* 22:413–443.

Thursday, November 17th: Orientation to Navajo Traditions
Response papers on Chinese Traditions due (for those writing them).

WEEK TWELVE

November 22 and 24: Thanksgiving Week—No class

WEEK 13

Tuesday, November 29: Navajo Healing Traditions

• Required Readings (to be completed for November 29th class)

Tom Csordas. 2005. Gender and Healing in Navajo Society. In *RHA*,
pp. 291–304.

Maureen Trudelle Schwarz. 1997. *Molded in the Image of Changing
Woman: Navajo Views on the Human Body and Personhood*, pp. xi–14.
Tucson: University of Arizona Press.

Karl W. Luckert, 1979. *Coyoteway: A Navajo Holyway Healing Ceremonial*,
pp. 3–30. Tucson: University of Arizona Press.

Mary Wheelwright, 1988. The Myth of the Coyote Chant. In *The Myth*

and Prayers of the Great Star Chant and the Myth of the Coyote Chant,
pp. 97–107. Tsaile, AZ: Navajo Community College Press.

Thursday, December 1: Orientation to Pluralism and Hybridity
Response papers on Navajo Traditions due (for those writing them).

WEEK FOURTEEN

Tuesday, December 6: Pluralism and Hybridity

- Required Readings (to be completed for December 6th class)

Bradley P. Stoner. 1985. Understanding Medical Systems: Traditional,
Modern, and Syncretic Health Care Alternatives in Medically Pluralistic Societies. *Medical Anthropology Quarterly*, 17(2):44–48.

Johannes Triebel. 2002. Living Together with the Ancestors: Ancestor
Veneration in Africa as a Challenge for Missiology. *Missiology: An International Review* 30(2):187–197.

Mei-Mei Sanford. 2001. Living Water: Òsun, Mami Wata, and Olókùn in
the Lives of Four Contemporary Nigerian Christian Women. In *Osun
Across the Waters: A Yoruba Goddess in Africa and the Americas*, ed. Joseph M. Murphy and Mei-Mei Sanford, pp. 237–250. Bloomington: Indiana University Press.

Julianne Cordero. 2005. The Gathering of Traditions: The Reciprocal Alliance of History, Ecology, Health, and Community among the Contemporary Chumash. In *RHA*, pp. 139–157.

Linda M. Hunt. 1993. The Metastasis of Witchcraft: The Interrelationship between Traditional and Biomedical Concepts of Cancer in
Southern Mexico. *Collegium Antropologicum* 17:249–255.

Lori Arviso Alvord and Elizabeth Cohen van Pelt. 1999. *The Scalpel and
the Silver Bear: The First Navajo Woman Surgeon Combines Western
Medicine and Traditional Healing*, pp. 1–4, 90–115, 137–149. New York:
Bantam Books.

Thursday, December 8: Conclusions
Response papers on Pluralism and Hybridity due (for those writing them).

Resource Bibliographies

Judaism and Healing

Susan S. Sered and Linda L. Barnes

Azamra Institute. 1996. *Call to live: Jewish guidance on healing.* Jerusalem: Azamra.

Barilan, Y. M. 2003. Revisiting the problem of Jewish bioethics: The case of terminal care. *Kennedy Institute of Ethics Journal* 13(2):141–68.

Bleich, David J., ed. 2002. *Judaism and healing: Halakhic perspectives.* Hoboken, NJ: Ktav Publishing House.

Brener, Anne. 2001. *Mourning and mitzvah: A guided journal for walking the mourner's path through grief to healing,* 2nd ed. Woodstock, VT: Jewish Lights Publishing.

Broyde, M. J. 1997. Cloning people and Jewish law: A preliminary analysis. *Journal of Halacha and Contemporary Society* 34(fall):27–65.

Buetow, S. 2003. The ethics of public consultation in health care: an Orthodox Jewish perspective. *Health Care Analysis* 11(2):151–60.

Cohen, A. 1996. Whose body? Living with pain. *Journal of Halacha and Contemporary Society* 32(fall):39–64.

Cowan, Neil M., and Ruth Schwarz Cowan. 1989. *Our parents' lives: The Americanization of Eastern European Jews.* New York: Basic Books.

Dein, Simon. 2004. *Religion and healing among the Lubavitch community in Stamford Hill, North London: A case study of Hasidism.* Lewiston, ME: E. Mellen Press.

Drake, D. C. 2001. Siamese twins—the surgery: An agonizing choice—parents, doctors, rabbis in dilemma. *Assia. Jewish Medical Ethics* 4(1):14–21.

Feld, J. P. Sherbin, and E. Cole. 1998. Barriers to organ donation in the Jewish community. *Journal of Transplant Coordination* 8(1):19–24.

Feldman, David M. *Health and medicine in the Jewish tradition: L'hayyim—to life* New York: Crossroad Press, 1986.

Fine, Lawrence. 2003. *Physician of the soul, healer of the cosmos: Isaac Luria and his kabbalistic fellowship.* Stanford, CA: Stanford University Press.

Flug, J. 2004. Halachic perspectives on alternative medicine. *Journal of Halacha and Contemporary Society* 47 (spring): 60–80.

Frankel, Estelle. 2003. *Sacred therapy: Jewish spiritual teachings on emotional healing and inner wholeness.* Boston: Shambhala.

Freedman, Benjamin, ed. 1999. *Duty and healing: Foundations of a Jewish bioethic.* New York: Routledge.

Freeman, David L., and Judith Z. Abrams, eds. 1999. *Illness and healing in the Jewish tradition: Writings from the Bible to today.* Philadelphia: Jewish Publication Society.

Friedman, Dayle A., ed. 2001. *Jewish pastoral care: A practical handbook from traditional and contemporary sources.* Woodstock, VT: Jewish Lights Publishing.

Glazerson, Matityahu. 1993. *Torah, light, and healing: Mystical insights into healing based on the Hebrew language.* Jerusalem: Lev Eliahu.

Greenbaum, Avraham. 1995. *The wings of the sun: Traditional Jewish healing in theory and practice.* Jerusalem: Breslov Research Institute.

Halperin, M. 2001. Siamese twins: Rav Feinstein's ruling and the subsequent controversy. *Assia. Jewish Medical Ethics* 4(1):26–27.

Herle, Peter. 2004. Ritual medical lore of Sephardic women: Sweetening the spirits, healing the sick. *Journal of American Folklore* 117(463):111–12.

Heynick, Frank. 2002. *Jews and medicine: An epic saga.* Hoboken, NJ: Ktav Publishing House.

Hirsh, Richard. 1999. Reflections on "healing" in contemporary liberal Judaism. *Reconstructionist* 63(2):16–25.

Inwald, D., I. Jakobovits, and A. Petros. 2000. Brain stem death: Managing care when accepted medical guidelines and religious beliefs are in conflict. Consideration and compromise are possible. *British Medical Journal* 320(7244): 1266–67.

Isaacs, Ronald H. 1998. *Divination, magic, and healing: The book of Jewish folklore.* Northvale, NJ: Jason Aronson.

Isaacs, Ronald H., *Judaism, medicine, and healing.* Northvale, NJ: Jason Aronson, 1998.

Kark, J. D., et al 1996. Does religious observance promote health? Mortality in secular vs religious kibbutzim in Israel. *American Journal of Public Health* 86(3): 341–46.

Lantos, J. D. 2001. Hope and responsibility in clinical settings: Two reflections on Jewish life and death. Are scientific truths the only truths? *Update* 17(1):1, 4–8

Lerner, Michael. 1995. *Jewish renewal: A path to healing and transformation.* New York: Harper Perennial.

Lesses, Rebecca. 1998. *Ritual practices to gain power: Angels, incantations, and revelation in early Jewish mysticism.* Harrisburg, PA: Trinity.

Lev, Rachel. 2003. *Shine the light: Sexual abuse and healing in the Jewish community.* Boston: Northeastern University Press.

Levin, Yoske. 1996. *Chasidic healing* (videotape). New York: Bea Moss Productions.

Mackler, Aaron L., ed. 2000. *Life and death responsibilities in Jewish biomedical ethics.* New York: Louis Finkelstein Institute, The Jewish Theological Seminary of America.

Mosenkis, A. 1997. Genetic screening for breast cancer susceptibility: A Torah perspective. *Journal of Halacha and Contemporary Society* 34(fall):5–26.

Ochs, Carol. 2004. *Reaching Godward: Voices from Jewish spiritual guidance.* New York: UAHC Press.

Okun, B.S. 2000. Religiosity and contraceptive method choice: The Jewish population of Israel. *European Journal of Population* 16(2):109–32.

Person, Hara E., ed. 2003. *The mitzvah of healing: An anthology of Jewish texts, meditations, essays, personal stories, and rituals.* New York: UAHC Press.

Polsky, Howard W., and Yaella Wozner. 1989. *Everyday miracles: The healing wisdom of Hasidic stories.* Northvale, NJ: J. Aronson.

Praglin, Laura J. 1999. The Jewish healing tradition in historical perspective. *Reconstructionist* 63(2):6–15.

Rauch, Eduardo. 1994. Redeeming the holy sparks: Evil, healing, and the soul of the world. In *The Parabola book of healing,* pp. 37–44. New York: Continuum.

Resnicoff, S. H. 1998–99. Jewish law perspectives on suicide and physician-assisted dying. *Journal of Law and Religion* 13(2):289–349.

Rosin, A. J., and M. Sonnenblick. 1998. Autonomy and paternalism in geriatric medicine. The Jewish ethical approach to issues of feeding terminally ill patients, and to cardiopulmonary resuscitation. *Journal of medical ethics* 24(1):44–48.

Rosman, Steven M. 1997. *Jewish healing wisdom.* Northvale, NJ: Jason Aronson.

Rosner, Fred, ed. 1994. *Medicine in the Bible and the Talmud: Selections from classical Jewish sources,* Hoboken, NJ: KTAV Publishing House.

———. 2002. The Jewish view of healing. *Cancer Investigation* 20(4):598–603.

Schostak, Z. 1995. Is there patient autonomy in Halacha? *Assia. Jewish medical ethics* 2(2):22–7

Sefer, Carmen Caballero-Navas, ed. and trans. 2004. *The Book of women's love and Jewish medieval medical literature on women* [Sefer ahavat nashim]. New York: Kegan Paul.

Sered, Susan S. 1992. *Women as ritual experts: The religious lives of elderly Jewish women in Jerusalem.* New York: Oxford University Press

———. 2000. *What makes women sick? Maternity, modesty, and militarism in Israeli society.* Hanover, NH: Brandeis University Press

———. 2005. Healing as Resistance: Reflections upon new forms of American Jewish healing. In *Religion and Healing in America,* ed. Linda L. Barnes and Susan S. Sered, pp. 231–52. New York: Oxford University Press.

Singer, Isaac Bashevis, 1981. Demons by choice: An interview. *Parabola* 6(4):68–74.

Spitz, E. 1996. Through her I too shall bear a child: Birth surrogates in Jewish law. *Journal of Religious Ethics* 24(1):65–97.

Steinberg, A. 2001. Halakhic guidelines for physicians in intensive care units. *Assia. Jewish Medical Ethics* 4(1):5–6.

Tendler, M. D. 2001. Siamese twins—the surgery: So one may live. *Assia. Jewish Medical Ethics* 4(1):22–25.

Umansky, Ellen M. 2005. *From Christian Science to Jewish science: Spiritual healing and American Jews* New York: Oxford University Press.

Weintraub, Simkha Y., ed. 1994. *Healing of soul, healing of body: Spiritual leaders unfold the strength and solace in Psalms.* Woodstock, VT: Jewish Lights Publishing.

Werber, S. J. Ancient answers to modern questions: Death, dying, and organ transplants—a Jewish law perspective. *Journal of Law and Health* 11(1–2):13–44.

Zeller, David. 2003. *Ruah=Ruach: Inspiring, healing, relaxing and meditative Jewish music.* Jerusalem: D. Zeller.

Zwebner, Bat Tova, and Chana Shofnos. 1989. *The healing visit: Insights into the mitzvah of bikur cholim.* Southfield, MI: Targum Press.

Christian Traditions of Healing

Linda L. Barnes

EARLY CHRISTIANITY

Amundsen, Darrel W., and Gary B. Ferngren. 1986. The early Christian tradition. In *Caring and curing: Health and medicine in the Western religious traditions*, ed. Ronald L. Numbers and Darrel W. Amundson. New York: Macmillan Publishing.

Barrett-Lennard, R. J. S. 1994. *Christian healing after the New Testament: Some approaches to illness in the second, third, and fourth centuries.* Lanham, MD: University Press of America.

Beck, James R. 1993. *The healing words of Jesus.* Grand Rapids, MI: Baker Book House.

Bostock, D G. 1985. Medical theory and theology in Origen. In *Origen Tertia*, pp. 191–99. Rome: Edizioni dell'Ateneo.

Dawson, George Gordon. 1977. *Healing: Pagan and Christian.* New York: AMS Press.

Halliburton, John. 1993. Anointing in the early church. In *The oil of gladness*, pp. 77–91. London: SPCK.

Hamilton, Mary. 1906. *Incubation; or, the cure of disease in pagan temples and Christian churches.* London: Simpkin, Marshall, Hamilton, Kent and Co.

Kee, Howard Clark. 1989. Magic and messiah. In *Religion, science, and magic: In concert and in conflict*, pp. 121–41. New York: Oxford University Press.

Leeper, Elizabeth A. 1993. The role of exorcism in early Christianity. *Studia Patristica* 26:59–62

Pherigo, Lindsey P. 1991. *The great physician: Luke, the healing stories.* Nashville: Abingdon Press.

Stapleton, Ruth Carter. 1979. *In his footsteps: The healing ministry of Jesus, then and now.* San Francisco: Harper and Row.

Thomas, Zach. 1994. *Healing touch: The church's forgotten language.* Louisville, KY: Westminster/John Knox Press.

ROMAN CATHOLIC

Amundsen, Darrel W. 1986. The Medieval Catholic Tradition. In *Caring and curing: Health and medicine in the Western religious traditions*, ed. Ronald L. Numbers and Darrel W. Amundsen, pp. 65–107. New York: Macmillan.

Bax, Mart. 1990. The madonna of Medjugorje: Religious rivalry and the formation of a devotional movement in Yugoslavia. *Anthropological quarterly* 63(2):63–75.

Beckwith, Barbara. 1977. The new rite of anointing the sick. In *Living our faith after the changes: Explaining Catholic thinking since Vatican II.* Cincinnati: St. Anthony Messenger Press.

Bentley, James. 1985. *Restless bones: The story of relics* London: Constable and Company Ltd.

Biller, Peter, and Joseph Ziegler, ed. 2001. *Religion and medicine in the Middle Ages.* Rochester, NY: York Medieval Press.

Catholic Health Association. 1993. *Care of the dying: A Catholic perspective.* St. Louis: Catholic Health Association of the United States.

Chauvet, Louis-Marie, and Miklós Tomka, ed. 1998. *Illness and healing.* Maryknoll, NY: Orbis Books.

Chocran, Tracy. 1994. Mary visions: A virgin in the sky with diamonds. *Omni* 17(1):54–59.

Collins, Mary. 1991. The Roman ritual: Pastoral care and the anointing of the sick. In *The pastoral care of the sick,* ed. Mary Collins and David N. Power, pp. 3–18. London: Trinity Press International.

Coffey, Thomas F., Linda Kay Davidson, and Maryjane Dunn, trans. 1996. *The miracles of Saint James: Translations from the Liber sancti Jacobi.* New York: Italica Press.

Darling, Frank C. 1990. *Christian healing in the Middle Ages and beyond.* Boulder, CO: Vista Publications.

Ditchfield, Simon. 1993. Martyrs on the move: Relics as vindicators of local diversity in the Tridentine church. In *Martyrs and martyrologies,* pp. 283–94. Oxford: Blackwell.

Dudley, Martin, and Geoffrey Rowell, eds. 1993. *The oil of gladness: Anointing in the Christian tradition.* London: Liturgical Press.

Durham, Michael S. 1995. *Miracles of Mary: Apparitions, legends, and miraculous works of the blessed Virgin Mary.* San Francisco: HarperSanFrancisco.

Garvey, Mark. 1998. *Searching for Mary: An exploration of Marian apparitions across the U.S.* New York: Plume.

Griese, Orville N. 1987. *Catholic identity in health care: Principles and practice* Braintree, MA: Pope John Center.

Helm, Jürgen, and Annette Winkelmann, eds. 2001. *Religious confessions and the sciences in the sixteenth century* Boston: Brill.

Kelly, David F. 1979. *The emergence of Roman Catholic medical ethics in North America.* New York: Edwin Mellen Press.

———. 2004. *Contemporary Catholic health care ethics.* Washington, DC: Georgetown University Press.

Kselman, Thomas A. 1983. *Miracles and prophecies in nineteenth-century France.* New Brunswick, NJ: Rutgers University Press.

Laurentin, Rene. 1994. *Pilgrimages, sanctuaries, icons, apparitions: An historical and scriptural account.* Milford, OH: The Foundation.

Marnham, Patrick. 1980. *Lourdes: A modern pilgrimage.* London: Heinemann.

Marty, M., and Kenneth Vaux, eds. 1982. *Health/medicine and the faith traditions: An inquiry into religion and medicine.* Philadelphia: Fortress Press.

McCormick, Richard A. 1984. *Health and medicine in the Catholic tradition: Tradition in transition.* New York: Crossroad.

Miller, Elliot, and Kenneth R. Samples. 1992. *The cult of the Virgin: Catholic Mariology and the apparitions of Mary.* Grand Rapids, MI: Baker Book House.

Molina, Caroline. 1994. Illness as privilege: Hildegard von Bingen and the condition of mystic writing. *Women's Studies* 23(1):85–91

Nabhan-Warren, Kristy. 2005. *The Virgin of el barrio: Marian apparitions, Catholic evangelizing, and Mexican American activism.* New York: New York University Press.

O'Connell, Marvin R. 1986. The Roman Catholic tradition since 1545. In *Caring and curing: Health and medicine in the Western religious traditions,* ed. Ronald L. Numbers and Darrel W. Amundsen, pp. 108–45. New York: Macmillan.

Orsi, Robert A. 1996. *Thank you, St. Jude: Women's devotion to the patron saint of hopeless causes.* New Haven, CT: Yale University Press.

———. 2002. *The Madonna of 115th Street: Faith and community in Italian Harlem, 1880–1950,* 2nd ed. New Haven, CT: Yale University Press.

_____. 2005. *Between heaven and earth: The religious worlds people make and the scholars who study them*. Princeton, NJ: Princeton University Press.

Pagel, Walter. 1985. *Religion and Neoplatonism in renaissance medicine*, ed. Marianne Winder. London: Variorum Reprints.

Rollason, David W. 1989. *Saints and relics in Anglo-Saxon England*. Oxford: Blackwell.

Seward, Desmond. 1993. *The dancing sun: Journeys to the miracle shrines*. London: Macmillan.

Snoek, Godefridus J. C. 1995. *Medieval piety from relics to the Eucharist: A process of mutual interaction*. Leiden; New York: E.J. Brill.

Sox, David. 1985. *Relics and shrines*. London: Allen and Unwin.

Sweetinburgh, Sheila. 2004. *The role of the hospital in medieval England: Gift-giving and the spiritual economy*. Portland, OR: Four Courts Press.

Taylor, Therese. 1995. "So many extraordinary things to tell": Letters from Lourdes, 1858. *Journal of Ecclesiastical History* 46(3):457–81.

Toner, Patrick J. 1974. Exorcism and the Catholic Faith. In *Exorcism through the ages*, ed. St. Elmo Nauman Jr., pp. 31–41. New York: Philosophical Library.

Ulrich, Ingeborg. 1993. *Hildegard of Bingen: Mystic, healer, companion of the angels*, trans. Linda M. Maloney. Collegeville, MN: Liturgical Press.

Van Dam, Raymond. 1993. *Saints and their miracles in late antique Gaul*. Princeton, NJ: Princeton University Press.

Wasyliw, Patricia Healy. 1996. *Martyrdom, murder, and magic: Child saints and their cults in medieval Europe*. New York: P. Lang.

Watling, Catherine T. 1993. *Lourdes: City of the sick*. Slough: St. Pauls.

Wojcik, Daniel. 1996. "Polaroids from heaven": Photography, folk religion, and the miraculous image tradition at a Marian apparition site. *Journal of American Folklore* 109(432):129–48.

Woodward, Kenneth L. 1990. *Making saints: How the Catholic Church determines who becomes a saint, who doesn't, and why*. New York: Simon and Schuster.

Ziegler, Joseph. 1998. *Medicine and religion, c. 1300: The case of Arnau de Vilanova*. New York: Oxford University Press.

Zimdars-Swartz, Sandra. 1991. *Encountering Mary: From La Salette to Medjugorje* Princeton, NJ: Princeton University Press.

ANGLICAN AND EPISCOPALIAN

Brown, Deborah A., ed. 2000. *Christianity in the twenty-first century*. New York: Crossroad.

Cowles, Edward Spencer. 1925. *Religion and medicine in the church*. New York: Macmillan.

Gifford, Sanford. 1997. *The Emmanuel movement (Boston, 1904–1929): The origins of group treatment and the assault on lay psychotherapy*. Boston: Francis A. Countway Library of Medicine.

Grell, Ole Peter, and Andrew Cunningham, eds. 1996. *Religio medici: Medicine and religion in seventeenth-century England*. Brookfield: Ashgate Publishing Company.

Gusmer, Charles W. 1974. *The ministry of healing in the Church of England: An ecumenical-liturgical study*. Great Wakering, England: Mayhew-McCrimmon.

Nunnally, J. Ellen. 2003. *Deep peace: Healing in our lives*. Cambridge, MA: Cowley Publications.

Smith, David H. 1986. *Health and medicine in the Anglican tradition: Conscience, community, and compromise.* New York: Crossroad.

Taylor, Barbara Brown. 1995. *Gospel medicine.* Cambridge, MA: Cowley Publications.

Worcester, Elwood, and Samuel McComb. 1931. *Body, mind, and spirit,* Boston: Marshall Jones Co.

EASTERN ORTHODOX

Ambrosius, Bishop of Joensuu. 1990. "Jesus Christ—the life of the world" in Orthodox iconography. In *Icons, windows on eternity,* pp. 205–11. Geneva: WCC Publications.

Antony, of Choziba. 1994. *Life of Saint George of Choziba; and, the miracles of the Most Holy Mother of God at Choziba,* trans. Tim Vivian and Apostolos N. Athanassakis. San Francisco: International Scholars Publications.

Bigham, Stephane. 1992. Allegorical personification in Orthodox iconography. *Sacred Art Journal* 13(June):58–67.

Bigham, Stephen. 1985. Death and Orthodox iconography. *Saint Vladimir's theological quarterly* 29(4):325–41.

Bowes, Marie. 1986. Evidence of the kingdom: The New York weeping icons. *Epiphany* 6(4):37–39.

Cavarnos, Constantine. 1978. *St. Arsenios of Paros: Remarkable confessor, spiritual guide, educator, ascetic, miracle-worker, and healer: An account of his life, character, message, and miracles.* Belmont, MA: Institute for Byzantine and Modern Greek Studies.

———. 1987. *St. Methodia of Kimolos, remarkable ascetic, teacher of virtue, counselor, comforter, and healer (1865–1908): An account of her life, character, miracles, and influence.* Belmont, MA: Institute for Byzantine and Modern Greek Studies.

Cavarnos, Constantine, and Mary-Barbara Zeldin. 1980. *St. Seraphim of Sarov: Widely beloved mystic, healer, comforter, and spiritual guide.* Belmont, MA: Institute for Byzantine and Modern Greek Studies.

Chirban, John T. 1991. *Healing: Orthodox Christian perspectives in medicine, psychology, and religion.* Brookline, MA: Holy Cross Orthodox Press.

———. 1993. Healing and Orthodox spirituality. *Ecumenical Review* 45(3):337–44.

———, ed. 2001. *Sickness or sin: Spiritual discernment and differential diagnosis.* Brookline, MA: Holy Cross Orthodox Press.

Connor, Carolyn L. 1991. *Art and miracles in medieval Byzantium: The crypt at Hosios Loukas and its frescoes.* Princeton, NJ: Princeton University Press.

Constantelos, Demetrios J. 1967. Physician-Priests in the Medieval Greek Church. *Greek Orthodox theological review* 14: 141–53.

———. 1982–1989. "Medicine, Byzantine," and "Hospitals, Byzantine." In *Dictionary of the Middle Ages,* ed. Joseph R. Strayer. New York: Scribner.

Crisafulli, Virgil S., and John W. Nesbitt. 1997. *The miracles of St. Artemios: A collection of miracle stories by an anonymous author of seventh century Byzantium,* trans. Virgil S. Crisafulli. New York: E.J. Brill.

Darling, Frank C. 1990. Healers in the Eastern Orthodox Church (fourth and fifth centuries). In *Christian healing in the Middle Ages and beyond,* pp. 95–113. Boulder, CO: Vista Publications.

Dubisch, Jill. 1990. Pilgrimage and popular religion at a Greek holy shrine. In *Religious orthodoxy and popular faith in European society,* pp. 113–139. Princeton, NJ: Princeton University Press.

————. 1991. Men's time and women's time: History, myth, and ritual at a modern Greek shrine. *Journal of Ritual Studies* 5:1–26.

Duncan-Flowers, Maggie. 1990. A pilgrim's ampulla from the shrine of St. John the Evangelist at Ephesus. In *The blessings of pilgrimage,* ed. Robert Ousterhout, pp. 125–39. Urbana: University of Illinois Press.

Edelstein, Ludwig. 1966. The distinctive Hellenism of Greek medicine. *Bulletin of the history of medicine* 40:197–225.

Groen, Basilius. 1991. The anointing of the sick in the Greek Orthodox Church. In *The pastoral care of the sick,* ed. Mary Collins and David N. Power, pp. 50–59. London: Trinity Press International.

Hall, Christine. 1993. The use of holy oils in the Orthodox churches of the Byzantine tradition. In *The oil of gladness: Anointing in the Christian tradition,* ed. Martin Dudley and Geoffrey Rowell, pp. 101–12. London: Liturgical Press.

Harakas, Stanley S. 1986. The Eastern Orthodox tradition. In *Caring and curing: Health and medicine in the Western religious traditions,* ed. Ronald L. Numbers and Darrel W. Amundsen, pp. 146–72. New York: Macmillan.

————. 1990. *Health and medicine in the Eastern Orthodox tradition: Faith, liturgy, and wholeness.* New York: Crossroad.

Harvey, Susan Ashbrook. 1984. Physicians and ascetics in John of Ephesus: An expedient alliance. In *Symposium on Byzantine medicine,* ed. John Scarborough. Vol. 38 of *Dumbarton Oaks papers.* Washington, DC: Dumbarton Oaks.

Horden, Peregrine. 1982. Saints and doctors in the early Byzantine empire: The case of Theodore of Sykeon. In *The Church and healing,* ed. W. J. Sheils. Vol. 19 of *Studies in church history.* Oxford: Basil Blackwell.

Iwaszewicz, Martha. 1992. The visit to Argentina of the miraculous Iveron myrrh-streaming icon to the Mother of God. *Orthodox Life,* 42(May–June):36–49.

Keenan, Mary Emily. 1941. Gregory of Nazianzus and early Byzantine medicine. *Bulletin of the History of Medicine* 9:8–30.

————. 1944. St. Gregory of Nyssa and the medical profession. *Bulletin of the History of Medicine* 15:150–61.

Lambertsen, Isaac E., trans. An account of the miraculous icons of the Holy Great-martyr George. *Living orthodoxy,* 16(March–April):3–5.

Magoulias, Harry J. 1964. The lives of the saints as sources of data for the history of Byzantine medicine in the sixth and seventh centuries. *Byzantinische zeitschrift* 57: 127–50.

Maguire, Henry. 1996. *The icons of their bodies: Saints and their images in Byzantium.* Princeton, NJ: Princeton University Press.

Papademetriou, George C. 1974. Exorcism and the Greek Orthodox Church. In *Exorcism through the ages,* ed. St. Elmo Nauman Jr., pp. 43–56. New York: Philosophical Library.

Phougias, Metropolitan Methodios G. 1990. Icons in patristic theology and spirituality, eastern and western. *Sacred Art Journal* 11(March):7–10.

Scarborough, John, ed. 1985. *Symposium on Byzantine medicine.* Washington, DC: Dumbarton Oaks Research Library and Collection.

Talbot, Alice-Mary. 1983. *Faith healing in late Byzantium: The posthumous miracles of the patriarch Athanasios I of Constantinople by Theoktistos the Stoudite.* Brookline, MA: Hellenic College Press.

Vsevolod, Monk. 1995. Seven hundredth anniversary of the wonderworking Kursk Root Icon of the Sign. Photos. *Orthodox Life* 45(November–December):7–10.

PROTESTANT EXAMPLES

Lutheran

Beckmen, Richard J., and Steven J. Nerheim. 1985. *Toward a healing ministry: Exploring and implementing a congregational ministry.* Minneapolis: Augsburg.

Buehler, David A. 1981. Caring, curing, calling: The minister and the ministry of healing. *LCA Partners* 3:7–9, 25.

Christenson, Larry 1976. *The charismatic renewal among Lutherans.* Minneapolis: Lutheran Charismatic Renewal Services.

Linberg, Carter. 1986. The Lutheran tradition. In *Caring and curing: Health and medicine in the Western religious traditions,* pp. 173–203. New York: Macmillan.

Liotta, Matthew A. 1935. *The connection between religion and medicine.* New York: J. J. Little and Ives.

Marty, Martin E. 1983. *Health and medicine in the Lutheran tradition: Being well.* New York: Crossroad.

Tillich, Paul, et al. 1958. *Religion and health: A symposium,* ed. Simon Doniger. New York: Association Press.

———. 1984. *The meaning of health: Essays in existentialism, psychoanalysis, and religion,* ed. Perry LeFevre. Chicago: Exploration Press.

Vaux, Kenneth. 1980. *Lutheran General Hospital: An institution intent on a moral purpose.* Chicago: Park Ridge.

Reformed Tradition

Baxter, Richard. 1981. The cure of melancholy and overmuch sorrow, by faith and physic. In *Puritan sermons, 1659–1689,* ed. James Nichols. Wheaton, Ill.: R.O. Roberts.

———. 1838. Directions for the sick. In *The practical works of Richard Baxter,* Vol. 1, pp. 522–47. London: G. Virtue.

Beall, Otho, T., Jr. and Richard H. Shryock. 1954. *Cotton Mather: First significant figure in American medicine.* Baltimore: John Hopkins University Press.

Ely, Ezra Stiles. 1829. *Visits of mercy; or, the journals of the Rev. Ezra Stiles Ely written while he was stated preacher to the hospital and alms-house, in the city of New York,* 6th ed. Philadelphia: Samuel F. Bradford.

Foster, Charles I. 1960. *An errand of mercy.* Chapel Hill: University of North Carolina.

Frazier, Claude Albee, ed. 1974. *Healing and religious faith.* Philadelphia: United Church Press.

Hiltner, Seward. 1966. Christian understanding of sin in the light of medicine and psychiatry. *Medical Arts and Sciences* 20(2):35–49.

———. 1943. *Religion and health.* New York: Macmillan.

———. 1968. Salvation's message about health. *International Review of Missions* 57: 157–74.

Holifield, E. Brooks. 1983. *A history of pastoral care in America: From salvation to self-realization.* Nashville: Abingdon Press.

McNeill, John Thomas. 1951. *A history of the cure of souls.* New York: Harper.

Mather, Cotton. 1691. *Memorable providences relating to witchcrafts and possessions . . . clearly manifesting, not only that there are witches, but that good men (as well as others) may possibly have their lives shortned by such evil instruments of Satan.* London: Thomas Parkhurst.

Parker, Gail Thain. 1969. Jonathan Edwards and melancholy. *New England Quarterly* 41:193–212.

Rosenberg, Charles E. 1979. Inward vision and outward glance: The shaping of the American hospital, 1880–1914. *Bulletin of the History of Medicine* 53:346–91.

Rosenberg, Charles E., and Carroll S. Rosenberg. 1968. Pietism and the origins of the American Public Health Movement. *Journal of the History of Medicine and Allied Sciences* 23:16–35.

Ryan, Frank Jamieson. 1899. *Protestant miracles high orthodox and evangelical authority for the belief in divine interposition in human affairs: Some account of marvelous cures of illness, rescue from danger, death, poverty and suffering, through faith and prayer, in recent centuries.* Stockton, CA: Record.

Smylie, James H. 1986. The reformed tradition. In *Caring and curing: Health and medicine in the Western religious traditions,* ed. Ronald L. Numbers and Darrel W. Amundson, pp. 204–39. New York: Macmillan.

United Presbyterian Church in the U.S.A. 1960. *The relation of Christian faith to health.* Philadelphia: United Presbyterian Church in the U.S.A.

Vaux, Kenneth L. 1978. *This mortal coil: The meaning of health and disease.* San Francisco: Harper and Row.

———. 1984. *Health and medicine in the reformed tradition: Promise, providence, and care.* New York: Crossland.

Wesleyan-Methodist Tradition

Bardell, Eunice Bonow. 1979. Primitive physick: John Wesley's receipts. *Pharmacy in History* 21:111–21.

Hill, A. Wesley. 1958. *John Wesley among the physicians: A study of eighteenth-century medicine.* London: Epworth Press.

Holifield, E. Brooks. 1986. *Health and medicine in the Methodist tradition: Journey toward wholeness* New York: Crossroad.

Rack, Henry D. 1982. Doctors, demons, and early Methodist healing. In *The church and healing,* ed. W.J. Sheils, pp. 137–52. Vol. 19 of *Studies in church history.* Oxford: Basil Blackwell,

Rousseau, G. S. 1968. John Wesley's Primitive Physick (1747). *Harvard Library Bulletin* 16:242–56.

Vanderpool, Harold Y. 1986. The Wesleyan-Methodist tradition. In *Caring and curing: Health and medicine in the Western religious traditions,* eds. Ronald L. Numbers and Darrel W. Amundson, pp. 317–353. New York: Macmillan.

Wesley, John. 1746. *A collection of receipts for the use of the poor.* Bristol, England: Felix Farley.

———. 1774. *A Primitive Physick: Or, an easy and natural method of curing most diseases.* London: R. Hawes.

———. 1789. *The duty and advantage of early rising.* London.

Evangelical and Pentecostal Traditions

Allen, Norm R., Jr. 1993. Faith healing in the black community. *Free Inquiry* 14(1):14.

Barnhart, Joe. 1988. Faith healers in a naturalistic context. *The Humanist* 48(5):5–8.

Blair, Barbara, and Susan E. Cayleff, ed. 1993. *Wings of gauze: Women of color and the experience of health and illness.* Detroit: Wayne State University Press.

Bringle, Mary Louise. 1990. *Despair, sickness or sin? Hopelessness and healing in the Christian life.* Nashville: Abingdon Press.

Buehler, David A. 1985. *Health and healing in the Bible,* ed. Raymond Tiemeyer. Philadelphia: Parish Life Press.

Cain, John Milton. 1959. *You can work miracles; a nonsectarian discussion of faith healing.* [Riverside, CT]: N.p.

Clark, Charles S. 1992. Faith healers and freedom of religion. *CQ researcher* 2(4):87.

Csordas, Thomas J. 1988. Elements of charismatic persuasion and healing. *Medical Anthropology Quarterly* 2:121–42.

————. 1994. *The sacred self: A cultural phenomenology of charismatic healing.* Berkeley: University of California Press.

Dickason, C. Fred. 1987. *Demon possession and the Christian: A new perspective.* Chicago: Moody Press.

Edwardes, Phil, and James McConnell. 1985. *Healing for you: The story of Phil Edwardes, a healer with remarkable power.* Wellingborough, England: Thorsons.

Eugene, Toinette M. There is a balm in Gilead: Black women and the black church as agents of a therapeutic community. *Women and Therapy* 16(2–3):55–71.

Fuller, Elizabeth. 1986. *The touch of grace.* New York: Dodd, Mead.

Hall, David A., ed. 1991. *Healing ministries of the Holy Spirit.* Memphis, TN: COGIC Publishing Board.

Harper, Michael. 1984. *Spiritual warfare* Ann Arbor, MI: Servant Books.

Harpur, Tom. 1994. *The uncommon touch: An investigation of spiritual healing.* Toronto: McClelland and Stewart.

Harrell, David Edwin, Jr. 1975. *All things are possible: The healing and charismatic revivals in modern America.* Bloomington: Indiana University Press.

Johnson, Paul, with Larry Richards. 1987. *Spiritual secrets to physical health.* Waco, TX: Word Books.

Koch, Kurt E. 1971. *Occult bondage and deliverance; advice for counselling the sick, the troubled, and the occultly oppressed.* Grand Rapids, MI: Kregel Publications.

Kuhlman, Kathryn. 1962. *I believe in miracles.* Englewood Cliffs, NJ: Prentice-Hall.

Levack, Brian P. 1992. *Possession and exorcism.* New York: Garland Publishing.

Martin, Malachi. 1992. *Hostage to the devil: The possession and exorcism of five living Americans.* San Francisco: HarperSanFrancisco.

Melinsky, Michael Arthur Hugh. 1968. *Healing miracles; an examination from history and experience of the place of miracle in Christian thought and medical practice.* London: A. R. Mowbray.

Percy, Martyn. 1997. The Gospel miracles and modern healing movements. *Theology* 99(793):8–17.

Randi, James. 1987. *The faith healers.* Buffalo, NY: Prometheus Books.

Sanford, Agnes Mary White. 1969. *The healing power of the Bible.* Philadelphia: Lippincott.

Schwarz, Ted. 1993. *Healing in the name of God: Faith or fraud?* Grand Rapids, MI: Zondervan.

Smedes, Lewis B., ed. 1987. *Ministry and the miraculous: A case study at Fuller Theological Seminary,* Waco, TX: Word Books.

Stapleton, Ruth Carter. 1979. *In His footsteps: The healing ministry of Jesus, then and now.* San Francisco: Harper and Row.

Sweet, Leonard I. 1994. *Health and medicine in the evangelical tradition.* Valley Forge, PA: Trinity Press International.

Wimber, John, with Kevin Springer. 1987a. *Power healing*. San Francisco: Harper and Row.

———. 1987b. *Study guide to power healing*. San Francisco: Harper and Row.

Wimberly, Edward P. 1997. *Recalling our own stories: Spiritual renewal for religious caregivers*. San Francisco: Jossey-Bass.

Witty, Robert Gee. 1989. *Divine healing*. Nashville: Broadman Press.

MEDICAL MISSIONS

Bate, Stuart C. 1999. *Inculturation of the Christian mission to heal in the South African context*. Lewiston, NY: Edwin Mellen Press.

Choa, Gerald H. 1990. *"Heal the sick" was their motto: The Protestant medical missionaries in China*. Hong Kong: Chinese University.

Crane, Sophie. 1998. *A legacy remembered: A century of medical missions*. Franklin, TN: Providence House.

Fisher, James T. 1997. *Dr. America: The lives of Thomas A. Dooley, 1927–1961*. Amherst: University of Massachusetts Press.

Gates, Tom. 1998. *Sickness, suffering, and healing: More stories from another place*. Wallingford, PA: Pendle Hill Publications.

Gelfand, Michael. 1988. *Godly medicine in Zimbabwe: A history of its medical missions*. Gweru, Zimbabwe: Mambo Press.

Gulick, Edward Vose. 1973. *Peter Parker and the opening of China*. Cambridge, MA: Harvard University Press.

Krimsky, Joseph. 1977. *Pilgrimage and service*. New York: Arno Press.

Romig, Ella Mae Ervin. 1997. *When the geese come: The journals of a Moravian missionary Ella Mae Ervin Romig 1898–1905, Southwest Alaska*, ed. Phyllis Demuth Movius. Fairbanks: University of Alaska Press.

Wanless, W. J. 1898. *The medical mission: Its place, power, and appeal*. Philadelphia: Westminster.

Wilkinson, John. 1990. *Making men whole: The theology of medical missions*. London: Christian Medical Fellowship.

TWO LATIN AMERICAN EXAMPLES: CHRISTIANITY AND INDIGENOUS TRADITIONS

Mexico

Curcio-Nagy, Linda A. 1996. Native icon to city protectress to royal patroness: Ritual, political symbolism and the Virgin of Remedies. *Americas* 52(3):367–91.

Curley, Daniel. 1991. *The curandero: Eight stories*. Kansas City, MO: BKMK Press.

Drufovka, Ivan. 2004. *Yo soy hechicero* [I am a sorcerer] Videotape. Narberth, PA: Drufovka/Stanford.

Harvey, H. R. 1991. Pilgrimage and shrine: Religious practices among the Otomi of Huixquilucan, Mexico. In *Pilgrimage in Latin America*, pp. 91–107. New York: Greenwood Press.

Heinrich, Michael. Herbal and symbolic medicines of the lowland Mixe (Oaxaca, Mexico): Disease concepts, healer's roles, and plant use. *Anthropos* 89(1–3):73–83.

Kay, Margarita Artschwager. 1977. Health and illness in a Mexican American barrio.

In *Ethnic medicine in the Southwest*, pp. 99–166. Tucson: University of Arizona Press.

Lok, Rossana 1991. *Gifts to the dead and the living: Forms of exchange in San Miguel Tzinacapan, Sierra Norte de Puebla, Mexico.* Leiden: Centre of Non-Western Studies, Leiden University.

Macklin, J. J., and Perez de Ayala. 1980. *Tigre Juan and el curandero de su honra.* London: Grant and Cutler

Marcos, Sylvia. 1991. Healing Rituals and popular medicine in Mexico. In *The pastoral care of the sick*, pp. 108–21. London: SCM Press.

Marino, Daniela. 1997. Prayer for a sleeping child: Iconography of the funeral ritual of little angels in Mexico. *Journal of American Culture* 20(2):37–49.

Nutini, Hugo G. 1988. *Todos santos in rural Tlaxcala: A syncretic, expressive, and symbolic analysis of the cult of the dead.* Princeton, NJ: Princeton University Press.

Oktavec, Eileen. 1995. *Answered prayers: Miracles and milagros along the border.* Tucson: University of Arizona Press.

Ortiz Echaniz, Silvia. 1990. *Una religiosidad popular: El espiritualismo trinitario mariano.* Mexico, D.F.: Instituto Nacional de Antropología e Historia.

Poole, Stafford. 1995. *Our Lady of Guadalupe: The origins and sources of a Mexican national symbol, 1531–1797.* Tucson: University of Arizona Press.

Prieto, Jorge. 1989. *Harvest of hope: The pilgrimage of a Mexican-American physician.* Notre Dame, IN: University of Notre Dame Press.

Rodriguez, Jeanette. 1994. *Our Lady of Guadalupe: Faith and empowerment among Mexican-American women.* Austin: University of Texas Press.

Sandstrom, Alan R. 1986. Paper spirits of Mexico; elaborate rituals, long hidden in remote Indian villages provide a glimpse of Aztec cosmology. *Natural History* 95(January):66–73.

Slade, Doren L. 1992. *Making the world safe for existence: Celebration of the saints among the Sierra Nahuat of Chignautla, Mexico.* Ann Arbor: University of Michigan Press.

Villoro, Luis. 1992. The unacceptable otherness. (Spanish and Aztec religious views). *Diogenes* 159:57–68.

Puerto Rico

Adler, Leonore Loeb. 1995. *Spirit versus scalpel: Traditional healing and modern psychotherapy.* Westport, CT: Bergin and Garvey/Greenwood Publishing Group.

Angel, Ronald, and Peter J. Guarnaccia. 1989. Mind, body, and culture: Somatization among Hispanics. *Social Science and Medicine* 28(12)229–238.

Berthold, S. Megan. 1989. Spiritism as a form of psychotherapy: Implications for social work practice. *Social Casework* 70(8):502–509.

Delgado, Melvin. 1996. Religion as a caregiving system for Puerto Rican elders with functional disabilities. *Journal of Gerontological Social Work* 26(3–4):129–44.

Garrison, Vivian. 1977a. Doctor, espiritista or psychiatrist? Health-seeking behaviour in a Puerto Rican neighborhood of New York City. *Medical anthropology* 1(2):65–191.

———. 1977b. The "Puerto Rican syndrome" in psychiatry and espiritismo. In *Case studies in spirit possession*, ed. Vincent Crapanzano and Vivian Garrison, pp. 383–449. New York: John Wiley and Sons.

Gleason, Judith, and Elisa Mereghetti. 1992. *The king does not lie: The initiation of a priest of Shango* Videotape. New York: Filmakers Library.

Guarnaccia, Peter J., Victor DeLaCancela, and Emilio Carrillo. 1989. Multiple meanings of *ataques de nervios* in the Latino community. *Medical Anthropology* 11(1):47–
62.

Harwood, Alan. 1977. Puerto Rican spiritism. *Culture, Medicine, and Psychiatry*, Part 1:
1(1):69–95; Part 2: 1(2);135–54.

———. 1981. Mainland Puerto Ricans. In *Ethnicity and medical care*, pp. 397–481.
Cambridge, MA: Harvard University Press.

Harwood, Alan. 1987. *Rx, spiritist as needed: A study of a Puerto Rican community mental health resource*. Ithaca, NY: Cornell University Press.

Koss-Chioino, Joan. 1992. *Women as healers, women as patients: Mental health care and
traditional healing in Puerto Rico*. Boulder, CO: Westview Press.

Olmos, Margarite Fernández, and Lizabeth Paravisini-Gebert, ed. 2001. *Healing cultures: Art and religion as curative practices in the Caribbean and its diaspora*. New
York: Palgrave.

Orsi, Robert. 1992. The religious boundaries of an inbetween people: Street Feste and
the problem of the dark-skinned Other in Italian Harlem, 1920–1990. *American
Quarterly* 44(3):313–46.

Ortiz, Manuel. 1988. The rise of spiritism in North America. *Urban Mission* 5(March):
11–17.

Singer, Merrill. 1989. Becoming a Puerto Rican espiritista: Life history of a female
healer. In *Women as healers: Cross-cultural perspectives*, ed. Carol Shepherd Mc-
Clain, pp. 157–85. New Brunswick, NJ: Rutgers University.

AFRICAN CHRISTIANITIES

Aderibigbe, Gbola, and Deji Ayegboyin, ed. 1995. *Religion, medicine, and healing* (Nigerian Association for the Study of Religions and Education Conference). Ikeja,
Lagos: Free Enterprise Publishers.

Berinyuu, Abraham Adu. 1988. *Pastoral care to the sick in Africa: An approach to transcultural pastoral theology*. New York: P. Lang.

Byaruhanga-Akiiki, A.B.T., and Obed N.O. Kealotswe. 1995. *African theology of healing:
The infinite oneness*. Gaboroni: University of Botswana Press.

Chavunduka, G. L. 1977. Traditional medicine and Christian beliefs. In *Christianity
south of the Zambezi*, Vol. 2, ed. M.F.C. Bourdillon, pp. 131–46. Gwelo, Rhodesia:
Mambo Press.

Daneel, M L. 1992. Exorcism as a means of combating wizardry liberation or enslave-
ment. [Zimbabwean independent churches] In *Empirical studies of African inde-
pendent/indigenous churches*, ed. G. C. Oosthuizen and Irving Hexham, pp. 195–
238. Lewiston, NY: Edwin Mellen Press.

Ela, Jean M. 1977. Ancestors and Christian faith: an African problem. In *Liturgy and
cultural religious traditions*, ed. Herman Schmidt and David Power, pp. 34–50.
New York: Seabury Press.

Fashole-Luke, Edward W. 1974. Ancestor veneration and the communion of saints. In
New Testament Christianity for Africa and the world, pp. 209–21. London: SPCK.

Hagan, George P. 1988. Divinity and experience: The trance and Christianity in
southern Ghana. In *Vernacular Christianity: Essays in the social anthropology of religion*, ed. Wendy James and Douglas H. Johnson, pp. 146–56. New York: Lilian
Barber Press.

Hammond-Tooke, W. D. 1989. The aetiology of spirit in southern Africa. In *Afro-

Christian religion and healing in southern Africa, ed. G.C. Oosthuizen, pp. 43–65. Lewiston, NY: Edwin Mellen Press.

Hebga, Meinrad P. 1991. Healing in Africa [Christianization of healing rites.] In *The pastoral care of the sick*, ed. Mary Collins and David N. Power, pp. 60–71. Philadelphia: Trinity Press International.

Kealotswe, O.N.O. 1991. Spiritual healing and traditional medicine in Botswana. In *Afro-Christian religion at the grassroots in southern Africa*, ed. G. C. Oosthuizen, pp. 184–90. Lewiston, NY: Edwin Mellen Press.

Kyeyune, David. 1975. Dialogue between Christianity and African religion in Uganda: Relation between the spirits and the living relatives. In *Dialogue with the African traditional religions*, ed. Association of Episcopal Conferences of Anglophone West Africa. Kampala, Uganda: Gaba Publications.

Masamba ma Mpolo 1979. Community and cure: The therapeutics of the traditional religions and the religion of the prophets in Africa. In *Christian and Islamic contributions towards establishing independent states in Africa south of the Sahara*, ed. Institut für Auslandsbeziehungen, pp. 125–38. Tübingen: Laupp and Gobel.

Oosthuizen, G. C., ed. 1989. *Afro-Christian religion and healing in southern Africa*. Lewiston, NY: E. Mellen Press.

———. 1992. *The healer-prophet in Afro-Christian churches*. Leiden: E.J. Brill.

Pobee, John S. 1994. Healing—an African Christian theologian's perspective. *International review of mission* 83(329):247–55.

Friedson, Steven. 1989. *Prophet healers of northern Malawi* [Videotape.] Seattle: University of Washington Press.

Singleton, Michael. 1978. Spirits and "spiritual direction": The pastoral counselling of the possessed. In *Christianity in independent Africa*, ed. Edward Fusholé-Luke. pp. 471–78. London: Rex Collings.

HEALTH MINISTRIES

Chase-Ziolek, Mary. 2005. *Health, healing, and wholeness: Engaging congregations in ministries of health*. Cleveland, Ohio: Pilgrim Press.

Dunkle, Rosene M. 1996. Parish nurses help patients—body and soul. *RN* 59(5):55–57

Evans, Abigail Rian. 1999. *The healing church: Practical programs for health ministries*. Cleveland: United Church Press.

Fichter, Joseph Henry. 1986. *Healing ministries: Conversations on the spiritual dimensions of health care*. New York: Paulist Press.

Kimble, Melvin A., ed. 1995. *Aging, spirituality, and religion: A handbook*. Minneapolis: Fortress Press.

Lumsdon, Kevin. 1994. Parish nurse programs strengthen community links. *Hospitals and Health Networks* 68(11):74.

Myers, Margaret Elizabeth. 2002. *Parish nursing speaks: The voices of those who practice, facilitate, and support parish nursing*. Toronto: Opus Wholistic Publications.

VandeCreek, Larry, and Sue Mooney, ed. 2002. *Parish nurses, health care chaplains, and community clergy: Navigating the maze of professional relationships*. New York: Haworth Pastoral Press.

Westberg, Granger E., with Jill Westberg McNamara, *The parish nurse: Providing a minister of health for your congregation*. Minneapolis: Augsburg, 1990.

CHRISTIANITY AND PHYSICIANS

Anderson, Douglas. 1990. The physician's experience: Witnessing numinous reality. *Second Opinion* 13(March):111–22.

Barnard, David. 1982. The gift of trust: Psychodynamic and religious meanings in the physician's office. *Soundings* 65(summer):213–32.

———. 1985. The physician as priest, revisited. *Journal of Religion and Health* 24(winter):272–86.

Barton, Julie, Marita Grudzen, and Ron Zielske. 2003. *Vital connections in long-term care: Spiritual resources for staff and residents.* Baltimore: Health Professions Press.

Beadle, E. R. 1865. *The sacredness of the medical profession.* Philadelphia: James S. Claxton.

Bull, Malcolm. 1990. Secularization and medicalization. *The British Journal of Sociology* 41(2):245–61.

Cates, Diana Fritz, and Paul Lauritzen, ed. 2001. *Medicine and the ethics of care.* Washington, DC: Georgetown University Press.

Cerrato, Paul L. 1998. Spirituality and healing. *RN* 61(2):49–50.

Christy, John H. 1998. Prayer as medicine. *Forbes* 161(6):136–37.

Cowles, Edward Spencer. 1925. *Religion and medicine in the church, representing the principle of the work in the scientific cooperation of physicians and clergymen in the body and soul medical and mental clinic, New York City.* New York: Macmillan.

Daaleman, Timothy P. 1994. Patient attitudes regarding physician inquiry into spiritual and religious issues. *Journal of Family Practice* 39(6):564–68.

DesAutels, Peggy, Margaret P. Battin, and Larry May.1999. *Praying for a cure: When medical and religious practices conflict.* Lanham, MD: Rowman and Littlefield.

Foster, Daniel W. 1982. Religion and medicine: The physician's perspective. In *Health/ medicine and the faith traditions,* pp. 245–70. Philadelphia: Fortress Press.

Gaines, Atwood D. 1985. The once- and the twice-born. In *Physicians of Western medicine: Anthropological approaches to theory and practice,* ed. Robert A. Hahn, and Atwood D. Gaines. Boston: D. Reidel Publishing Company.

Galanter, Marc. 1997. Spiritual recovery movements and contemporary medical care. *Psychiatry: Interpersonal and Biological Processes* 60(3):211–23.

Hanford, Jack Tyrus. 2002. *Bioethics from a faith perspective: Ethics in health care for the twenty-first century.* New York: Haworth Pastoral Press.

Hauerwas, Stanley. 1985. Salvation and health: Why medicine needs the church. In *Theology and bioethics,* ed. Earl E. Shelp, pp. 205–24. Dordrecht, Holland: D Reidel Publishing.

Haynes, William F. 1990. *A physician's witness to the power of shared prayer.* Chicago: Loyola University Press.

Hurley, Patricia Shields. 1985. *Religion and medicine: A medical subject analysis and research index with bibliography.* Washington, DC: ABBE Publishers Association.

Kepler, Milton O. 1968. Importance of religion in medical education. *Journal of Religion and Health* 7:358–67.

Kilner, John F., C. Christopher Hook, and Diann B. Uustal. 2002. *Cutting-edge bioethics: A Christian exploration of technologies and trends.* Grand Rapids, MI: Eerdmans.

King, Dana E. 1994. Beliefs and attitudes of hospital inpatients about faith healing and prayer. *Journal of Family Practice* 39(4):349–52.

King, Michael, Peter Speck, and Angela Thomas. 1994. Spiritual and religious beliefs in acute illness—is this a feasible area for study?" *Social Science and Medicine* 38(4):631–36.

Knight, James A. 1982. The minister as healer, the healer as minister. *Journal of religion and health* 21(summer):100–14.

Koenig, Harold George. 1999. *The healing power of faith: Science explores medicine's last great frontier.* New York: Simon and Schuster.

_____. Lucille B. Bearon, and Richard Dayringer. 1989. Physician perspectives on the role of religion in the physician-older patient relationship. *Journal of Family Practice* 28(4):441–48.

_____. 1999. *The healing power of faith: Science explores medicine's last great frontier.* New York: Simon and Schuster.

_____. 2004. *Faith in the future: Healthcare, aging, and the role of religion.* Philadelphia: Templeton Foundation Press.

Krebs, John M. 1847. *The reciprocal relations of physicians and clergymen.* New York: Henry Ludwig.

Lefebure, Marcus, ed. 1985. *Human experience and the art of counselling: Further conversations between a doctor and a priest.* Edinburgh: T and T Clark.

Mahoney, John. 1984. *Bio-ethics and belief: Religion and medicine in dialogue.* Westminster, MD: Christian Classics.

Mangan, Katherine S. 1997. Blurring the boundaries between religion and science (medical school programs on the healing role of spirituality). *Chronicle of Higher Education* 43(26):A14.

Maretzki, W. 1985. Including the physician in healer-centered research. In *Physicians of Western medicine: Anthropological approaches to theory and practice,* ed. Robert A. Hahn and Atwood D. Gaines, 23–50. Boston: D. Reidel Publishing Company.

Marwick, Charles. 1995. Should physicians prescribe prayer for health? Spiritual aspects of well-being considered. *JAMA* 273(20):1561–62.

May, William F. 1983. *The physician's covenant: Images of the healer in medical ethics.* Philadelphia: Westminster Press.

McKee, Denise. 1990. Comparing a Christian physicians' support group with the Balint group. *Journal of Family Practice* 30(1):65–68.

McKenny, Gerald P., and Jonathan R. Sande, ed. 1994. *Theological analyses of the clinical encounter.* Dordrecht: Kluwer Academic Publishers.

Midgley, Mary. 1995. Visions, secular and sacred. *Hastings Center Report* 25(5):20–27.

Mohrmann, Margaret E. 1995. *Medicine as ministry: Reflections on suffering, ethics, and hope.* Cleveland: Pilgrim Press.

Nicholi, Armand M. 1989. How does the world view of the scientist and the clinician influence their work? *Perspectives on science and Christian faith* 41:214–20.

Numbers, Ronald L., and Ronald C. Sawyer. 1982. Medicine and Christianity in the modern world. In *Health/medicine and the faith traditions,* ed. Martin E. Marty and Kenneth L. Vaux. Philadelphia: Fortress Press.

Pellegrino, Edmund D. 1986. Health care: A vocation to justice and love. In *The professions in ethical context,* ed. Victor W. Sidel, pp. 97–126. Villanova, PA: Villanova University Press.

Ross, Linda A. 1997. *Nurses' perceptions of spiritual care.* Brookfield, VT: Avebury.

Sansone, Randy A., Khatain, Kenneth, and Paul Rodenhauser. 1990. The role of religion in psychiatric education: A national survey. *Academic Psychiatry* 14(1):34–38.

Schreiber, Katrina. 1991. Religion in the physician-patient relationship. *JAMA* 266(21): 3062–63.

Scott, Edward M. 1979. Combining the roles of "priest" and "physician": A clinical case. *Journal of Religion and Health* 18(April):160–63.

Sevensky, Robert L. 1982. The religious physician. *Journal of Religion and Health* 21(fall):254–63.

Shannon, Thomas A. 2003. *The new genetic medicine: Theological and ethical reflections.* Lanham, MD: Rowman and Littlefield Publishers.

Shriver, Donald W. 1980a. How shall religion be defined in relation to medical education? In *Medicine and religion*, pp. 133–48. Pittsburgh: University of Pittsburgh.

———, ed. 1980b. *Medicine and religion: Strategies of care* Pittsburgh: University of Pittsburgh.

Smith, David H., ed. 2000. *Caring well: Religion, narrative, and health care ethics.* Louisville, KY: Westminster John Knox Press.

Stacey, James. 1993. *Inside the new temple: The high cost of mistaking medicine for religion.* Winnetka, IL: Conversation Press.

Stephens, James T., and Edward LeRoy Long. 1960. *The Christian as a doctor* New York: Association Press.

Tan, Siang-Yang, 1996. Religion in clinical practice: Implicit and explicit integration. In *Religion and the clinical practice of psychology*, ed. Edward P. Shafranske, pp. 365–87. Washington, DC: American Psychological Association.

Westberg, Granger E. 1961. *Minister and doctor meet.* New York: Harper.

White, Bowen Faville, and John A. MacDougall. 2001. *Clinician's guide to spirituality.* New York: McGraw-Hill.

Wirth, Daniel P. 1993. Implementing spiritual healing in modern medical practice. *Advances* 9(4):69–81.

ADDITIONAL RESOURCES

Ammicht-Quinn, Regina, and Elsa Tamez, eds. 2002. *The body and religion.* London: SCM.

Bush, Lester E. Jr. 1993. *Health and medicine among the Latter-Day Saints: Science, sense, and Scripture.* New York: Crossroad.

Fraser, Gary E. 2003. *Diet, life expectancy, and chronic disease: Studies of Seventh-Day Adventists and other vegetarians.* New York: Oxford University Press.

Judd, Daniel K., ed. 1999. *Religion, mental health, and the Latter-Day Saints.* Provo, UT: Religious Studies Center, Brigham Young University.

Kellehear, Allan. 1996. *Experiences near death: Beyond medicine and religion.* New York: Oxford University Press.

McCall, Junietta Baker. 2002. *A practical guide to hospital ministry: Healing ways.* New York: Haworth Pastoral Press.

Plante, Thomas G., ed. 2001. *Faith and health: Psychological perspectives.* New York: Guilford Press.

Snyder, Graydon F. 1995. *Health and medicine in the Anabaptist tradition: Care in community.* Valley Forge, PA: Trinity Press International.

TenBrook, Gretchen W. 2000. *Broken bodies, healing hearts: Reflections of a hospital chaplain.* New York: Haworth Pastoral Press.

Teaching Islam and Healing

Lance D. Laird

ISLAMIC MEDICAL TRADITIONS: HISTORICAL OVERVIEWS

Allan, N. 1990. Hospice to hospital in the Near East: An instance of continuity and change in late antiquity. *Bulletin of the History of Medicine* 64(3):446–62.

Antes, Peter. 1989. Medicine and the living tradition of Islam. In *Healing and restoring: Health and medicine in the world's religious traditions*, ed. Lawrence Sullivan, pp. 173–202. New York: Macmillan.

Bayrakdar, M. 1985. The spiritual medicine of early Muslims. *Islamic quarterly* 29(1): 1–28.

Conrad, Lawrence I. 1995. Medicine: Traditional practice. In *The Oxford encyclopedia of the modern Islamic world*, ed. J. L. Esposito. Vol. 3, pp. 85–91. New York: Oxford University Press.

Dols, M. W. 1987. The origins of the Islamic hospital: Myth and reality. *Bulletin of the History of Medicine* 61(3):367–90.

Dols, Michael W. 1992. *Majnun: The madman in medieval Islamic society*. New York: Oxford University Press.

Dols, M. W. 1987. Insanity and its treatment in Islamic society. *Medical history* 31(1):1–14.

O'Connor, Kathleen. 1999. Prophetic medicine and Qur'anic healing: Religious healing systems in Islam. In *Studies in Middle Eastern health*, ed. Robin Barlow and Joseph W. Brown, pp. 39–77. Ann Arbor, MI: Center for Middle Eastern and North African Studies.

Perho, Irmeli. 1995. *The prophet's medicine: A creation of the Muslim traditionalist scholars*. Vol. 74 of *Studia Orientalia*. Helsinki: Kokemaki.

Rahman, Fazlur. 1987. *Health and medicine in the Islamic tradition: Change and identity*. New York: Crossroads.

ISLAMIC MEDICINE: HISTORICAL BIOGRAPHICAL AND PRIMARY SOURCE MATERIAL

Avicenna. 1963. *Avicenna's poem on medicine*, trans. Haven C. Krueger. Springfield, IL: Charles C Thomas.

Bray, Julian Ashtiany. 1999. Third and fourth century bleeding poetry. *Arabic and Middle Eastern Literatures* 2:75–92.

Elgood, Cyril. 1962. Tibb-Ul-Nabbi or Medicine of the prophet, trans. Cyril Elgood. *Osiris* 14:33–192.

Ibn Qayyim al-Jawzīyah 1998. *Muhammad ibn Abī Bakr. Medicine of the prophet*, trans. Penelope Johnstone. Cambridge, England: Islamic Texts Society.

Iskandar, A.Z. 1990. Al-Razi. *Religion, learning, and science in the Abbasid period*, ed. M.J.L. Young, J. D. Latham, and R. B. Serjeant, pp. 370–77. Cambridge: Cambridge University Press.

Mahdi, M., and D. Gutas. 1992. Avicenna. In *Encyclopaedia Iranica*, ed. Ehsan Yar-Shater. Vol. 3, pp. 66–110. Costa Mesa, CA: Mazda Publishers.

Sezgin, Fuat, ed. 1967. al-Razi. In *Geschichte Des Arabischen Schrifttums*, ed. Fuat Sezgin. Vol. 3, pp. 274–94. Leiden: E.J. Brill.

Rāzī, Abū Bakr Muhammad ibn Zakarīyā. 1950. *The spiritual physick of Rhazes*, trans. Arthur J. Arberry. London: J. Murray.

Richter-Bernburg, L. 1994. Abu Bakr Muhammad Al-Razi's (Rhazes) medical works. *Medicina Nei Secoli* 6(2):377–92.

TRADITIONAL HEALING PRACTICES IN MUSLIM COMMUNITIES: ANTHROPOLOGICAL INSIGHTS

Asefzadeh, S., and F. Sameefar. 2001. Traditional healers in the Qazvin region of the Islamic republic of Iran: A qualitative study. *Eastern Mediterranean Health Journal* 7(3):544–50.

Beckerleg, S. 1994. Medical pluralism and Islam in Swahili communities in Kenya. *Medical Anthropology Quarterly* 8(3):299–313.

Betteridge, Anne H. 2002. Muslim women and shrines in Shiraz. *Everyday life in the Muslim Middle East*, ed. Donna Lee Bowen and Evelyn A. Early, pp. 276–89. Bloomington: Indiana University Press.

Bowen, John Richard. 1993. Return to sender: A Muslim discourse of sorcery in a relatively egalitarian society, the Gayo of northern Sumatra. In *Understanding witchcraft and sorcery in Southeast Asia*, ed. C. W. Watson and R. F. Ellen, pp. 179–90. Honolulu: University of Hawaii Press.

———. 1993. Spells, prayer, and the power of words. In *Muslims through discourse: Religion and ritual in Gayo society*, pp. 77–105. Princeton, NJ: Princeton University Press.

Claisse, R. 1985. Traditional therapeutic system in Morocco. *Journal of Ethnopharmacology* 13(3):301–306.

Doumato, Eleanor Abdella. 2000. *Getting God's ear: Women, Islam, and healing in Saudi Arabia and the Gulf.* New York: Columbia University Press.

Flueckiger, Joyce Burkhalter. 1998. Storytelling in the rhetoric of a Muslim female healer in South India. In *Spiritual traditions: Essential visions for living*, ed. David Emmanuel Singh, pp. 226–52. Bangalore: UTC.

al-Krenawi, A. 1999. Explanations of mental health symptoms by the Bedouin-Arabs of the Negev. *International Journal of Social Psychiatry* 45(1):56–64.

al-Krenawi, Alean, and John R. Graham. 1997. Spirit possession and exorcism in the treatment of a Bedouin psychiatric patient. *Clinical social work journal* 25:211–22.

MacPhee, M. 2003. Medicine for the heart: The embodiment of faith in Morocco. *Medical Anthropology* 22(1):53–83.

Owusu-Ansah, David. 2000. Prayer, amulets, and healing. In *The history of Islam in Africa*, ed. Nehemia Levtzion and Randall L. Pouwels, pp. 477–88. Athens: Ohio University Press.

Pfleiderer, B. 1988. The semiotics of ritual healing in a North Indian Muslim shrine. *Social Science and Medicine* 27(5):417–24.

Saeed, K., et al. 2000. The prevalence, classification, and treatment of mental disorders among attenders of native faith healers in rural Pakistan. *Social Psychiatry and Psychiatric Epidemiology* 35(10):480–85.

Sanni, A. 2002. Diagnosis through rosary and sand: Islamic elements in the healing custom of the Yoruba (Nigeria). *Medicine and Law* 21(2):295–306.

Wikan, U. 1988. Bereavement and loss in two Muslim communities: Egypt and Bali compared. *Social Science and Medicine* 27(5):451–60.

Woodward, M. R. 1985. Healing and morality: A Javanese example. *Social Science and Medicine* 21(9):1007–21.

MODERNITY, TRADITION, AND REVIVAL: DEBATE AND ADAPTATION IN "ISLAMIC MEDICINE"

Adib, SM. 2004. From the biomedical model to the Islamic alternative: A brief overview of medical practices in the contemporary Arab world. *Social Science and Medicine* 58(4):697–702.

Baasher, T. A. 2001. Islam and mental health. *Eastern Mediterranean Health Journal* 7(3):372–76.

Ewing, Katherine Pratt. 1997. *Arguing sainthood: Modernity, psychoanalysis, and Islam.* Durham, NC: Duke University Press.

Horikoshi, A. 1980. An Islamic psychiatric institution in West Java. *Social Science and Medicine* 14B(3):157–65.

al-Issa, Ihsan, ed. 2000. *Al-Junun: Mental illness in the Islamic world.* Madison, CT: International Universities Press.

Morsy, S. 1988. Islamic clinics in Egypt: The cultural elaboration of biomedical hegemony. *Medical Anthropology Quarterly* n.s. 2(4): 355–69.

Pugh, J. F. 2003. Concepts of arthritis in India's medical traditions: Ayurvedic and Unani perspectives. *Social Science and Medicine* 56.2 (2003): 415–24.

Stenberg, Leif. 1996. Seyyed Hossein Nasr and Ziauddin Sardar on Islam and science: Marginalization or modernization of a religious tradition. *Social Epistemology* 10(3–4):273–87.

Swartz, M. J. 1997. Illness and morality in the Mombasa Swahili community: A metaphorical model in an Islamic culture. *Culture, Medicine, and Psychiatry* 21(1):89–114.

ETHICAL AND LEGAL DIMENSIONS OF ISLAMIC HEALING

Ajlouni, K. M. 2003. Values, qualifications, ethics, and legal standards in Arabic (Islamic) medicine. *Saudi Medical Journal* 24(8):820–26.

Asman, O. 2004. Abortion in Islamic countries—legal and religious aspects. *Medicine and Law* 23(1):73–89.

Atighetchi, D. 2000. Islamic tradition and medically assisted reproduction. *Molecular and Cellular Endocrinology* 169(1–2):137–41.

Brockop, J. E. 2002. Islamic ethics of saving life: A comparative perspective. *Medicine and Law* 21(2):225–41.

Ebrahim, A. F. 1998. Islamic jurisprudence and the end of human life. *Medicine and Law* 17(2):189–96.

Francesca, E. 2002. AIDS in contemporary Islamic ethical literature. *Medicine and Law* 21(2):381–94.

Gatrad, A. R., and A. Sheikh. 2001. Medical ethics and Islam: Principles and practice. *Archives of Disease in Childhood* 84(1):72–75.

Ilkilic, I. 2002. Bioethical conflicts between Muslim patients and German physicians and the principles of biomedical ethics. *Medicine and Law* 21(2):243–56.

Nanji, A. A. 1988. Medical ethics and the Islamic tradition. *Journal of Medicine and Philosophy* 13(3):257–75.

Rispler-Chaim, V. 1989. Islamic medical ethics in the twentieth century. *Journal of Medical Ethics* 15(4): 203–208.

Sachedina, A. A. 1988. Islamic views on organ transplantation. *Transplantation Proceedings* 20(supp 1):1084–88.

MUSLIMS AND HEALING IN CONTEMPORARY WESTERN CONTEXTS

Chishti, Abu Abdullah Ghulam. 1991. *The book of Sufi healing*. Rochester, VT: Inner Traditions International.

Hermansen, Marcia. 2004. Dimensions of Islamic religious healing in America. In *Religion and healing in America*, ed. Linda L. Barnes and Susan S. Sered. New York: Oxford University Press.

Hoffer, C.B.M. 1992. The practice of Islamic healing. In *Islam in Dutch society: Current developments and future prospects*, ed. W.A.R. Shadid and P. S. Koningsveld, pp. 40–53. Kampen, The Netherlands: Kok Pharos.

Kassamali, Noor. 2004. Healing rituals and the role of Fatima. In *Religious healing in Boston: Body, spirit, community*, ed. Susan Sered, p. 45. Cambridge, MA: Center for the Study of World Religions, Harvard University.

Kobeisy, Ahmed Nezar. 2004. *Counseling American Muslims: Understanding the faith and helping the people. Contributions in psychology*, vol. 48. Westport, CT: Praeger.

Manderson, L., and P. Allotey. 2003. Storytelling, marginality, and community in Australia: How immigrants position their difference in health care settings. *Medical Anthropology* 22(1):1–21.

Sheikh, Aziz, and Abdul Rashid Gatrad, eds. 2000. *Caring for Muslim patients*. Abingdon: England: Radcliffe Medical Press.

African and African Diaspora Traditions and Healing

Linda L. Barnes

AFRICAN TRADITIONS

(For African Christian traditions, see bibliography on Christianity and Healing.)

Appiah-Kubi, Kofi. Religion and healing in an African community: The Akan of Ghana. In *Healing and restoring: Health and medicine in the world's religious traditions*, ed. Lawrence Sullivan, pp. 203–23. New York: Macmillan.

Ayim-Aboagye, Desmond. 1993. *The function of myth in Akan healing experience: A psychological inquiry into two traditional Akan healing communities*. Uppsala, Sweden: Uppsala University Press.

Badenberg, Robert. 2003. *Sickness and healing: A case study on the dialectic of culture and personality*. Nuremberg: VTR.

Dei, George J. Sefa, Budd L. Hall, and Dorothy Goldin Rosenberg, eds. 2000. *Indigenous knowledges in global contexts: Multiple readings of our world*. Buffalo; Toronto: University of Toronto Press.

Elia, Nada. 2001. *Trances, dances, and vociferations: Agency and resistance in Africana women's narratives*. New York: Garland Publishing.

Feierman, Steven, and John M. Janzen, eds. 1992. *The social basis of health and healing in Africa*. Berkeley: University of California Press.

Fink, Helga. 1989. *Religion, disease, and healing in Ghana: A case study of traditional Dormaa medicine*, trans. Volker Englich. Munich: Trickster Wissenschaft.

Foblets, Marie-Claire, and Trutz von Trotha, eds. 2004. *Healing the wounds: Essays on the reconstruction of societies after war*. Portland, Ore.: Hart Publishing.

Goduka, Ivy, with Beth Blue Swadener. 1999. *Affirming unity in diversity in education: Healing with ubuntu*. Johannesburg: Thorold's Africana Books.

Harvey, Graham, ed. 2000. *Indigenous religions: A companion*. New York: Cassell.

Janzen, John. 1989. Health, religion, and medicine in central and southern African traditions. In *Healing and restoring: Health and medicine in the world's religious traditions*, ed. Lawrence Sullivan, pp. 225–54. New York: Macmillan.

Janzen, John, Adrien Ngudiankama, and Melissa Filippi-Franz. 2005. Religious healing among war traumatized African immigrants. In *Religion and healing in America*, ed. Linda L. Barnes and Susan S. Sered, pp. 159–172. New York: Oxford University.

Keeney, Bradford, ed. 2003. *Ropes to God: Experiencing the Bushman spiritual universe*. Philadelphia: Ringing Rocks Press.

Obeng, Cecilia Sem. 2004. *Voices of affliction: Aspects of traditional healing and their impact on Akan families in Ghana*. Cologne: Köppe.

Orubu, A. O., ed. 2001. *African traditional religion*. Benin City, Nigeria: Institute of Education, University of Benin.

Peek, Philip M., ed. 1991. *African divination systems: Ways of knowing*. Bloomington: Indiana University Press.

Pfeiffer, James. 2002. African independent churches in Mozambique: Healing the afflictions of inequality. *Medical Anthropology Quarterly* 16(2):176–99.

Simpson, George Eaton. 1980. *Yoruba religion and medicine in Ibadan*. Ibadan, Nigeria: Ibadan University Press.

Somé, Malidoma Patrice. 1999. *The healing wisdom of Africa: Finding life purpose through nature, ritual, and community*. London: Thorsons.

Taylor, Robert Joseph, Linda M. Chatters, and Jeff Levin. 2004. *Religion in the lives of African Americans: Social, psychological, and health perspectives*. Thousand Oaks, CA: Sage Publications.

Thomas, Linda E. 1999. *Under the canopy: Ritual process and spiritual resilience in South Africa*. Columbia: University of South Carolina Press.

Ugwu, Chinọnyelu Moses. 1998. *Healing in the Nigerian church: A pastoral-psychological exploration*. New York: Peter Lang.

AFRICAN AMERICAN TRADITIONS

Anderson, Alita, ed. 2001. *On the other side: African Americans tell of healing*. Louisville, KY: Westminster John Knox Press.

Badenberg, Robert. 2003. *Sickness and healing: A case study on the dialectic of culture and personality*. Badenberg: VTR.

Bair, Barbara, and Susan E. Cayleff, eds. 1993. *Wings of gauze: Women of color and the experience of health and illness*. Detroit: Wayne State University Press.

Burack, Cynthia. 2004. *Healing identities: Black feminist thought and the politics of groups*. Ithaca, NY: Cornell University Press.

Burgess, Norma J., and Eurnestine Brown, ed. 2000. *African-American women: An ecological perspective*. New York: Falmer Press.

Byrd, W. Michael. 2000–2002. *An American health dilemma: The medical history of African Americans and the problem of race*. New York: Routledge.

Chireau, Yvonne Patricia. 2003. *Black magic: Religion and the African American conjuring tradition*. Berkeley: University of California Press.

Fett, Sharla M. 2002. *Working cures: Healing, health, and power on southern slave plantations.* Chapel Hill: University of North Carolina Press.

hooks, bell. 2004. *We real cool: Black men and masculinity.* New York: Routledge.

King, J. L., with Courtney Carreras. 2005. *Coming up from the down low: The journey to acceptance, healing, and honest love.* New York: Crown Publishers.

Rastogi, Mujdita, and Elizabeth Wieling, eds. 2005. *Voices of color: First-person accounts of ethnic minority therapists.* Thousand Oaks, CA: Sage Publications.

Townes, Emilie M. 1998. *Breaking the fine rain of death: African American health issues and a womanist ethic of care.* New York: Continuum.

Williams, Olgen. 2005. *Healing the heart, healing the 'hood.* West Lafayette, IN: Purdue University Press.

American Mind Cure and New Thought

Linda L. Barnes

Anderson, C. Alan. 1993. *Healing hypotheses: Horatio W. Dresser and the philosophy of New Thought.* New York: Garland.

Becker, Carl B. 1990. Religious healing in nineteenth-century "new religions": The cases of Tenrikyo and Christian Science. *Religion* 20(3):199–231.

Byars, Robert Lee. 1931. *New psychology and humanism; a mind science; a new interpretation of the powers that be for human welfare; is nature a blind accidental force or a sentient intelligent reality?* Columbia, MO: New Psychology Publishing Company.

Christian Science Publishing Society. 1966. *A century of Christian Science healing.* Boston: Christian Science Publishing Society.

Davis, Andrew Jackson. 1883 [1859]. *The great harmonia: Being a progressive revelation of the eternal principles which inspire mind and govern matter,* Vol. 5, 8th ed. Boston: Colby and Rich, Banner of Light Publishing House.

Davis, Andrew Jackson. 1886. *The history and philosophy of evil; with suggestions for more ennobling institutions and philosophical systems of education.* Boston: Colby and Rich, Banner of Light Publishing House.

Dresser, Horatio W. 1908. *A physician to the soul.* New York: G.P. Putnam's Sons.

———. 1917. *Handbook of the New Thought.* New York: G.P. Putnam's Sons.

———. 1922. *Spiritual health and healing.* New York: Thomas Y. Crowell Company.

Eddy, Mary Baker. 1971 [1903]. *Science and health with key to the Scriptures* Boston: First Church of Christ, Scientist.

Higgins, Paul Lambourne, ed. 1976. *Frontiers of the spirit: Studies in the mystical and psychical areas in observance of the twentieth anniversary of the founding of Spiritual Frontiers Fellowship.* Minneapolis: T. S. Denison.

Hufford, David J. 1993. Epistemologies in religious healing. *Journal of Medicine and Philosophy* 18(2):175–94.

Judah, J. Stillson. 1967. *The history and philosophy of the metaphysical movements in America.* Philadelphia: Westminster Press.

Meyer, Donald. 1988. *The positive thinkers: Popular religious psychology from Mary Baker Eddy to Norman Vincent Peale and Ronald Reagan.* Middletown, CT: Wesleyan University Press.

Osborn, Arthur Walter. 1926. *Occultism, Christian Science and healing,* 2nd ed. Melbourne, Australia: Solar Publications.

Parker, Gail Thain. 1973. *Mind cure in New England*. Hanover, N.H.: University Press of New England.

Peel, Robert. 1988. *Health and medicine in the Christian Science tradition: Principle, practice, and challenge.* New York: Crossroad.

Richardson, James T., and John Dewitt. 1992. Christian Science spiritual healing, the law, and public opinion. *Journal of Church and State* 34(3):549–61.

Schoepflin, Rennie B. 1988. Christian Science healing in America. In *Other Healers: Unorthodox Medicine in America*, ed. Norman Gevitz, pp. 192–214. Baltimore: Johns Hopkins University Press.

———. 2003. *Christian Science on trial: Religious healing in America.* Baltimore: Johns Hopkins University Press.

Twain, Mark. 1897. Mental telegraphy, and mental telegraphy again. In *Literary Essays*, pp. 111–47. New York: Harper and Brothers Publishers.

Useful Anthologies, Collections, and Journals

Linda L. Barnes

ANTHOLOGIES AND COLLECTIONS

Barnes, Linda L., and Susan S. Sered. 2005. *Religion and healing in America.* New York: Oxford University Press.

Coyle, J. Kevin, and Steven C. Muir. 1999. *Healing in religion and society, from Hippocrates to the Puritans: Selected studies.* Lewiston, NY: Edwin Mellen Press.

Crépeau, Pierre, ed. 1985. *Médicine et religion populaires* [Folk medicine and religion]. Ottawa: National Museums of Canada.

Csordas, Thomas J. 2002. *Body/meaning/healing.* New York: Palgrave, 2002.

Hinnells, John R., and Roy Porter, eds. 1999. *Religion, health, and suffering.* New York: Kegan Paul International.

Leavitt, Judith Walzer. 1999. *Women and health in America: Historical readings,* 2nd ed. Madison: University of Wisconsin Press.

Lehmann, Arthur C., and James E. Myers, comp. 2001. *Magic, witchcraft, and religion: An anthropological study of the supernatural,* 5th ed. Mountain View, CA: Mayfield Publishing Company.

Marland, Hilary, and Margaret Pelling, ed. 1996. *Task of healing: Medicine, religion, and gender in England and the Netherlands, 1450–1800.* Rotterdam: Erasmus Publishing.

Numbers, Ronald L., and Darrel W. Amundsen, eds. 1998. *Caring and curing: Health and medicine in the Western religious traditions.* Baltimore: Johns Hopkins University Press.

Sered, Susan Starr, ed. 2002. *Religious healing in Boston: Reports from the field.* Cambridge, MA: Center for the Study of World Religions, Harvard University.

———. 2004. *Religious healing in Boston: Body, spirit, community* Cambridge, MA: Center for the Study of World Religions, Harvard University.

Sered, Susan Starr, and Linda L. Barnes, ed. 2001. *Religious healing in Boston: First findings.* Cambridge, MA: Center for the Study of World Religions, Harvard University.

Skultans, Vieda, and John Cox, ed. 2000. *Anthropological approaches to psychological medicine: Crossing bridges.* Philadelphia: Jessica Kingsley Publishers.

Sullivan, Lawrence, ed. 1989. *Healing and restoring: Health and medicine in the world's religious traditions*. New York: Macmillan.

JOURNALS

The following journals are extremely useful sources for course design. They are also potential venues for students and faculty to pursue publishing their work.

Annual report—Institutes of religion and health
Anthropology and medicine
British journal for the history of science
Bulletin of the history of medicine
Bulletin of the Indian Institute of the History of Medicine
Bulletin of the Institute of the History of Medicine
Chinese science
Culture, illness, and healing
Culture, medicine, and psychiatry
Curare
Ethos
Healing journal
Health and healing
History of medicine
History of science
Indian journal of history of medicine
Isis
Journal of Christian healing
Journal of religion and health
Journal of religion, disability, and health
Journal of the history of medicine
Journal of the history of medicine and allied sciences
Justice as healing
Medical anthropology
Medical anthropology quarterly
Mental health, religion, and culture
Religion and health
Routledge studies in the social history of medicine
Second opinion
Social history of medicine
Social science and medicine
Society for ancient medicine newsletter
Spirituality and health
Studies in history of medicine and science
Studies in the history of medicine
Transcultural psychiatry

Index

biomedicine (*continued*)
  as pluralistic, 8
  and religious healing, 49
  religious overtones of, 8
  vis à vis medicine, 3
biopsychosocial approach, 171, 173, 174
birthing traditions, 33, 51, 74
Bloom, Benjamin, 30
body, 12, 14, 29–44, 249–51
Bordo, Susan, 31
Boston University School of Medicine, 307, 309, 310, 315
Brady, Jeff, 7
Branch, William, 320
Broyles-Gonzalez, Yolanda, 142
Buddhist medicine, 34–35, 84, 212–13, 255

Cameron, Julia, 256
caregiving, 287
Carman, John, 9
Carr, Christopher, 12, 19, 20
Carrasco, Davíd, 141, 142, 144
Catholicism, 37, 53, 139–40, 144, 146, 148, 255
causality, 99
change, 99
chantways, 34–35, 36
chaplains, 267, 270
Charaka, 62, 64
chi. See qi
Chicanas/Chicanos, 127, 128, 139–55
children, 122
Chinese healing, 96–108
Chinese history, 98
Chinese medicine, 33–34, 88, 249, 250
Chinese religious traditions, 83–85
Chinese traditional medicine. *See* traditional Chinese medicine
Christianity, 116, 118, 119, 147, 159, 163–64, 249, 272
  Bibliography, 356–370
clinicians, 315–19
colonization, 119, 121, 142

community, 236–37, 289
community wisdom, 282–83
Comparative Healing Systems (course), 48–56
comparative study, 8–16, 49, 87, 171, 172
Compendium (Charaka), 62
complementarity, 34
complementary and alternative medicine, 15, 49, 53, 321–22
Complementary Bodies (course unit), 33–34
Confucianism, 85, 96, 280
congregations, 253
contract learning. *See* covenant learning
conviction, 263–64
cooperative learning, 297
core shamanism, 19, 171, 173, 174
correspondence, 34
cosmology, 141, 264, 267
counseling, 289
covenant learning, 296–97
Crawford, Suzanne, 6, 12, 16–17, 20
creativity, 22
critical incident group approach, 320
cross-cultural communication, 288
cross-cultural psychiatry, 10
cross-cultural study, 32, 49, 171–74, 177, 207–18, 248
Csordas, Tom, 10, 12, 31, 37
cultural competence, 8, 308, 321–22
cultural counterpoints, 248
cultural genograms, 316–19
cultures, 32, 49, 50, 161, 174, 231, 300, 316
  See also specific cultures
curandera, 147–48
curing, 50–51, 248, 270
custom narrative and practice, 62–64

dance, 75–76
Daoism, 96, 99
Davis-Floyd, Robbie, 33, 38, 51
Days of the Dead, 22, 132–33, 144–45